Cyber-Physical Systems
Solutions to Pandemic Challenges

Editors

Tushar Semwal and Faiz Iqbal
School of Engineering
University of Edinburgh
Edinburgh, UK

CRC Press
Taylor & Francis Group
Boca Raton   London   New York

CRC Press is an imprint of the
Taylor & Francis Group, an **informa** business

A SCIENCE PUBLISHERS BOOK

First edition published 2022
by CRC Press
6000 Broken Sound Parkway NW, Suite 300, Boca Raton, FL 33487-2742

and by CRC Press
2 Park Square, Milton Park, Abingdon, Oxon, OX14 4RN

© 2022 Taylor & Francis Group, LLC

CRC Press is an imprint of Taylor & Francis Group, LLC

ISBN: 978-1-032-03037-1 (hbk)
ISBN: 978-1-032-03046-3 (pbk)
ISBN: 978-1-003-18638-0 (ebk)

DOI: 10.1201/9781003186380

Typeset in Times New Roman
by Innovative Processors

Preface

A Cyber-Physical System (CPS) is an integration of cyber components with their physical counterparts. A cyber unit could be either a software or hardware. At the same time, the physical components are those objects, which are governed by the law of physics. CPSs have transformed how we interact with the physical world, ranging from sensing the environmental parameters to controlling a complex manufacturing industry.

The profound implication of a pandemic situation is devastating to both the economy of the world and the health of the people. The COVID-19 pandemic is a prominent example of one of the most comprehensive and tragic catastrophes in a century. The book *Cyber-Physical Systems: Solutions to Pandemic Challenges* presents the significance and practicality of CPS amidst a pandemic situation. It provides a strong foundation to CPS while also incorporating latest theoretical advances and practical applications to alleviate the state of a pandemic. The scope of the book covers:

- Theoretical background and application-oriented overview of the different CPS models
- Impact of COVID-19 and similar pandemic situations on engineering aspects of various industries and organisations
- Exciting and impactful CPS based solutions to different pandemic situations
- Covers security and privacy in CPS when applied to critical and sensitive pandemic affected environment
- Describes government-funded projects and work using CPS in real-world scenarios

Cyber-Physical Systems: Solutions to Pandemic Challenges, for the first time, provides a unique and fresh exposure to CPSs employed in a pandemic situation. This comprehensive book promotes high-quality research and applied work on the impact of CPSs during a pandemic. The book brings together researchers, practitioners, academics, experts, and industry professionals from around the world to share their knowledge and experience. The book is for the academic researchers, industry practitioners, and aspiring graduates to delve into the importance of Cyber-Physical Systems to tackle a pandemic situation. The book will encompass core research topics to industry implementations of CPS especially tailored to control the effect of a pandemic such as COVID-19.

Tushar Semwal
Faiz Iqbal

Contents

Part IV: Frameworks and Perspectives

Part V: Use Cases of Solutions to Pandemic Challenges

List of Contributors

Abid Haleem: Department of Mechanical Engineering, Jamia Millia Islamia, New Delhi, India.

Abhishek Bhatnagar: Department of Mechanical Engineering, Indian Institute of Technology Delhi, New Delhi, India.

Adam Stokes: Soft Systems Group, Institute of Integrated Micro and Nano Systems, School of Engineering, The University of Edinburgh, Edinburgh, Scotland, UK.

Alistair McConnell: Soft Systems Group, Institute of Integrated Micro and Nano Systems, School of Engineering, The University of Edinburgh, Edinburgh, Scotland, UK.

Ashish Siddhartha: Department of Mechanical Engineering, Indian Institute of Technology (Indian School of Mines) Dhanbad, Dhanbad, Jharkhand, India.

Bao Jinsong: College of Mechanical Engineering, Donghua University Shanghai, China.

Bożena Gajdzik: Department of Industrial Informatics, Silesian University of Technology, Poland.

Chase Smith: Leeds Business School, Leeds Beckett University, Leeds, UK.

Daniel Mitchell: Smart Systems Group, Institute of Sensors, Signals and Systems, School of Engineering and Physical Sciences, Heriot-Watt University, Edinburgh, Scotland, U.K.

David Flynn: Smart Systems Group, Institute of Sensors, Signals and Systems, School of Engineering and Physical Sciences, Heriot-Watt University, Edinburgh, Scotland, U.K.

Elvis Hozdić: Department of Control and Manufacturing Systems, Faculty of Mechanical Engineering, University of Ljubljana, Ljubljana, Slovenia.

Faiz Iqbal: Soft Systems Group, Institute of Integrated Micro and Nano Systems, School of Engineering, The University of Edinburgh, Edinburgh, Scotland, UK.

Hajar Fatorachian: Leeds Business School, Leeds Beckett University, Leeds, UK.

Jamie Blanche: Smart Systems Group, Institute of Sensors, Signals and Systems, School of Engineering and Physical Sciences, Heriot-Watt University, Edinburgh, Scotland, U.K.

Jitin Malhotra: Department of Mechanical Engineering, Indian Institute of Technology Delhi, New Delhi, India.

Karen Donaldson: Soft Systems Group, Institute of Integrated Micro and Nano Systems, School of Engineering, The University of Edinburgh, Edinburgh, Scotland, UK.

Li Jei: College of Mechanical Engineering, Donghua University Shanghai, China.

Lu Yuqian: Department of Mechanical Engineering, The University of Auckland, New Zealand.

Lv Qibin: College of Mechanical Engineering, Donghua University Shanghai, China.

Mohammad Javaid: Department of Mechanical Engineering, Jamia Millia Islamia, New Delhi, India.

Madhur Shukla: Department of Mechanical Engineering, Indian Institute of Technology, New Delhi, India.

Maximilian Nicolae: Department of Automation and Industrial Informatics, Faculty of Automation and Computers, University Politehnica of Bucharest.

Nomesh B. Bolia: Department of Mechanical Engineering, Indian Institute of Technology Delhi, New Delhi, India.

Radoslaw Wolniak: Department of Organization and Management, Silesian University of Technology, Poland.

Radu Pietraru: Department of Automation and Industrial Informatics, Faculty of Automation and Computers, University Politehnica of Bucharest.

Rajiv Suman: G.B. Pant University of Agriculture & Technology, Pantnagar, Uttarakhand, India.

Sam Harper: Smart Systems Group, Institute of Sensors, Signals and Systems, School of Engineering and Physical Sciences, Heriot-Watt University, Edinburgh, Scotland, U.K.

Sandra Grabowska: Department of Production Engineering, Silesian University of Technology, Poland.

Sebastian Saniuk: Department of Engineering Management and Logistic Systems, University of Zielona Góra, Zielona Góra, Poland.

Shrushti Maheshwari: Department of Mechanical Engineering, Indian Institute of Technology (Indian School of Mines) Dhanbad, Dhanbad, Jharkhand, India.

Stefan Mocanu: Department of Automation and Industrial Informatics, Faculty of Automation and Computers, University Politehnica of Bucharest.

Sulejman Kendić: Medicooral-AS, Bihac, Džemala Bijedica, Bihac, Bosnia and Herzegovina.

Sunil Jha: Department of Mechanical Engineering, Indian Institute of Technology Delhi, New Delhi, India.

Theo Lim: Smart Systems Group, Institute of Sensors, Signals and Systems, School of Engineering and Physical Sciences, Heriot-Watt University, Edinburgh, Scotland, U.K.

Tushar Semwal: Soft Systems Group, Institute of Integrated Micro and Nano Systems, School of Engineering, The University of Edinburgh, Edinburgh, Scotland, UK.

Zafar Alam: Department of Mechanical Engineering, Indian Institute of Technology (Indian School of Mines) Dhanbad, Dhanbad, Jharkhand, India.

Zhang Rong: College of Mechanical Engineering, Donghua University, Shanghai, China.

Zoran Jurković: University of Rijeka, Department of Industrial Engineering and Management, Rijeka, Croatia.

Introduction to Cyber-Physical Systems and Challenges Faced due to the COVID-19 Pandemic

Faiz Iqbal, Jitin Malhotra, Sunil Jha and Tushar Semwal*

1. Introduction

The economic world has been affected over all its sectors due to the ongoing COVID-19 pandemic. It is a health crisis that has defined the situation in the health sector. However, the health sector is not the only affected sectorial entity due to this pandemic. With its unprecedented effect across all dimensions the pandemic has become a worldwide crisis in all forms of social and economic reforms delivering potentially everlasting effects on each and every country it has its presence on. The pandemic also brought scaled organizational modifications in almost all aspects of life forcing enterprises both private and government to adapt to the new normal. Governments were and still are tasked at saving lives at the cost of a lot of other things and a balance must be found. The balance meant restrictions at various levels for businesses which led to financial problems amounting to a cosmic scale and with challenges to create conditions safe for everyone. Work from home for the vast majority of companies became the new normal as employees were asked to stay home and hone a new set of skills to deal with digital platforms on top of their own skills. Despite the best efforts from many companies to keep employee health and wellbeing a top priority the conditions are just not desirable and leading to frustrated moods. With this being a global crisis, the effects of COVID-19 are being felt across many industrial sectors. None of the companies worldwide have a proven strategy for this extremely rare and new nature of working conditions. Every company has had to individually fight the pandemic challenges they are in front of in these difficult times.

The concept of Industry 4.0 (I4.0) started as an industry development strategy for economies around the world at the end of the first decade of this twenty-first century. From an economic point of view, industry acts as the growth engine for every country. Technological development of various aspects including production

---

*Corresponding author: tusharsemwal@outlook.com

has been extremely rapid of late, and very recently having been coupled with digital advancements it has enabled the creation of cyber-physical systems (CPS). The cyber part of CPS is able to deal with the physical processes through the use of advanced sensors, sophisticated controllers, and interactive user interfaces, enabling the use of cyber worlds to manipulate physical standalone systems remotely, reliably, and in real-time. Tasks such as communication, computing, control, and self-maintenance are feasible with the advent of CPS. Industry 4.0 has been looked upon as a medium to enhance production rates and competitive strategies. From its conception in 2010-2011 until the present it is a big challenge for many industries around the world.

The COVID-19 pandemic in the beginning led to the cessation of work in almost all industries. Especially in the small and medium-sized enterprises (SMEs) and micro-SMEs, reduced production efficiency further aggravated scarcity of various essential products as well. The number of SMEs is large and dominant in the current market. These types of enterprises usually work with a traditional work force and lack the latest advancements of I4.0 knowledge and skills. Therefore, owing to their lack of intelligence within this domain, primarily all the work is still dominated by manual interventions. The pandemic introduced the sudden and unexpected shortage of manual labour and enterprises could not come up with solutions to these pandemic challenges in the short term. With the advancements of I4.0 it was already becoming essential for SMEs to develop, change and adapt to the new regime of less humans and more automation. Simultaneously, the COVID-19 pandemic meant that the same change are now even more vital to survival of these small entities viz. micro, small, and medium scale enterprises. This, transforming the existing micro-SMEs into I4.0 compliant enterprises has also become a pandemic challenge.

The pandemic has also affected the education system in a huge way and schools, colleges, universities, none have been spared. With every country looking to spend significant amounts of money and time in developing the next generation it is a very challenging and daunting task to keep the education system going. The pandemic may last for years and children's years of education are extremely vital for their knowledge and growth and quick solutions are required to the education specific pandemic challenges. Same is the case for undergraduate and postgraduate studies especially in engineering. With their laboratories being forced to close, it is vital to bring new solutions to remote learning giving the same feel and knowledge to students to learn from and become the outstanding engineers of the future.

Supply chains (SCs) are another area that have been affected by the pandemic, although most of the activities in this domain have been rendered essential and can carry out their operations but they do not operate just by the logistics and there exists a huge workforce that makes every operation as smooth as it seems. The pandemic having affected this behind-the-scenes workforce has had its effect on SCs as well. The advancements in CPS are capable of addressing the issues faced by SCs through the implementation of I4.0 technological advancements. With the pandemic affecting many of the SC aspects there has arisen new challenges in this domain that need tackling for the supply chain world to be running in an advanced manner coping up with rapid technological challenges and the challenges the pandemic brings.

New manufacturing technologies, such as additive manufacturing (AM), are consistent in producing a versatile variety of products reliably. The performance of AM has seen drastic improvements in recent years and producing spares or replacement parts has been enabled through AM. The pandemic challenges of unprecedented demand for spares have somewhat been overcome by AM in producing new pandemic related products such as Face masks, Face shields, Swabs, and Ventilator parts. AM remains at the core of these latest advancements and also brings solutions to pandemic challenges.

With growing levels of customization, I4.0 and CPS are capable of providing solutions to the various COVID-19 Pandemic challenges few of which are listed in previous paragraphs. The following section lays out a comprehensive review of recent archival literature in CPS domain to find out how the recent work reported on CPS is still viable in a pandemic situation.

2. Cyber-Physical Systems – Recent Advancements and Technologies

The current section will introduce the readers to CPS and its related technologies. This section will present an overview of each technology to the reader with few key applications in 5 major domains (Fig. 1.1) i.e., agriculture, energy needs, healthcare, manufacturing, and transportation. These domains have been selected based on the needs of humans in difficult times like the COVID-19 pandemic.

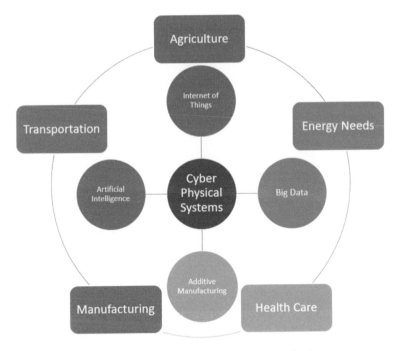

Figure 1.1: CPS and core technologies, with applications.

2.1 Cyber Physical Systems (CPS)

Cyber-Physical Systems (CPS) are aone of a kind, large-scale networked system, formed by uniting cyber and physical elements. They are multi-scale, spatially distributed, time-sensitive, networked systems which connect cyber elements to physical systems through sensors and actuators [1, 2]. Figure 1.2 shows a basic block diagram of the cyber-physical system having three major functional components [3]:

i. First is the cyberspace which is formed with capabilities of smart data conversion and management; data analysis & inference; and computational capabilities.

ii. Second is the physical space having capabilities of real time data acquisition from physical entities, to receive feedback from the cyber world through highly advanced communication systems and implement actuation actions in the real world.

iii. Third is the communication network which connects both physical and cyber spaces.

CPS term first came into existence at US National Science Foundation in 2006 [4], and from then on has gained a lot of attraction. These networked systems are of huge interest in academia, industries and even top the government priority lists because of its significant impact on society, environment and in economic sectors. In the US, the President's Council of Advisors on Science and Technology (PCAST) suggested putting CPS as one of the top items of the research agenda [5]. Also, the National Science Foundation (NSF) has promoted the CPS by providing funding opportunities to the scientific community [6, 7]. Talking about European Union's initiatives, Advanced Research and Technology for Embedded Intelligence Systems (ARTEMIS) has heavily invested in CPS with a vision of making physical systems to

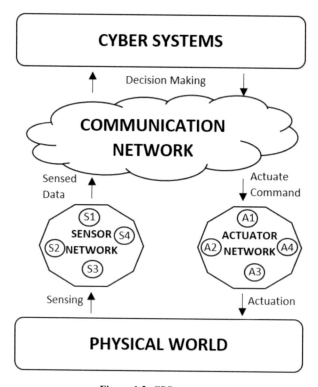

Figure 1.2: CPS components.

be smart and physically aware by connecting cyber elements to them, communicate with them and get benefited by digital information and services [8]. The EU has also launched a R&D program called Horizon 2020, with almost a budget of 80 billion euros. This program primarily targets the CPS and its related technologies to advance the research and innovation in various domains like manufacturing, agriculture, green energy, transportation, healthcare etc. [9].

The CPS aims to boost the realization of smart networked systems with features like accuracy, adaptability, availability, compositionality, compossibility, confidentiality, dependability, efficiency, heterogeneity, integrity, interoperability, maintainability, predictability, reliability, reconfigurability, resilience, robustness, safety, scalability, security, and sustainability [2].

CPS applications in major domains:

(a) *Agriculture:* CPS can play a major role in creating modern and precision agriculture by collecting data about the environment like weather, soil, humidity, and climate and based on data inference which suggests what plants can be grown on land, are profitable, and are currently in demand [10]. In addition to making suggestions, it can make various predictions regarding using AI regarding the market needs based on previous knowledge and current data [11]. Livestock management can also be one of the applications which can be better managed by CPS. Various applications in agriculture are available using CPS which are smart farming [12], smart crop cutting machines, smart logistics or intelligent supply chain for crops [13], smart irrigations systems [14, 15], smart waste disposal systems, and smart biomass systems, etc.

(b) *Energy Needs:* With technological advancements, the energy needs are also increasing day by day, which makes us think more about renewable energy sources and incorporating some smart systems which can provide us ways to save energy and utilize them in an efficient manner. One of the best examples of CPS in this sector are smart grids, which is a smart way of modernizing the grids by combining communication and information technologies with power systems engineering in a homogenous manner resulting in a distributed, responsive, and cooperative technology for consumers [16–18]. CPS further helps in blackouts monitoring, large scale (statewide) or smaller scale (street wide) energy needs monitoring by smart sensors, communication technologies and controlling at a centralized location for a better management of resources [19, 20]. Another application is in water or gas distribution smart meters having wireless connectivity capability, wireless meter reading reporting, meter fault monitoring & reporting, theft reporting like features which make them smart and user friendly [21].

(c) *Healthcare:* CPS in the health care sector addresses the issues related to the real-time and remote monitoring of the physiological conditions of patients [22, 23]. The research opportunities in Medical applications includes the smart portable medical devices customized to patients' needs like pacemakers, infusion pumps, and smart wearables; also, to add to the list there would be smart operation theatres, smart home cares and smart prescriptions [24]. The concept of Medical Cyber-Physical Systems also summarizes more promising directions for research and mostly tries to solve the problems by integrating specialized software into medical devices [25]. Also, the use of robots in operating rooms have given rise to some new terminologies which are quite popular in medical world viz.

telesurgery, medical robotics, robots assisted surgeries, rehabilitation robots, etc. [25–29]. The key benefits of robotic surgery are increasing in patient safety, decreasing patient recovery time, leading to a decrease in operating times, a decrease in surgeon fatigue as robots largely play the key role and surgeons just act as the supervisors to them [30].

(d) *Manufacturing:* Most of the applications of CPS are in the manufacturing domain. CPS plays a key role in making the current manufacturing setup a smarter, efficient, autonomous, and optimize the factories for continuous production, with zero downtime [31]. CPS has the capabilities to improve the processes by sharing the real time useful information to other machines installed locally or in some remote locations for further actions, various suppliers of raw materials in case of shortage of raw material onan need basis, to customers indicating the status of their ordered product, to logistics vendors for shipping of products, and to the waste disposal vendors to collect the waste material from factory on timely basis [32–38].

(e) *Transportation:* The CPS plays an important role in all kinds of transportation services whether it be military or civilian related. Starting from self-driving fully autonomous cars having onboard sensors, computation capabilities, communication links to the base stations [39, 40]. These applications have the tendency to improve the safety of passengers onboard and outside the vehicle, and efficiently manage traffic as autonomous vehicles itself are learning and taking the decisions based on current data and previous knowledge. The collision avoidance systems equipped on the vehicles make them safer for the humans [41]. More advanced applications can be lane keeping assistance, distance keeping assistance, potholes detection and reporting systems [42–44]. CPS will not only be managing the land traffic but can also in air and water. Better control of drones or UAVs with full autopilot capabilities and providing assistance to airplane pilots in efficient decision making soon will be a reality and comes under the reign of CPS [45].

2.2   Internet of Things (IOT)

Internet of Things was coined by Kevin Ashton in 1999, while linking the RFID in Procter & Gamble's supply chain with the internet [46]. Further getting deep into the meaning of Internet of Things, we get two different constituting terms *"Internet"* and *"Things"*, when combined results in a disruptive level of innovation in today's ICT focused world. Various researchers have defined IOT in different ways like Atzori et al. [47] added a perspective to IOT meaning by adding a perspective on *semantic oriented* (focus on the data and the knowledge acquired by analyzing), in addition to *internet oriented* (focusing on network components), and *things oriented* (focusing on different sensors available and their interconnection) already known in literature, which gives a new meaning to IOT; and Working RFID group defined IOT as *"The worldwide network of interconnected objects uniquely addressable based on standard communication protocols"* [48]; Acc. to CERP, IOT 2010 the IOT is defined as *"an integrated part of Future Internet and could be defined as a dynamic global network infrastructure with self-configuring capabilities based on standard and interoperable communication protocols where physical and virtual "things" have identities, physical attributes, and virtual personalities and use intelligent interfaces, and are seamlessly integrated into the information network"* [49]. As per predictions, in the next decade the internet will be a backbone of everything. And, when all the physical things are enhanced by electronics, it makes them smarter and when connected over the internet creates a path for new services and applications to come into existence involving both physical and virtual worlds. Key enablers for IOT are identifying technologies, sensors, communication, computing capabilities, services, and semantics [50].

Few applications of IOT are, but are not limited to these only:

(a) *Agriculture:* IOT in conjunction with CPS plays an important role in major initiatives in the agriculture domain like precision agriculture, and smart farming [12]. Further IOT contributes to a lot in the agriculture domain in all three sub-domains i.e., livestock management, precision farming [10], and greenhouse monitoring. All three sub-domains have applications like in livestock management: animal health monitoring, heart rate, GPS based monitoring; precision farming: climate condition monitoring, pest and crop disease monitoring and predictions, irrigation monitoring system [14, 15], farm management systems; greenhouse monitoring: water management, plant monitoring, weather monitoring, drones-based surveying [51].

(b) *Energy Needs:* With the integration of IOT technologies to buildings or homes, these buildings are on a path of becoming self-aware, and smarter which decreases resource consumption and an efficient management of devices available in home from entertainment to security, giving humans an overall improvement in satisfaction level and moving towards the concept of green buildings [52, 53]. Utilizing the sensors data and processing them can also predict the energy requirements for the future and helps in managing the areas where usually the resources i.e., electricity, water, or gas are wasted [54–57]. The concept of smart homes/buildings further contributes to the future smart cities [58]. Starting from the service sectors like smart governance, smart buildings, smart utilities to smart parking, smart street lighting, traffic monitoring, air quality monitoring, waste management, noise monitoring are some of the key features of smart cities [59]. All these mentioned features are achieved by adding sensors with the embedded devices connected to all components of this smart city having the capability to transmit real time information to the cloud and also utilize this information in a real time for decision making tasks [60–62].

(c) *Healthcare:* IOT applications in health care ranges from smart wearable devices to monitoring the patient health and drug delivery in case of emergencies [63–65]. The IOT enhances the current state of living by continually monitoring the body temperature, blood pressure, breathing patterns, blood sugar levels using the wearable sensors [66] or through fixed sensors on the body and further transmitting these data to cloud for storage and analysis by medical specialists [67, 68]. Also, by studying the data relayed by sensors the medical staff can take immediate actions which can help in stopping the further deterioration of health of patients [69, 70]. Now-a-days some new and cheap smart wearables are commonly available in market in various forms which can give a brief about the daily activities done by human like exercises performed, calories burned, steps taken, and ECG patterns, etc., to help in betterment of daily lifestyle and mitigating the health problems [71, 72].

(d) *Manufacturing:* The IOT when applied in the industrial setup it is commonly termed as Industrial Internet of Things (IIOT) and is a major element of the fourth industrial revolution (Industry 4.0). Its application areas range from the development of smart factories, smart products, and smart services, etc. Also, various IIOT architectural frameworks are proposed by researchers like [73–76], which can act as a reference for implementing these smart technologies in industry scenarios for achieving the goals of Industry 4.0. The IIOT plays its role in various capacities during the complete product life cycle, starting from design, production, maintenance and lastly disposal. In-fact sometimes IIOT is synonymously used for CPS in manufacturing, as they both work towards the goals of efficient and smart production facilities. Various applications like digital twins [77], prognostics and health monitoring [78], smart logistics [79], digital supply chain [80], self-optimization [81], self-awareness [82], etc. the list is not exhaustive, but without IIOT and its related technologies, such smartness cannot be achieved.

(e) *Transportation:* IOT plays an important role in the automotive sector, where it can help the manufacturers in simplifying the production process by improving raw material/components order tracking, improving logistics for smooth transfer of finished vehicles, controlling quality of vehicles with more stringent rules, and finally improving the services to the customer by letting them track their orders [83–85]. In addition to easing the production process, the IOT can play roles in various communications like Vehicle to Vehicle (V2V) and Vehicle to Infrastructure (V2I) which can help in the better management of traffic and can make a contribution to the development and running of Intelligent Transportation Systems applications [86]. Also, in case of emergencies like accidents or breakdown of vehicles, the vehicle itself can relay its locations and other information to a centralized system or to the nearby facilities for help [87]. In case of the aviation sector, IOT covers the areas in which embedded devices can be introduced in the systems with having onboard sensing capabilities and communication capabilities to wirelessly monitor the status of the airplanes, helps the companies in condition-based maintenance, and facilitates maintenance planning as the systems become self-serving assets [88]. Introduction of RFID technology in this sector helps in checking for the counterfeit parts used in the aircrafts during maintenance which may hamper the safety of humans on board. Also, RFID can be used for easy tracking of luggage/passengers/crew/cargos can help in safety of the aircrafts and ease the process of commuting for passengers and companies [89].

2.3   Big Data Analysis

Big Data's most cited definition includes 3V's i.e., Volume, Variety, and Velocity which was presented by Doug Laney in 2001[90]. In brief, the term Big Data is applicable to information which cannot be extracted from raw data for analysis and decision-making purposes using conventional processes or tools available [91]. Various researchers and organizations have given different definitions by adding some more V's to this basic definition provided by Laney. The additional V's are Value [92], and Veracity [93]. So, going in depth of the Big Data V's:

i. *Volume:* It mainly points to the magnitude of data, which has and will be exponentially increasing, questioning the availability of capacity on existing storage devices [94].

ii. *Variety:* this parameter refers to the fact that the data is generated from heterogeneous sources like different kinds of sensors, various social media networks, mobile devices, etc. in a format which can be either un-structured, semi-structured or fully structured formats [95].

iii. *Velocity:* it defines the speed at which the data is generated and delivered, which is usually processed in real time, or near real-times, in a stream-line fashion or in batch format [96].

iv. *Value:* it refers to the process of unveiling the unexplored or under-utilized values from big data to help in making decisions in a more efficient manner [92].

v. *Veracity:* this parameter focuses on the data quality and level of trust which can be made on big data as many sources like social networking sites have uncertainties and unreliability in data available on them [93].

Big Data applications are:

(a) *Agriculture:* CPS and IOT provides a platform to move towards modernizing agriculture and initiatives like precision agriculture and smart farming are an example to it [10, 12]. But all the applications which these platforms provide are based on one thing "*data*", and in absence of data, nothing is possible. Major applications related to monitoring and predictions in livestock management, precision farming, and farm management are all based on previous knowledge and current data [11, 15, 51]. The ubiquitous data collected from farms is utilized and based on it the decisions are taken. Also, in case of supply chain and logistics of farm produce, Big data plays a huge role, and all planning and management actions are based on this huge data inferences [13, 97].

(b) *Energy Needs:* Big Data provides many visible benefits to utilities and electricity users like an increase in stability and reliability of systems, increase in asset utilization and its efficiency, and full customer satisfaction and experience [16, 17]. Further applications of Big Data are the monitoring, analyzing & predicting of energy needs throughout the grids, various events classification and detection like faults, line tripping, load shedding, oscillation, etc. The Big Data can also come in handy for power plant models validation and calibrations, load forecasting, distribution network verifications, demand response management, parameter estimations for distribution systems, system security and protection purposes [18–20].

(c) *Healthcare:* Big Data technologies play a bigger role in biomedical and health care informatics research as the data is being generated at a very high speed and scale. Big Data finds its applications in four major biomedical sub-divisions i.e., Bioinformatics: which deals with managing the genome data, analyses it and associates it with common diseases. Clinical informatics: which deals with intelligent decision making based on vast amounts of patient data. It further includes activity-based research, analyzing relationships among patients' main diagnosis & underlying cause of death, and manages the storage of data from electronic health records (EHR) and other sources like EEG data. Imaging-informatics: which deals with generation, management, and representation of medical imaging data. This domain focuses on personalized healthcare applications and incorporates imaging data to EHR in the cloud. Last is Public Health Informatics: which deals with 3 core functions i.e., assessment, policy development and assurance for public health. It has application areas in the surveillance of infectious diseases, population health management, mental health management and chronic disease management [98, 99].

(d) *Manufacturing:* Industry 4.0 which aims to digitize the manufacturing sector, has three main components and data is one of them. It is expected that Big Data will grow exponentially in this sector and almost all the applications targeted to modernize this sector will include data [100]. In fact data will be the base to all applications like digital twins [77], prognostics and health monitoring [78], smart logistics [79], smart supply chain [80], self-optimization [81], self-awareness [82], etc. and CPS with its related technologies will play a key role in achieving successfully implement them.

(e) *Transportation:* Big Data finds its application in Intelligent Transportation System (ITS), which is a transportation management system formed by integration of sensors, electronics, and IT systems to transportation infrastructure with an aim to make transportation systems efficient, environment friendly, safe & accessible to users [42, 43]. Big Data is mostly utilized in real-time traffic information collection and management, urban planning activities, and analyses of near misses and collision related mis-happenings on roads [101, 102]. Big Data also finds its application in autonomous vehicles paying an important role in CPS platforms for autonomous vehicles.

2.4   Additive Manufacturing

Additive Manufacturing (AM) or commonly called 3D printing is an advanced manufacturing process to fabricate components by adding material to it instead of a conventional subtraction machining process (milling, turning, etc.) to obtain desired shapes [103]. In AM, precision geometric shapes are produced from a computer-aided-design (CAD) model by slicing it and feeding it to an AM machine, followed by a post processing process. For making prototypes or in part improvement process by trial-and-error process AM technology is quite straight forward, faster and comes in handy. Also, this technology offers an easy way to fabricate complex geometries in a single step without any additional assemblies, resulting in lower manufacturing costs and lead times, which encourages researchers and industry people to use it extensively [104].

The AM process accepts various inputs like a 3D CAD, 2D CAD drawing, point cloud data from reverse engineering or MRI/CT scan data, these are all converted to a standard 3D cad model and converted to STL format which carries all the layer-by-layer information for 3D printing of the parts. To this STL data, machine and process parameters with support structure data is added and a single file is compiled which is fed to the AM machines and parts are manufactured according to it [105]. The raw material for AM machines can be either solid, liquid, gas or can be paste. Most common AM techniques are [104]:

i. *Stereolithography:* This technique utilizes a photosensitive liquid resin which solidifies into a solid polymer when exposed to an ultraviolet light source. Because of absorption and scattering of beam, the reaction only takes place near the surface of resin. It works in a layer-by-layer form, where the laser scans and solidifies resin first then its lowered down equivalent to one slice thickness and resin is again solidified. This is a continuous process till the full part is manufactured.

ii. *Selective Laser Sintering:* This technique is quite like stereolithography, but the raw material is now in fine polymeric powder form and a CO_2 laser acts as a source for solidification. After one layer of powder is cured a roller comes into action and spreads the powder which is to be cured and is repeated until the part is fabricated.

iii. *Fused Deposition Modelling:* In this technique, a nozzle with an in-built heater heats the solid polymeric material is heated and extruded out on a platform, and once the material is deposited on a platform it solidifies very quickly. Here mostly the nozzle moves in a plane (X-Y) and the platform moves up-down (Z), so a solid 3D part can be manufactured.

As AM technology utilizes various materials to print 3D parts like polymers, ceramics, and metals, so they find applications in many applications, some of them are:

(a) *Agriculture:* AM techniques has applications in agriculture in 5 major categorizes i.e., manufacturing hand tools like the tri-claw apple picker, custom shovel handle, hand shovel, and pulleys; in food processing like manufacturing water testers, pH testers, corn sheller, cassava press, and sausage funnels for meat grinders; in animal management like chicken feed holder, ant trap, gutting tool, and field dressing tool; in water management like manufacturing of garden hose splitters, gaskets, and contoured spigot for 5 gallon bucket; in hydroponics like manufacturing of hydroponic halo ring, plant pot, peristaltic pump, and 3D Ponics [106].

(b) *Energy Needs:* AM technology contributes mostly to producing electrodes and devices for electrochemical energy-storage devices (EESD) i.e., batteries and supercapacitors [107]. The EESD have widely been used in aerospace, constructions, electronics, energy, biosensors, etc. [108]. 3D printing provides an innovative approach to fabricate these technologies from nanoscale to macroscale with a complete control over the device geometry i.e., dimensions, porosity, and morphology [109]. In addition to EESD, AM is widely utilized in printing wearable bio-electronic devices, which are flexible bioelectronic structures having integrated life-long power source [110, 111].

(c) *Healthcare:* In healthcare, the AM has a huge number of applications, even in the difficult pandemic times the AM played an important role. Major medical applications are in surgical planning, where the surgeon's 3D print the bone structure of patients and study before surgery to reduce operations time, risk to life and costs during operation [112]. In medical education and training, 3D models of internal and external human anatomy structures help in studying surgical procedures and problems [113]. In customized implants and bone replicas, 3D printing plays a key role, as complex knee joints, spinal implants and dental implants can be manufactured with precision [114, 115]. For scaffoldings and tissue engineering, FDM, & SLS are the common contributing 3D printing technologies as they can produce complex geometry with higher accuracy [116]. Prosthetics and orthotics also use a lot of 3D printed components as these models provide comfort and stability with precision [117].

(d) *Manufacturing:* AM plays an important role in the product life cycle majorly in designing and manufacturing in various capacities. Major design applications are CAD model verification, visualization purposes, proof of concepts for marketing and commercial applications. Further looking at the parts from engineering perspectives applications include scaled prototypes e.g., perfume bottles with different holding capacities, part form and fit related considerations e.g., like a new rear view mirror design testing or door handle design testing, thermal fluid flow analysis, stress analysis, pre-production parts, jig-fixtures manufacturing, and rapid tools manufacturing, etc. [103].

(e) *Transportation:* AM techniques are mostly utilized in manufacturing of automotives in the transportation domain, where major areas include prototype printing of components using varied materials i.e., plastics, metals, composites, etc. during the design and pre-production phases [118, 119]. One interesting application is a 3D printed complete car, which actually works has also been presented [120]. The contribution of 3D printing in the automotive sector is mainly in five ways i.e., flexible optimized designs, rapid tooling, fast customizations, production aids and real-world testing phases [121]. Prototyping complex gearbox housings, to advanced driver control systems, creating metallic engine blocks to production tools, everywhere the AM finds its applications [103]. In the aerospace industry also 3D printing finds its applications in manufacturing complex geometry parts e.g., fuel nozzles; printing difficult to machine parts; custom parts production; on-demand manufacturing of old parts; and high performance to weight ratio products mostly in space travel [122].

2.5 Artificial Intelligence

Artificial Intelligence (AI) term was first used by John McCarthy (Dartmouth College), Marvin L. Minsky (MIT), Nathaniel Rochester (IBM), and Claude Shannon (Bell Laboratories) in 1956, when they conducted the Dartmouth Summer Research Project on Artificial Intelligence, which shaped this field [123]. Considering the postwar traditions of systems engineering and cybernetics with mathematical logic and a philosophical approach aimed at formally describing human thinking, the brain takes symbolic information as input, processes it using a set of formal rules and doing so can solve problems, make decisions, and even formulate certain judgments. After the 1956 workshop, researchers started working towards identifying formal processes to replicate human behavior in an automated fashion in various defined problems like medical diagnosis, chess, mathematics, language processing, etc. [124, 125]. However, currently researchers are designing automated systems that can perform even better than humans in complex problem domains [126].

AI is divided majorly into two categories i.e., supervised, and unsupervised type of learning. Supervised learning refers to models where the data is given as input with their expected outputs and the model needs to generate a relationship between input features and expected values (can be discrete or continuous values). This category has two sub-categories i.e., regression where the training labels are continuous and classification where training labels are discrete. In case of unsupervised learning, the models are formulated in an unsupervised manner i.e., labels are not provided, and models need to recognize patterns and formulate a relationship among input features and expected output values. This category also has two sub-categories i.e., clustering where the models are created based on similarity among the input objects and distinct categories, second is statistical estimation which uses principles of probability and statistics to create a distribution function among input objects and specific parameters [127].

AI applications in various domains are:

(a) *Agriculture:* AI application in agriculture mostly focused on providing meaning and value to the data collected from the farm, like weather, soil, humidity, and climate and based on this data inference and making predictions regarding the produce, which is one of the goals of smart farming [10, 11]. Also, in drone imagery data analysis of farms, AI algorithms play their role [128, 129], and by merging both data i.e., image and sensor, results in digital twins of farms which digitally replicates the complete farm and opens a wide variety of new dimensions to precision farming [130, 131]. AI is also helping in defining the way plants need to be sowed to reduce overlap and excessive gap between two plants [132].

(b) *Energy Needs:* The smart grid technology generates a lot of data and feeding this data to AI algorithms helps in predicting the required load, and efficiently managing it [20]. AI provides tools for designing, simulation, diagnosing faults, and embed fault tolerance into these smart grids [133]. AI also plays its part in discovery of new materials and chemistry i.e., catalysis, batteries, solar cells, and crystal discovery etc. [134]. AI can come in handy in reviewing short-term load demand forecasting techniques for smart grids and building based on load, weather, humans, previous knowledge, and current data [135], further some AI algorithms are utilized in modelling the heating and cooling loads in energy-efficient buildings [136]. Overall, all the data collected is converted into useful information for decision making using AI algorithms [137].

(c) *Healthcare:* AI algorithms are very good at making predictions, doing simulations and optimization tasks, so the best application in the healthcare domain would be the prediction of risk of diseases, predictions of epidemics and disease outbreaks. Also, by implying a three-fold technique of acquisition, analyzing and visualization can help in tackling the problems of current medical setup like deficient infrastructure, deficient manpower, unmanageable patient load, equivocal quality of services, high expenditure, etc. [65]. One other application is precision medicine, where based on the patient's previous health records and treatment context, predictions are made regarding the treatment protocols which are likely to succeed on a particular patient [138]. The AI is also being used for detecting clinically relevant elements from the imaging data, and even some chatbots also came into existence for providing the telemedicine services [139].

(d) *Manufacturing:* Industry 4.0 is creating waves in this sector and is mostly about connecting the physical machine to the cyber world and utilizing this data generated out of the machine for making these machines smarter [31]. Various application come into existence this Industry 4.0 hat, which is not possible without utilizing AI algorithms like digital twins [77], prognostics and health monitoring [78], smart logistics [79], digital supply chain [80], self-optimization [81], self-awareness [82], etc. Further, AI can also come in handy during the complete product life cycle, starting from design, where AI can do simulations and give suggestions on product designs, perform optimization & keep an eye on machines during manufacturing, and report in case of any abnormality, based on current data and state can trigger maintenance activities and when product life is near, order replacement and inform necessary people for disposal [32–38].

(e) *Transportation:* With the trend of modernizing transportation systems, Intelligent Transportation Systems (ITS) came into existence which integrates sensors, electronics, and IT to transportation infrastructure with an aim to make transportation systems efficient, environment friendly, safe and accessible to users [42, 43]. But to successfully implement ITS, AI plays an important role as all the data which is generated is converted to useful information by these algorithms, predictions based on that data are made by it and finally management of transportation infrastructure is done by it [101, 102]. In case of emergencies like accidents or breakdown of vehicles, the vehicle itself can relay its locations and other information to a centralized system or to the nearby facilities for help which is done by AI algorithms running in the vehicles [87]. More advanced applications like lane keeping assistance, distance keeping assistance, potholes detection and reporting systems are all realized by AI using the plethora of sensors and network elements [42–44].

3. Conclusion

This chapter introduced Cyber-Physical Systems (CPS) and its strong interconnection with various technologies. We described the several forms in which a pandemic such as COVID-19 has affected different sectors. The pandemic has taken its toll on multiple industries ranging from teaching institutions, manufacturing, workspaces, machining, production, and supply chain to name a few. Both Industry 4.0 and CPS can aid in mitigating and suppressing the adverse effect of COVID-19 pandemic in these sectors. However, the current CPS solutions need to be formally designed to cater to the industrial needs during the pandemic. The rest of the chapters are described as follows. Chapters 2, and 3 meticulously describe the adverse effect of COVID-19 pandemic on the steel industries, and SMEs, all around different geographic areas, respectively, while Chapter 4 introduces and describes Industry 4.0 standards against countering the pandemic situation. With most industry personnel forced to work remotely, a CPS-based solution leveraging the concepts of human-robot assembly is presented in Chapter 5. Chapter 6 picks on an interesting CPS perspective to mitigate the pandemic issues in teaching carried out in engineering laboratories, while Chapter 7 discusses the impact of using CPS in enhancing the resilience of supply chain during dynamism due to pandemic. Manufacturing industries play a crucial role for progress of a country or region. Chapters 8, 9, and 10 describes CPS and Industry 4.0 based solutions for various manufacturing systems. Advanced frameworks for improving the production systems and online education are presented in Chapters 11, and 12 respectively. Finally, chapters 14, and 15 present two vital use-cases in workplaces, and machine tools.

References

1. Ahmadi, A., C. Cherifi, V. Cheutet and Y. Ouzrout. A review of CPS 5 components architecture for manufacturing based on standards. *In*: 2017 11th International Conference on Software, Knowledge, Information Management and Applications (SKIMA), IEEE. (2017, December): 1–6).
2. Gunes, V., S. Peter, T. Givargis and F. Vahid. A survey on concepts, applications, and challenges in cyber-physical systems. KSII Transactions on Internet & Information Systems, 8(12): (2014).

3. Chen, H. Theoretical foundations for cyber-physical systems: A literature review. Journal of Industrial Integration and Management, 2(03), (2017): 1750013.
4. Lee, E.A. Cyber-physical systems – are computing foundations adequate. *In*: Position paper for NSF workshop on Cyber-physical Systems: Research Motivation, Techniques and Roadmap, 2, (2006) Citeseer, 1–9.
5. Marburger, J.H., E.F. Kvamme, G. Scalise and D.A. Reed. Leadership under challenge: Information technology R&D in a competitive world. An assessment of the Federal Networking and Information Technology R&D Program. Executive office of the president Washington DC. President's Council of Advisors on Science and Technology (2007).
6. CPS Steering Group. Cyber-physical systems executive summary. http://precise.seas.upenn.edu/events/iccpsll/_doc/CPS-Executive-Summary.pdf (2008).
7. Cyber-Physical Systems Virtual Organization (CPS-VO). Retrieved on April 09, 2021 from: http://cps-vo.org/
8. The Artemis Embedded Computing Systems Initiative. Retrieved on April 09, 2021 from: https://artemis-ia.eu/
9. The EU Framework Program for Research and Innovation (Horizon2020). Retrieved on April 09, 2021 from: http://ec.europa.eu/programmes/horizon2020/
10. Rad, C.-R., O. Hancu, I.-A. Takacs and G. Olteanu. Smart monitoring of potato crop: A cyber-physical system architecture model in the field of precision agriculture. Agriculture and Agricultural Science Procedia, 6, (2015): 73–79.
11. Chukkapalli, S.S.L., S. Mittal, M. Gupta, M. Abdelsalam, A. Joshi, R. Sandhu, and K. Joshi. Ontologies and artificial intelligence systems for the cooperative smart farming ecosystem. IEEE Access, 8, (2020): 164045–164064.
12. Zamora-Izquierdo, M.A., J. Santa, J.A. Martínez, V. Martínez and A.F. Skarmeta. Smart farming IoT platform based on edge and cloud computing. Biosystems Engineering, 177, (2019): 4–17.
13. Zhang, Ning. Smart logistics path for cyber-physical systems with internet of things. IEEE Access, 6, (2018): 70808–70819.
14. Selmani, A., H. Oubehar, M. Outanoute, A. Ed-Dahhak, M. Guerbaoui, A. Lachhab and B. Bouchikhi. Agricultural cyber-physical system enabled for remote management of solar-powered precision irrigation. Biosystems Engineering, 177, (2019): 18–30.
15. Namala, K.K., K.K. Prabhu AV, A. Math, A. Kumari and S. Kulkarni. Smart irrigation with embedded system. IEEE Bombay Section Symposium (IBSS), (2016): 1–5.
16. Yu, X. and Y. Xue. Smart grids: A cyber–physical systems perspective. Proceedings of the IEEE, 104(5), (2016): 1058–1070.
17. Yu, X., C. Cecati, T. Dillon and M. Godoy Simoes. The new frontier of smart grids. IEEE Industrial Electronics Magazine, 5(3), (2011): 49–63.
18. Xu, L., Q. Guo, T. Yang and H. Sun. Robust routing optimization for smart grids considering cyber-physical interdependence. IEEE Transactions on Smart Grid, 10(5), (2018): 5620–5629.
19. Li, H., A. Dimitrovski, J.B. Song, Z. Han and L. Qian. Communication infrastructure design in cyber physical systems with applications in smart grids: A hybrid system framework. IEEE Communications Surveys & Tutorials, 16(3), (2014): 1689–1708.

20. Alazab, M., S. Khan, S.S.R. Krishnan, Q.-V. Pham, M.P.K. Reddy and T.R. Gadekallu. A multidirectional LSTM model for predicting the stability of a smart grid. IEEE Access, 8, (2020): 85454–85463.
21. Mogles, N., I. Walker, A.P. Ramallo-González, J.H. Lee, S. Natarajan, J. Padget, E. Gabe-Thomas, T. Lovett, G. Ren, S. Hyniewska, E. O'Neill, R. Hourizi and D. Coley. How smart do smart meters need to be? Building and Environment, 125, (2017): 439–450.
22. Zhang, Y., M. Qiu, C.-W. Tsai, M.M. Hassan and A. Alamri. Health-CPS: Healthcare cyber-physical system assisted by cloud and big data. IEEE Systems Journal, 11(1), (2015): 88–95.
23. Roy, A., C. Roy, S. Misra, Y. Rahulamathavan and M. Rajarajan. Care: Criticality-aware data transmission in CPS-based healthcare systems. IEEE International Conference on Communications Workshops (ICC Workshops), (2018): 1–6.
24. Haque, S.A., S.M. Aziz and M. Rahman. Review of cyber-physical system in healthcare. International Journal of Distributed Sensor Networks, 10(4), (2014): 217415.
25. Dey, N., A.S. Ashour, F. Shi, S.J. Fong and J.M.R. Tavares. Medical cyber-physical systems: A survey. Journal of Medical Systems, 42(4) (2018): 1–13.
26. Yang, G., Z. Pang, M.J. Deen, M. Dong, Y.-T. Zhang, N. Lovell and A.M. Rahmani. Homecare robotic systems for healthcare 4.0: Visions and enabling technologies. IEEE Journal of Biomedical and Health Informatics, 24(9) (2020): 2535–2549.
27. Jin, M.L., M.M. Brown, P. Dhir, A. Nirmalan and P. A. Edwards. Telemedicine, Telementoring, and Telesurgery for Surgical Practices. Current Problems in Surgery, (2021): 100987.
28. Sedaghat, S. and A.H. Jahangir. RT-TelSurg: Real time telesurgery using SDN, fog, and cloud as infrastructures. IEEE Access, (2021).
29. Taylor, R.H., A. Menciassi, G. Fichtinger, P. Fiorini and P. Dario. Medical robotics and computer-integrated surgery. Springer Handbook of Robotics, (2016): 1657–1684.
30. Diana, M. and J. Marescaux. Robotic surgery. Journal of British Surgery, 102(2), (2015): e15-e28.
31. Jazdi, N. Cyber physical systems in the context of Industry 4.0. *In*: 2014 IEEE International Conference on Automation, Quality and Testing, Robotics, IEEE, (2014): 1–4.
32. Wan, J., M. Chen, F. Xia, L. Di and K. Zhou. From machine-to-machine communications towards cyber-physical systems. Computer Science and Information Systems, 10(3), (2013): 1105–1128.
33. Sadiku, M.N., Y. Wang, S. Cui and S.M. Musa. Cyber-physical systems: A literature review. European Scientific Journal. 13(36), (2017): 52–58.
34. Bagheri, B., S. Yang, H.-A. Kao and J. Lee. Cyber-physical systems architecture for self-aware machines in industry 4.0 environment. IFAC-PapersOnLine, 48(3), (2015): 1622–1627.
35. Liu, C. and P. Jiang. A cyber-physical system architecture in shop floor for intelligent manufacturing. Procedia Cirp, 56, (2016): 372–377.
36. Chaves, A., R. Maia, C. Belchior, R. Araújo and G. Gouveia. Khrono Sim: A platform for complex systems simulation and testing. *In*: 2018 IEEE 23rd International Conference on Emerging Technologies and Factory Automation (ETFA). IEEE, vol. 1, (2018): 131–138.

37. Muccini, H., M. Sharaf and D. Weyns. Self-adaptation for cyber-physical systems: A systematic literature review. *In*: Proceedings of the 11th International Symposium on Software Engineering for Adaptive and Self-managing Systems, (2016): 75–81.
38. Jirkovský, V., M. Obitko, P. Kadera and V. Mařík. Toward plug&play cyber-physical system components. IEEE Transactions on Industrial Informatics, 14(6), (2018): 2803–2811.
39. Yongfu, L., S. Dihua, L. Weining and Z. Xuebo. A service-oriented architecture for the transportation cyber-physical systems. *In*: Proceedings of the 31st Chinese Control Conference, IEEE, (2012): 7674–7678.
40. Rawat, D. B., C. Bajracharya and G. Yan. Towards intelligent transportation cyber-physical systems: Real-time computing and communications perspectives. *In*: SoutheastCon 2015, IEEE, (2015): 1–6.
41. Sun, Y. and H. Song (Eds). Secure and trustworthy transportation cyber-physical systems. Springer Singapore, (2017).
42. Dimitrakopoulos, G. and P. Demestichas. Intelligent transportation systems. IEEE Vehicular Technology Magazine, 5(1), (2010): 77–84.
43. Zhang, J., F.-Y. Wang, K. Wang, W.-H. Lin, X. Xu and C. Chen. Data-driven intelligent transportation systems: A survey. IEEE Transactions on Intelligent Transportation Systems, 12(4), (2011): 1624–1639.
44. Cook, W., A. Driscoll and B. Tenbergen. Airborne CPS: A simulator for functional dependencies in cyber physical systems: a traffic collision avoidance system implementation. *In*: 2018 4th International Workshop on Requirements Engineering for Self-Adaptive, Collaborative, and Cyber Physical Systems (RESACS), IEEE, (2018): 32–35.
45. Vierhauser, M., J. Cleland-Huang, S. Bayley, T. Krismayer, R. Rabiser and P. Grünbacher. Monitoring CPS at runtime – A case study in the UAV domain. *In*: 2018 44th Euromicro Conference on Software Engineering and Advanced Applications (SEAA), IEEE, (2018): 73–80.
46. Ashton, K. That 'internet of things' thing. RFID Journal, 22(7), (2009): 97–114.
47. Atzori, L., A. Iera and G. Morabito. The internet of things: A survey. Computer Networks, 54(15), (2010): 2787–2805.
48. INFSO, DG. Internet of Things in 2020: Roadmap for the Future. INFSO D 4 (2008).
49. Al-Fuqaha, A., M. Guizani, M. Mohammadi, M. Aledhari and M. Ayyash. Internet of things: A survey on enabling technologies, protocols, and applications. IEEE Communications Surveys & Tutorials, 17(4), (2015): 2347–2376.
50. Sundmaeker, H., P. Guillemin, P. Friess and S. Woelfflé. Vision and challenges for realising the Internet of Things. Cluster of European research projects on the internet of things. European Commision, 3(3), (2010): 34–36.
51. Farooq, M.S., S. Riaz, A. Abid, K. Abid and M.A. Naeem. A survey on the role of IoT in Agriculture for the implementation of smart farming. IEEE Access, 7, (2019): 156237–156271.
52. Martins, J.F., J.A. Oliveira-Lima, V. Delgado-Gomes, R. Lopes, D. Silva, S. Vieira and C. Lima. Smart homes and smart buildings. *In*: 2012 13th Biennial Baltic Electronics Conference, IEEE, (2012): 27–38.
53. Aldrich, F.K. Smart homes: Past, present and future. Inside the Smart Home, Springer, London, (2003): 17–39.

54. Plageras, A.P., K.E. Psannis, C. Stergiou, H. Wang and B.B. Gupta. Efficient IoT-based sensor BIG Data collection-processing and analysis in smart buildings. Future Generation Computer Systems, 82, (2018): 349–357.

55. Hong, S.H., M. Yu and X. Huang. A real-time demand response algorithm for heterogeneous devices in buildings and homes. Energy, 80, (2015): 123–132.

56. Akkaya, K., I. Guvenc, R. Aygun, N. Pala and A. Kadri. IoT-based occupancy monitoring techniques for energy-efficient smart buildings. *In*: 2015 IEEE Wireless Communications and Networking Conference Workshops (WCNCW), IEEE, (2015): 58–63.

57. Chen, S.-Yeh, C.-F. Lai, Y.-M. Huang and Y.-L. Jeng. Intelligent home-appliance recognition over IoT cloud network. *In*: 2013 9th International Wireless Communications and Mobile Computing Conference (IWCMC), IEEE, (2013): 639–643.

58. Minoli, D., K. Sohraby and B. Occhiogrosso. IoT considerations, requirements and architectures for smart buildings—Energy optimization and next-generation building management systems. IEEE Internet of Things Journal, 4(1), (2017): 269–283.

59. Zanella, A., N. Bui, A. Castellani, L. Vangelista and M. Zorzi. Internet of things for smart cities. IEEE Internet of Things Journal, 1(1), (2014): 22–32.

60. Mitton, N., S. Papavassiliou, A. Puliafito and K.S. Trivedi. Combining Cloud and sensors in a smart city environment. (2012): 1–10.

61. Petrolo, R., N. Mitton, J. Soldatos, M. Hauswirth and G. Schiele. Integrating wireless sensor networks within a city cloud. *In*: 2014 Eleventh Annual IEEE International Conference on Sensing, Communication, and Networking Workshops (SECON Workshops). IEEE, (2014): 24–27.

62. Suciu, G., A. Vulpe, S. Halunga, O. Fratu, G. Todoran and V. Suciu. Smart cities built on resilient cloud computing and secure internet of things. *In*: 2013 19th International Conference on Control Systems and Computer Science, IEEE, (2013): 513–518.

63. Alagöz, F., A.C. Valdez, W. Wilkowska, M. Ziefle, S. Dorner and A. Holzinger. From cloud computing to mobile Internet, from user focus to culture and hedonism: The crucible of mobile health care and wellness applications. *In*: 5th International Conference on Pervasive Computing and Applications. IEEE, (2010): 38–45.

64. Kulkarni, A. and S. Sathe. Healthcare applications of the Internet of Things: A Review. International Journal of Computer Science and Information Technologies, 5(5), (2014): 6229–6232.

65. Bhatt, C., N. Dey and A.S. Ashour (Eds). Internet of things and big data technologies for next generation healthcare. (2017): 978–3.

66. Akyildiz, I.F., W. Su, Y. Sankarasubramaniam and E. Cayirci. A survey on sensor networks. IEEE Communications Magazine, 40(8), (2002): 102–114.

67. Fortino, G., D. Parisi, V. Pirrone and G. Di Fatta. BodyCloud: A SaaS approach for community body sensor networks. Future Generation Computer Systems, 35, (2014): 62–79.

68. Doukas, C. and I. Maglogiannis. Bringing IoT and cloud computing towards pervasive healthcare. *In*: 2012 Sixth International Conference on Innovative Mobile and Internet Services in Ubiquitous Computing. IEEE, (2012): 922–926.

69. Doukas, C. and I. Maglogiannis. Managing wearable sensor data through cloud computing. *In*: 2011 IEEE Third International Conference on Cloud Computing Technology and Science. IEEE, (2011): 440–445.

70. Fernandez, F. and G.C. Pallis. Opportunities and challenges of the Internet of Things for healthcare: Systems engineering perspective. *In*: 2014 4th International Conference on Wireless Mobile Communication and Healthcare-Transforming Healthcare Through Innovations in Mobile and Wireless Technologies (MOBIHEALTH). IEEE, (2014): 263–266.

71. Jimenez, F. and R. Torres. Building an IoT-aware healthcare monitoring system. *In*: 2015 34th International Conference of the Chilean Computer Science Society (SCCC). IEEE, (2015): 1–4.

72. Yeole, A.S. and D.R. Kalbande. Use of Internet of Things (IoT) in healthcare: A survey. *In*: Proceedings of the ACM Symposium on Women in Research 2016, (2016): 71–76.

73. Liao, Y., E. de Freitas Rocha Loures and F. Deschamps. Industrial Internet of Things: A systematic literature review and insights. IEEE Internet of Things Journal, 5(6), (2018): 4515–4525.

74. Alexopoulos, K., S. Koukas, N. Boli and D. Mourtzis. Architecture and development of an Industrial Internet of Things framework for realizing services in Industrial Product Service Systems. Procedia CIRP, 72, (2018): 880–885.

75. Wan, J., S. Tang, Z. Shu, D. Li, S. Wang, M. Imran and A.V. Vasilakos. Software-defined industrial internet of things in the context of industry 4.0. IEEE Sensors Journal, 16(20), (2016): 7373–7380.

76. Boyes, H., B. Hallaq, J. Cunningham and T. Watson. The industrial internet of things (IIoT): An analysis framework. Computers in Industry, 101, (2018): 1–12.

77. Kritzinger, W., M. Karner, G. Traar, J. Henjes and W. Sihn. Digital twin in manufacturing: A categorical literature review and classification. IFAC-PapersOnLine, 51(11), (2018): 1016–1022.

78. Zonta, T., C.A. da Costa, R. da Rosa Righi, M.J. de Lima, E.S. da Trindade and G.P. Li. Predictive maintenance in the Industry 4.0: A systematic literature review. Computers & Industrial Engineering, (2020): 106889.

79. Zhang, Y., Z. Guo, J. Lv and Y. Liu. A framework for smart production-logistics systems based on CPS and industrial IoT. IEEE Transactions on Industrial Informatics, 14(9), (2018): 4019–4032.

80. Büyüközkan, G. and F. Göçer. Digital supply chain: Literature review and a proposed framework for future research. Computers in Industry, 97, (2018): 157–177.

81. Permin, E., F. Bertelsmeier, M. Blum, J. Bützler, S. Haag, S. Kuz, D. Özdemir, S. Stemmler, U. Thombansen, R. Schmitt, C. Brecher, C. Schlick, D. Abel, R. Poprawe, P. Loosen, W. Schulz and G. Schuh. Self-optimizing production systems. Procedia Cirp, 41, (2016): 417–422.

82. Liao, L., R. Minhas, A. Rangarajan, T. Kurtoglu and J. De Kleer. A self-aware machine platform in manufacturing shop floor utilizing MTConnect data. Palo Alto Research Center Palo Alto United States (2014).

83. McFarlane, D. and Y. Sheffi. The impact of automatic identification on supply chain operations. Department of Engineering, University of Cambridge (2003).

84. Aris, I.B., R. Kalos, Z. Sahbusdin and A.F.M. Amin. Impacts of IoT and big data to automotive industry. *In*: 2015 10th Asian Control Conference (ASCC), IEEE, (2015): 1–5.

85. Liu, T., R. Yuan and H. Chang. Research on the Internet of Things in the Automotive Industry. *In*: 2012 International Conference on Management of e-Commerce and e-Government. IEEE, (2012): 230–233.

86. Martínez de Aragón, B., J. Alonso-Zarate and A. Laya. How connectivity is transforming the automotive ecosystem. Internet Technology Letters, 1(1), (2018): e14.

87. Panga, G., S. Zamfir, T. Balan and O. Popa. IoT diagnostics for connected cars. International Scientific Committee, (2016): 287.

88. Brintrup, A.M., D.C. Ranasinghe, S. Kwan, A. Parlikad and K. Owens. Roadmap to self-serving assets in civil aerospace. *In*: Proceedings of the 19th CIRP Design Conference – Competitive Design. Cranfield University Press, (2009).

89. Singh, A., S. Meshram, T. Gujar and P.R. Wankhede. Baggage tracing and handling system using RFID and IoT for airports. *In*: 2016 International Conference on Computing, Analytics and Security Trends (CAST). IEEE, (2016): 466–470.

90. Laney, D. 3D data management: Controlling data volume, velocity and variety. META Group Research Note, 6(70), (2001): 1.

91. Zikopoulos, P. and C. Eaton. Understanding big data: Analytics for enterprise class hadoop and streaming data. McGraw-Hill Osborne Media, (2011).

92. Gantz, J. and D. Reinsel. Extracting value from chaos. IDC Iview, 1142, (2011): 1–12.

93. Zikopoulos, P.C., D. Deroos and K. Parasuraman. Harness the power of big data: The IBM big data platform. McGraw-Hill, (2013).

94. Chen, CL.P. and C.-Y. Zhang. Data-intensive applications, challenges, techniques and technologies: A survey on Big Data. Information Sciences, 275, (2014): 314–347.

95. Tan, K.H., Y.Z. Zhan, G. Ji, F. Ye and C. Chang. Harvesting big data to enhance supply chain innovation capabilities: An analytic infrastructure based on deduction graph. International Journal of Production Economics, 165, (2015): 223–233.

96. Assunção, M.D., R.N. Calheiros, S. Bianchi, M.A.S. Netto and R. Buyya. Big Data computing and clouds: Trends and future directions. Journal of Parallel and Distributed Computing, 79, (2015): 3–15.

97. Lee, C.K.M., Y. Lv, K.K.H. Ng, W. Ho and K.L. Choy. Design and application of Internet of things-based warehouse management system for smart logistics. International Journal of Production Research, 56(8), (2018): 2753–2768.

98. Luo, J., M. Wu, D. Gopukumar and Y. Zhao. Big data application in biomedical research and health care: A literature review. Biomedical Informatics Insights, 8, (2016): BII–S31559.

99. Hulsen, Tim, Saumya S. Jamuar, Alan R. Moody, Jason H. Karnes, Orsolya Varga, Stine Hedensted, Roberto Spreafico, David A. Hafler and Eoin F. McKinney. From big data to precision medicine. Frontiers in Medicine, 6, (2019): 34.

100. Tao, F., Q. Qi, A. Liu and A. Kusiak. Data-driven smart manufacturing. Journal of Manufacturing Systems, 48, (2018): 157–169.
101. Lv, Y., Y. Duan, W. Kang, Z. Li and F-Y. Wang. Traffic flow prediction with big data: A deep learning approach. IEEE Transactions on Intelligent Transportation Systems, 16(2), (2014): 865–873.
102. Khazaei, H., S. Zareian, R. Veleda and M. Litoiu. Sipresk: A big data analytic platform for smart transportation. Smart City 360°, Springer, Cham, (2016): 419–430.
103. Chua, C.K., K.F. Leong and C.S. Lim. Rapid prototyping: Principles and applications (with companion CD-ROM). World Scientific Publishing Company, (2010).
104. Gibson, I., D. Rosen, B. Stucker and M. Khorasani. Additive Manufacturing Technologies. Vol. 17. New York: Springer, (2014).
105. Gebhardt, A. Rapid Prototyping. (2003).
106. Pearce, J. Applications of open source 3-D printing on small farms. Organic Farming, 1(1), (2013): 19–35.
107. Browne, M.P., E. Redondo and M. Pumera. 3D printing for electrochemical energy applications. Chemical Reviews, 120(5), (2020): 2783–2810.
108. Tian, X., J. Jin, S. Yuan, C.K. Chua, S.B. Tor and K. Zhou. Emerging 3D-printed electrochemical energy storage devices: A critical review. Advanced Energy Materials, 7(17), (2017): 1700127.
109. Zhang, F., M. Wei, V.V. Viswanathan, B. Swart, Y. Shao, G. Wu and C. Zhou. 3D printing technologies for electrochemical energy storage. Nano Energy, 40, (2017): 418–431.
110. Krishnadoss, V., B. Kanjilal, A. Hesketh, C. Miller, A. Mugweru, M. Akbard, A. Khademhosseini and I. Noshadi. In situ 3D printing of implantable energy storage devices. Chemical Engineering Journal, 409, (2021): 128213.
111. Zhang, Y., T. Ji, S. Hou, L. Zhang, Y. Shi, J. Zhao and X. Xu. All-printed solid-state substrate-versatile and high-performance micro-supercapacitors for in situ fabricated transferable and wearable energy storage via multi-material 3D printing. Journal of Power Sources, 403, (2018): 109–117.
112. Tejo-Otero, A., I. Buj-Corral and F. Fenollosa-Artés. 3D printing in medicine for preoperative surgical planning: A review. Annals of Biomedical Engineering, 48(2), (2020): 536–555.
113. Li, K.H.C., C. Kui, E.K.M. Lee, C.S. Ho, S.H.S. Hei, W. Wu, W.T. Wong et al. The role of 3D printing in anatomy education and surgical training: A narrative review. MedEdPublish, 6(2), (2017).
114. Popov, V.V., G. Muller-Kamskii, A. Kovalevsky, G. Dzhenzhera, E. Strokin, A. Kolomiets and J. Ramon. Design and 3D-printing of titanium bone implants: Brief review of approach and clinical cases. Biomedical Engineering Letters, 8(4), (2018): 337–344.
115. Dawood, A., B.M. Marti, V. Sauret-Jackson and A. Darwood. 3D printing in dentistry. British Dental Journal, 219(11), (2015): 521–529.
116. Tan, X.P., Y.J. Tan, C.S.L. Chow, S.B. Tor and W.Y. Yeong. Metallic powder-bed based 3D printing of cellular scaffolds for orthopaedic implants: A state-of-the-art review on manufacturing, topological design, mechanical properties and biocompatibility. Materials Science and Engineering: C, 76, (2017): 1328–1343.

117. Nickel, E., K. Barrons, B. Hand, A. Cataldo and A. Hansen. Three-dimensional printing in prosthetics: Method for managing rapid limb volume change. Prosthetics and Orthotics International, 44(5), (2020): 355–358.

118. Savastano, M., C. Amendola, D. Fabrizio and E. Massaroni. 3-D printing in the spare parts supply chain: An explorative study in the automotive industry. *In:* Digitally Supported Innovation. Springer, Cham, (2016): 153–170.

119. Hackney, P.M. and R. Wooldridge. 3D sand printing for automotive mass production applications. International Journal of Rapid Manufacturing, 6(2–3), (2017): 134–154.

120. Nichols, M.R. How does the automotive industry benefit from 3D metal printing? Metal Powder Report, 74(5), (2019): 257–258.

121. Lecklider, T. 3D printing drives automotive innovation. Technology, 4, (2019): 3D.

122. Ngo, T.D., A. Kashani, G. Imbalzano, K.TQ. Nguyen and D. Hui. Additive manufacturing (3D printing): A review of materials, methods, applications and challenges. Composites Part B: Engineering, 143, (2018): 172–196.

123. McCarthy, J., M.L. Minsky, N. Rochester and C.E. Shannon. A proposal for the Dartmouth summer research project on artificial intelligence, August 31, 1955. AI Magazine, 27(4), (2006): 12–14.

124. Kline, R.. Cybernetics, automata studies, and the Dartmouth conference on artificial intelligence. IEEE Annals of the History of Computing, 33(4), (2010): 5–16.

125. Kline, R.R. The cybernetics moment: Or why we call our age the information age. JHU Press, (2015).

126. Dick, S. Artificial Intelligence. (2019).

127. Lee, J. Industrial AI: Applications with Sustainable Performance, (2020).

128. Sundmaeker, Harald, C.N. Verdouw, J. Wolfert and Luis Perez Freire. Internet of food and farm 2020. Digitising the Industry, vol. 49, River Publishers, (2016): 129–150.

129. Migdall, S., P. Klug, A. Denis and H. Bach. The additional value of hyperspectral data for smart farming. *In:* 2012 IEEE International Geoscience and Remote Sensing Symposium. IEEE, (2012): 7329–7332.

130. Lottes, P., R. Khanna, J. Pfeifer, R. Siegwart and C. Stachniss. UAV-based crop and weed classification for smart farming. *In:* 2017 IEEE International Conference on Robotics and Automation (ICRA). IEEE, (2017): 3024–3031.

131. Chukkapalli, S.S.L., A. Piplai, S. Mittal, M. Gupta and A. Joshi. A smart-farming ontology for attribute-based access control. *In:* 2020 IEEE 6th Intl Conference on Big Data Security on Cloud (BigDataSecurity), IEEE Intl Conference on High Performance and Smart Computing, (HPSC) and IEEE Intl Conference on Intelligent Data and Security (IDS). IEEE, 2020: 29–34.

132. AutoTrac, Jul. (2020), [online] Available: https://www.deere.com/sub-saharan/en/technology-products/precision-ag/autotrac/.

133. Bose, B.K. Artificial intelligence techniques in smart grid and renewable energy systems—Some example applications. Proceedings of the IEEE, 105(11), (2017): 2262–2273.

134. Gu, G.H., J. Noh, I. Kim and Y. Jung. Machine learning for renewable energy materials. Journal of Materials Chemistry A, 7(29), (2019): 17096–17117.

135. Raza, M.Q. and A. Khosravi. A review on artificial intelligence-based load demand forecasting techniques for smart grid and buildings. Renewable and Sustainable Energy Reviews, 50, (2015): 1352–1372.
136. Chou, J.-S. and D.-K. Bui. Modeling heating and cooling loads by artificial intelligence for energy-efficient building design. Energy and Buildings, 82 (2014): 437–446.
137. Jin, D., R. Ocone, K. Jiao and J. Xuan. Energy and AI. Energy AI, 1, (2020): 100002.
138. Lee, S-I., C. Safiye, B.A. Logsdon, S.M. Lundberg, T.J. Martins, V.G. Oehler, E.H. Estey, C.P. Miller, S. Chien, J. Dai, A. Saxena, C.A. Blau and P.S. Becker. A machine learning approach to integrate big data for precision medicine in acute myeloid leukemia. Nature Communications, 9(1), (2018): 1–13.
139. Davenport, T. and R. Kalakota. The potential for artificial intelligence in healthcare. Future Healthcare Journal, 6(2), (2019): 94.

Part I
The Effect of Covid-19 on Industries

Sensitivity of the Steel Sector to Economic Crises: Impact of the Covid-19 Crisis on Steel Production in Poland

Bożena Gajdzik* and Radosław Wolniak

1. Introduction

The determinants of the vulnerability of national economies to external influences have recently been the subject of interest of modern economics. The increasing number of empirical researches on the impact of economic crises on businesses took place in the 1990s and beyond. Most studies deal with the financial effects of the 1990s (analysis concentrated on the so-called "contagion" effect). The 1990s and beyond are the times of the rise of globalization. Cooperation within individual companies has turned into international cooperation. Economic and industrial processes are global in the sense of direct cooperation between enterprises or through links between enterprises. Industries started to form business network structures. Globalization with business network linkages is a feature of a mature industrial economy. Economic crises in a networked economy move quickly from country to country, economy to economy and industry to industry. The strong development of the market economy and the progressive processes of capital concentration changed the rules of economic crisis. Further, it started changes in the rules of the management of capital, industrial production and services of increasingly large global corporations, as well as the development of transport and communications, digitization of business, development of automation and robotization. All mentioned processes have influenced the internationalization of economic activity and have an impact on the formation of international and global markets. As a result of these processes, economic crises covered increasingly vast areas of many countries' business activities, and also the world economy.

The existing processes of economic, social and cultural development in recent years have been significantly undermined by the negative effects of the 2008–2009

*Corresponding author: bozena.gajdzik@polsl.pl

financial crisis, which entailed an international economic crisis and in the next decade by the SARS-CoV-2 virus epidemic (outbreak – December 2019), which covered the entire world and resulted in an economic crisis starting from the first half of 2020. Although publications still refer to the traditional concepts of crisis, for example J. Schumpeter conception (1982) [1], which assumes that the economic crisis is due to the exhaustion of innovation processes, mainly technical and organizational, J.M. Keynes (1936) [2], who assumes that the economic crisis is associated with decreasing demand, and J. Estey (1956) [3], who explains the economic crisis with the help of the theory of cyclical fluctuations, the modern explanation of economic crises is more complex and is often a result of the overlap of many factors.

The dynamic business environment makes us increasingly think of "abnormal crises", i.e. crises whose causes cannot be foreseen or understood. The virus that took over the world changed the existing forms of business functioning, and the rigid patterns of conduct in a crisis situation did not apply. Now the new ones had to be applied, starting from remote working through production limitations, to the creation of new (replacement) structures in entire supply chains.

The purpose of this chapter is to analyze the industry, specifically the steel sector dimension of the economic slowdown in Poland, following the effects of the COVID-19 crisis. The availability of data covering the period of the consecutive months of the 2020 slowdown in the steel market in Poland, conditioned to some extent by the situation in the European and global steel markets, will allow us to see how sensitive the situation in the steel industry in Poland was during the period of changes in the economic situation. For comparison purposes, statistics on steel production in 2020 in Poland were compared to the period of the 2008–2009 – the time of earlier financial crisis.

2. Literature Review

The coronavirus COVID-19 pandemic has a big impact on the now existing global health crisis. The pandemic is not only a health crisis, but we can also define it as a type of unprecedented socio-economic crisis. This crisis has the potential to create deep, devastating, and longstanding effects. Those effects can be political, social or economic, and can play an influence on each of the affected countries. Although we don't know exactly where the source of the existing outbreak is we can say that many of the earliest identified cases of the COVID-19 pandemic have been identified among people who had earlier visited the Huanan Seafood Wholesale Market which is located in Wuhan, Hubei, China [4]. This disease was named by the World Health Organization (WHO) on 11 February 2020, as "COVID-19". This name, is a shortened name for coronavirus disease 2019 [5]. The pandemic situation started in early March 2020. On the basis of data we can consider Europe as the active center of the COVID-19 pandemic since March 13, 2020. At this time the number of new cases became greater in European Union countries compared to China [6]. This outbreak can be considered as a major destabilizing threat that is very dangerous and has a large negative impact on the global economy.

Many industrial sectors are struggling with the effects of a severe economic slowdown. The steel sector is also one of these sectors. There has been a decline in steel production worldwide, in Europe and in many other countries. Poland is one of these countries.

With the exception of the 2008–2009 financial crisis, the decline in global crude steel in 2009, from 2010 to 2019, global steel production grew [7]. Average growth rates in 2010–2015 was 2.5%, in 2015–2019 was 3.6% [7]. The amount of world crude steel production on the basis of WorldSteel (for the 64 countries) in particular months of 2020 is presented in Table 2.1.

Table 2.1: World crude steel production (for the 64 countries) in particular months of 2020

Month	Total steel production in million tonnes (Mt)	Comparison to the month of 2019 (m-o-m)
January	154.4	+2.1%
February	143.3	+2.8%
March	147.1	−6.0%
April	137.1	−13.0%
May	148.8	−8.7%
June	148.3	−7.0%
July	152.7	−2.5%
August	156.2	+0.6%
September	156.4	+2.9%
October	161.9	+7.0%
November	158.3	+6.6%
December	160.9	+5.8%

Source: Based on monthly reports by WorldSteel.

The first month of 2020, which was the start of a decline in world crude steel production, was March. The decline in world crude steel production continued until August 2020. The last months of the year are an increase in world steel production in comparison to 2019. But global world crude steel production although for the year 2020 reached 1,864.0 million tonnes (Mt), down by 0.9% compared to 2019 [8]. The situation is worse in the EU steel sector. Following the global financial crisis (2008–2009), steel production in the EU (28 countries) is declining overall, except for 2014 and 2017 [9]. From a level above 170 million tonnes (in 2010, EU crude steel was 173 million tonnes) to 157 million tonnes in 2019 [9]. The situation in the individual months of 2020 was presented in Table 2.2.

In the EU, from January to October 2020, there was a decrease in steel production. Throughout 2020, the European Union (with the United Kingdom) recorded production of 138.8 million tonnes, a decrease of 12% from the previous year [8]. The COVID-19 outbreak has a big impact on many industries in the world. It changes the business operating conditions and with it a rise of many problems with operating management and supply chain management [11–13].

The pandemic especially has an important impact on mining and metal companies [14–16]. There are many vulnerabilities in the value chain which due to this, which can be highlighted in the following points [17, 18]:

- Worldwide trade disruption due to logistics restrictions and limited availability of critical consumables and machine components
- Uncertain future demand due to unknown length of the pandemic

Table 2.2: EU crude steel production (for the 28 countries) in particular
months of 2020

Month	Total steel production in thousands of tonnes	Comparison to the month of 2019 (m-o-m)
January	12,293	−12.0%
February	12,277	−9.0%
March	12,029	−20.4%
April	10,729	−22.9%
May	10,485	−26.8%
June	10,156	−24.6%
July	9,817	−24.4%
August	9,315	−16.6%
September	11,111	−14.0%
October	12,610	−5.6%
November	12,809	+5.5%
December	11,757	+3.5%

Source: Based on monthly reports by WorldSteel and Eurofer [8–10].

- Unbalanced and un-optimal production operations due to lack of flexibility in the mining and metal industry operations
- Continuous risk of exposure to the miners and health and wellbeing of workers, suppliers, and other supply chain partners

We are able to distinguish many actions which government and businesses can take to deal with the crisis. We can divide potential action to take on six types which we characterized in the Table 2.3:

- Empower people and use the human capital with purpose,
- Assess liquidity of assets,
- Assure reliability of supply and delivery,
- Secure continuity of all organizational operations,
- Uncover opportunities and new potential opportunities,,
- Try to digitalize enterprise activities,

On the basis of the presented actions an organization functioning in the mining or metal industry should deliver strategic plans and rethink about all of their activities. The COVID-19 pandemic outbreak can be an opportunity where the company can fast adjust operations and chain management to a new situation [23–25]. For example, besides the pandemic outbreak in Poland incomes of industrial companies were already higher in the third quarter 2020 than a year ago, and profits were much higher [26]. This is an example that a pandemic can be an opportunity for organizations to grow if their managers can use the opportunities properly.

Table 2.3: Action which can be taken by industrial companies to deal with
problems of the COVID-19 outbreak

Category	Potential actions
Empower people and operate with purpose	• Rethinking the way companies operate. Rethink how companies build trust among workers, communities and suppliers. • Try to honor the company's value despite the outbreak situation. • Think that difficult times can be a chance to start many potentially innovative and creative solutions.
Assess liquidity	• Secure your company's cash flow. • Evaluate opportunities from the financial point of view. Think about possible strategic purchases and a proper pricing strategy. • Try to seek out new strategic alliances to accelerate production. • Try working with suppliers to build better long-term partnerships.
Assure supply and delivery	• Company should strength the collaboration with customers and distributors to increase the level of understanding of their economic demands. • Company should find out the balance between its growth and try to avoid unprofitable growth. • Try to adjust your supply change system to be more flexible. It will allow the company to switch between a disruptive situation and normal operations when needed. • Company should establish system to allow an automated identification and also evaluation of risk in disruptive situations.
Secure operational continuity	• Adjust the resiliency and production capabilities to minimize risk of future disruption. • Think holistically about all activities of the company. Analyze the impact of the pandemic situation on all activities. • Secure the access of the company to critical supplies needed to ensure the continuity of production. Try to form strategic alliances across suppliers.
Uncover opportunities	• Rethink what capabilities can you maintain in-house and what the company should buy-in. • Try to update the company policies and union agreements to the new, pandemic situation. • Think strategically about the future. Analyze what actions are sustainable. • Think about your value chain. Is it possible to achieve any new partnership, merger or acquisition across value chain?
Replatform for a digital world	• Define the future architecture of the whole business. Think about changes in business in term of some years. Analyze limitations of your system. • Analyze the system of company data collection. The data should have the right quality because it is needed to establish a good digital strategy. • Company should analyze current workforce strengths. Managers can create a proper talent management conception to meet the future company needs.

Source: On Basis [17–22].

3. Analysis of Sensitivity of Steel Production in Poland to Economic Crises

A characteristic feature of the market economy is the cyclical nature of its economic conditions. The reasons for alternating periods of economic growth and recession are connected with internal conditions of the country and region, as well as, what is 'imported' from outside in a conditions of progressing globalization. The last period of crisis, which Poland and its steel producers entered in 2009, was determined by external factors and for the first time showed in such a clear way the impact of globalization on the functioning of individual countries. Another crisis was caused by the COVID-19 pandemic. This pandemic led to a catastrophic collapse of the world economy. The 2019-nCov coronavirus, was discovered in late 2019 in Wuhan, and the effects of the crisis were manifesting in 2020. The crisis is still ongoing and health institutions around the world are starting a program of mass vaccination of their populations (from January 2021).

The main objective of the study is to analyze the sensitivity of steel production in Poland to the global economic crisis, taking into account the variation of steel production in different months of 2020. COVID-19 crisis was initiated at the end of 2019 by the SARS-Cov-2 virus epidemic. The performed analysis covers the shorter and longer periods of steel production trends.

4. Research Methodology

To determine the sensitivity of the steel sector in Poland to the global economic downturn during the COVID-19 crisis, data analysis was performed. The scheme of the research procedure includes four stages:

(1) Gathering data on the volume of crude steel production in Poland.
(2) Analysis of steel production volumes, including characteristics of changes:
  - crude steel production in individual months of 2020 (thousand tonnes)
  - crude steel production by month in 2017–2019 (thousand tonnes).
(3) The calculation of the dynamics of production decline was done according to the formula (1):

$$\Delta Y_{it} = \frac{(Y_{it} - Y_{it-1;t-2;t-3})}{Y_{it-1;t-2;t-3}} \times 100\% \tag{1}$$

where:

Y_t – crude steel production in the current year (2020);

$Y_{t-1;t-2;t-3}$ – average crude steel production for previous years (2019-2018, 2017)

i – months: Jan., Feb. March, Apr. May, Jun. Jul. Aug. Sep. Oct. Nov. Dec.

t – crisis year: 2020

$t-1;t-2;t-3$ – previous years: 2008, 2007, 2006

(4) Comparison of steel production from the COVID-19 crisis with steel production in Poland during the 2008–2009 global financial crisis was done by comparing the dynamics of production decline in 2009 and in 2020. The dynamics of production decline in 2009 was calculated according to formula (1) for the collected data:

Y_t – crude steel production in the current year (2009);

$\underline{Y}_{t-1;\,t-2;\,t-3}$ – average crude steel production for previous years (2008, 2007, 2006)

i – months: Jan., Feb. March, Apr. May, Jun. Jul. Aug. Sep. Oct. Nov. Dec.

t – crisis year: 2009

$_{t-1;t-2;t-3}$ – previous years: 2008, 2007, 2006

Synthetic analysis of the impact of crisis and economic downturn on crude steel production in Poland, based on the identified dynamics of change in the case of the COVID-19 crisis and global financial crisis 2008–2009 (global economic and financial crisis was initiated on 14 September 2008 by the collapse of Lehman Brothers Bank in the USA, and its impact became visible in 2009).

The spatial scope of the study covers the area of Poland, focusing on crude steel production volume (tonnes). The time range of steel production volume covers the periods 2000–2020 – steel production in individual years, while in the case of sensitivity analysis of steel production – dynamics of changes (formula 1), it refers to the state in 2017–2020 years and 2006–2009 years, steel production in individual months.

The results of the analysis confirmed the existence of the impact of global economic crises on the volume of steel production in Poland.

5. Analysis of the Volume of Steel Production in Poland in Periods of Economic Crises

To determine the impact of the two global economic crises on steel production volumes, the analysis started with a juxtaposition of steel production volumes in Poland over the period from 2000 to 2020, shown in Table 2.4.

Table 2.4: Crude steel production in Poland in the period from 2000 to 2020 (in million tonnes)

2000	10.5	2011	8.8
2001	8.8	2012	8.4
2002	8.4	2013	8
2003	9.1	2014	8.6
2004	10.6	2015	9.2
2005	8.3	2016	9
2006	10	2017	10.3
2007	10.6	2018	10.2
2008	9.7	2019	9
2009	7.1	2020	7.9
2010	8		

Source: Based on [27–28]: World Steel, *World Steel in Figures 2000, 2001…2019*, World Steel Association, Brussels, 2019, and *Polish Steel Industry*. Report of Polish Steel Association in Katowice, Poland.

The average crude steel production in the period from 2000 to 2020 was 9.1 million tonnes. The effects of the global financial crisis, are visible as a sharp decline in steel production in Poland, were recorded in 2009. In 2009, steel production in

Poland dropped to 7.1 million tonnes, i.e. by 2 thousand tonnes of steel less compared to the average production in previous years. In 2020, crude steel production decreased by 1.2 million tonnes. The analysis of the steel production trend in the long term shows that during the global economic crises (2009 and 2020), crude steel production in Poland decreased sharply, compared to the average – 9.1 million tonnes, this is a decrease by 21.98% in 2009 and by 13.19% in 2020 (Fig. 2.1).

A detailed monthly analysis of the volume of steel production in the periods of global economic crises is presented in Fig. 2.2.

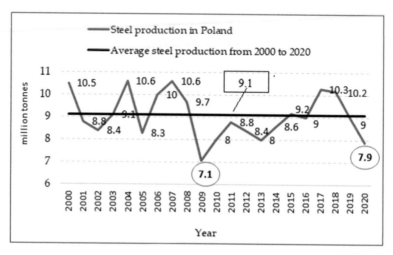

Figure 2.1: Steel production in Poland from 2000 to 2020 – Yearly/
Source: Own analysis based on data from the Polish Steel Association.

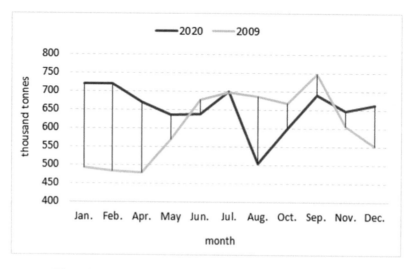

Figure 2.2: Steel production in Poland in 2009 and in 2020 – Monthly.
Source: Own analysis based on data from the Polish Steel Association.

Based on the trend analysis, it can be concluded that in the first months of 2020 (COVID-19 crisis), crude steel production in Poland was higher compared to steel production in Poland in 2009 (financial crisis). The situation changed in May, then crude steel production during the COVID-19 crisis dropped sharply compared to the steel production in Poland in 2009. At the end of 2020 – November and December, crude steel production in Poland was increasing. In 2020, the largest decrease in production was recorded in August, then 505 thousand tonnes of steel were produced in Poland. The average monthly production in 2020 was 654 thousand tonnes. In August 2020, crude steel production decreased by 22.78% compared to the monthly average. The total crude steel production in 2020 was 7.9 million tonnes. The volume of this production was compared with that of steel in 2019-2017 (Fig. 2.3).

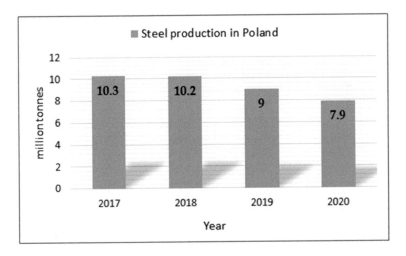

Figure 2.3: Steel production in Poland in the period from 2017 to 2020 – Yearly.
Source: Own analysis based on data from World Steel [27].

2017 saw the highest volume of crude steel production in Poland in the last decade. The average annual crude steel production for 2010–2020 was 8.9 million tonnes. Comparing the average steel production for the period 2010–2020 with the production in 2020, which is the year of COVID-19 crisis, we noted a decrease in crude steel production by 1 million tonnes. Steel production in 2020 was the lowest for the entire 2010-2020 period (Fig. 2.4).

A comparative analysis of monthly steel production from 2017 to 2020 was performed to calculate the dynamics of the sensitivity of steel production volumes in the case of economic tightening and a general economic slowdown in 2020 (Fig. 2.5).

The trend analysis above (Fig. 2.5) allows us to confirm once again the conclusion that steel production in Poland in 2020 decreased and, compared to steel production in previous years, only November and December showed an increase compared to 2019 production.

At this stage of the analysis, the dynamics of change was calculated (according to formula 1). In Fig. 2.6 there are the changes in the volume of steel production in Poland 2020 with relations to the average monthly production volume for the period from 2017 to 2019. The average dynamics of the decrease in steel production in

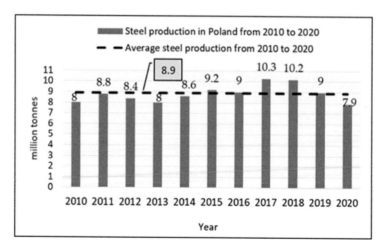

Figure 2.4: Steel production in Poland in the period from 2010 to 2020 – Yearly.
Source: Own analysis based on data from World Steel and the Polish Steel Association [27–28].

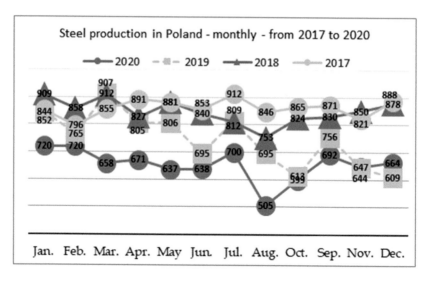

Figure 2.5: Steel Production in Poland in the period from 2017 to 2020 – Monthly.
Source: Own analysis based on data from the Polish Steel Association.

Poland in 2020 (according to formula 1) was 20%. Based on the data (Table 2.5, there was a decline in steel production in each month in 2020.

The final stage of the analysis was to calculate the dynamics of change for crude steel production in 2009 in comparison with the average steel production for previous years – the period from 2006 to 2009. The results are summarized in Table 2.6.

On the basis of the obtained results (the last row from Table 2.5 and the last row from Table 2.6), in Fig. 2.7 a summary of the dynamics of change was made.

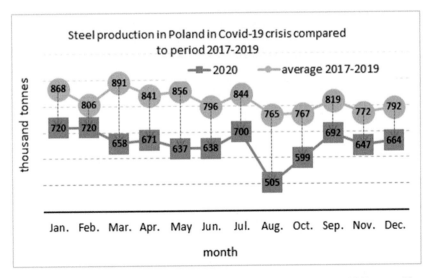

Figure 2.6: Steel production in Poland in 2020 – compared to average 2017-2019 – monthly.

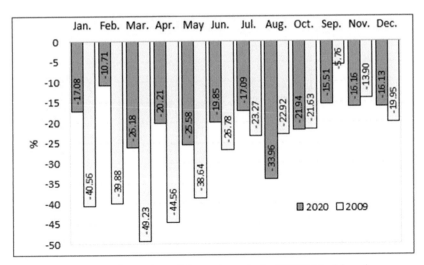

Figure 2.7: Comparison of change dynamics in COVID-19 crisis and financial crisis in 2009.

6. Conclusion

Based on the performed analysis, the decreasing dynamics of steel production in Poland in 2020 is weaker compared to the decreasing dynamics in 2009. The effects of the global financial crisis in 2009 was therefore more severe for the steel sector in Poland than the current COVID-19 downturn. The sensitivity of the steel sector in Poland was greater in the case of the fall in the financial market which lead to increases in the interest rates on loans and fluctuations in the price markets in 2009 than to the effects of the economic slowdown caused by the exclusion of some areas

Table 2.5: Monthly steel production in Poland in 2020 compared to average production in 2017-2019 (in thousands of tonnes) and dynamics of change (in %) [28]

2020	720	720	658	671	637	638	700	505	599	692	647	664
Average for 2019-2017	868	806	891	841	856	796	844	765	767	819	772	792
Dynamics	-17.08	-10.71	-26.18	-20.21	-25.58	-19.85	-17.09	-33.96	-21.94	-15.51	-16.16	-16.13

Table 2.6: Monthly steel production in Poland in 2009 compared to average production in the years 2006–2009 (in thousands of tonnes) and change dynamics (in %) [28]

2009	492	483	473	479	569	677	697	686	669	747	607	551
Average for 2006-2008	828	803	932	864	927	925	908	890	854	793	705	688
Dynamics	-40.56	-39.88	-49.23	-44.56	-38.64	-26.78	-23.27	-22.92	-21.63	-5.76	-13.90	-19.95

of the economy from "normal" functioning during the lockdown period. COVID-19 crisis hits individual industries in Poland (as well as globally) with different intensity. It has a more selective effect than the global financial crisis. Some industries were hit very strongly, others less severely. In contrast, the financial crisis of 2008–2009 hit many branches of industry very hard. The economic impact of the 2008–2009 crisis had a greater impact on the decline in steel production than the COVID-19 crisis. However, the signals and effects of the COVID-19 crisis cannot be ignored because it is still ongoing.

The most important issue in times of crisis is to be pro-active and predictive. Doing analysis, albeit such as this, gives a picture of the situation. There is nothing worse than acting blindly. Every decision should be taken in a thoroughly considered manner, observing and drawing the right conclusions and taking appropriate countermeasures is the key to success. Making the wrong decisions will result in inefficient operations for steel producers. In creating scenarios for the steel sector in Poland one should assume that we are dealing with a serious crisis and significant strategic uncertainty. In addition to industry analysis, market analysis, GDP analysis and forecasts should be carried out and many economic factors, e.g. interest rates, inflation, should be taken into account to determine the strategy of an organization. The industry analysis performed by the company is an element of the analyses that should be performed for strategic purposes. The value of the analysis results from relating the situation of the steel sector in Poland in 2020, from the first year of the pandemic in Poland to the financial crisis at the end of the previous decade. The authors' analysis complements the research already published in Resources (2021) [15]. A new element of this analysis was the reference to the averaged steel production volumes for the period of 3 years preceding the crisis year both for the COVID-19 crisis for 2020 and the financial crisis from 2009.

References

1. Schumpeter, J.A. The Theory of Economic Development: An Inquiry into Profits, Capital, Credit, Interest, and the Business Cycle (1912/1934). Transaction Publishers. January 1 (1982).
2. Keynes, J.M. The General Theory of Employment, Interest, and Money. (1936).
3. Estey, J.A. Business Cycles: Their Nature, Cause, and Control. New York: Prentice-Hall. (1956).
4. Sun, J., W. He, L. Wang, A. Lai, X. Ji, X. Zhai, G. Li, M.A. Suchard, J. Tian, J. Zhou, M. Veit, S. Su. COVID-19: Epidemiology, evolution, and cross-disciplinary perspectives. Trends in Molecular Medicine, 26(5) (2020): 483–495. doi:10.1016/j.molmed.2020.02.008. PMC 7118693. PMID 32359479.
5. Lovelace Jr., B. World Health Organization names the new coronavirus: COVID-19. CNBC. (2020). Retrieved 23 October 2020. https://www.cnbc.com/2020/02/11/world-health-organization-names-the-new-coronavirus-COVID-19.html
6. Fredericks, B. WHO says Europe is new epicenter of coronavirus pandemic. New York Post. (2020). Retrieved 9 May 2020. https://nypost.com/2020/03/13/who-says-europe-is-new-epicenter-of-coronavirus-pandemic/

7. 2020 World Steel in Figures. WorldSteel Association. Report. Data finalised 30 April 2020.
8. WorldSteel Association. Statistics. https://www.worldsteel.org/more-items.html?tag=%2Fstatistics&page=1&origin=%2Fzh%2Fmedia-centre%2Fblog.html
9. European Steel in Figures. Axel Eggert, Director General, The European Steel Association (EUROFER). (2020). https://www.eurofer.eu/assets/Uploads/European-Steel-in-Figures-2020.pdf
10. Trading Economics: European Union Steel Production 1990-2020 Data. https://tradingeconomics.com/european-union/steel-production: based on WorldSteel Association
11. Gregurec, I., M.T. Furjan and K. Tomičić-Pupek. The impact of covid-19 on sustainable business models in SMEs. Sustainability (Switzerland), 13(3) (2021): 1098, 1-24.
12. Jiang, P., Y.V. Fan, J.J. Klemeš. Impacts of COVID-19 on energy demand and consumption: Challenges, lessons and emerging opportunities. Applied Energy, 285 (2021): 116441.
13. Nakat, Z. and C. Bou-Mitri. COVID-19 and the food industry: Readiness assessment. Food Control, 121 (2021): 107661.
14. Wolniak, R. Search for information on suspension of business activities and dismissal of employes on the Internet as a result of coronavirus pandemic in Poland. Zarządzaniei Jakość, 2 (2020): 120–130.
15. Gajdzik, B. and R. Wolniak. Influence of the COVID-19 crisis on steel production in Poland compared to the financial crisis of 2009 and to boom periods in the market. Resources, 10(1) (2021): 1–17.
16. Zhou, C., G. Yang, S. Ma, Y. Liu and Z. Zhao. The impact of the COVID-19 pandemic on waste-to-energy and waste-to-material industry in China. Renewable and Sustainable Energy Reviews, 139 (2021): 110693.
17. Responding to COVID-19. Navigating the impact on the mining and metals industries. Accenture, (2020), https://www.accenture.com/_acnmedia/PDF-121/Accenture-Navigating-Impact-COVID-19-Mining-Metals.pdf, [access data: 12.02.2021].
18. Uddin, M.M., A. Akter, A.B.M. Khaleduzzaman, M.N. Sultana and T. Hemme. Application of the Farm Simulation Model approach on economic loss estimation due to Coronavirus (COVID-19) in Bangladesh dairy farms—strategies, options, and way forward. Tropical Animal Health and Production, 53(1) (2021): 33–43.
19. Powerful profit growth for industrial companies, https://spotdata.pl/blog/2020/12/02/potezny-wzrost-zysku-firm-przemyslowych/, [access data: 12.02.2021].
20. Perrin, A. and G. Martin. Resilience of French organic dairy cattle farms and supply chains to the COVID-19 pandemic. Agricultural Systems, 190 (2021): 103082.
21. Belhadi, A., S. Kamble, C.J.C. Jabbour, N.O. Ndubisi, M. Venkatesh. Manufacturing and service supply chain resilience to the COVID-19 outbreak: Lessons learned from the automobile and airline industries. Technological Forecasting and Social Change, 163 (2021): 120447.

22. Bragatto, P., T. Vairo, M.F. Milazzo and B. Fabiano. The impact of the COVID-19 pandemic on the safety management in Italian Seveso industries. Journal of Loss Prevention in the Process Industries, 70 (2021): 104393.
23. Dube, K., G. Nhamo and D. Chikodzi. COVID-19 pandemic and prospects for recovery of the global aviation industry. Journal of Air Transport Management, 92 (2021): 102022.
24. Sarfraz, Z., A. Sarfraz, H.M. Iftikar and R. Akhund. Is COVID-19 pushing us to the fifth industrial revolution (Society 5.0)? Pakistan Journal of Medical Sciences, 37(2) (2021): 1–4.
25. COVID-19: The impact on industry, https://www.incae.edu/sites/default/files/coronavirus-report-v4-1.pdf, [access data: 12.02.2021].
26. Bąk, P., M. Kapusta and M. Sukiennik. Mining company management in case of the epidemic emergency. Journal of the Polish Mineral Engineering Society, 2(2) (2020): 231–235.
27. WorldSteel, World steel in figures 2000, 2001...2019, World Steel Association, Brussels. (2019).
28. Polish Steel Industry. Report of Polish Steel Association in Katowice, Poland.

The State of SME Enterprises in the Face of the Crisis Caused by the Covid-19 Epidemic

Sebastian Saniuk, Sandra Grabowska* and Bożena Gajdzik

1. Introduction

The Covid-19 pandemic caused enormous changes in the organization of social, professional, and private lives. Companies and governmental institutions have had to quickly adapt their operations to the prevailing conditions during the crisis. A crisis is a time of fear, uncertainty, ambiguity, volatility, austerity, and cost cutting. Government restrictions aimed at curbing the epidemic caused technical, organizational, and financial problems for companies. Creating a new, safe work environment was a challenge for companies. Many companies directed employees to work from home offices, equipping them with computers and mobile devices. Some companies have introduced financial allowances (compensation) for working from home. However, even the best-organized remote work can affect overall employee dissatisfaction, decreased motivation, and sometimes even frustration [1].

Managing in a crisis requires focusing on strategic actions to survive the crisis. The scope of anti-crisis measures taken by companies depends on many different factors, e.g., the strength of the crisis, the main symptoms of the crisis, the economic characteristics of the sector, the type of business, the structure of the supply chain, the cost structure and the organization of processes. The foundation for managing a crisis in a company is a well-constructed crisis management program (CMP). Its development should include the diagnosis stage, indicating the type of threat, the causes of the crisis and its symptoms, determining ways of counteracting the negative effects of the crisis, and strategies of returning to the state of homeostasis, "normality".

The Covid-19 outbreak is a global crisis, and its effects are being felt across many industry sectors. Companies do not have a proven strategy for the entirely new nature of the crisis. Each company individually must confront the challenges it will face during this difficult time. To determine the key anti-crisis measures of SME, a

---

*Corresponding author: sandra.grabowska@polsl.pl

survey was conducted. The research provided information on the ways of introducing changes in the functioning of enterprises, especially in the field of organization and communication.

One way to counteract the negative effects of pandemics is to organize remote working where possible and to use the potential of ICT to create cyber-physical supply chains linking the customer, suppliers, and manufacturers in a network. The need for research in the organization and management of business networks is also evidenced by the numerous benefits of collaboration identified in the literature for both the companies themselves and the customer [2–4]. Nowadays, the participation of a company in a network is particularly attractive for small and medium enterprises. Such cooperation creates an opportunity to build a competitive advantage through access to all kinds of resources (capital, competencies, know-how, etc.) using ICT. During networking, the level of technology used, the level of competence of the staff employed, and the openness to unrestricted communication using, among others, communication networks or the Internet of Things will be essential. By combining the potential of partners as a network organization, it will be possible to offer more complex, innovative products and services tailored to customer needs [5].

The main aim of the study is to analyze the situation of Polish enterprises in the SME sector in the face of the COVID-19 pandemic and to adapt the enterprises to the new modus operandi based on the creation of cyber-physical networks of cooperating small and medium enterprises.

2. Managing an Enterprise in a Crisis

Enterprises operate in an environment where, in addition to positive events, there are also negative ones, causing a state of internal imbalance in the conducted business. The functioning of enterprises is inextricably linked to business cycles, after periods of economic growth, there is a crisis. The crisis is considered as a strong threat to competitiveness and a disruption to the achievement of objectives, due to the high unpredictability of its effects and the disintegration of previous reference systems [6–8]. Over the years, the operating conditions of companies have changed significantly, processes such as globalization, networking, and consumerism facilitate the migration of crisis – moving from country to country. As the negative effects of the crisis and economic downturn on a global scope increase, organizations develop anti-crisis strategies [9]. Crisis management with an emphasis on preventive measures, is not an easy activity because each crisis is different and the triggering sources are difficult to predict in a global economy [10]. Companies are constantly learning crisis management by identifying and analyzing a specific situation. The success of anti-crisis measures depends on many factors, including [11]:

- the actual causes of the crisis and their correct identification,
- the main symptoms of the crisis,
- the strength of severity,
- the duration of the crisis,
- the company's previous strategy and its adaptation to the requirements of the environment,
- the development phases of the organization,
- the structure and culture of the organization,

- the economic characteristics of the sector and the current economic situation on a national scale,
- the structure of costs and prices,
- the structure of anti-crisis strategies applied.

The classical approach to crisis and crisis management focuses on four issues referred to as the 4Cs [12]:

- **Cause** – causes are considered in terms of internal and external conditions that directly trigger difficult situations,
- **Consequences** – effects considered in the short and long term,
- **Caution** – a warning system that focuses on actions that minimize the effects of the crisis,
- **Coping** – solutions, i.e., such actions that are taken after the crisis as a reaction to a specific event.

Individual crisis management practices are adopted as standards of operation [13]. Crisis management plans and procedures should detail roles and activities, modes of information transfer, tasks of anti-crisis teams, resources, and even schedules. The selection of actions is determined (at the initial stage) by the phase of the crisis. The phases of crisis management can be organized by stages: pre-crisis prevention, crisis management, and post crisis outcomes [14]. Anti-crisis activities must include all levels of the organization, from strategic to operational. The following levels of crisis management can be distinguished [15]:

- strategic crisis management (requirement to reorganize operating strategy and reduce investments),
- operational crisis management (cost reduction)
- financial crisis management (pursuit of liquidity).

Taking preventive or corrective actions is possible when the company is aware of the effects of the crisis. If it so happens that managers (leaders) adopt a passive attitude (example of attitudes: denial, rejection, fragmentation), it will be difficult to talk about crisis actions and their effectiveness. Anti-crisis programs should focus not so much on defending the past as on seeking the ability to shape the future of the organization. In essence, these are decisions that radically change the face of the company, or at least shatter its current order. A deep crisis of the company usually requires revolutionary undertakings, radically changing the status quo [16]. The experience of various crisis situations and the knowledge of how to counter their effects can be helpful in a crisis related to the COVID 19 pandemic.

3. Analysis of the Situation of Enterprises in the Conditions of Covid-19 – Crisis

3.1 Materials and Methods

The research material consisted of the results of a survey conducted among Polish enterprises from the SME sector. The research was conducted in the period from September 1 to December 20, 2020. The period covered the effects of the first and second waves of Covid in Poland. At that time, it was difficult to predict how long the epidemic would last and whether there would be further waves of the disease. The research was carried out using the CAWI method (Computer Assisted Web Interview), 96 enterprises took part in it (the sample was purposive). All small and medium enterprises that agreed to fill in the questionnaire participated in the study. The study covered all industries without exceptions. The only criterion for selecting companies for the study was their size. The structure of questions in the questionnaire was built according to the stages of crisis management, from diagnosis, through strategies and action programs. The questionnaire was validated, a pilot study was conducted among 15 experts with knowledge of enterprise management in crisis. The questionnaire was revised with their comments. The questionnaire consisted of 22 questions. For the presentation of the results, several answers were selected that indicate changes in the behavior of enterprises under the influence of a crisis. It began by identifying all the possible effects of the Covid-19 crisis to which the participating companies are susceptible and determining the impact of each of them on the company, employees and customers. The results of the research covers the period of the first and second wave of the disease.

3.2   Results of Research

The occurrence of two waves of diseases and sanitary restrictions introduced by the governments of individual countries, including the periodically announced lockdown in the economy, brought a lot of difficulties in the normal functioning of enterprises. In the sector of small and medium enterprises, about 35% of respondents declared negative effects of the epidemic on the company. Respondents perceive the crisis as a temporary situation (26%), and about 23% of respondents indicate no negative impact of the pandemic on their business. Only 13% of the surveyed enterprises declare a negative impact of the pandemic and take countermeasures. Few, about 3% of enterprises declare drastic crisis management steps, including liquidation or suspension of operations. Such results may indicate the selective nature of the pandemic's impact on the SME sector. Restaurants, hotels, cinemas, theatres, large-format stores, so-called shopping malls, etc., are in the most difficult situation because for most of the duration of the outbreak, they are completely prohibited from operating. Figure 3.1 shows the impact of the COVID-19 pandemic on the situation of the surveyed companies.

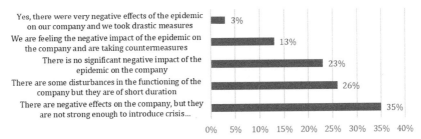

Impact of the COVID-19 pandemic on the situation of surveyed companies

Figure 3.1: The impact of the COVID-19 pandemic on the situation of the surveyed companies.

Most respondents (over 30%) emphasized organizational crisis (standstill, switching off part of administration) and technical and production crises (limited investments, switching off unnecessary production capacity). Moreover financial crisis (decrease in enterprise value, worse financial results) (23%) and marketing crisis (limitations of advertising, PR activities) (16%). The detailed results of the survey are presented in Fig. 3.2.

Types of crises that occurred in the company in connection with the COVID-19 epidemic

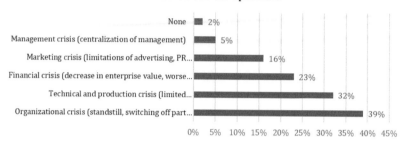

Figure 3.2: Types of crises that occurred in the company in connection with the COVID-19 epidemic.

The occurrence of emergencies related to the increase in diseases and the restrictions imposed by the government caused companies to take ad hoc measures to limit the operation of the business. Actions focused on ensuring core business were taken by 42% of respondents. Approximately 35% of companies have not implemented elements of crisis management in their companies. Only 12% of companies have developed and implemented a Crisis Management Program (CMP) (see Fig. 3.3).

Elements of crisis management that were introduced in the enterprise during the COVID-19 epidemic

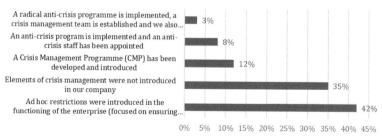

Figure 3.3: Elements of crisis management that were introduced in the enterprise during the COVID-19 epidemic.

One of the ways to counter the threat of the spread of the Covid-19 virus was to introduce remote working in positions where such work was possible. Only 18% of the companies that participated in the study said they had not introduced remote working – including 14% of respondents who indicated that it was impossible. An interesting observation is that as many as 22% of respondents indicate improvement in employee productivity in this form of work. About 33% of the respondents indicated the same level of productivity, while about 13% of the respondents reported a decrease in productivity. The detailed findings in this regard are shown in Fig. 3.4.

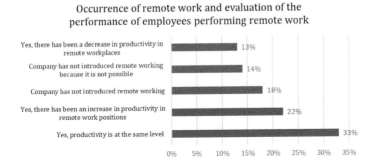

Figure 3.4: Occurrence of remote work and evaluation of the performance of employees performing remote work.

The enterprises responded by adjusting their work organization to the crisis, mobilizing appropriate additional resources to counteract the effects of the crisis (35% of respondents) made identification of weaknesses and threats, systematic monitoring of business activities, systematic adjustment of business plan assumptions and systematic controlling of economic results (33% of respondents). About 24% of the enterprises participating in the survey declared that they had developed actions that would restore the normal mode of operation of the organization (i.e., removing the effects of the crisis, closing reports on the effects of the crisis, using the lessons learned to secure the future of the company). Only a few enterprises (about 8%) declared the appointment of anti-crisis personnel, assignment of appropriate competencies and responsibilities to them, and preparation of an anti-crisis action program (i.e. actions that rationalize the economic account by counteracting the negative effects of the pandemic). Figure 3.5 presents the detailed results.

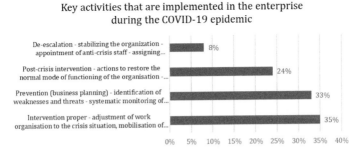

Figure 3.5: Key activities that are implemented in the enterprise during the COVID-19 epidemic.

One of the key aspects that can be applied to the impact of a pandemic and its impact on business operations is the uncertainty about changes in business growth strategies. Uncertainty for companies about the duration of the threat and its impact on consumer behavior and business partners raises concerns about the choice of post-pandemic growth strategy. More than half of the companies indicate introducing remote working where possible (58% of respondents), a significant proportion of them plan to limit investments in new technologies due to the uncertainty of development and changes in demand for products/services (39%). The companies indicate increased interest in implementing the concept of Industry 4.0 enabling the reduction of direct production staff (27% respondents). The details of the remaining results are shown in Fig. 3.6.

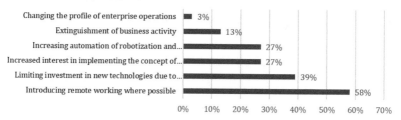

Figure 3.6: Changing the company's development strategy as a result of problems related to the COVID-19 pandemic.

An important question might be: will the COVID-19 pandemic change the way small- and medium-sized enterprises operate in the future? After periods of successive lockdowns, the direction of changes in the activities of enterprises can be noticed. Detailed answers are presented in Fig. 3.7. Some of them are:

- the use of e-commerce in commercial and customer contact activities (72% of respondents),
- increased pressure on enterprises to cooperate with the use of ICT technologies (57% of respondents),
- increasing flexibility of product and service offerings (68% of respondents),
- increasing the share of remote work in relation to stationary work (47% of respondents).

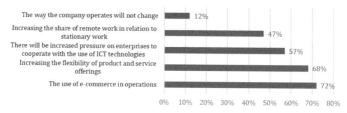

Figure 3.7: The expected impact of the COVID-19 pandemic on changing the functioning of enterprises in the SME sector.

4. Discussion and Summary

The survey conducted among the companies clearly indicates the changes in the activities of small and medium enterprises, which have suffered from the introduction of successive lockdowns and sanitary restrictions. Crisis actions in SMEs should be characterized by the following features; flexibility and adaptability, which are characteristic for the organic structures of the surveyed companies. In the SME sector, as opposed to large companies, informal organizational ties prevail, which favors the individual activities - of the managerial staff. The scope of the served market also determines the effectiveness of solutions in a crisis. The lack of knowledge about the possibilities of new ICT, B2B, B2C technologies combined with the lack of financial resources to invest in new technologies becomes a serious problem for these companies. Paradoxically, small and medium enterprises have begun to see some opportunities for development in changing their modus operandi and take advantage of the potential offered by Internet-related technologies. A significant growth of the e-commerce market is observed, as well as the need to shift from labor- to capital-intensive activities in production and to support services with ICT systems (e.g., logistics).

A positive sign is the phenomenon of quick reactions to crisis situations in the SME sector observed in the research. Unfortunately, most companies do not have adequate knowledge in the field of crisis management, which resulted in the lack of a developed and introduced Crisis Management Program (CMP). Decentralization of companies and their flexibility improves the speed of responding to changes in the situation and solving unexpected problems that arise. Simple organizational structures in SMEs favor independent initiatives of the management.

In the situation of the emergence of an increase in disease, companies reacted relatively quickly to the introduction of remote working and the application of a sanitary regime at stationary workplaces. In the situation of the introduction of remote working, they reported an increase or the same level of employee productivity. Managers of these companies see the positive effects of virtual work. Organization of telework, teleconferences, and realization of joint projects in virtual teams has so far been reserved for large corporations and companies in the IT sector. Nowadays, the entire society, which is forced to stay indoors, communicates through ICT systems. Shopping in online stores, doing official business, working remotely is a pandemic-enforced stage of society digitalization. The emergence of the concepts of Industry 4.0 and Society 5.0 is becoming a fact. Small and medium enterprises are already aware of the need for change and investment in new technologies identified with the fourth industrial revolution.

Forming group ties is easier, especially in family businesses and related companies. Hence, there is a need for businesses to cooperate, enabling the transfer of knowledge and experience and mutual support in crisis situations. Hence, the identified directions of change presented in the research. Orientation towards greater use of e-commerce in commercial activities and customer contact, interest in Industry 4.0 technologies, and greater pressure on enterprise cooperation using ICT technologies.

The cooperation of small and medium enterprises in the cyber-physical network creates new opportunities and enables the use of modern technological and organizational solutions, which have a significant impact on the increase in the efficiency of operations manifested by process orientation, decentralization of management, professional development of employees, and innovation. In addition, the involvement of enterprises in multiple alliances allows for better use of production capacity and increased productivity of available production and human resources of the enterprise. Functioning in a network also positively influences the learning process through the acquisition of experience, know-how, and knowledge based on the mutual relations of cooperating enterprises [3, 17]. The application of ICT solutions and well-known and applied communication technologies like Internet of Things, Cloud Computing, and Big Data to this network approach would eventually allow the whole process to occur automatically. This means that the development of network forms of cooperation, provides an excellent basis for rapid implementation of the currently developed concept of Industry 4.0, especially at the level of small and medium enterprises.

The idea of a manufacturing network called Cyber Industry Network (CIN) means the production of common production orders using a fully automated processes of individual network partners, where communication occurs over the Internet and the necessary data is stored in the cloud (cloud technology). As a result, all network participants have constant access to the selected, necessary information from anywhere in the world. Thus, the opportunity for growth is born in the creation of partnerships involving the combination of specialized competencies and the ability to change to better meet customer expectations and enable effective competitive advantage in the marketplace.

The development of e-business platforms that allow for the combination of resources and competencies of enterprises from the SME sector in order to implement joint ventures for the needs of a modern consumer based on the available resources is a way to facilitate the rapid formation of networks. The e-business platform should support enterprises in creating and managing the Cyber Industrial Network (CIN) in the event of emerging business opportunities requiring the involvement of resources, know-how and the specialist knowledge of employees located in geographically dispersed enterprises [18]. A general diagram of the platform's operation is shown in Fig. 3.8.

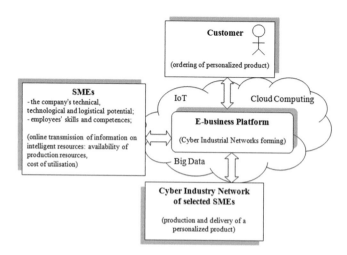

Figure 3.8: Schema of Cyber Industry Network (CIN) [18].

Future research in this field requires the development of new business models that should support the design of the cooperation of enterprises within the network and the customer with the network especially with the use of new technologies like IoT, Big Data, Cloud Computing, etc.

The research conducted allowed us to determine the impact of the economic crisis caused by the COVID-19 virus epidemic on the engineering and organizational aspects of Polish enterprises of the SME sector. The enterprises were examined with regard to the organization of remote work and the possibilities of creating cybernetic physical networks of cooperating enterprises. As a result of the research, it was possible to indicate that the new conditions of society and business caused by the Covid-19 virus epidemic have forced, among other things, a number of organizational changes, the need to digitize many processes, and even the construction of new cybernetic supply chains. The small and medium enterprises participating in the survey emphasized the need to use e-commerce, ICT and to make the offer more flexible. In addition, they introduced remote work and focused on cooperation with other enterprises. As a result, it is necessary to create new business models dedicated to companies cooperating within cyber-physical networks oriented towards electronic logistics customer service.

References

1. Nowacki, K., S. Grabowska and K. Łakomy. Activities of employers and OHS services during the developing COVID-19 epidemic in Poland. Safety Science, 131 (2020): 104935. doi:10.1016/j.ssci.2020.104935 (n.d).
2. Zastempowski, M. and N. Przybylska. Cooperation in creating innovation in Polish small- and medium-sized enterprises in the light of empirical studies. Journal of Competitiveness, 8(2) (2016): 42–58, DOI: 10.7441/joc.2016.02.04
3. Jordão, R. and J. Novas. Knowledge management and intellectual capital in networks of small- and medium-sized enterprises. Journal of Intellectual Capital, 18(3) (2017): 667–692, https://doi.org/10.1108/JIC-11-2016-0120
4. Perechuda, K. Zarządzanie przedsiębiorstwem przyszłości. Koncepcje, modele, metody. Agencja Wydawnicza Placet, Warszawa, (2002): 53–54.
5. Walters, D. and J. Buchanan. The new economy, new opportunities and new structures. Management Decision, No. 39/10 (2001): 822–823D.
6. Caponigro, J. Crisis Counselor Step-By-Step Guide to Managing Business. London, (2000): 12.
7. Barton, L. Crisis in Organizations: Managing and Communicating in the Heat of Chaos. Cincinnati, OH: South-Western Publishing Company, (1993).
8. Leupin, U. Turnaround von Unternehmen: von der Krisenbewältigungzur Erflogssteigerung, einpraktischer Fűhrungsbehelf für Unternehmen, Banken und Berater. Bern – Stuttgart – Wieden, (1998): 39.
9. Taneja, S., M. Pryor, S. Sewell and A. Recuero, Strategic crisis management: A basis for renewal and crisis prevention. J. Manag. Policy Pract., 15 (2014): 78–85.
10. Krystek, U. Unternehmungskrisen. Beschreibung, Vermeidung und Bewältigung Überlebenskrisischer Prozessein Unternehmungen. Wiesbaden, (1987): 89–90.

11. Slatter, Stuart, Lovett, David. Restrukturyzacjafirmy. Zarządzanie przedsiębiorstwem w sytuacjach kryzysowych. Warszawa, (2001).
12. Person, C. and J. Clair. Reframing crisis management. Academy of Management Review, 23 (1988): 59–76.
13. PAS200. Crisis Management: Guidance and Good Practice. British Standards Institute (BSI): Cabinet Office: UK (2011).
14. Bundy, J., M. Pfarrer, C. Short and T. Coombs. Crises and Crisis Management: Integration, Interpretation, and Research Development. J. Manag., 43 (2017): 1661–1692.
15. Zelek, A. Zarządzanie kryzysem w przedsiębiorstwie – perspektywa strategiczna. Warszawa (2003): 142.
16. Taylor, B. Turnaround, recovery and growth: The way through the crisis. Journal of General Management, 8(2) (1982): 5–13. https://doi.org/10.1177/030630708200800201
17. Urbaniak, M. Wybrane elementy gospodarczych organizacji wirtualnych. Akademia Ekonomiczna, Poznań (2001): 36.
18. Saniuk, S. The concept of utilizing SMEs network e-business platforms for customized production in the industry 4.0 perspective. Scientific Papers of the Silesian University of Technology. Organization and Management Series, No. 136 (2019): 523–533, DOI: 10.29119/1641-3466.2019.136.40

Towards Industry 4.0 versus the Covid-19 Crisis – The Use of Selected Technologies (ICT) in Business

Bożena Gajdzik

1. Introduction

At the beginning of the 21st Century, the concept of Industry 4.0 appeared as an industry development strategy for economies around the world, especially highly developed economies [1]. For any economy, industry is the engine of economic growth. The development of production technology in the last quarter of a century has been very fast, and in combination with digitization it enables the creation of cyber-physical production systems (CPPS) [2, 3]. Industry 4.0 is seen by governments and enterprises as an opportunity to increase productivity and competitiveness. Industry 4.0, from the moment it appeared in 2011 (as an initiative of the German government), is a big challenge for the producers of many industries around the world. In this industry, production is carried out by intelligent and digital factories – smart factories [4]. Computerized production systems are equipped with network links with established digital twin systems. Computers communicate with other objects and provide information about the operation of machines. Robots equipped with artificial intelligence create production cells. Personalized products are manufactured in such modern factories. Customers can participate in their design, monitoring the progress of work and tracking the logistic path by which the product reaches them [5].

A decade after the Industry 4.0 and its strong popularization by political and business circles, the world is entering the next decade with problems caused by COVID-19. At the end of 2019, the first cases appeared, an epidemic (pandemic) caused by the SARS-CoV-2 virus. In 2020, countries around the world saw an increasing increase in incidence among their populations. The effects of the pandemic – restrictions on the movement and contact of people, were felt by manufacturers, customers, and suppliers around the world. Due to the spread of the COVID-19 coronavirus, all organizations had to quickly adapt to economic restrictions. The COVID-19 crisis has caused enormous changes in and around business. Companies had to develop new rules of work organization, change the methods of producing and delivering products to customers [6].

Email: bozena.gajdzik@polsl.pl

Digitalization is a very broad and capacious concept. It can refer to many areas of business and the digital transformation process itself can take place in different ways. In a crisis, people will appreciate the importance of IC technology as it becomes part of their professional and private lives. ICT enables unlimited communication and the performing of many activities remotely (remotely), ranging from simple activities, e.g., sending documents, to more complex ones, e.g., controlling devices. According to Cambridge Dictionary: the use of computers and other electronic equipment and systems to collect, store, use, and send data electronically is called ICT. A digital company is described by "the application of Information and Communication Technologies (ICT) for the integration of activities in different functional areas as well as the so-called extended enterprise or partnering firms in the supply chain" [7]. The beginning of digitization is seen in the Third Industrial Revolution that is the first programmable logic controller (PLC) in 1969. Changes from the first PLC until the development of electronics, computers, and ICT (Information and Communication Technology) to automate production processes, it entered the third industrial revolution is known as "Electronic automation" [8]. The Third Industrial Revolution is characterized by computing power and replacing manual work by robots. The Fourth Industrial Revolution is called "smart automation" with "smart digitalization". Progresses in the new revolution are as follows: the use of cyber-physical systems (CPS); the cyber-physical mechanisms and interfaces to digitize, smart end-to-end processes, smart factories; learning machines and artificial intelligence (AI) [9]. The industry created from the technology of the Fourth Industrial Revolution is the "Industry 4.0". Industry 4.0 needs requires investments in automation and ICT [10].

The main objective of this chapter is to present the level of use (application) of IC technologies in the processing industry. The scope of the analysis covers the Polish metal industry. Statistical data were used for the analysis. The analysis provides information on the level of maturity of the Polish metallurgy industry. Innovations in production and the development of ICT technologies are preparing steel mills for Industry 4.0. Unfortunately, the COVID-19 pandemic shook the development of the steel production market (decrease in production), but ICT technology proved to be useful in the period when people had problems with contact (face to face meetings).

2. Background for Analyzed Topic

Internet information technologies is used in industrial sectors, economies, and societies [10]. Over the years, Information and Communications Technologies (ICT) have grown. From its beginnings in facilitating tabulation and record keeping, to applications for myriad needs including: automating and repetitive processes; control of processes and Just-in-Time management; the use of Enterprise Resource Planning (ERP); Customer Relationship Management (CRM) and Supply Chain Management (SCM).

Digitization precedes the emergence of the Industry 4.0 [11]. Since the 1990s, the rank (importance) of projects related to various areas of digitization has been growing [11]. Technological progress facilitates changes in the functioning of companies, markets, societies and economies. Information and computer technology (equipped with ICT) is a determinant of the quality of life of modern societies [12] and the building of the knowledge economy [13]. The fourth industrial revolution strengthens and extends ICT functions. For business, modern ICT is a network of communication and connections for implemented processes, by creating efficient interfaces and integrated data exchange. The Internet of Things (IoT) and big data are becoming a new area of business activity, cloud computing (CC) is becoming a new data centre, and data exchange takes place in real time. Information reaches all participants of the global value chains [14], and thanks to increased connectivity, it is possible to build intelligent ecosystems [15]. Using new technologies creates sustainable strategies of production. Sustainability is a basic paradigm of Industry 4.0 [16].

In Industry 4.0, which builds on the technological advances of the last revolution, digitalization is smarter than in the third industrial revolution, and its application is moving out of companies and into entire supply chains. Cyber physical systems coupled with digitalization advances are creating new opportunities for supply chains [17]. Smart products and CPS will be of importance when it comes down to digital changes and to shaping the (digital) supply chain of the future. Products are the final forms of hardware, sensors, data storage, microprocessors, software, and connectivity. Smart products create a new value [18].

The realization of smart products requires the digitization of production and the full digitization of the entire enterprise, and in conjunction with the digitization of services and IC mega-trends this carries over to the supply chain. The authors of the publication [17] analyzed the maturity levels of digitalized from production (enterprises) to supply chain. The first maturity level is called "Digitalization awareness". The second one, smart networked products, implemented microelectronics in physical objects according to the CPS. The third level is digitization of the company until fully digitalization enterprises. The fourth is CPS going increasingly beyond the enterprise. The fifth level of maturity is fully digitized supply chains. The ecosystem involves new and digital technologies, IoT (the Internet of Things) and data anywhere and everywhere in the companies and supply chains. Innovation ecosystems are collaborative networks focused on the concretion of value [19]. This new value needs strong IC technology support. Social and market changes in Industry 4.0 are (first of all) connected with communication and personalization [20]. IC technology, which has been developed for many years, is useful for businesses, societies, and economies during periods of economic growth and during the crisis. It was particularly useful during the COVID-19 crisis. There are several reasons for the use of information systems in crisis situations, the most important of which is the increasing complexity of crises, the growing role of knowledge, the geographical scope and cooperation of crises, as well as globalization and openness (mobility) of societies [21]. During crises, the use of ICT is each time adapted by companies to the existing conditions. IC technology streamlines communication paths, ensuring the continuity of data transfer and production control and supply chain management. The use of IC technology on a larger scale in the COVID-19 crisis than in previous crises was made possible by earlier investments and spending by companies and governments. In recent years, many scientists have studied the importance of communication technologies used in crisis and risk management. Michalewski, and Witkowski [22] cites research on the use of IC technology in various types of crises, e.g. during an earthquake [23] and natural disasters [24, 25]. The effectiveness of crisis resolution forms, e.g., mediation [26], the type of methods and tools used [27]and the level of risk reduction [28]. Many studies have shown that individual OI technologies support different stages of crisis management. In crisis management, the use of ICT by companies is adapted to the effects and strength of the crisis. ICT technologies, computers, mobile devices, Internet access, cloud computing, ERP and CRM systems, integrate individual components of crisis management. ICT enables both functioning inside the company and its cooperation with the environment. The use of ICT improves communication paths, especially in conditions of limited face to face contact. ICT in crisis management facilitates the exchange of information and helps in making decisions. Computers, networks, and information systems have an impact on the efficiency, security, and continuity of information. The flow of information, thanks to IC technology, is carried out from any place and at any time [22]. ICT provides companies with operational and technical capabilities to maintain the continuity of cooperation between all participants of crisis response and support by the higher level of technology. IC technology reduces the risk of disrupting the supply chain. IC technology evolves with technological advances. In Industry 4.0, IC technologies support: smart communication, a big data environment, smart analytics [29]smart product, smart chain, smart factory, and integrated operations ecosystems [30].

The year 2020 will be remembered in history by the COVID-19 pandemic. The pandemic caused an increase in morbidity and mortality. The actions of governments, by enforcing lockdowns on their populations caused a drop in production in many industrial sectors. The crisis has also affected the steel sector in Poland. In 2020, steel production amounted to 7.951 million tonnes and was down by 12.78% compared to the previous year but the production was higher than in the financial crisis of 2009. 7.1 million tonnes of crude steel was produced in Poland in 2009 (a drop of about 9.55% compared to crude steel production in 2020) [31]. The reduction in production translated into a freeze in investments (lower investment expenditures). According to estimates the investment expenditure in the Polish steel industry decreased 16.7% compared to investment realized in 2018 (in 2018, the steel industry in Poland invested PLN 870 million). In 2020, raw material and energy prices increased. These price increases have pushed up production costs. Average price of exported steel products was 3168 PLN/tonne and 3157 PLN/tonne for imported products [32]. Supply chains have been broken, particularly the raw material supply problems in the period of March to June 2020. The steel sector has a strong relationship with steel customer markets. The largest decrease was recorded in the automotive market a decrease in the production of cars in Poland about 31% compared to the production of cars in 2019 [33]. More data about situation of the Polish steel industry during the COVID-19 crisis is presented in Table 4.1.

Table 4.1: Steel Industry in Poland in 2020 compared to 2019 [34]

Crude steel production	Finished steel products	Exports	Imports	Apparent steel use	Potential productivity
7.851 million tonnes	7.160 million tonnes	5.122 million tonnes	10.750 million tonnes	12.865 million tonnes	10.6 F million tonnes
-13%	-8%	-11%	-3%	-6%	74%

Besides of the many negative impacts of the crisis on the metal sector in Poland, a positive factor related to the use of IC technology can also be noted. COVID-19 opened the way to the digitalization of this sector not only by forcing companies to change their work systems or communication, but also by overturning previous barriers and fears related to the digitalization of operations.

The need to communicate and do business within the constraints and economic restrictions around the world has become a fundamental determinant for deciding whether to invest in ICT in various enterprises. In order to determine the level of application of IC technologies in the industry, an own analysis was made about ICT investments in the metal sector in Poland. The performed analysis concerns one industry and should be treated as an example of changes on the way to digitalization of industry in Poland.

3. Analysis of using ICT in the Metal Industry in Poland

The area of research being the use of ICT by the Polish industrial sector: metals production (chapter 24 according to the Polish Classification of Activities) and production of metal products (chapter 25 according to the classification) as a total of enterprises of a given type of activity (%). The final analysis was performed on the data from statistical reports. The scope of the analysis covered selected ICT technologies: computers; Internet access, including broadband and mobile; a businesses-own website; e-government/administration; enterprises purchasing cloud computing services; enterprises using social media; ERP systems; CRM systems. The time range for the analysis concerned annual data from 2010–2018 and a comparison between 2014 and 2019 (some of the data has been supplemented by more recent data from 2020). The analysis is focused on the presentation of the situation right through the COVID-19 pandemic. Information on the use of selected information and communication technologies (ICT) in plants was obtained from the studies of the Statistics by generalizing the results of surveys conducted by this institution using the representative method according to the harmonized methodology used in European Union countries. In 2018, the study covered 7.2 thousand industrial enterprises (37.4% of the total number of enterprises). The survey in these enterprises included entities with at least 10 employees and other organizations and users [35].

3.1   Enterprises using Computers and Internet

The use of computers in industrial enterprises belonging to metal industry in Poland with access to the Internet are common (all surveyed companies are indicated). In recent years, companies' access to broadband Internet with a high information flow rate measured in Mb/s megabits per second has been growing. Broadband access is provided by technologies from the DSL family (ADSL, SDSL etc.), cable television networks (cable modem), satellite connections, wireless connections via modem or telephones. Access to broadband Internet was recorded in all surveyed enterprises (100% in the last three years). Mobile Internet connections, which are realized by means of mobile devices connecting to the Internet (cellular telecommunications network for business purposes), are used in 76.7% of the surveyed companies. It should be noted, however, that in the last decade industrial enterprises belonging to analysed sector saw a rapid growth in the users of mobile connections. In 2011, the number of mobile connection users were 29.8% of users, currently there are over twice as many users (76.7%). In the last 5 years (the period from 2014 to 2019), the number of employees equipped with mobile devices allowing mobile Internet access increased by 7.4%. In 2014, the share of companies that equipped their employees with mobile devices with Internet access (laptops, smartphones) was 67.2%, and in 2019, 74.6% were equipped. The development of the Internet, bypassing printed sources when searching for information, and the development of voice and image transmission technologies over the Internet have weakened the strength of traditional telecommunications. The data analysing the use of computers and Internet by industrial enterprises in metal industry in Poland is presented in Table 4.2.

Table 4.2: Usage of both computers and Internet by enterprises in the metal industry in Poland [35]

Tools	Year								
	2010	**2011**	**2012**	**2013**	**2014**	**2015**	**2016**	**2017**	**2018**
	%	**%**	**%**	**%**	**%**	**%**	**%**	**%**	**%**
Computers	100	100	98.1	98.2	97.7	100	100	100	100
Access to Internet including:	100	97.4	96.5	96.5	95.8	100	100	100	100
Broadband Internet	76.7	87.2	81.1	89.5	93.8	100	100	100	100
Mobile Internet	-	29.8	49.4	55.6	76.5	51.2	64.2	72.9	76.7

3.2   Enterprises with Websites

The share of enterprises from the analyzed sector using their own website ranges from 76.2% in 2010 to 83.4% in 2018 (Fig. 4.1).

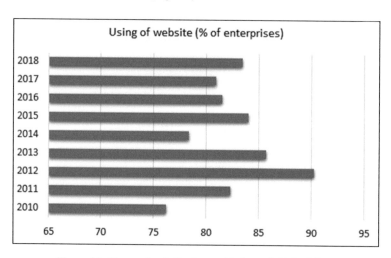

Figure 4.1: Usage of websites in metal industry in Poland [35].

Over 80% of companies that have their own website use it for tasks such as online ordering or booking, e.g. "basket", presentation of products, goods or services and price list, checking the status of their order online, enabling users to order products according to their own specifications, personalization of website content for frequent/regular users, links or references to company profiles on social media, information about vacancies or the ability to send online application documents, collecting and analyzing information on the behaviour of website visitors (comparison of the list in Table 4.3).

Table 4.3: Using of functions of website in metal industry in Poland [35]

Tools and functions	Year		
	2014	2019	2020
	%	%	%
Enterprises with website	78.0	81.2	82.2
Online ordering or booking, e.g. "basket"	9.4	9.1	8.3
Presentation of products, goods or services and price lists	73.4	77.8	77.9
Checking the status of your order online	5.5	5.6	5.2
Enabling users to order products according to their own specifications	17.0	8.7	10.2
Personalization of website content for frequent/regular users	4.4	5.4	5.1
Links or references to company profiles on social media	8.8	15.2	21.8
Information about vacancies or the ability to send online application documents	15.3	19.1	22.6
Enterprises collecting and analyzing information on the behaviour of website visitors	-	11.1	-

Explanation of the Table 4.3, the usage of: "-" means that there is no access to the data.

3.3 Enterprises using Social Media

The use of social media by enterprises of the analyzed industry in Poland in communication processes was recorded for the first time in 2016. Only 6.9% of all surveyed companies had FB or other forms of social media. In the following year, 15% of people using social media for business purposes were recorded. The doubling of users took place in 2018 where 32.4% of social media participants among the surveyed companies were recorded (Table 4.4).

In the analyzed industry section, social media is used for: social networking sites, creating the image of an enterprise or marketing products (e.g. advertising products), to receive or respond to customer comments/comments and questions, customer involvement in the process of product development or innovation (products, services), cooperation with business partners or other organizations (e.g. public administration bodies, non-governmental organizations), recruitment of employees, exchange of views, opinions or knowledge within the enterprise.

3.4 Enterprises using E-administration and E-sales

E-administration is a popular form of customer and employee service (gov.pl). Almost all industrial enterprises belonging to analyzed industry use data and document transfer by using e-administration. In the period 2011-2018, among the group of surveyed enterprises, the share of companies with an e-administration system was almost 100% (Fig. 4.2). The most popular form of customer service is issuing and sending electronic invoices. Over 75% of the surveyed companies use this service (Table 4.5).

Table 4.4: Usage of functions of social media in the metal industry in Poland [35]

Tools and functions	Year	
	2014	2019
	%	%
Enterprises using social media	19.0	29.2
Social networking sites	13.9	26.9
Creating the image of an enterprise or marketing products (e.g. advertising products)	-	25.2
Receive or respond to customer comments/comments and questions	-	13.6
Customer involvement in the process of product development or innovation (products, services)	-	4.8
Cooperation with business partners or other organizations (e.g. public administration bodies, non-governmental organizations)	-	8.2
Recruitment of employees	-	12.0
Exchange of views, opinions or knowledge within the enterprise	-	7.4

Explanation of Table 4.4 usage of: "-" means that there is no access to the data.

Table 4. 5: Using of functions of e-sale in the metal industry in Poland [35]

Tools and functions	Year		
	2014	2019	2020
	%	%	%
Enterprises sending (issuing) electronic invoices	-	75.3	75.3*
Enterprises conducting e-sales through a website or mobile applications	5.3	7.8	10.8
Own website or mobile application	-	6.9	6.4
Online trading platforms, auctioning websites, e.g. Allegro, eBay and related mobile applications		3.0	4.2

Explanation of Table 4.5 usage of: "-" means that there is no access to the data, * data from previous research.

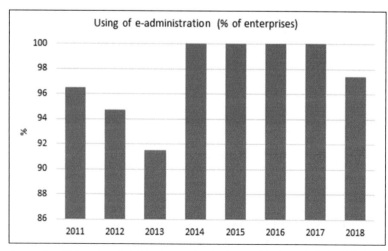

Figure 4.2: Using of e-administration section in the metal industry in Poland [35].

E-sales (e-commerce) is an additional form of access to customers for enterprises. E-sales in mills is carried out via a website or by mobile applications, but the actual share of companies using this method in the total of companies analyzed that use this e-service is small. In 2018, there were 5.3% of users, and 7.8% in the following year but in 2020, 10.8%. Fewer than 5% of companies sell through online trading platforms and auction sites. The low share of e-sales in the surveyed industry results from the specificity of steel products (large and heavy products) purchased by the construction, automotive, machinery and other sectors. In the analyzed sector, the dominant form of sale is the distribution of steel products by producers or distribution centres (companies intermediating in the sale of metal products) [36, 37].

3.5   Enterprises Using IC Systems

The steel companies (over 1/3) of the surveyed use ERP and CRM systems (Fig. 4.3). The ERP (Enterprise Resource Planning) system is a resource management software. It operates on the basis of a single database in which data and information from all areas of the company's operations are collected and processed. ERP and visual communication tools are used by management, equipment operators, employees, specialists, Lean practitioners, obtaining information on key performance indicators necessary to achieve the company's goals. Lean Management/Manufacturing, Reengineering, Six Sigma and Knowledge Management must be supported by ICT [38]. On the other hand, CRM (Customer Relationship Management) is used at the stage of building a relationship with the client. The system is used to acquire, sell and maintain relationships with customers. The task of the operational type CRM system is to automate the tasks and forms of interaction with the client. IT and computer systems support enterprises in the production of products, production planning and scheduling, process optimization, decision making and communication with the environment. These systems are used in large production companies and in distribution centres of steel products.

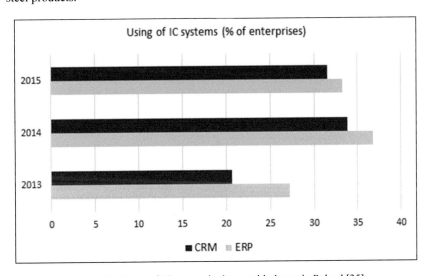

Figure 4.3: Using of IC system in the metal industry in Poland [35].

3.6 Enterprises using Cloud Computing

A new service that has been used by steel companies in recent years is cloud computing services. In 2016, the first industrial enterprises belonging to the analyzed chapter took advantage of access to cloud computing for business purposes. According to data from 2018, less than 15% of all surveyed companies purchased cloud services but in 2020, 22.8% were buyers (Fig. 4.4). The prerequisite for using this service is the access of companies to the Internet and connection via virtual private networks VPN: Virtual Private Networks in order to access the software, use a certain computing power and the possibility of data storage.

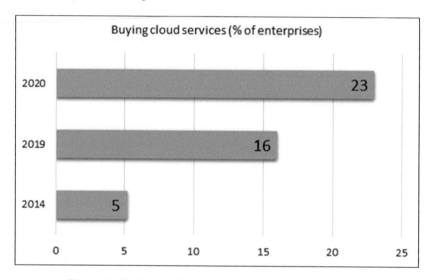

Figure 4.4: Buying cloud services in metal industry in Poland [35].

4. Expenditures on ICT and ICT Specialists

In the group of surveyed enterprises, over 40% invested in ICT: that is the purchase of computer equipment, both computers and peripheral devices (printers, scanners) and computer programs, purchase of digital network devices as well as IT and computer systems, expansion or modification of systems, purchase of services in CC (cloud computing), expenditure on training ICT specialists etc. More data is presented in Table 4.6.

In recent years, the number of employees that is ICT specialists who are employed in the steel sector in Poland has increased. In the group of surveyed enterprises, over 20% of companies employ ICT specialists, and the number of IT and computer departments in enterprises is growing [33]. Analyzed organizations provide their employees with training to improve ICT skills (13.9% in 2019 and 15.6% in 2020). In the last two years, the number of companies employing ICT specialists and providing them with training has doubled, thus for the category of employment of the ICT specialists it increased from 21.2 to 26.0%, for the category of training it increased from 13.9 to 15.6%.

Table 4.6: Technological expenditures and employment of ICT specialists in the metal industry in Poland [35]

Characteristics	Year		
	2014	2019	2020
	%	%	%
Enterprises invest in ICT	41.5	40.2	40.9
Enterprises employing ICT specialists	9.2	21.2	26.0
Enterprises providing employees with training in raising ICT skills	8.7	13.9	15.6
Enterprises equipping their employees with mobile devices enabling mobile Internet access	67.2	74.6	79.9

5. Development and Innovation

The results of the statistical analysis performed according to the presented IC technology components are summarized in Fig. 4.5. The technology used supports enterprises in their business activities and is a source of innovation.

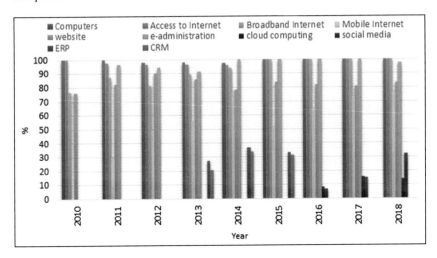

Figure 4.5: Using of ICT in the metal industry in Poland [35].

The analyzed branch is heading towards anew industry. The possibilities of using key technologies of Industry 4.0 in steel production were presented by Peters [39, 40]. ICT technologies are important for communication, optimization of processes design thinking, transfer of data in real time, analysis of Big Data, personalization of products, building of cyber-physical steel production system, stronger integration in value chain. By using CAD/CAM systems and related equipment, such as printers or 3D scanners, industrial companies in the analyzed sector are able to quickly develop various versions of products/designs for customers. According to the latest data, about 7.5% of companies in the analyzed sector use 3D printing in their activities [41]. On the other hand, 23.2% of companies use industrial or service robots, which also require support from ICT. OI technologies are used to support research and development (R&D) and innovation. Based on statistical data, it has been established that the expenditure on R&D increases year by year. A strong increase in expenditure on research activities was recorded in the metal sector after 2013. In 2014, the amount of 100 million PLN was exceeded for the first time, and in the following period, the expenditure was approx. PLN 100 million, while in the period from 2017 to 2018, the expenditure on research and development exceeded PLN 200 million (annually). The expenditure on innovations is much higher, which in 2020 amounted to PLN 421 million, and in 2018 increased by PLN 741 million (giving the amount of PLN 1,162 million) (Fig. 4.6).

ICT is used for technological, process, product and organizational innovations. ICT systematizes the accumulation of knowledge in databases and the codification of knowledge, and new technologies consequently facilitate the exchange of codified knowledge in the enterprise and outside it. Various ICT-based methods and tools have been developed that relate to users and are applicable to multi-user innovation. Every year, over 30% of organizations (producers) create new products, and over 40% of producers crate better products (data from Statistics Poland). For many years, the largest metallurgical companies in Poland have applied World Class Manufacturing standards [42]. They "climb higher and higher" and use new technologies. The link between ICT and their approach to innovation occurs in three general areas: information, ICT creates access to information;access, IT creates direct access to customers and other companies;networks, IT creates a network between entities from various industries and with competitors, as well as a network with customers.

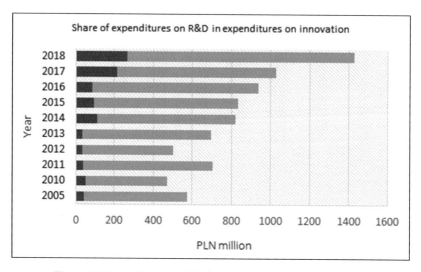

Figure 4.6: Expenditures on R&D in the metal industry in Poland [35].

6. Conclusion

The development of presented technologies underpins the growth of industries, economies and societies. The competitiveness of Polish steel (metal) enterprises is largely based on the availability and quality of ICT sector solutions. In the global world, it is one of the key investments for growth. Information and communication technology (ICT) solutions support the innovation and development of companies and have tremendously helped companies to cope with the uncertainty they experienced during the COVID-19 crisis. They allowed them to carry out many tasks remotely and maintain contacts through digital communication. In the transformation of companies to Industry 4.0, the importance of the ICT sector is growing dynamically, as shown by selected components of IC technology used in the metal industry in Poland. The key new trends in the ICT sector are cloud computing, Big Data, Internet of Things (IoT) and other technologies of Industry 4.0 [43]. IC technology is increasingly used in steel mills Digitalization allows business to be flexible in its relationships and ensures business continuity. At the time of a pandemic, digital communication, data management and digitalization of production have become even more important. Businesses today have huge volumes of data from a variety of sources. Data processing is focused on gaining a competitive advantage and aligned with the company's most important business needs. Business Intelligence (BI) is a complex process of transforming existing data into information that can be turned into knowledge. BI enables efficient and accurate planning, budgeting and reporting, as well as helping to predict trends and therefore inform decision making and subsequent monitoring of performance. Digitalization means eliminating paper documentation by introducing electronic archiving, document circulation and authorization, e-invoicing, etc. ERP systems used in steel mills allow the integration of processed information in related databases, and communication of systems without human intervention (including host-to-host solutions, platforms for communication with contractors, automatic invoicing between companies in the group, consolidation). The use of the Cloud, an as a service model, allows for easier and more flexible access to the latest tools and applications, without having to maintain expensive IT infrastructure. Mobile solutions increase accessibility to information and streamline processes with applications for mobile devices. IC technology in Industry 4.0 is used in the development of robots whose principles of operation can be written in the form of algorithms. Digital technologies make it possible to reach out in real time with relevant and selected information. Digitization is also about the digital customer. On the one hand, digitalization can help to understand and measure how satisfied customers are with their contact with a company and, on the other, make it far more efficient. Delivering a product or service, staying in touch with customers, handling complaints or recommending further purchases all require the use of IC technology. Digitization is also an opportunity for companies to build customer knowledge. The multitude of "traces" in the digital world left by customers at different stages of cooperation provides an opportunity to better understand the context of customer decisions and choices and to develop a personalised approach. The IC technology in blockchain allows for secure transactions between network participants, guaranteeing the integrity of its register, simple verification and data transparency. The implementation of IC solutions is becoming increasingly easy due to the growing availability and variety of offerings on the market. IC technology has made its way into business and will continue to be promoted and developed because it works well in economic boom times as well as downturns and crisis situations such as COVID-19.

References

1. Hermann, M., T. Pentek and B. Otto. Design principles for Industries 4.0 scenarios. A literature review. Working Paper 01 (2015), Technische Universität Dortmund Fakultät Maschinenbau. Available online: http://www.iim.mb.tu-dortmund.de/cms/de/forschung/Arbeitsberichte/Design-Principles-for-Industrie-4_0-Scenarios.pdf

2. Lee, J., B. Bagheri and H-A. Kao. Research letters: A cyber-physical systems architecture for Industry 4.0-based manufacturing systems. Manufacturing Letters, 3 (2015): 18–23.

3. Liu, Y., Y. Peng, B. Wang, S. Yao and Z. Liu. Review on cyber-physical systems. IEEE, CAA, J. Autom. Sin., 4(1) (2017): 27–40.

4. Kagermann, H., W. Wahlster and J. Helbig (eds.) Recommendations for implementing the strategic initiative Industrie 4.0: Final report of the Industrie 4.0 Working Group, (2013).

5. Bauernhansl, T., M. ten Hompel and B. Vogel-Henser. Industrie 4.0 in Produkten. Automatisierung und Logistik. Wiesbaden Springer: Fachmedien, (2014).

6. Lovelace Jr., B. (11 February 2020). World Health Organization names the new coronavirus: COVID-19. CNBC. Retrieved 23 October 2020.

7. Gunasekaran, A. and E.WT. Ngai Managing digital enterprise. International Journal of Business Information Systems, 2(3) (2007): 266–275.

8. Schlick, J., P. Stephan and D. Zuhkle. Produktion 2020. Auf dem Weg zur 4.0 industriellen Revolution. IM – Fachzeitschrift fur Information Management und Consulting. (August 2012).

9. Germany Trade and Invest, INDUSTRIE 4.0—Smart manufacturing for the future, July 1, 2014; National Academy of Science and Engineering, Securing the future of German manufacturing industry: Recommendations for implementing the strategic initiative Industry 4.0, (April 2013).

10. Davies, R. EPRS – European Parliamentary Research Service. Members' Research Service PE 568.337, (2015).

11. Arens, M., C. Neef, B. Beckert and S. Hirzel. Perspectives for digitising energy intensive industries – Findings from the European iron and steel industry. ECEEE INDUSTRIAL SUMMER STUDY PROCEEDINGS. INDUSTRIAL EFFICIENCY, (2018): 259–268. Available online: https://www.eceee.org/library/conference_proceedings/eceee_Industrial_Summer_Study/2018/2-sustainable-production-towards-a-circular-economy/perspectives-for-digitising-energy-intensive-industries-findings-from-the-european-iron-and-steel-industry/2018/2-118-18_Arens.pdf/.

12. Stolterman, E. and A.C. Fors. Information technology and the good life. IFIP Advances in Information and Communication Technology, 143 (2004): 687–692.

13. Eliasson, G., S. Floster, T. Lindberg, T. Pousette and E. Taymaz. The Knowledge Based Information Economy. Industrial Institute of Economic and Social Research. Stockholm, (1990).

14. Fonseca, L.M. Industry 4.0 and the digital society: Concepts, dimensions, and envisioned benefits, doi: 10.2478/picbe-2018-0034, PICBE – Proceedings of the 12th International Conference on Business Excellence, (2018): 386–397.

15. Peraković, D., M. PeOriša and P. Zorić. Challenges and Issues of ICT in Industry 4.0. In Design, Simulation, Manufacturing: The Innovation Exchange DSMIE

(2019): Advances in Design, Simulation and Manufacturing II, Springer (2019): 259–266.

16. Gajdzik, B., S. Grabowska, S. Saniuk and T. Wieczorek. Sustainable Development and Industry 4.0: A Bibliometric Analysis Identifying Key Scientific Problems of the Sustainable Industry 4.0. Energies, 13, 4254 (2020), doi:10.3390/en13164254

17. Klötzer, C. and A. Pflaum. Toward the Development of a Maturity Model for Digitalization within the Manufacturing Industry's Supply Chain. Proceedings of the 50th Hawaii International Conference on System Sciences, 2017, 4210–4219.

18. Porter, M.E. and J.E. Heppelmann. How smart connected products are transforming competition. Harvard Business Review, 92(11) (2014): 64–88.

19. Russell, M.G. and N.V. Smorodinskaya. Leveraging complexity for ecosystemic innovation. Technol. Forecast. Soc. Change (2018): 1–18. https://doi.org/10.1016/j.techfore.2017.11.024

20. Saniuk, S., S. Grabowska and B. Gajdzik. Social expectations and market changes in the context of developing the Industry 4.0 concept. Sustainability 12, 1362 (2020): doi:10.3390/su12041362.

21. Kulkarni, S.R. and S. Campus. Role of social media in crisis communication: Case study on garbage crisis. Journal of Xi'an University of Architecture & Technology (2020): 1006–7930.

22. Michalewski, G. and M. Witkowski. Role of networks and ICT systems in decision making in crisis situations. Collegium of Economic Analysis Annals, 49 (2018): 319–332.

23. Aryankhesal, A., S. Pakjouei and M. Kamali. Safety needs of people with disabilities during earthquakes. Disaster Medicine and Public Health Preparedness, 12(5) (2017): 615–621; https://doi.org/10.1017/dmp.2017.121

24. Bennett, D.M., B.D. Phillips and E. Davis. The future of accessibility in disaster conditions: How wireless technologies will transform the life cycle of emergency management. Futures, 87 (2017): 122–132.

25. Lichter, M., A. Yair Grinberger and D.l Felsenstein. Simulating and communicating outcomes in disaster management situations. SPRS International Journal of Geoinformatics, 4(4) (2015): 1827–1847.

26. Díaz, P., C. John., M. Paloma and I. Aedo Cuevas. Coproduction as an approach to technology-mediated citizen participation in emergency management. Future Internet, 8(3) (2016): 41. Available online: https://doi.org/10.3390/fi8030041

27. Stary, Christian and Stefan Cronholm. Method transfer across domains and disciplines: Enriching universal access development. Universal Access in the Information Society, 14 (2015): 145–150.

28. Radianti, J., T. Gjøsæter and W. Chen. Universal design of information sharing tools for disaster risk reduction. *In:* Universal access in human-computer interaction: Methods, technologies, and users. Antona M. & C. Stephanidis (eds.), UAHCI, 2018: 63–74. Lecture Notes in Computer Science, 10907. Cham, Switzerland: Springer (2017).

29. Lee, J., H.-A. Kao and S. Yang. Service innovation and smart analytics for Industry 4.0 and big data environment. Procedia CIRP, pp. 3–8. Elsevier B.V., Windsor, Ontario, Canada (2014).

30. Wollschlaeger, M., T. Sauter and J. Jasperneite. The future of industrial communication: Automation networks in the era of the Internet of Things

and Industry 4.0. IEEE Ind. Electron. Mag. 11(1) (2017): 17–27 https://doi. org/10.1109/MIE.2017.2649104

31. Gajdzik, B. and R. Wolniak. Influence of the COVID-19 crisis on steel production in Poland compared to the financial crisis of 2009 and to boom periods in the market. Resources, 10 (1-4) (2021): 1–17 , doi: 10.3390/resources10010004

32. Gajdzik, B. Pandemic year in the Polish steel sector: Steel production and apparent steel use in 2020 compared to previous year. IBIMA (2021).

33. Gajdzik, B. Steel industry in Poland – Trends in production, employment and productivity in the period from 2004 to 2019. Metalurgija, 60(1-2) (2021): 165–168.

34. Steel Industry in Poland. Polish Steel Association (in Polish: HIPH), Poland, Katowice, March (2021).

35. Statistics Poland (in Polish: GUS): Use of information and communication technologies in enterprises in 2020 or 2019 (2014). Available online:https://stat.gov.pl/obszary-tematyczne/nauka-i-technika-spoleczenstwo-informacyjne/spoleczenstwo-informacyjne/wykorzystanie-technologii-informacyjno-komunikacyjnych-w-jednostkach-administracji-publicznej-przedsiebiorstwach-i-gospodarstwach-domowych-w-2020-roku,3,19.html

36. Gajdzik, B. Strategie zmian w dystrybucji wyrobów hutniczych. Logistyka, 6 (2008): 62–64.

37. Gajdzik, B. Transformacja dystrybucji wyrobów hutniczych w Polsce. Gospodarka Materiałowa i Logistyka, 63(10) (2011): 20–27.

38. Houy, T. ICT and Lean Management: Will They Ever Get Along? Communications & Strategies September (2005).

39. Peters, H. Application of Industry 4.0 concepts at steel production from an applied research perspective. Presentation at 17th IFAC Symposium on Control, Optimization, and Automation in Mining, Mineral and Metal Processing (2016). Accessed online: ttps://tc.ifac-control.org/6/2/files/symposia/vienna-2016/mmm2016_keynotes_peters

40. Peters, H. How could Industry 4.0 transform the Steel Industry? Presentation at Future Steel Forum, Warsaw, 14-15 June 2017. Available online: https://futuresteelforum.com/content-images/speakers/Prof.-Dr-Harald-Peters-Industry-4.0-transform-the-steel-industry.pdf

41. Sorli, M. and D. Stokic. Innovating in Product/Process Development. London: Springer, (2009).

42. Gajdzik, B. World Class Manufacturing in metallurgical enterprise. Metalurgija, 52(1) (2013): 131–134.

43. Branca, T.A., B. Fornai, V. Colla and M.M. Murri. The challenge of digitalization in the steel sector. Metals, 10 (March 2020). DOI:10.3390/met10020288

Part II

CPS Based Solutions during the Pandemic

Human-Robot Collaborative Assembly based on CPS

Zhang Rong, Bao Jinsong*, Lu Yuqian, Li Jie and LvQibin

1. Introduction

In early 2020, COVID-19 broke out in full force and spread rapidly across the globe. In the face of this sudden and highly contagious disease, medical products and supplies are in short supply. Before a reasonable and efficient treatment plan could be found, countries had to order forced home isolation to reduce physical contact in order to prevent the further spread of Covid-19 [1]. However, due to the formulation of the home isolation scheme, workers could not go to work due to the shortage of epidemic prevention materials and were unable to ensure their own safety, leading to the cessation of work in almost all manufacturing industries. This was true especially in the medical equipment manufacturing industry and its related enterprises, and reduced production efficiency further aggravates medical products scarcity. The number of small and medium-sized enterprises (SMEs) is large and dominant in the current manufacturing market. Due to the low level of intelligence within this type of enterprises, most operations are still dominated by manual operations. Faced with the sudden shortage of labor force, enterprises couldn't take effective measures in the short term. Therefore, it is vital for the survival of SMEs to adopt the new model of machine replacement, increase robot investment, reduce human demand, give full play to the respective advantages of collaborative robots and humans. Simultaneously, it enhances the intelligence, information, and digitalization of SMEs, strengthening their adaptability to the dynamic market and establishing a comprehensive CPS [2].

As a product of human intelligence, robots act as a tool to replace and complete human capabilities. Robots have replaced humans in large numbers to perform simple, repetitive and physically demanding tasks, significantly improving production efficiency and quality [3]. In the age of intelligence, with the support of advanced information technology, the interaction between the physical space and cyber space has become possible. At the same time, with the development and maturation of various intelligent algorithms, robots will be more deeply integrated into the operation space. However, they will never be able to replace humans. Therefore, the Human-robot

*Corresponding author: bao@dhu.edu.cn

collaboration (HRC), which integrates humans and robots' advantages, has become the optimal manufacturing industry solution [4].

As an intelligent system integrating computing, communication and control, CPS can interact with physical processes through the sensor, the controller and user interfaces (UI), using cyber spaces to manipulate physical entities in a remote, reliable, real-time, secure and collaborative manner [5]. The enterprise with a CPS system can make the physical system perform computing, communication, control, and self-coordination based on the operating environment's perception. However, the CPS system focuses on the interaction and integration of physical space and cyber space, which is suitable for automatic workshops and does not consider the new scene of HRC. HRC not only reduces the number of workers needed but also ensures higher productivity. Therefore, CPS is further deployed in the HRC of manufacturing enterprises, aiming to form the human-in-loop CPS to realize the integration of human-robot-physics-cyber. HRC is considered a critical research object to promote the development and reform of the current manufacturing industry. The ventilator assembly problem under the epidemic's influence is the most representative. This chapter provides a detailed introduction to Human-robot collaborative Assembly (HRCA) based on CPS.

This chapter is organized as follows. In Section 2, advances in current research are presented. Section 3 discusses the framework of HCPS and the environment of HRCA. In Section 4, the perceptual and cognitive processes in the case of HRCA are discussed. Then, in Section 5, taking the PB-560 ventilator as an example, the vectorization expression of assembly tree and the self-decision updating strategy of assembly sequence based on reinforcement learning are introduced. Finally, the summary and prospects are made in Section 6.

2. Advances in Current Research

Facing the uncertainty of labor and market demand, an enterprises' development goal is to realize flexible production and intelligent manufacturing. Similarly, to break away from the impact of COVID-19 on the market, the demand for an intelligent manufacturing solution is rising, especially in the manufacturing industry [6, 7]. Using robots to replace humans and HRC is adopted to reduce manpower and improve enterprises' productivity.

In the area of human-robot collaborative assembly based on CPS, some of these aspects have been studied. Nikolakis et al. combined several physical and software systems to establishing human safety while performing near robots [5]. Moreover, Kim et al. propose a new manufacturing system optimization strategy through the CPS and Internet of Things (IoT) [8]. Based on CPS, Liu et al. presented a structured design framework to support the biologically inspired design of context-aware smart products [9]. The framework is developed based on the theoretical foundations of the situated function–behavior–structure ontology. To achieve a combination of robot repeatability and accuracy with operator adaptability and intelligence, the HRC-based system architecture is proposed, combined with a new method of vision sensing and control, high precision and fast intelligent solutions are realized [10].

Zhou et al. agree that an intelligent manufacturing system is a composite intelligent system consisting of humans, cyber systems, and physical systems, and this kind of intelligent system is called a human-cyber-physical system (HCPS) [11].

However, human operators cannot enter a hazardous manufacturing environment, but there is still a need for human collaboration in many cases [12]. To address this issue, Liu et al. introduced a remote human-robot collaboration system that follows the concept of CPS [13]. To solve similar problems, Wang et al. proposed a CPS with a layered architecture, which allows a robot to assist human operators in performing welding. The spatial separation of human and robot is achieved by interacting in a virtual environment [14].

In the early stage, humans dominate HRC. The operator can manipulate the robotic arm by pushing and pulling the force sensor, and force sensors play a big part in control [15, 16]. Zheng et al. realized off-line control of the robot through a trajectory planning algorithm [17]. Germi et al. propose an adaptive GA-based potential field algorithm for collision-free path planning [18]. However, robots will never be able to do all the work independently, and humans are irreplaceable in some scenarios [19].

The self-organization and self-decision ability of robots relies on two key technologies, the perception of the collaborative environment and the corresponding decision-making based on cognitive ability. In particular, perception usually needs to provide effective environmental information using external equipment. Vision is widely used because of its low cost, high efficiency, good continuity, high precision, a wide range of applications and other advantages [20-24]. To achieve context awareness on the shop floor, Nikolakis et al. proposed a cyber-physical context-aware system and collaborative or individual assembly operations via event-driven controllers [25]. Considering the random movement of the human operator in collaboration, Liu et al. proposed generating a motion transition probability matrix using a hidden Markov model in the motion sequence [26]. Understanding human intentions can provide appropriate cognitive aids [27]. To improve the visual cognitive function of intelligent robots, Jian et al. studied the intelligent cognitive function of robots based on ant colony algorithms. By learning knowledge autonomously and accumulating it into long-term memory, robots achieve self-learning, memory and intelligence development similar to human beings [28]. In the specific assembly environment, Wang et al. presented a review of human-robot collaboration research and defined the classification schemes concerning agent multiplicity, initiative, and alignment of human actions with the nominal process definition [29].

The above studies show that most scholars attach great importance to the irreplaceable importance of humans in intelligent manufacturing systems and show that HRC research in the intelligent manufacturing system is of great significance. By integrating the respective strengths of human, cyber systems and physical systems, HCPS-based HRC can improve its intelligence, efficiency, product quality, robustness and the ability to solve complex problems. At the same time, the intensity of humans is significantly reduced, and the production cost also shows a downward trend. Besides, the transfer of human knowledge and experience of the HRC system effectively improves the transmission and utilization of human experiential knowledge while enhancing the robot's intelligence.

3. Framework and Environment of HRCA

3.1 From CPS to HCPS

Intelligent manufacturing is a large concept that is constantly evolving and developing. In the traditional manufacturing system, which contains only two parts, the human and the physical system, as shown in Fig. 5.1, almost all the work is performed by a human directly either by hand or by operating the machine. Although machines and equipment greatly reduces human physical labor, in the early manufacturing system, many tasks such as perception, decision analysis, control and learning were completed by human beings.

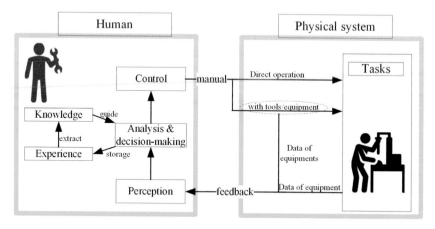

Figure 5.1: Human-physical system.

In the traditional manufacturing system, this has high requirements for people and a high work intensity, leading to the system's low efficiency. With the improvement of the level of information technology, machines' automation ability is gradually improved, and the concept of CPS is put forward. Human beings will pay more attention to higher-level tasks. As shown in Fig. 5.2, robots can initially solve simple decision-making problems under different conditions and realize manufacturing automation based on various sensor technologies.

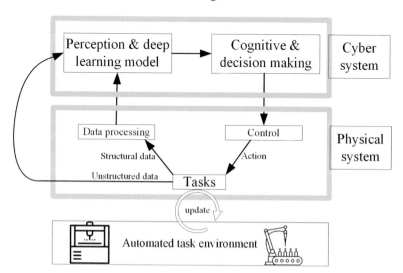

Figure 5.2: Cyber-physical system promotes automated manufacturing.

Many scholars nationally and internationally agree that technology, people and data need to be integrated to be genuinely effective and thus generate benefits. Nunes et al. argue that the role of the human has been overlooked in most current CPS studies and proposed a human-in-the-loop CPS [30]. The role of a human in CPS mainly includes data acquisition, state inference, drive, control, detection and so on. HCPS was proposed by Zhou et al. They believe that the physical system is the main body of the intelligent manufacturing system. The cyber system is the dominant one, and the human being is the master [11, 31]. HCPS reveals the technical mechanism of intelligent manufacturing and constitutes the technical system of intelligent manufacturing.

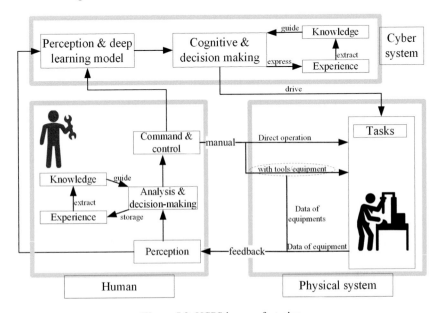

Figure 5.3: HCPS in manufacturing.

In the CPS concept, humans play a dominant role in the system. Furthermore, as physical systems and cyber systems are also designed and built by humans, the relevant models and algorithms are likewise done by R&D personnel. As manufacturing systems move from automation to digitalization and intelligence in all areas, the role of humans in the system is gradually changing from "operator" to "supervisor". Due to the limited workforce and the increasing cost of labors, the unmanned factory has become the ultimate goal of intelligent manufacturing. However, due to intelligence limitations, an unmanned model is not yet possible, and in some manufacturing processes, the collaboration between humans and robots aims to reduce the workforce while increasing productivity. Moreover, some robots' inability to perform tasks on their own is also one reason to promote the development of HRC, which often includes too complex or flexible assembly work. In the case of HCPS, the focus of the human is on completing complex and challenging tasks alone or with the robot's assistance. In contrast,most collaborative assembly tasks and decision making will be carried out by the robot, which realizes the liberation of human in physical and mental labor. Therefore, HCPS based HRC requires robots to have the ability to perceive and recognize the task environment, extract the semantic information of assembly task, understand the behavior of assembly task, and then make reasonable HRC strategy planning.

3.2 HCPS based Collaborative Environment

3.2.1 Definition of a Collaborative Environment

The collaborative environment refers to the human-robot collaborative space for specific tasks. In the environment, there is no isolation between human and robot by protective equipment. Instead, human and robot will work in a shared space. Generally, a variety of sensors will be used to provide vision, voice, and touch capabilities for robots to ensure the safety of humans and make the manufacturing process smoothly.

The HRC environment for assembly tasks is shown in Fig. 5.4. Firstly, the type of current task is defined. After which the robot will obtain all the assembly parts in the HRC environment through the visual sensing device. They will be compared with the existing information of 3D model in a library to identify the label information. Secondly, the related operation tools and action information are extracted based on the task attribute information. At the same time, the task of HRCA will be divided into several subtasks which human and robot complete. During the operation of human, the robot can provide corresponding tools for human according to the identified information. For some simple tasks, such as peg-in-hole assembly, the turnover of sub-assembly and so on, the robot takes the initiative to complete them. The working intention (what action the robot will do next) is displayed through the graphical UI, so that human can judge whether the working behavior of robot is reasonable or not. For unreasonable behavior, human should take the initiative to avoid and give the corresponding signal prompt.

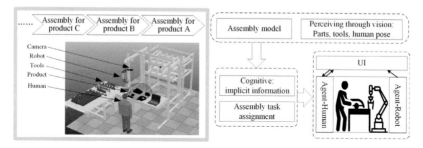

Figure 5.4: HRC environment for assembly tasks.

3.2.2 Elements of a Collaborative Environment

In real process of HRCA, it is necessary to analyze the elements of the collaborative environment for a better flow of data between the human and physical system.

(1) Physical Space

In physical space, it can be further divided into executor and executed objects. Executors refer to robots and human workers. The operators have high flexibility, substantial autonomy and a strong sense of task planning. Besides, human workers are good at using experience and knowledge to deal with new situations. However, persistent and high-intensity work will lead to the decline of human energy, attention, making the possibility of mistakes increased.

In comparison, robots are better at performing high-intensity and straightforward work. Besides this, the repetition accuracy and stability of a robot are much higher than that of a human. However, the adaptability of the robot is very poor, making it impossible to complete the difficult task alone. Therefore, the advantages of human and robot is complemented to form the HRC assembly mode. They work as the co-executor of assembly tasks to complete all kinds of tasks together.

The executed objects are the parts to be assembled, connectors and operation tools. Through the direct or indirect operation of the components and connectors with the help of tools, the assembly task of each sub-module can be completed. The type of operation tools should belong to limited dataset for humans and robots to choose from. Accordingly, the number and type of parts should match the corresponding file of model.

(2) Cyber Space

The state of interaction among humans, robots and the environment mainly depends on the flow of data and information. Generally, the executor takes the initiative to obtain the data information and then processes it to extract the useful information, which can be used as the judgment basis of the execution action. Among them, robots need additional auxiliary equipment to obtain external information, such as vision sensor, tactile sensor, voice sensor and so on. The voice sensor makes the interaction between human and robot more natural and efficient. However, the noise will be severe in industrial scenes, and there will be some faults, such as pronunciation inaccuracy, recognition error and semantic understanding error in interaction, making the safety and controllability poor. The use of tactile sensors has huge limitations because it can only work in the covered area, which does not broadcast. The realization of all-round contact detection needs a large area of sensor coverage. Besides, the tactile sensors will work after contact, and the type of contact (active contact or passive contact) can not be determined. Although the tactile sensor has high security, it can only obtain less information and therefore lessen the improvement of the robot's interaction ability. The visual equipment can obtain a large amount of information, which is the two-dimensional feature information, semantic information from RGB, and the three-dimensional pose information from RGB-D. Through feature recognition, the different object recognition and scene segmentation can be realized. In comparison, visual way is the better approach with non-contact and high safety.

In the HRC scene, the intention of human behavior will be extracted from the image information by visual module. Then the position and pose of other parts or tools will be obtained in the HRC environment, which can be further used to calculate workspace occupation. According to the demand of assembly tasks and occupation of workspace, the subtasks of current assembly will be generated after the assembly tree relating to the product's process information is transformed as vector. Then the safe and efficient trajectory of cooperative assembly is planned to complete the assembly task. In the information interaction model of human-robot integration, the robot will infer the intention of human behavior by processing the sequence of human poses and carry out the cooperative task which is in line with the intentionof the human. Besides, the robot recognizes the state of target object and judge the progress of current assembly task in HRC environment. After getting the position of assembly part and tools, the robot will pick up and transfer them in time, which improves the efficiency of HRC.

4. Perception and Cognition Approach of HRCA

In HRC based on HCPS, the robot needs to constantly interact with the surrounding environment and humans participating in collaboration and adjust its behavior in time according to the environment and human state changes. The implementation of this process is inextricably linked to the robot's situational awareness. It can identify the changing part of the environment, understand the scene, and make decisions. It can be determined that accurate perception and correct cognition of the collaborative environment are essential for safe HRC.

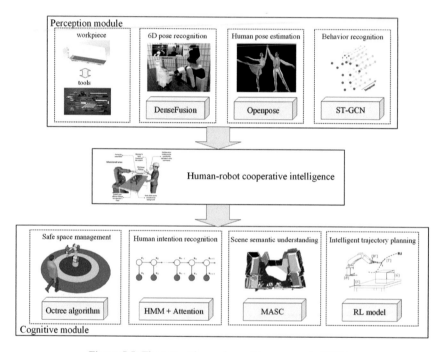

Figure 5.5: The perception and cognition process in HRCA.

4.1 Perception Process

Perception is the premise of information interaction. Perception comes from neuroscience, which refers to the stimulation of sensory organs by the external environment to form a pulse signal in the neural network. And the signal is transmitted to the brain and interacts with the memory block to produce a kind of feedback. In the abstract, the perception behavior of robot agents can be regarded as acquiring the surrounding environments information through external sensor devices and forming a particular understanding. The memory module of the brain can be compared with the trained recognition network model. The same input can achieve different feature expressions in different feature presentation models, which is similar to the diversity of the human perception of the environment. In summary, in a specific scene, we need a specific perception function.

The acquisition and initial processing of environmental information by the robot's external sensing devices can be considered the robot's perception process, including object detection and instance segmentation, pose calculation, human motion recognition, etc. Ultimately, different perceptual results are ultimately different extracted. While objection is to extract and classify the objects in the scene, and instance segmentation is to separate the individuals in the image based on the pixel processing of different parts of the image based on object detection. The classical segmentation algorithm mainly uses edge operators, clustering analysis, and wavelet transformation to segment the region of an image. In contrast, the current algorithms based on deep learning mainly include CNN, Mask-RCNN, Yolo, PointNet, etc. Pose calculation is to obtain the object's position information and the pose and orientation information under the current working plane based on object detection and determine the robot's contact pose when grasping. The main algorithms include PVNet, NOCs, Pix2Pose and deep-6DPose. Similarly, in RGB-D images, human skeleton information is acquired based on OpenPose and then the current action behavior is estimated by methods such as LSTM or Pose Tracking.

4.2   Cognitive Process

An essential feature of the new generation of the intelligent manufacturing system is that the agent's learning and cognitive ability can be improved. The robot participating in the cooperative task not only has a more powerful ability to perceive, calculate, analyze and execute actions but also has the ability to learn, improve and generate cognition. As the upper structure of the perception module, the cognitive system's decision module can make in-depth analysis based on the information obtained by the perception system, mine the potentially useful information, and carry out autonomous learning combined with logical reasoning and meta reinforcement learning.

For the position, posture and distribution information of parts acquired by the perception layer, and the sequential behavior information of human body, the attention method is adopted to excavate human behavior intention and combine with task state to further improve the accuracy of human operation behavior discrimination. In terms of HRC strategy, the robot can analyze the current scene based on transfer learning method, and independently choose the cooperation strategy suitable for the current state. Based on reinforcement learning method, the robot can continuously interact with the environment and learn more suitable task execution actions. The "knowledge base" in the cognitive system is built by the combination of human expert experience and intelligent learning cognitive system, which contains all kinds of knowledge that human workers can access and includes implicit knowledge that is difficult for humans to master or describe. Moreover, in practical use, the robot can continuously populate and update the knowledge base by self-learning to mine new implicit knowledge and enhance the experience store.

5.   Case Study

In this section, we take a PB560 ventilator as an example, as shown in Fig. 5.6, the simulation experiment of human-robot collaborative assembly based on CPS is carried out. Firstly, a digital representation model corresponding to the physical structure model of the ventilator is established. Secondly, a reinforcement learning framework with a human-robot collaboration strategy is introduced. Finally, in the cyber space, the optimal collaboration strategy is obtained by continuously interacting with the

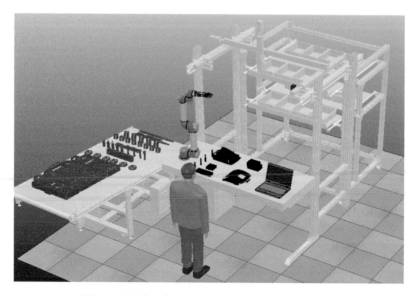

Figure 5.6: Virtual HRC assembly experimental platform.

physical space through reinforcement learning methods. And the adaptability of CPS-based HRCA in a dynamic environment is demonstrated.

The ventilator is made up of over 100 components, with more than 40 connectors. Moreover, there are 15 flexible connectors, including 10 hoses and 5 cables. It is difficult for a robot to control these kinds of parts accurately, so it needs to cooperate with humans or be executed by humans alone. Besides, some screws can be regarded as a collaborative task, robot transfer tools and a human carries out the assembly work. The assembly of rigid parts, such as battery insertion, panel mounting and module turnover, can be completed by robot. The simplified ventilator assembly tree is shown in Fig. 5.7, with the nodes representing components and the edges representing the connection between components.

According to the properties of each part and its connection mode, the assembly state is represented as: $H_i = \{(D_H, D_R, T_H, T_R), (D_H^m, D_R^m, T_H^m, T_R^m, D_H^t, D_R^t, T_H^t, T_R^t)\}$.

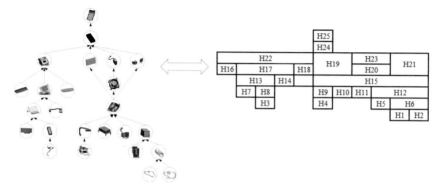

Figure 5.7: Simplified ventilator assembly tree.

D_H represents the difficulty of the operator to complete the task alone, D_R represents the difficulty of the robot to complete the task alone, T_H and T_R represent the time taken by each to complete the task respectively (since there is no real ventilator product, the values for time and difficulty were defined by manual estimation). For some assembly tasks that cannot be performed by a robot or a human alone or that require the operation of an additional tool to perform, the difficultly of performing the part D_H^m and the difficulty of performing the operating tool D_H^t are defined, respectively, as well as the time taken to operate the tool for the assembly task T_H^m. The reward function is set to be related to the difficulty and time of the task, and the state of the agent can be described as:

$$S = \begin{cases} (0, i+1) & \text{finish, select next target} \\ (1, i, T-t) & \text{assembly in progress} \\ (-1, i) & \text{waiting for collaborators} \end{cases}$$

The reinforcement learning method of HRC strategy for assembly tasks is shown in Fig. 5.8. Agent-Human and Agent-Robot perform corresponding actions, a reward is then given according to the status of the respective task. Moreover, continue to new actions until all sub-tasks are completed, denoted as one learning period. Through continuous iterative learning, and trying different collaborative strategies. Finally, the results of our experiments are presented using Gantt plots. As shown in Fig. 5.9, the tasks obtained through the collaborative reinforcement learning network were assigned to the human and the robot in a time sequence. The tasks were executed in an orderly manner, with a total assembly time in 6 minutes.

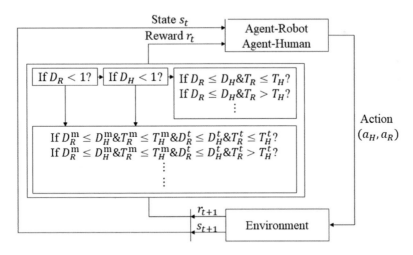

Figure 5.8: Reinforcement learning method for assembly task assignment.

6. Summary and Prospect

The human-robot collaborative assembly approach based on the CPS proposed in this chapter is applied in a task allocation sequence optimization for the assembly of ventilators. The robot obtains the assembly task information through perception and

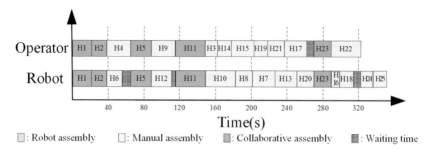

Figure 5.9: The HRC assembly sequences of a ventilator.

cognition, and realizes the adaptability of the HRC system to the dynamic assembly scene through reinforcement learning algorithm, which greatly improves the work efficiency of the HRC system and the anti-interference ability to the dynamic work scene. Especially when responding to new assembly tasks, the proposed approach can be adapted to new tasks without substantial changes. At the same time, the reduction in human labour reduces the impact of worker turnover on the factory.

In the future, more natural interaction and collaboration can be achieved by further refining and enriching the state information in HRC scenarios and through deeper cognitive functions that facilitate the robot's understanding of human behavior beyond the assembly task.

References

1. Rapaccini, M., N. Saccani, C. Kowalkowski, M. Paiola and F. Adrodegari. Navigating disruptive crises through service-led growth: The impact of COVID-19 on Italian Manufacturing Firms. Industrial Marketing Management, 88 (1 July 2020): 225–237. https://doi.org/10.1016/j.indmarman.2020.05.017
2. Papadopoulos, T., K.N. Baltas and M.E. Balta. The use of digital technologies by small and medium enterprises during COVID-19: Implications for theory and practice. International Journal of Information Management, 55 (1 December 2020): 102192. https://doi.org/10.1016/j.ijinfomgt.2020.102192
3. Vogel, C., M. Fritzsche and N. Elkmann. Safe human-robot cooperation with high-payload robots in industrial applications. *In:* 11th ACM/IEEE International Conference on Human-Robot Interaction (HRI), (2016): 529–530. https://doi.org/10.1109/HRI.2016.7451840
4. Wang, W., R. Li, Y. Chen, Z.M. Diekel and Y. Jia. Facilitating human–robot collaborative tasks by teaching-learning-collaboration from human demonstrations. IEEE Transactions on Automation Science and Engineering, 16(2) (April 2019): 640–653. https://doi.org/10.1109/TASE.2018.2840345
5. Nikolakis, N., V. Maratos and S. Makris. A Cyber Physical System (CPS) approach for safe human-robot collaboration in a shared workplace. Robotics and Computer-Integrated Manufacturing, 56 (1 April 2019): 233–243. https://doi.org/10.1016/j.rcim.2018.10.003

6. Zimmerling, A. and X. Chen. Innovation and possible long-term impact driven by COVID-19: Manufacturing, personal protective equipment and digital technologies. Technology in Society, 65 (1 May 2021): 101541. https://doi.org/10.1016/j.techsoc.2021.101541

7. Belhadi, A., S. Kamble, C. Jose, C. Jabbour, A. Gunasekaran, N.O. Ndubisi and M. Venkatesh. Manufacturing and service supply chain resilience to the COVID-19 outbreak: Lessons learned from the automobile and airline industries. Technological Forecasting and Social Change, 163 (1 February 2021): 120447. https://doi.org/10.1016/j.techfore.2020.120447

8. Kim, S.H. and S. Park. CPS (Cyber Physical System) based manufacturing system optimization. Procedia Computer Science, 5th International Conference on Information Technology and Quantitative Management (ITQM) 2017, 122 (1 January 2017): 518–524. https://doi.org/10.1016/j.procs.2017.11.401

9. Liu, A., I. Teo, D. Chen, S. Lu, T. Wuest, Z. Zhang and F. Tao. Biologically inspired design of context-aware smart products. Engineering, 5(4) (1 August 2019): 637–645. https://doi.org/10.1016/j.eng.2019.06.005

10. Wang, X.V., X. Zhang, Y. Yang and L. Wang. A human-robot collaboration system towards high accuracy. Procedia CIRP, 53rd CIRP Conference on Manufacturing Systems 2020, 93 (1 January 2020): 1085–1090. https://doi.org/10.1016/j.procir.2020.04.085

11. Zhou, J., Y. Zhou, B. Wang and J. Zang. Human-Cyber-Physical Systems (HCPSs) in the context of new-generation intelligent manufacturing. Engineering, 5(4) (1 August 2019): 624–636. https://doi.org/10.1016/j.eng.2019.07.015

12. Robla-Gómez, S., V.M. Becerra, J.R. Llata, E. González-Sarabia, C. Torre-Ferrero and J. Pérez-Oria. Working together: A review on safe human-robot collaboration in industrial environments. IEEE Access, 5 (2017): 26754–26773. https://doi.org/10.1109/ACCESS.2017.2773127

13. Liu, H. and L. Wang. Remote human–robot collaboration: A cyber–physical system application for hazard manufacturing environment. Journal of Manufacturing Systems, 54 (1 January 2020): 24–34. https://doi.org/10.1016/j.jmsy.2019.11.001

14. Wang, Q., W. Jiao, R. Yu, M.T. Johnson and Y. Zhang. Virtual reality robot-assisted welding based on human intention recognition. IEEE Transactions on Automation Science and Engineering, 17(2) (April 2020): 799–808. https://doi.org/10.1109/TASE.2019.2945607

15. Lin, H.-I. and Y.-C. Ho. Adaptive gain control for a steady human-robot cooperation. In: Proceedings – 2019 IEEE International Conference on Industrial Cyber Physical Systems, ICPS 2019, Taipei, Taiwan, (2019): 325–330. http://dx.doi.org/10.1109/ICPHYS.2019.8780293.

16. Wei, W., H. Peng, J. Pang and Q. Yu. Impedance control in uncertain environment using reinforcement learning. In: 9th IEEE International Conference on Cyber Technology in Automation, Control and Intelligent Systems, CYBER 2019, 1203–1208. Suzhou, China, (2019). http://dx.doi.org/10.1109/CYBER46603.2019.9066697

17. Zheng, X., Y. Zheng, Y. Shuai, J. Yang, S. Yang and Y. Tian. Kinematics Analysis and Trajectory Planning of 6-DOF Robot. In: 2019 IEEE 3rd Information Technology, Networking, Electronic and Automation Control Conference (ITNEC), (2019): 1749–1754. https://doi.org/10.1109/ITNEC.2019.8729280

18. Germi, S.B., M.A. Khosravi and R. FesharakiFard. Adaptive GA-based potential field algorithm for collision-free path planning of mobile robots in dynamic environments. *In:* 2018 6th RSI International Conference on Robotics and Mechatronics (IcRoM), (2018): 28–33. https://doi.org/10.1109/ICRoM.2018.8657601

19. Cimini, C., F. Pirola, R. Pinto and S. Cavalieri. A human-in-the-loop manufacturing control architecture for the next generation of production systems. Journal of Manufacturing Systems, 54 (1 January 2020): 258–271. https://doi.org/10.1016/j.jmsy.2020.01.002

20. Bergamini, L., M. Sposato, M. Pellicciari, M. Peruzzini, S. Calderara and J. Schmidt. Deep learning-based method for vision-guided robotic grasping of unknown objects. Advanced Engineering Informatics, 44 (1 April 2020): 101052. https://doi.org/10.1016/j.aei.2020.101052

21. Kulik, S. and A. Shtanko. Using convolutional neural networks for recognition of objects varied in appearance in computer vision for intellectual robots. Procedia Computer Science, Postproceedings of the 10th Annual International Conference on Biologically Inspired Cognitive Architectures, BICA 2019 (Tenth Annual Meeting of the BICA Society), held August 15-19, 2019 in Seattle, Washington, USA, 169 (1 January 2020): 164–167. https://doi.org/10.1016/j.procs.2020.02.129

22. Wang, W., W. Tian, W. Liao and B. Li. Pose accuracy compensation of mobile industry robot with binocular vision measurement and deep belief network. Optik, 238 (1 July 2021): 166716. https://doi.org/10.1016/j.ijleo.2021.166716

23. Wang, H., C. Yuan, J. Shen, W. Yang and H. Ling. Action unit detection and key frame selection for human activity prediction. Neurocomputing, 318 (27 November 2018): 109–19. https://doi.org/10.1016/j.neucom.2018.08.037

24. Chen, C., T. Wang, D. Li and J. Hong. Repetitive assembly action recognition based on object detection and pose estimation. Journal of Manufacturing Systems, 55 (1 April 2020): 325–333. https://doi.org/10.1016/j.jmsy.2020.04.018

25. Nikolakis, N., K. Sipsas and S. Makris. A cyber-physical context-aware system for coordinating human-robot collaboration. Procedia CIRP, 72 (2018): 27–32. https://doi.org/10.1016/j.procir.2018.03.033

26. Liu, H. and L. Wang. Human motion prediction for human-robot collaboration. Journal of Manufacturing Systems, Special Issue on Latest Advancements in Manufacturing Systems at NAMRC, 45, 44 (1 July 2017): 287–294. https://doi.org/10.1016/j.jmsy.2017.04.009

27. Chien, S.-Y., Y.-L. Lin, P.-J. Lee, S. Han, M. Lewis and K. Sycara. Attention allocation for human multi-robot control: Cognitive analysis based on behavior data and hidden states. International Journal of Human-Computer Studies, Cognitive Assistants, 117 (1 September 2018): 30–44. https://doi.org/10.1016/j.ijhcs.2018.03.005

28. Jian, Y. and Y. Li. Research on intelligent cognitive function enhancement of intelligent robot based on ant colony algorithm. Cognitive Systems Research, 56 (1 August 2019): 203–212. https://doi.org/10.1016/j.cogsys.2018.12.014

29. Wang, X.V., Z. Kemény, J. Váncza and L. Wang. Human-robot collaborative assembly in cyber-physical production: Classification framework and implementation. CIRP Annals, 66(1) (1 January 2017): 5–8. https://doi.org/10.1016/j.cirp.2017.04.101

30. Nunes, D., J. Sa Silva and F. Boavida. A Practical Introduction to Human-in-the-Loop Cyber-Physical Systems. Hoboken, NJ: Wiley-IEEE Press, (2018).
31. Zhou, J., P. Li, Y. Zhou, B. Wang, J. Zang and L. Meng. Toward new-generation intelligent manufacturing. Engineering, Cybersecurity, 4(1) (1 February 2018): 11–20. https://doi.org/10.1016/j.eng.2018.01.002

A CPS Perspective on Teaching Engineering Laboratories during Pandemics

Maximilian Nicolae*, Radu Pietraru and Stefan Mocanu

1. Some in Depth Context as to Who Will Develop Future Innovations

The pandemic has shown us many of the shortcomings of society, shortcomings that even if we knew about them, we did not consider them so important, or that could have an immediate impact. The same can be said about global warming, the prospect of which for some is imminent and very close and for others it is a problem that can wait. Without entering such controversies, however, the present material aims to provide an opinion of the authors about the implications of automation on the future when we are faced with situations that even if we anticipate we are not prepared for them. Because it is about society's response to certain problems, society needs to be prepared, and education could ultimately be responsible for that preparation. We will not discuss how education should specialize engineers in making high-performance weapons to protect us from various threats, but we intend to discuss education in the context of automation, in the context of "total connectivity and integration" (interdisciplinary), practically, in the context of Cyber-Physical Systems (CPS). And to add substance to the following, we chose to present a case study from the experience of the authors, professors from a top faculty* that prepares future specialists in the field of CPS. Even if the case study is a technical and very applied one, we consider that it can be extended by analogy to global aspects related to CPS, aspects whose importance and challenges were highlighted to us with the appearance of the pandemic.

No matter how many definitions we find for CPS or similar approaches (see Industry 4.0) the name is relevant enough to make sure that these approaches exist among us and cannot disappear. The benefits of interconnecting between physical and software-driven systems are as clear as can be, and they can cover the whole

---

* Faculty of Automation and Computers, University "Politehnica" of Bucharest.

*Corresponding author: max.nicolae@upb.ro

spectrum, starting with reducing the waste of redundant activities, not putting people to work on robotic tasks (see scientific management and Taylorism) to systems whose performance cannot be matched in "natural" ways. It is enough to think about the famous film "Schindler's List" and we can get an idea of where the performance indicators (KPIs) and the "standardization"* of human work can lead. Of course, there is nothing free in this world and automation comes with costs. Among the estimated costs of automation are those related to labour. "Many bright, perfectly capable humans will find themselves the new horse: unemployed through no fault of their own" is an excerpt from the well-known video entitled "Humans need not apply" [1, 2] and in which automation and artificial intelligence (also with the role of automation) are presented as means that will make many jobs (in most fields, including creative fields) no longer open to people. On the other hand, we are told in every way that the CPS field will create a lot of other jobs. If we consider the opinion of an acclaimed and so-called "visionary", Elon Musk (a model for young generations) who supports the guaranteed minimum income, we can get an idea of the context in which education must prepare generations to keep up with this accelerated trend in the field of technology and, at the same time, able to innovate. If we are to talk about innovation, then there are some issues. The field of engineering, the one responsible for the technological advance that led to approaches such as CPS and Industry 4.0, should be largely characterized by creativity or, perhaps, ingenuity, if we go by the play on words and etymology. In fact, we will continue to speculate in this direction and refer to the etymology of the word "engineer" which seems to have its roots in the Latin "ingenium", or "genius" which, in turn (according to the same dictionary†), is outside the meaning of talented and special abilities it can also be translated as a guardian spirit. So, engineers must behave like true geniuses and continue to design and support systems that help and protect people and nature in general.

Nowadays the time-to-market (TTM) seems to be one of the most important features for developing of new products and services (NPSD), many times overpassing some quality aspects or even standard compliance. The new advancement in artificial intelligence, cloud virtualization and Internet of things exerts a lot of pressure on many other industrial fields which are characterized by large inertia in the adoption of novel technology. CPS and its European counterpart approach applied in industry, i.e. Industry 4.0, are in the front line of such adoption. Another domain with high inertia, but with a critical importance in development of the CPS system as we can see, is the education in engineering. Education seems to be not so different from what happens in other domains when it comes to TTM. Therefore, engineering universities tend to integrate in their laboratories the latest technologies and they are proud of that. Afterall, this becomes a means to advertise on the education market (expensive endowments). Our students are attracted to work with the last development in technology, but will they be able to preserve their competitiveness on the labor market without a deeper knowledge? Before the pandemic we were able to attract students in engineering to understand the fundamentals by designing practical labs for them,with the aim of "teaching fundamentals". The key factor was the physical interaction with those lab platforms and the activities they had to do.

---

* In the film there is a scene in which a worker is taken out of the workshop and with his pistol at his head he is timed while he manages to complete his task.

† engineer. (n.d.) American Heritage® Dictionary of the English Language, Fifth Edition. (2011). Retrieved March 25 2021 from https://www.thefreedictionary.com/engineer

As teachers we are often asked by student's parents or even by students about the curriculum and how it is adapted to the "new requirements" of the labor market. For example, we are regularly warned that we do not use the latest released equipment on the market. In the context of the above introductions, we can now say that we usually respond to such challenges not by indicating an underfunding but rather by explaining that the actual modern equipment will be followed by some newer generation equipment that will no longer have the need for a human operator and that we want our students to be the ones to design such equipment. Of course, engineers mean not only design, but also operation. In education there is a whole inflation of diplomas and scientific degrees that we can understand especially in the context of approaches such as "lifelong learning". However, the question arises as to whether education becomes an industry by itself that is parallel to society's goals. Just as in quality management there is a certification industry with titles inspired by martial arts, certifications that do not necessarily attest the quality of the holder except in the context of standardized procedures, so it is very possible that education, especially higher education, can prepare most graduates for an industry that will be artificially maintained by bureaucratic means, an industry parallel to the "natural" needs of society. "Functional illiteracy" is still being discussed at the pre-university level. We can't help but wonder at the university level if even in the field of information technology there can be a functional illiteracy and what form it would take. In this paper we will not develop this topic, but we want to introduce a context of how education could evolve, including at the highest level. The increased pressures for developing future CPS systems risk turning so-called specialists into personnel whose duty it is to assist machines equipped with artificial intelligence and not the other way around. It is known that engineering education considers the qualifications of two types of engineers, those who design and those who operate. Neither qualification should be seen as inferior to the other. Rather, the difference should be made between what a higher education institution would be and what a vocational (or professional) school would be. These things can be reduced to solving a much older compromise in education, the compromise between "quick fix" and "teaching fundamentals". The methodology and capacity for abstraction should be defining in higher education, but how could these things be made attractive in the context of current social pressures, pressures that have been briefly mentioned above.

This paper offers a practical perspective of education in this context, also offering a case study as a model on how CPS provided a solution in a borderline situation. The perspective is that of seeing the process of teaching an engineering laboratory as a CPS but, at the same time, expecting students to be the ones who will carry forward the technological advancement of the CPS field. We want our students to learn the basics, critical thinking, and the ability to abstract and develop methodologies for solving various problems even in the context where society needs them as operators of very complex systems. We want to develop their practical sense and sense of proportion, extremely important characteristics for engineers, and at the same time to develop their teamwork skills, confidence in colleagues and passion for this profession. We will call all these as "feelings" and consider them very important resources in their profession. But all these aspects, sometimes referred as transversal to the discipline, have been challenged with the COVID–19 pandemic. The lockdown sent us to consider activities in the online environment and then we found out how engineering can be done from home, where all the intense laboratory activities that are involved can be done. In fact, we unwittingly learned a lot of things that could change the way education is done, and more interestingly, we got here with the help of CPS. The rest of the chapter is structured as follows: we continue with the difference of implications for a "quick fix" and "teaching fundamentals" approaches on designing CPS when it comes to the education of students that are increasingly connected and subscribed to the distractions of social networks, we will present our case study that we consider relevant and how it migrated online due to CPS approaches. Some discussions and the lessons learned conclude the chapter.

2. The "quick fix" Approach

Information technology (IT) is an area that is experiencing extremely rapid development. This makes the demand for a skilled work force well beyond the training capacity of the education system. We could even go so far as to make a comparison with the demand for medical staff in pandemic conditions. In both cases we can ask how long it will take and what the solutions are? Education is a system of great inertia and as Sir Ken Robinson referred to, in many of his talks on the TED platform [3] and appreciated by millions of followers, education was designed on the principles of the Enlightenment and the Industrial Revolution and many things have changed since then. Moreover, even if the company needs a large staff with a certain qualifications, can that staff be motivated only based on financial gains? Interestingly, many of these so-called skilled jobs involve following procedures and too little creativity, which makes them exposed as being the first jobs to be taken over by robots. Returning to the IT field, where the standardization is at a very high level, the integration of library modules and the use of predefined templates transforms many of the IT engineers into users whose activity could disappear in the future. Their utility is very necessary now, given the extremely high demand, but we could ask ourselves how long this trend will remain? What will be their reconversion capacity when many of the companies that hire them now, hire them for certain tasks that in the future will be done by robots (software bots)? Without generalization we still must discuss the pressure we feel from the IT companies which are willing to assume much of the training of specialists, which is not bad, but there may be discussions about qualifications,their acknowledgement, who should be held accountable, and what will be the competencies in the long run in the case of unexpected events such as those that we seem to face more and more often. As we mentioned at the beginning, the CPS field exists and must offer solutions to such problems that have social implications. We want to also discuss the perspective of implications in innovation and technological advancements that aims to serve humanity. There is much discussion about the creative possibilities of robots but so far advancements in this direction are largely debatable. The writing of film scripts or the composition of songs by robots are still at the algorithmic level and do not convey the author's feelings as in the case of works made by humans. The fact that a voice assistant tells a joke does not mean that it is empathetic in any way with the interlocutor. That is why there are good actors and less talented actors. But the chances are that these technologies will become a part of our lives and we will get used to interacting with them as our second nature [4]. Our problem is how to prepare future engineers who are not to assist these technologies but become the technology creators. The educational curriculum in the field of science (including engineering) requires practical laboratory classes, which no one disputes. Moreover, the engineering curriculum tends to focus more on skills and not at all on the reproduction of so-called "knowledge", which is self-evident. It is curious as to why the education was once focused on reproduction. The problem with skills is that they are difficult to quantify, especially at the utility level over a certain time perspective. Companies that hire graduates will be able to say that they need certain skills at that particular moment, but they do not say how they guarantee the necessary retention of that skill for a longer period (neither could they). As such, engineering must adapt its curriculum in such a way as to develop several skills for students, among which we return and emphasize the aspects related to creativity and practical sense. We do not intend to discuss an engineering curriculum or the basics of an engineering laboratory. For the latter, the paper [5] provides a fundamental analysis of the role of laboratory activities in engineering education. As mentioned, we intend to present our experience with one of the laboratories that we taught during the pandemics, but we sought to place the laboratory in a relevant context so that it can be used to be extended as a methodology to other disciplines.

3.   Teaching Fundamentals in "The Social Dilemma"

The globalization of communication brings with it the submission of its users to the most attractive and demanding information. Geographical boundaries are no longer barriers to the spread of "brilliant" ideas that hold the user captive in opposition to "boring" information, without immediate practical applicability, such as fundamental theoretical notions. The notion of "going viral" defines to some extent the ability to spread information but, at the same time, it also shows how much of this time is spent consuming this information. The film "The Social Dilemma" (2020) through the statements of some of the creators of social networks reveals somewhat the levels reached in the desire to keep the users captive. In this context it only takes a few enlightened minds for their creations to have an impact globally. Some followers of evolutionism might go so far as to say that this is a challenge that the adapted ones must survive. Others would draw parallels with the idea that people should be busy with something. Instead, education suffers greatly and needs to adapt in a way that turns threats into opportunities. To some extent this is what we propose with our laboratories and ideas such as gamification are common. They are related to the fact that students are attracted to show their achievements and to be subjected to a "jury" of acquaintances who judge by their likes which makes social networks contribute towards the training of students in various activities. But this is not enough if the laboratory is not attractive. As such, the laboratory must be attractive to current generations of students, but also provide basic engineering skills. According to [5] the practical work falls into four broad groups: cognitive learning, inquiry methodology, vocational aims, and the development of personal skills. In the following we will focus on an aspect that engineering laboratories should provide, namely practice. We can make an analogy between this practical sense and the sense of dimension, the ability to perceive through the prism of some experiences, some feelings. The expression of "common sense" is often use in relation to this situation, but in engineering this "common" should be developed. We consider this experience extremely important and its lack can lead to many problems, from some without major implications to some whose subtlety we may not immediately notice but can lead to major long-term consequences. Within the "innocent" implications we can give as an example more and more often met in our teaching activity. We refer here to the results obtained by students after some calculation errors, results about which the students do not have the capacity to check their feasibility because those values do not tell them anything at all. It so happens that they leave written on their papers some aberrant results without raising any doubts. On the other hand, if those results had referred to some physical quantities with which they are accustomed from the experience of their feelings (such as time, distance, mass) then the aberrant results would immediately rise suspicions. The subtle implications are those related to the capacity for innovation. Creativity comes down only to experience with a sheet of paper or a system that could be a more modern sheet of paper probably (a text on a window) as much as communication would only mean the voice. Creativity depends on several factors among which is the way we interact with the involved phenomena, especially when we are referring to CPS, so it is important to develop the experimental side. The importance of practical activity has been analyzed by many authors and ideas such as "practice by doing" and "teach others" have been considered the most effective teaching methods (according to studies in [6, 7]) performing lectures, reading and even the demonstration. This last aspect becomes especially important in the context in which the pandemic made the students have access to some laboratories only by watching remote demonstrations.

The engineering curriculum laboratories are designed to provide support for the notions presented in the course. Thus, the main objective seems to be cognitive learning, an objective that can be assimilated with the combination of theory and practice [5]. However, related activities should also target other more general activities (often identified by transversal competencies). Such skills, as will be seen in the case study below, help students to develop methodologies for their projects which are, in fact, CPS. Approaches such as automatic verification, digital twin, hardware in the loop, design for manufacturing are aspects that do not only belong to a certain discipline and they can be practiced on laboratories from several disciplines, and not necessarily imposed, but adopted with the conviction that by doing so they will save a lot of time and focus on only the important things. At the same time, let us not forget that we want to train their "feelings", their practical sense and, why not, to nourish their passion. The major implications of the pandemic in education are related to the deprivation of students from contacting natural phenomena. Without initially being aware, the migration to the online laboratory activities revealed this implication to us. The way the students adapted made us deepen some aspects that we will present towards the end of the material.

4. The Pandemic Implications

We have all witnessed the effects of the pandemic on everyday life. Most likely a long time from now we will discover various implications of which we are not yet aware. In terms of education, the most visible change is the transition from face-to-face to distance learning. This transition brought to the light both positive and negative aspects of the interaction between teachers and students, as well as between students. As presented in [8] and [11], the transition to online education required the intensive use of technology but, most importantly, a much higher degree of student involvement in the education process. Not only did the students suffer, in turn the professors had to reconsider their work. To get an idea from this perspective, it is enough to list the need to readjust the teaching materials, rethink the work tasks and the evaluation method, etc. And with the long interruption of the teaching process will eventually require a reconsideration of the entire teaching process [9, 10].

In many countries the material cost that had to be borne by students is significant given the standard of living associated with that country [12]. Among the components of this cost we can refer to communication and internet services, the purchase of multimedia equipment (video cameras, graphics tablets) but also educational materials specific to that particular field. The pleasant surprise we experienced in this context was that although we were unable to run our practical laboratories in face-to-face conditions and had to move to online simulators, our students bought components based on their own initiatives, components with which they assembled at home parts of their laboratory work.

5. Our Case Study

5.1 Before the Pandemic

The laboratory presented below belongs to a course on Digital Design (DD) taught to 2nd year students from the Faculty of Automation and Computers within the University "Politehnica" of Bucharest. Both the content and the methodology is used to serve as a good example for CPS from at least two reasons: first, the perspective of the equipment and methodology used for the laboratory activities and, second and more important, for the skills acquired by students for the future design of cyber-physical systems. As mentioned in previous sections, the constraints of the pandemic have revealed other benefits of such an approach.

The main objective of the laboratory is in line with the general objectives of engineering laboratories (cognitive learning) and provides support for the notions presented in the course. The course is dedicated to the fundamentals of digital circuit design and follows a classic approach in this field. First the numerical representations for the digital system are introduced, followed by the principles of fundamental logic gates and then the methods for analysis and synthesis of the functional components that are encountered in microprogrammed circuits or hardware configurable structures are developed. In the case of combinational logic circuits, examples of such components would be logic gates, multiplexers, encoders, decoders, adders, etc. In the case of sequential logic circuits, we could list flip-flops, shifting registers, counters, finite state algorithmic machines, etc. Many of these circuits and the methodologies used for design are found and applied to field programmable logic gates arrays (FPGAs), microprocessors, specialized circuits (ASICs) and other complex integrated circuits. The most common way to develop laboratories for this discipline taught in technical universities is to use development kits with FPGAs. If we refer to the need for skills that students should develop to be competitive in the labor market that method is probably the most effective way and the most appropriate. That is why we do not want to deprive students of this experience and in the second part of their lab they use FPGA-based development kits, namely Nexys 4DDR. In Fig. 6.1. such a kit is illustrated.

Our experience has shown us that there are some inconveniences in introducing this kit at the beginning of the laboratory, inconveniences caused mostly by the current level of involvement of students, especially those in the first years of study. Among these drawbacks we would like to list (without seeking in any way to affect the image

Figure 6.1: FPGA development board.

of the manufacturer, clearly stating that the main causes are the attitude of students that we understand to some extent, as we presented in the section on teaching the basics in the world of distractions generated by social networks):

- Such equipment can be easily damaged by inexperienced and inattentive students and is quite expensive (even with all the discounts given by the manufacturer to universities). For example, it is easy to create a short circuit.
- Even using high-performance personal computers (state-of-the-art processor, SSD, large RAM) synthesizing some circuits takes a long time for a student who often makes mistakes.
- Many of the fundamental elements of logical design are somehow hidden from the student who should develop that practical sense, that experience with those low-level bit streams, an experience about whose importance we argued in a previous section.

All the disadvantages that we have identified above pale in comparison to the advantages that such a platform offers to students in their future development. As a result, we continue to use such platforms but not from the first part of the laboratory. For the beginning of the laboratory, we wanted to use something closer to the fundamental engineering values that we mentioned in this paper. In the CPS field, where it is imperative that information technology blends properly with the process, not as in the case of rigorously approached theory with mathematical tools, the boundary between the ability to do something and the ability to reproduce something is quite fragile and things can easily be confused. Probably now the reader will better understand why we had to bore him with the elaborated context from the beginning of the chapter. For example, we could interface a sensor very well without clearly understanding that interface, instead we could only call some library functions. This is not wrong, but will we be able to maintain our competitiveness in front of a "machine" if we limit ourselves to working strictly procedurally without using other senses with which we have been endowed. And to be even more precise, we will present a joke that one of the authors makes to the students when they work with certain industrial sensors, a joke known from one employer of our graduates when they are interviewed for a job: "Don't touch that sensor wire because it uses unified current and you risk injury." Even if it seems like an innocent joke, the lack of measure can have very important consequences, especially if we must design a new product or system, when experience provides us with a first estimate of the expected results and helps us to keep our course, or we have to change it in time if the implications require it. We need to estimate correctly the resources involved, including those related to time and labor. All these are part of the engineers' life and they must contribute with passion and with all the senses they have. On this occasion we remember a famous reply given by a politician (engineer and prime minister of Romania in the early twentieth century) when asked in the Assembly of Deputies about what an engineer can provide to politics, he answered briefly and firmly: "measure, the sense of measure".

Returning now to our laboratory, we had to find a solution that would give students that feeling of the phenomenon and, at the same time, follow the course plan. There are many teaching platforms that aim to experiment with fundamental logic circuits (not FPGAs). However, these platforms do not solve the problems related to short circuit protection and come with high costs. Another problem that we saw on these platforms is the lack of automatic verification. We will describe this last issue when we introduce the platform we propose and used.

Even from the beginning of the introduction for the platform that we propose as a CPS approach we want to mention clearly that it is not a commercial platform. It is an open platform that anyone who reads this material and has knowledge in the field can quickly implement with components off the shelf and with one exception. The exception is given by a printed circuit board (PCB) whose project we can make available with pleasure but can be extremely simple to design based on other specific needs. In our case the PCB was initially thought of in an intermediate stage to achieve the solution very quickly and to identify shortcomings to develop a new corresponding version. The interesting experience for us was that 6 years after the introduction of that platform (at the time of writing) we had absolutely no operating problems and there were always other priorities than to bring out an improved version. The need is the biggest motivation and as it was not imperative need for an improved version, we find ourselves in this situation. Afterall "right the first time" is a desired manufacturing concept.

In the case of the fundamentals of digital design (DD) many aspects can be reduced to systemic approach of a black box (see Fig. 6.2) in which the inputs and outputs are discrete time functions (signals) that can have two possible states (1 and 0). There are cases when a third state is introduced (high impedance) but this can be treated separately by considering the respective signal disconnected from the system.

Students working on DD lab will either need to analyze or design the system designated by the "?" in Fig. 6.3. If this system has number of M inputs, then students

	$x_{M-1}(t)$	...	$x_1(t)$	$x_0(t)$	$y_{N-1}(t+\tau)$	...	$y_1(t+\tau)$	$y_0(t+\tau)$
0	0	...	0	0	1	...	0	0
1	0	...	0	1	0	...	0	1
2	0	...	1	0	1	...	1	0
:	:	:	:	:	:	:	:	:
2^M-1	1	...	1	1	0	1	...	1

Figure 6.2: Systemic approach of logic circuits (left) functional described by the table of truth (right).

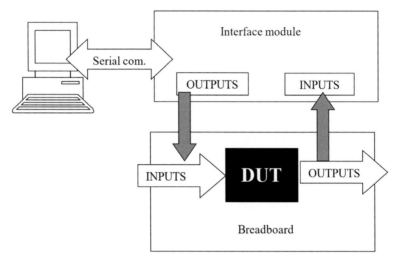

Figure 6.3: Digital design laboratory seen as a hardware in the loop (HiL)

will have to check their design by entering the 2^M possible combinations to check if the result is as expected (e.g.: for M = 5 there will be 32 combinations). Many of the platforms referred above generate the logic input variables from some switches. In this way, checking the operation becomes a waste of time. Imagine if students are asked to repeat this check several times until they get the correct result and, after that, the instructor is called to validate and score the result, in which case the instructor will have to witness that check. As a result, an automatic check is imperative. Automatic verification is common on platforms with FPGAs, but, as we mentioned, those platforms have other disadvantages for students who are new to the basics of digital design. The concept of automatic verification is very often associated with the concept of hardware in the loop (HiL) that characterizes CPS. The CPS can be calibrated in this way, tested during operation, or designed using HiL. In fact it is well known that CPS are often designed using model driven methodology and thus the steps used in verification are Model in the Loop (MiL), Software in the loop (SiL), processor in the loop (PiL) and then hardware in the loop (HiL). Precisely because one of the transversal objectives of the laboratory is to experiment with the physical phenomenon, it is necessary for students to have access to the "grass level", but time-consuming activities that do not provide added value (they are a waste) must be eliminated. In our case we refer to the time required for the generation of all input combinations from some switches. In conclusion, a HiL architecture is required as in Fig. 6.3 in which the device under test (DUT) is the black box designed by students (the one in Fig.

6.2) but whose verification is done at PC level through a module with a very simple interface. Of course, there are a lot of such interface modules and a lot of software (even professional applications) that facilitate the described approach. However, we find ourselves in the situation where we want to develop the autonomy of our students and not the dependence on a certain hardware. We also discuss fundamental issues at this level. We discuss the ability of students to be able to develop such test frameworks in their future projects. We discuss how the needs could require more specialized tools and what they must look for at dedicated suppliers. In our case, things are at basic level, and we designed the platform as an open-source framework.

The requirements for the interface in Fig. 6.5 were:

1. I/O: offering the possibility of acquiring digital signals (even analog) and programmatically generation of digital signals.
2. "Student proof" design: reduce the damage possibilities when operated by students on bases we mentioned early in this section.
3. Automatic verification: by using automation scripts in languages that students are already familiar with (Python, Matlab).
4. Low cost (materials and time): to be extremely cheap so that even students can afford to do it themselves.

When only the requirements 1 and 4 from above are considered, the hardware that immediately comes to mind is Arduino. We are not fans of "quick fix" and what Arduino means, but given the level of skills of the students we addressed we thought it was the fastest and most accessible platform (available at many stores at a price below 10 euros). Arduino involves a programming framework and a standardized platform which ultimately contains some microcontrollers for industrial use. We are often amused to see Arduino-type platforms used in the automation of processes that require other approaches. Arduino is largely a teaching platform designed to popularize access to some process automation solutions, so it can be used successfully at the high school level for beginners in the field of CPS. At the college level it may seem a little inappropriate. However, the economy of scale and replicas made in China have made platforms compatible with Arduino extremely cheap. The availability of a bootloader that eliminates the cost of an external programmer is a major advantage. The multitude of libraries, examples, and extension modules (shields) has made the Arduino approach a model to follow in many other fields. As such, Arduino can be used successfully at the faculty level but using methodologies appropriate to the respective training cycle (e.g., real time – interrupts driven and not pooling, algorithmic state machines and not ordinary sequential programming, integrated development environments – professional IDEs with increased productivity and not Arduino IDE, properly written function libraries and not those taken from the hobby community, etc.). Otherwise, if we kept the hobby approach promoted by the Arduino development framework at the faculty level, we would risk forming certain detrimental habits among the students (that "quick fix" that we kept mentioning). Students need to understand the basics because they can build on slippery foundations and their construction cannot move forward from a certain point on, which can have many consequences. In the case of our laboratory, the students did not interact with the code written on Arduino or with the respective development environment, so the above aspects were respected (during the pandemic this changed but we consider, as will be seen later in the text, the interaction is one as minor as possible). In conclusion, we chose to develop the interface module around the Arduino platform, endowing the latter with a shield properly designed to ensure the requirement 2 (Fig. 6.4). Requirement 3, as will be seen later, was solved partly in the Arduino software and partly on the PC in the scripting language. The latter is facilitated by the fact that the Arduino platform easily communicates with a PC via a USB port available on most PCs. Altium Designer was used to design the shield and the PCB was conceived on a single layer that was not exposed to students' access (Fig. 6.5).

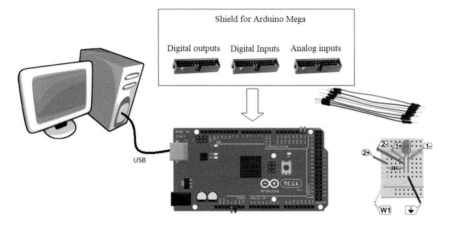

Figure 6.4: The architecture of the interface with the tested circuit, the module developed around the Arduino mega platform.

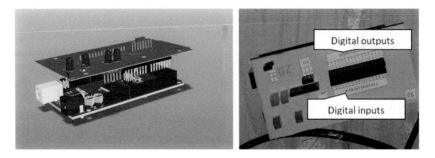

Figure 6.5: 3D model of the initial design developed in Altium Designer (left) and the outcome of the real platform (right).

The microcontroller's outputs on the Arduino platform were protected for short-circuiting by inserting resistors in series on the shield. This variant was chosen because the switching speeds are low and the circuits that make up the DUT (fundamental logic circuits) have high input impedances. The next variant is intended to be made with Mosfets to be able to secure higher currents without the risk of short circuits. Figure 6.6 shows the resulting platforms. It is interesting that the DUT circuit gets its power supply from the Arduino platform, which in turn is powered through the USB port from the PC, so no additional external power source is required. Moreover, the voltage regulators which equips the PCs' USB ports have overcurrent protection and thus, they manage to eliminate the damage of discrete circuits that students operate with on the breadboard (DUT). Forcing DUT circuits outputs to the power terminals or doing any other short circuit would lead to the protection mode of the PC's USB port and thus the discrete circuit would not be damaged. The students notice that it is a short circuit because the interface module is no longer powered, at which point they disconnect the suspicious wires, remove the USB cable that connects the Arduino to the PC and insert it back to have power again.

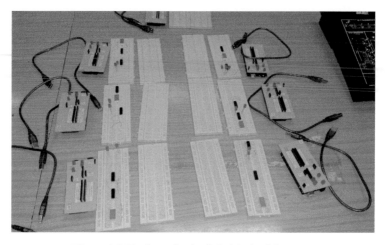

Figure 6.6: Platforms for the digital design laboratory

The software that we develop for the Arduino provides some simple text commands that give simple access to the pin states of the interface module. An example of commands is described in Table 6.1 below.

Table 6.1:

Command syntax	Description	Answer
dw*xxxx*	Configure the 16 output pins according to the xxxx parameter (4 hexadecimal characters: 0-9, A-F)	ACK or error
dr	Read the 16 inputs and display them as 4 hexadecimal characters preceded by the number 1.	1xxxx
bw*x v*	Configures the bit at position x (x = 0 - 9, a-f) with the value v (0 or 1).	ACK or error
br*x*	Read the value of the bit at position x (x = 0-9, a-f)	0 or 1
rs	Returns the system state (inputs and outputs) in both binary and hexadecimal format. All returned values are preceded by the number 1.	DO:1bbbbbbbbbbbbbbbb =0x1xxxx, DI:1bbbbbbbbbbbbbbbb =0x1xxxx
rv	Returns the version of the software running on uC.	0.3.0 beta

Students begin the lab by connecting the interface module to the PC and checking its availability in the PC operating system where they can also see the serial port that has been associated (Fig. 6.7).

> Keyboards
> Mice and other pointing devices
> Monitors
> Network adapters
∨ Ports (COM & LPT)
  USB-SERIAL CH340 (COM11)
> Print queues
> Processors
> Software devices
> Sound, video and game controllers
> Storage controllers

Figure 6.7: Serial communication port associated with the interface module.

The interaction with the interface module can be done from now on by sending commands to the respective serial port. In this sense, any terminal application can be used (e.g., in Fig. 6.8 the Termite application is used). However, a scripting language will be used to automate the verification process. We chose to exemplify with Python and Fig. 6.9 shows the first laboratory in which students use Jupyter Notebook to give commands to the interface board from the web browser. The advantage of this approach is that students will be able to interact with their test board in "immediate vicinity"to the theoretical notions described in the text associated with the laboratory (text also written in Jupyter Notebook).

With the help of some delays introduced and controlled in the software, it is very easy to make time diagrams that illustrate the dynamic operation of the tested circuits (Fig. 6.10).

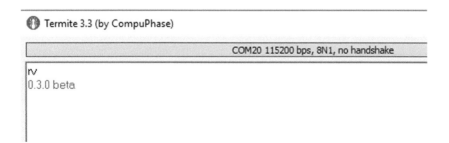

Termite 3.3 (by CompuPhase)

COM20 115200 bps, 8N1, no handshake

rv
0.3.0 beta

Figure 6.8: Serial interaction with the interface module through text commands.

Figure 6.9: Interfacing the module with Python (web based – Jupyter Notebook)

After this description, however, something should be mentioned. This way of wiring circuits on a breadboard does not seems to be appropriate for higher education and we use it only to develop that sense of measure and the HiL approach we have been talking about. Initially we wanted a maximum of 30% of all laboratories to be conducted in this way and the rest on platforms with FPGA. But the way the students in the 2nd year receive the assemblies they make on breadboards, the desire to buy their own such boards, wires and circuits are totally surprising. It is said that practice without theory is like when you sail on an uncharted sea but theory without practice is like when you are not sailing at all. In the field of information technology, the notion of practice may become quite vague but in the field of CPS the notion of practice must involve the physical process. Fueled by the desire of the students and their reaction when we had to change the platforms and move to those with FPGA, we allocated an inverse weight to the two types of platforms. We will return to these issues in the section dedicated to discussions.

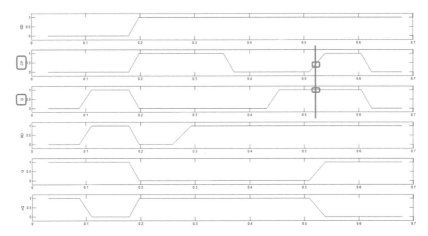

Figure 6.10: Example of a time diagram representation for D filp-flop made with the proposed platform.

5.2   During the Pandemic

The pandemic came and we had to move our activities online. Which seemed impossible given the hardware involved and especially the objectives we discussed at the beginning related to the practical experience with the process actually turned out to be quite simple precisely due to the CPS approach we used. Normally the objectives of the course could be experienced on well-known simulators, simulators whose complexity, accuracy and cost are largely correlated. In the following we only used free simulators that have many limitations. But even if we had used simulators with high accuracy and complexity (which involve costs) we still would not have been able to convey those transversal objectives that we presented in a previous section. The pandemic started when the students were already familiar with the way the platform worked and that may have mattered to some extent. But the migration of laboratories has shown us two aspects. One we already mentioned above, namely that we managed to migrate without compromising much of the proposed objectives and the second was that this way of doing the laboratory motivated students to acquire their own equipment and experiment at their places. If we had used complex simulators probably would not have identified this desire or the costs would have been inaccessible. But let us take them one at a time.

When we had to move online, it was out of the question for students to buy materials with their own money. We did not even know when we would return to face-to-face education, as a result we had to adapt in time and had no way to change radically. So, we looked for simulators that would keep the interactions we wanted as accurate as possible (between students and circuits). The first online simulation platform that came to mind was Autodesk's Tinkercad platform. It is a free platform, and we knew that it integrates breadboards and a few discrete logic circuits. In the case of circuits, its offer is very limited, but it was enough to make two laboratories. The first lab was dedicated to familiarizing students with the logic circuits and the connection between the functional diagrams, the symbolic descriptions, the datasheets, and the implementation aspects. The second lab was targeting the study of logical gates and methods of minimization. The issue of automatic verification appeared again. The major advantage of the circuit section of the Tinkercad platform is that it was developed around the Arduino concept and thus integrates Arduino. As such, the idea was to integrate the test part we had already developed around the Arduino (Fig. 6.11). Basically, the circuit that students analyze, and design (DUT) is made on a separate breadboard (2). The Arduino shield providing the interface with the DUT is implemented by another breadboard (1) in which the digital outputs of the Arduino (3) and the digital inputs (4) are legibly marked.

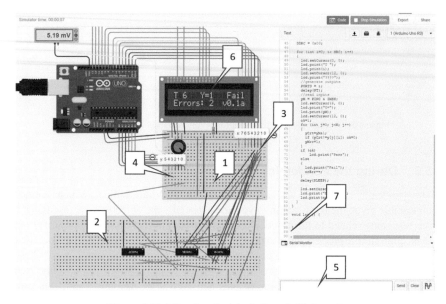

Figure 6.11: Migrating the lab platform in Tinkercad

To migrate to Tinkercad with our automatic verification solution we would have had to make a complicated Javascript interface that automatically interacts with the browser and sends text commands and reads in the window dedicated to the serial monitor (5). Since we did not know if it was worth the effort, we found a much simpler solution: attaching an LCD display (6) and writing a very simple code of only 90 lines (7) to perform automatic verification, a code in which students have to introduce only a description of the outputs from the table of truth. Additionally, students have the possibility to change some constants referring to the number of input and output variables as well as other parameters related to simulation times. To illustrate the simplicity and the lack of requirements for knowledge of embedded programming we illustrate this step in Fig. 6.12 with the code snippet where students need to make changes.

As we presented above, this platform covered only two laboratories. For the rest of the circuits, we had to use another simulator, also free. We chose Logisim. However, the fact that there was this background with automatic verification and how it was done allowed the introduction of a similar approach in Logisim even if we are talking about a simulator at a symbolic level and not at the level of physical circuits such as Tinkercad. Following Fig. 6.13, the circuit to be developed and tested (1 - DUT)

```
 3
 4  // -----------------------------------------
 5  // portion of code to be configured
 6
 7  // test speed
 8  #define SLEEP 1000 // the number of milliseconds between tests
 9  #define PT 50 // duration in ms for test before propagation
10
11  // number of input and output variables
12  #define M 3 // breadboard inputs (Arduino outputs)
13  #define N 1 // breadboard outputs (Arduino inputs)
14
15  #define NRC 1 << M // total number of combinations of input variables
16
17  // here is the truth table
18  int y[N][NRC]={{1, 1, 1, 0, 0, 1, 0, 0}
19                };
20  //-----------------------------------------
21
22  // defining the pins that emulate the input variables
23  // (to be outputs)
24  int x[8] = {0, 1, 2, 3, 4, 5, 6, 7};
25
26  // mask for inputs
27  #define IMSK ~(0xFF<<N)
28
```

Figure 6.12: The part of the Arduino code where students must make modifications.

will be able to receive inputs in an automatic manner by writing a ROM memory in advance (2). The outputs of the DUT will be stored in a RAM memory (3). All input combinations will be swiped using a counter (4) whose output will be used to address the memories. The synchronous clock signal for memories and counter is provided by the rectangular signal generator (5).

In this way we managed to migrate the entire laboratory without the students losing much of the specific competencies intended by the initial version held face to face. Additional, we managed to further transmit the transversal competencies that we have been discussing in the context of CPS.

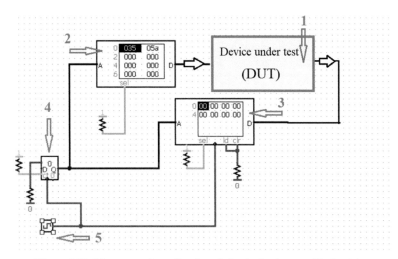

Figure 6.13: The automatic verification of circuits implemented in Logisim.

6. Discussions

The role and usefulness of simulators is undeniable, but when it comes to preparing young people, certain discussions are necessary. In electrical engineering and especially in computer engineering it is very easy to replace the physical processes with simulated ones and, in most cases, even the boundary between what is real and what is simulated can become confusing. Without drawing such a parallel to Orson Scott Card's famous novel, "Ender's Game," we could still draw a parallel between the time today's children spend playing computer and consoles games involving simulated worlds and the fact that we could only use simulators in engineering. Does that sense of measure and interaction with nature fade? Can simulators cultivate that sense? It is a topic often discussed in the field of SF literature and whether the authors of such literature were visionaries or simply influenced to some extent by the childhood of future engineers, the idea is that many of the systems presented by these authors have materialized in a form or other. This combination between the physical process and the cybernetic systems, even if it has clear objectives or simply investigates some possibilities, is becoming part of our nature that we tend to adopt, in some cases faster, in others reluctantly. From the perspective of designing such CPS, the question will arise whether a resonance between the physical process and the cyber system is necessary or if we can think of general recipes. Ultimately, these recipes are meant to provide quick and maybe even correct solutions. Take computer programming as an example. From a certain age of students,to be able to attract them in this field, it is necessary that the results of the programs they make to be spectacular. The idea of displaying the phrase "Hello world!" no longer brings satisfaction. As a result, a spectacular program whose results involved displaying something on the screen should integrate some very powerful libraries and which, through a short code, should have results that create that enthusiasm. In fact, this is the level of advance of cybernetics. We have specific artificial intelligence that can solve many problems such as image recognition, sound and so on, just a few lines of code away. A "Hello world" on the screen is demotivating. How could one be persuaded to study some old-fashioned things, even if fundamental, that could lead to the current technological advance after a lot of hard work and, especially, unjustified work at first sight. Can we accuse someone of using a shortcut? As such, we have a great advance in the field of computers, but how exactly can it be applied to physical systems? We could make a comparison between the advance of mathematical theory and the still lack of physical discoveries that are 100% associated with those theories (see string theory). In fact, we can make a lot of such speculations, but we will stop here with them. Returning to how do we educate future specialists who will have to harmonize the technological advancement of computers with physical systems and resume the question that to what extent should these specialists "feel" the processes with which they interact? Today, at engineering education we are still at the level where "hello world" in CPS systems arouses enthusiasm among students. This "hello world" in the field of CPS can be translated by simply making a movement by the axis of a motor or the lighting of a led. We are surprised at how fascinated our students are by such things. We believe that such things should be cultivated since high school and at the faculty level we should place much more emphasis on the development of abstraction and formalization skills. But until then, we cannot omit the phase of training the practical sense. We consider that a resonance between this practical sense and the skills of abstraction and formalization have a very large contribution in terms of creativity that we referred to when we mentioned it as a defining characteristic of engineers. Sir Ken Robinson defined creativity as the process of having original ideas that have value. The market value in the case of engineering involves aspects related to the manufacturing process (design for manufacture), the process of maintenance in operation, etc. All these concepts are integrated in the design of CPS and we believe that they should not be introduced to students only as design requirements, but students need to be aware through their experience of why and how such approaches can be implemented.

As we mentioned at the beginning of the chapter, the pressure to launch new products on the market causes many shortcuts in engineering, some being good and some having important negative consequences. The verification of the systems that are part of CPS is extremely important and the methodology in the case of verification is more industry-led and less theorized and grounded in universities. Each company tends to develop its own methodology for countless reasons, from issues related to competitiveness to issues related to labor management. We are surprised how many of our graduate's work in the field of verification only as beginners and then pursue a career in another field. This topic requires a separate discussion but their professional demotivation as well as unstimulated salaries in an extremely important field, which has some extremely important consequences, raises some questions about how the verification is done. There are many areas where engineers do not use tools, but tools use engineers and we seek to avoid this. We want to avoid it precisely by developing a sense among students that highlights certain aspects that are "against nature". Engineers in automation are the ones who design CPS and it is not just elements of CPS that still haven't been automated. The human ability to develop abstractions and formalisms was what contributed greatly to technological advancement. To what extent can these things be educated in the current context? As we said, computers themselves are a realm of abstraction, but when the interface with the process is other than an image on a display, a sound in speakers or a microphone, a text or touch input console, do things change?

In terms of digital design, configurable hardware resembles computers in that it hides much of the phenomena that take place there. The approach we had to the DD lab decoupling things exactly as a CPS does, keeping the process "visible" as stand-alone process, even if an electronic one, like any other physical process, we were able to apply the design techniques used in CPS involving MiL, SiL and HiL and we were able to easily migrate online when the times demanded it. The simplicity of the physical process as well as the interface with the cyber system determined the students, without us asking them to do so, to purchase components to replicate their laboratory at home. From what we discussed with the students we understood that their average investment was around 20 euros. In this way they were able to train their practical sense, an objective to which we were very attached, but they also developed certain skills in using a certain design methodology, specific to CPS design without anyone telling them about this thing.

7. Instead of Conclusions, Some Lessons That We Learned

We learned a long time ago about the Olin experiment [13] and we have even witnessed it so many times in the achievements of students who confirm that "Lots of stuff in engineering are done without a whole bunch of science. These students are quite capable of a lot of stuff now, and we don't need to deny that" [13]. We believe that we need to cultivate the students' passion and provide theory to support the problems they face.

We do not think we have to reinvent the wheel, be archaic in our approach and behave like actors in a history museum, but a descent to some roots helps us to keep our senses and use them. And the simplicity of approaches even for complex systems can help us to innovate by means other than brute force. Perhaps we should not forget that most current approaches to artificial intelligence are nothing more than an attempt to imitate a system that we do not understand (the model of a neuron used by AI algorithms is a model that we do not know how well it approximates the real phenomena that occur in the brain because when investigating such things some boundary conditions are set with which not all neuroscientists agree and they have their justified reasons [14]). In the end we get an interconnected network that involves a replication (of which we are not sure) of something that we expect evolution to have perfected (very possible). Training such a network is a process that involves enormous calculations (brute force with small shortcuts in places) and whose result works well only on small classes of problems.

As we mentioned at the end of the previous section, the CPS approach of the DD lab brought many benefits to the students and helped us when we had to migrate online determined by the circumstances. However, this migration has developed our experience and taught us some things and some of them we consider worthy of dissemination. Thus, we learned that:

- "Hello world" on an LCD display like the one in Fig. 6.11 has the effect that "Hello world" had on a CRT tube more than 40 years ago and not as a way of testing but more on the enthusiasm on the effect of a code. Although that LCD was used as a means of verification adapted to the possibilities of the simulator, it determined a lot of students to buy those components on their own initiative, each wanting to develop various ideas outside the laboratory.
- Although we thought that students might lose their enthusiasm as they progress through faculty, the fact that they found some challenges and became somewhat independent given the nature of the situation motivated them to experiment on their own.
- Students do not only invest in new smart phones but are willing to invest in their training, especially if it follows their passion without necessarily offering them a certification that will bring them a higher income.
- In the courses that followed this discipline they proved to be more interested and with the purchased hardware they continued to develop projects that can be classified as CPS.
- With simulators available, they were able to simulate some things before implementing them, thus avoiding ruining the hardware on which they gave money out of their own pockets. In opposition, being in the faculty's laboratory they would not have been as careful. In other words, motivated to protect their investment, they have developed a methodology.
- When working remotely the evaluation of students becomes very complicated because it is easy to cheat. One way to reduce this is to create different tasks for each student, but this approach creates a bottleneck on assessment stage. Through methods specific to the design and verification of CPS, we managed to

automatically evaluate some projects in such a way that we do not end up with our automatic system verifying the students' system designed to automatically solve parameterized problems that we gave.

In conclusion, we believe that laboratory activities cannot be carried out entirely online and laboratories designed as cyber-physical systems can offer an adaptable solution to many situations, including force majeure as in the case of pandemic and online activity. These approaches allow students to experiment in a way tailored to their needs and means without the need for instructor intervention. However, real life is not just about this type of interaction. That is why students should work in teams and benefit from the supervision of some professors and mentors, not only on technical aspects. And finally, the evaluation of students' results should express an objective way of the degree to which they are prepared to practice in real life (with all the implications arising from this), as the diploma they obtain entitles them not just to be prepared to practice on simulators. We hope that this material, even if adapted to a specific case study, will provide a point of view on how to approach also other laboratory activities and other disciplines in other fields. We believe that CPS are inevitable solutions in any field due to their generic nature, but they must be designed by humans for them and nature. There may be AI systems that design and optimize CPS, but these AI systems must have the functions objectively introduced by humans and this implies that humans must know their own nature, live it, experience it, and develop their senses that they develop us as humans, not those who develop us as machines or tools.

We end this chapter with a well-known joke that largely describes engineering pragmatism: if the optimist sees the full half of the glass, the pessimist sees the empty one, the engineer is bothered by the fact that the glass is twice as big, as necessary.

References

1. Grey, C.G.P. Humans Need Not Apply. Available on Youtube since August 13, (2014), https://www.youtube.com/watch?v=7Pq-S557XQU&t=8s Last access 25.03.2021
2. Kasanoff, B. If 'Humans Need Not Apply,' Will All Our Jobs Disappear? Forbes, (August 18, 2014).
3. Robinson, K. RSA Animate – Changing Education Paradigms. Available on Youtube since August 14, (2010), https://www.youtube.com/watch?v=zDZFcDGpL4U&t=362sLast access 25.03.2021
4. Pieraccini, R. and L. Rabiner. The Voice in the Machine – Building Computers That Understand Speech. The MIT Press, (2012).
5. Edward, N.S. The role of laboratory work in engineering education: Student and staff perceptions. International Journal of Electrical Engineering Education, SAGE Publishing, (2002), https://doi.org/10.7227/IJEEE.39.1.2
6. Surgenor, B. and Firth, K. The role of the laboratory in design engineering education. Proceedings of the Canadian Engineering Education Association (CEEA), (2006), https://doi.org/10.24908/pceea.v0i0.3848
7. Singhal, A.C., L. Bellamy and B. McNeill. A New Approach to Engineering Education. Arizona State University, Arizona, (1997): 88.

8. Vale, A., N. Coimbra, A. Martins and J. Oliveira. Education and innovation: Impacts during a global pandemic in a higher education institution. SHS Web of Conf., 92 (2021): 01053, DOI: https://doi.org/10.1051/shsconf/20219201053

9. Talanquer, V., R. Bucat, R. Tasker and P.G. Mahaffy. Lessons from a pandemic: Educating for complexity, change, uncertainty, vulnerability, and resilience, Journal of Chemical Education, 97(9) (2020): 2696–2700, DOI: 10.1021/acs.jchemed.0c00627

10. Vaimann, T., M. Stępień, A. Rassõlkin and I. Palu. Distance Learning in Technical Education on Example of Estonia and Poland. XI International Conference on Electrical Power Drive Systems (ICEPDS), St. Petersburg, Russia, (2020): 1–4, doi: 10.1109/ICEPDS47235.2020.9249317.

11. Malhotra, S., R. Dutta, A.K. Daminee and S. Mahna. Paradigm Shift in Engineering Education During COVID 19: From Chalkboards to Talk Boards, 12th International Conference on Computational Intelligence and Communication Networks (CICN), Bhimtal, India, (2020): 287–293, doi: 10.1109/CICN49253.2020.9242617

12. Bolu, C.A., J. Azeta, S.J. Mallo, S.O. Ismaila, J.O. Dada, S. Aderounmu, A. Ismail and E. Oyetunji. Engineering Students' Virtual Learning Challenges during COVID-19 Pandemic Lockdown: A Case Study, IFEES World Engineering Education Forum – Global Engineering Deans Council (WEEF-GEDC), Cape Town, South Africa, (2020): 1–5, doi: 10.1109/WEEF-GEDC49885.2020.9293681

13. Guizzo, E. The Olin Experiment. Can a tiny new college reinvent engineering education? IEEE Spectrum Magazine, May 2006. Available online at https://spectrum.ieee.org/at-work/education/the-olin-experiment

14. Patirniche, D.M. Nonconservative Neurobiology: A geometric perspective upon synaptic transmission, (2019). Available online on Researchergate.net https://www.researchgate.net/publication/332818326_Nonconservative_Neurobiology_A_geometric_perspective_upon_synaptic_transmission

Impact of CPS on Enhancing Supply Chain Resilience, with a Focus on Solutions to Pandemic Challenges

Hajar Fatorachian* and Chase Smith

1. Introduction

In recent decades, Supply Chains (SCs) have been exposed to disruptive changes (such as geopolitical threats (i.e., Brexit, US-China Tensions), economic recessions, and natural disasters) and have become increasingly vulnerable to these incidents, due to the increased collaboration and an intensified focus on supply chain efficiencies [1, 2, 3]. Pandemics and other systemic threats such as natural disasters, wars and political upheavals disrupt supply chains and global supply networks. COVID-19 is not only the most recent example of this, but it has also affected supply chains and economies across the entire globe, and has been among the most disruptive, in recent years, with upheaval occurring across social, economic, and political dimensions, in a very rapid fashion [1, 2, 4, 5, 6, 7].

The severity of the disease (as well as the fact that there is no cure/therapy yet) has resulted in lockdowns, restricting the movement of people and goods, which has substantially disrupted global supply networks and continues to heavily influence market trends (i.e. hoarding and price spikes; and reduced demand elsewhere), highlighting both the capability and fragility of supply chains and operational processes [1, 4, 6, 8, 9, 10, 11, 12, 13]. This, further, included the closing of non-essential businesses, restrictions on public gatherings, social distancing, shelter in place orders, postponed sporting events (for the foreseeable future), cancelled conferences, shortages of personal care products (i.e. toilet paper, hand sanitiser, and cotton swabs) and PPE, and commodities, such as wheat flour, being held at international borders, in order to discourage the further spread of the virus, affecting over 86 percent of (both manufacturing and service-based) supply chains [1, 4, 6, 9, 10, 11, 14].

These increasingly volatile environments are progressively being addressed through the implementation of technological innovations, such as those associated

*Corresponding author: h.fatorachian@leedsbeckett.ac.uk

with Industry 4.0, in order to increase flexibility and responsiveness, streamline/integrate business processes, and improve operational performance, not only in the long-term, but also during a crisis; some authors even propose that the pandemic will push the implementation of Industry 4.0 technologies, thus pushing us into society 5.0 [3, 5, 11, 15, 16].

The rest of this chapter is organized as follows: first, the impact of pandemics on supply chains is explored through the lenses of supply chain risk management and supply chain disruptions, followed by a discussion of how disruptions are managed; subsequently, the concept of Industry 4.0, and its associated technologies, are explained, followed by an analysis of how these technologies can be utilized to mitigate against supply chain disruptions from multiple perspectives; finally conclusions and recommendations are provided (Fig. 7.1).

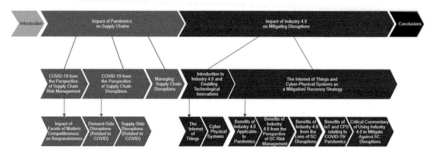

Figure 7.1: Chapter structure.

2. Impact of Pandemics on Supply Chains

This section first examines the COVID-19 pandemic from the lens of the supply chain risk management, as well as how the facets of modern competitiveness have worsened the responsiveness of supply chains. This is followed by a discussion surrounding Supply Chain Disruptions, and how COVID-19 can be rationalized from this perspective, on both the demand- and supply-sides of the chain. This section concludes with a discussion surrounding how Supply Chain Disruptions are managed.

2.1   Supply Chain Risk Management

Supply chains encounter risks from innumerable sources (such as natural disasters, infrastructural breakdowns, or acts of terrorism), which seriously disrupt a firm's abilities to effectively do business [17, 18, 19]. Disruptions are an inherent part of global supply chains, whether of natural or human origins – regardless of the products/services offered, or the business environment of the supply chain [8]. With regard to COVID-19 specifically, there are a few distinctive facets to consider: it is an unpredictable, long-term disturbance, which concurrently exists internally and externally, both up- and down-stream, where simultaneous disruptions befall supply, demand, and logistical infrastructures; this is true across every industry, with none being immune to the disruption [4, 8]. Although, there are a number of risks that will vary depending on the industry (i.e., food safety risks within the food retailing industry), the health of the population (including employees) is consistent. This not only necessitates increased testing and isolation measures, but also mandates a balance between production and worker protection, heavily impacting labour-intensive industries [20, 21].

Figure 7.2 demonstrates the impact of COVID-19 on various industries. As it can be seen, some industries' sales have still not recovered to pre-pandemic levels.

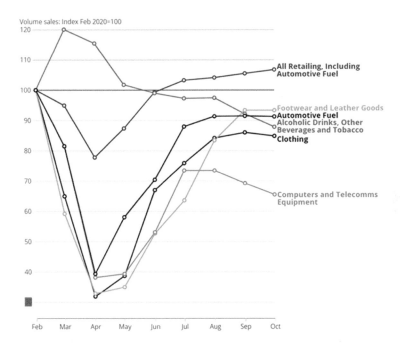

Figure 7.2: Indexed volume sales seasonally adjusted, Great Britain, February to October 2020. Source: Office for National Statistics – Monthly Business Survey - Retail Sales Inquiry

2.1.1 Impact on Supply Chain Responsiveness

The impact of the pandemic has been worsened by many facets of modern competitiveness, such as globalized and lengthened supply chains, intense price competition, and lean practices. Globalized supply chains, partaking in international trade, have been heavily impacted due to the worldwide restrictions of people and goods, an issue that worsens as the supply chain lengthens [1, 4, 6, 9, 14, 18, 22, 23, 24, 25, 26, 27, 28, 29, 30, 31, 32]. Additionally, while lean practices have aided firms' competitive advantage, they have made supply chains less agile, and thus, less flexible, and less able to cope with uncertainty, which is rife throughout the COVID situation [1, 6, 9, 10, 12, 33, 34]. Furthermore, the tendency for firms to compete as a member of the supply chain, as opposed to an individual organization, means that any ripple effects experienced are intensified, endangering operational performance levels across the entire supply network [2]. The ripple effect refers to a situation in which a disruption cascades downstream, impacting the supply chain performance [35]. This will lead to lower revenues, loss of market share and reputation, delivery delays, etc., which, in turn, will have significant impact on the performance and profitability of the supply chain [36].

2.2   Lens of Supply Chain Disruptions

Supply Chain Disruptions can be conceptualized as unexpected events within the supply chain, that significantly inhibit normal business operations; there are a few core types of disruptions, natural and man-made, which can either be random or premeditated [8, 11, 17, 18, 19, 22, 37, 38, 39, 40, 41, 42, 43, 44] (Fig. 7.3).

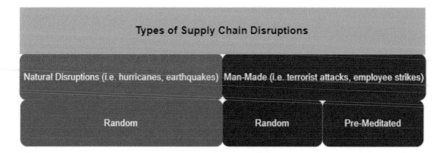

Figure 7.3: Types of supply chain disruptions.

The risks associated with disruptions are vast and vary between disruption types, leading to disrupted facilities, lost capacity, longer lead times, delivery delays, stockouts, price rigidity, inabilities to meet demand, reduced revenues and sales, decreased shareholder wealth, and increased costs or expenses; this not only has a significant impact on firms, but firms are also affected by the fact that the recovery process is often slow [13, 22, 25, 29, 37, 42, 45, 46]. The ability to effectively anticipate and mange SC disruptions is dependent upon the level of visibility, control, and transparency that organizations possess regarding a range of risk factors [47].

2.2.1 Demand-Side Disruptions (related to COVID)

The major demand-side shock surrounds panic buying and hoarding in some industries, and severe dips in demand in other industries. For instance, as it relates to the food industry, panic buying and hoarding, alongside a sharp increase in the demand for food, has been observed, due to increased unemployment, and feared disruptions to the food supply, resulting from movement restrictions; this has been self-perpetuating despite a steady food supply, and consumers have further responded by shifting some of the demand to foodbanks, and switching to online grocery shopping [10, 11, 12, 14, 33]. These behavioural changes and long-term market shifts (such as demand fluctuation) have caused innumerable issues within many supply chains, particularly those within the Fast-Moving Consumer Goods (FMCG) industry [10]. The demand spikes, caused by hoarding and panic buying, started the "crack" of a substantial bullwhip effect (as well as ripple effects), causing stock-outs in mass, across a variety of products, throughout the SC. This worsened firms' abilities to meet consumer demands effectively, or in other words, without increased time, effort, and costs [1, 4, 6, 12, 14, 18, 25, 33, 34, 41].

2.2.2 Supply-Side Disruptions (related to COVID)

COVID has also induced productivity issues, associated with lengthy, complex, and globalized networks, as well as changes in health and safety behaviour, which fall on the supply side. COVID has made it evident that most supply chains that are dependent on foreign suppliers and geographically dispersed locations (i.e. different countries), are left particularly vulnerable in environments where global travel restrictions are in place, affecting transportation and distribution networks [7, 11, 12, 33, 48]. Additionally, these travel limitations, as well as self-isolation and illness, have led to labour shortages; this, in addition to such dramatic changes in routine, hours, location etc., made productivity difficult to keep consistent; these problems contribute not only to delays, but also to errors within the production and delivery processes [7, 10, 12, 33]. Figure 7. 4 summarizes key demand and supply side disruptions related to COVID-19.

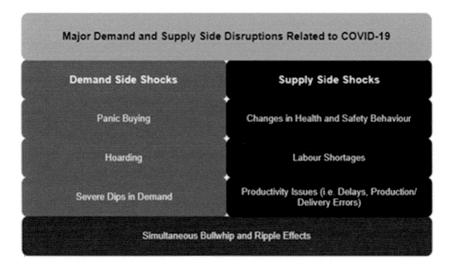

Figure 7.4: Demand and supply side disruptions related to COVID-19.

2.3   Managing Supply Chain Disruptions

Although, organizations may not be able to manage the disruption directly, the adoption of certain strategies can alleviate the eventual impact it will have on firm performance [49]. Disruption management strategies are categorized in two major ways; mitigation and recovery strategies, which occur pre and post-disruption, respectively [37]. Although, the decision to mitigate the risk of disruptions may seem obvious, such initiatives are resource-intensive; as such, firms typically respond to low-impact/high-probability risks, as they are the most pressing, and easiest to deal with [1, 19, 50] (Fig. 7.5).

Disruption discovery capabilities, mostly referred to as mitigation strategies, are the ability of an enterprise to create awareness surrounding disruptive events, where discovery and recovery are critical to its management [29]. Mitigation strategies are typically regarded as actions taken before the disruption occurs [22, 25, 28, 30, 31, 50, 51, 52] and can be categorized into two wide-ranging groups: redundancy (or buffering) and flexibility (or bridging) [4, 7, 31, 39, 50].

On the other hand, recovery strategies are considered to be those that are implemented post-disruption; these include, increased flexibility, advanced pay

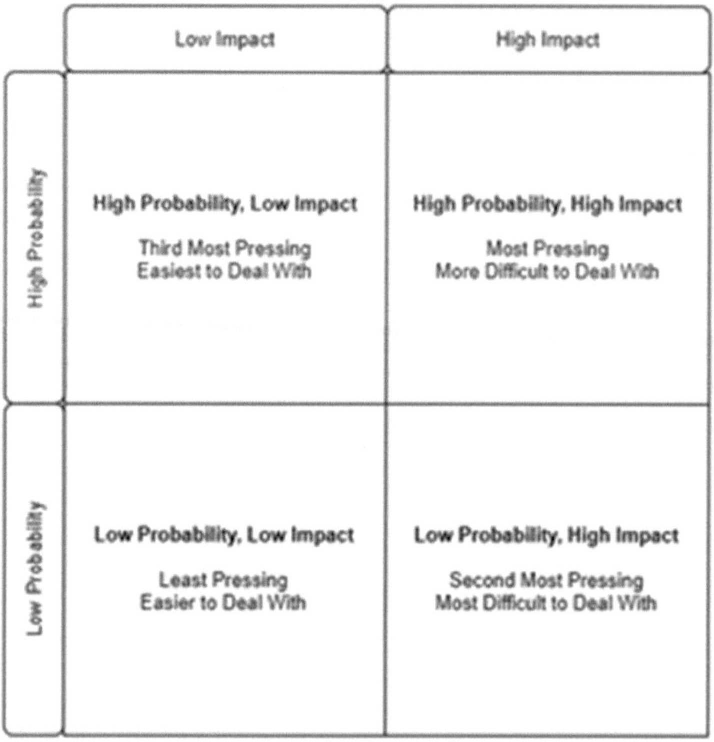

	Low Impact	High Impact
High Probability	**High Probability, Low Impact** Third Most Pressing Easiest to Deal With	**High Probability, High Impact** Most Pressing More Difficult to Deal With
Low Probability	**Low Probability, Low Impact** Least Pressing Easier to Deal With	**Low Probability, High Impact** Second Most Pressing Most Difficult to Deal With

Figure 7.5: Risk probability, impact matrix.

to bolster resilience, facilitation of worker movements, the growth of e-commerce (and different replenishment/order fulfilment processes, such as home delivery), technologies to improve hygiene and reduce customer-personnel interactions, business model changes, shortening and localizing the supply chain, dynamic pricing, transportation re-routing, and inventory management strategies, among many others [1, 4, 6, 8, 12, 14, 21, 22, 24, 25, 30, 31, 33, 37, 50, 51, 52, 53, 54, 55, 56].

In addition to these recovery strategies, others have been mentioned throughout the literature including back-up depots/suppliers, flexible transportation, capacity, and inventory buffers, postponement, capacity expansion/flexible supply, and facility fortification [19, 51, 57]. However, as Scheibe and Blackhurst (2018) point out, risks and supply chains are inherently intertwined, and as such, the employment of a given strategy may further propagate the disruption throughout the supply chain; thus, managers need to choose carefully when deciding to implement a recovery strategy.

It has also been noted that firms respond to crises by developing new initiatives and programmes, often discarding, or delaying their short-term plans to ensure recovery, reducing supply chain resilience [4, 6, 14]. Similarly, it has been argued that the typical management practice of making minute adjustments and changes, is no longer sufficient to deal with the rapidity of changes and the prevalence of uncertainty within the current market environment, and the level of disruption, which makes response strategies difficult to ascertain, particularly in the long-term [1, 4].

3. Impact of Industry 4.0 on Mitigating Supply Disruptions

This section begins by introducing the concept of Industry 4.0, and the technological innovations that enable it, before exploring the Internet of Things (IoT) and Cyber-Physical Systems (CPS) in depth. This is followed by an explanation of how these technologies can be utilized to mitigate against, and recover from, Supply Chain Disruptions, from four perspectives: the advantages of Industry 4.0 technologies that are applicable to pandemic-type disruptions; the advantages of Industry 4.0 technologies from the perspective of SC Risk Management and resilience; the advantages of Industry 4.0 technologies from the perspective of Supply Chain Disruption mitigation and recovery strategies; the advantages of IoT and CPS (specifically) as they relate to the COVID-19 situation/pandemics. This section concludes with some critical commentary regarding the use of Industry 4.0 technologies to mitigate against/recover from COVID-19.

3.1 Introduction to Industry 4.0 and Enabling Technological Innovations

In recent years, particularly among manufacturing sectors, there have been trends regarding the implementation of data exchanges, decentralized decision-making processes (that are supported or complemented by technology), automation, and technologies associated with Industry 4.0 [58]; these trends have the potential to not only impact the organizations implementing them, but also inspire significant improvements in the managerial discipline of supply chain and logistics [6, 14, 16, 59].

The fourth industrial revolution, brought about by the introduction of smart technologies into the manufacturing environment, follows the first three industrial revolutions, which brought about advances in mechanization, electricity, and information technology [58]. Industry 4.0, or the decentralization of business processes resulting from technological advances, is characterized by a series of technologies (i.e. Cyber Physical Systems, the Internet) that serve to integrate the physical and digital worlds (i.e. employees, enterprise systems, machinery and devices), to facilitate a more efficient, flexible, lower-cost, and a more sustainable processes (i.e. dynamic manufacturing), as well as new models of value creation and methods of communicating, developing practices, and overall, conducting business [5, 16, 59]. The process improvements enabled by such technologies are often associated with the introduction of dynamic/autonomous manufacturing, improved informational/technological infrastructures, transformed quality control systems, and improved product and service offerings, in addition to Industry 4.0 technologies, such as cloud computing, cognitive computing, additive manufacturing, cyber security, simulations, virtual/augmented reality, digital twins, Big Data and Analytics, Artificial Intelligence (including machine learning, hardware and software robotics, computer vision), machine to machine communications, RFID, blockchain, smart factories, horizontal/vertical integration, the Internet of Things (IoT), and Cyber-Physical Systems (CPS) [3, 6, 11, 14, 16, 25, 53, 59].

This chapter focuses on IoT and CPS (and their enabling technologies, i.e., Big Data and Analytics and Cloud Computing), which are core driving technologies of Industry 4.0, due to their particular abilities to bridge the gap between the digital and physical worlds, whilst also encouraging resource optimizations, increased productivity and efficiency (i.e. reducing errors, limiting energy usage), cost reductions, improved profitability, and customer loyalty [10, 16, 59].

3.1.1 The Internet of Things (IoT)

The Internet of Things (IoT) is a virtual platform based on RFID bar codes (Radio Frequency Identification), smart devices, and wireless sensors, that serve to combine, store, and process service- and production-based operational data, and integrate it with the products, people, and services among supply chain members [5, 10, 16, 25]. In other words, IoT is a globally accessible environment, where smart processes, devices, and systems are connected (via the Internet) in order to support decision making through constant communication and a real-time feedback generation [16]. Digital twins, another foundational principle of the IoT, is a data-driven framework, encompassing optimization, simulation, and data analytics, that represents the state of the supply network at any given moment, allowing for improved resilience and the virtual testing of contingency plans and process changes [25]. In addition, digital twins can allow for virtual representation of physical assets enabling real-time optimising, predicting, monitoring, and controlling, as well as improved decision making and leading to the improved efficiency of product design and process management. Furthermore, digital twin technologies can allow for remote installation, monitoring, testing, and maintenance of manufacturing equipment when the physical presence of engineers is not possible [60].

3.1.2 Cyber Physical Systems (CPS)

Cyber Physical Systems (CPS) are systems that integrate computing/communication capabilities with engineering/physical infrastructure and resources, which are aimed at easing communication/between humans, machines, processes, and products, leading to a merging of the physical and digital world, through hardware (including sensors) and software connectivity, as well as distributed knowledge/information [16]. The enhanced communication and information sharing enabled by CPS are also associated with more seamless and flexible operations, improved, more responsive and proactive decision making (via real-time data collection from various point throughout the supply chain), enhanced collaboration and cooperation (through a better understanding of party requirements), and improved customer satisfaction and product delivery; all of these have a profound impact on SC performance. Through the connection to the advanced computational technologies, CPS can lead to the creation of autonomous predictive capabilities, self-diagnosis/maintenance capabilities for risk avoidance, and collaborative production planning for improved performance [16]. Widespread, shared perceptions and communication are the key factors enabling effective collaborations; as such, technological innovations (i.e., IoT devices, sensors) can be adopted in order to facilitate the monitoring and visualization of manufacturing and logistics processes. The viability and resilience of supply chains and production lines, as well as the efficiency and speed of interactions among collaborative entities, are greatly enhanced by communication technologies, as they enable collaborative scheduling algorithms and models [58, 60].

At the individual business level, the application of Cyber Physical System-based technologies (such as Artificial Intelligence and Robotic Process Automation (RPA) technologies) on repeatable tasks (such as transactions) can help reduce the workload of overburdened personnel. Similarly, the adoption and implementation of simulations, as well as virtual and augmented reality technologies, can facilitate equipment set-up, fine-tuning, upkeep, etc. Businesses can also use AI to enhance their supplier relationship management and contract management through digitising their contracts and developing a contract database. This can help with monitoring performance of the suppliers by combining commercial transactional data and lead to identifying risky contracts and maximising impact of cost reduction programmes [61].

Similarly, operational control towers can be extended to include supply chain parties and allow for supply chain mapping to create a holistic picture of the supply network. This can lead to identification of potential problems/disruptions, and risky and vulnerable supply chain relationships. For instance, Procter & Gamble are able to develop a company-wide (shared) perspective across products and geographical distances, via their centralized control tower system. Effective planning and scheduling throughout the supply network is facilitated by the integration of diverse real-time data, from weather forecasts, and road delays, to more critical data, such as inventory levels. The system also assists with identification of most effective solutions through running through scenarios for potential problems [62].

3.2   The IoT and CPS as a Mitigation/Recovery Strategy

3.2.1 General Benefits of Industry 4.0 Applicable to Pandemics

IoT-based automation enables greater flexibility, proactivity, responsiveness, productivity, effectiveness, efficiency, production, and planning control (through real-time monitoring that considers machinery constraints and changeover times), sustainability (via fewer transactions and improved logistics management), and operational improvements throughout the supply chain, all of which are greatly beneficial to responding to pandemic-type disruptions. Cloud computing is a core enabler of the IoT, as large amounts of information is made accessible in a borderless, real-time fashion throughout the supply chain (via the high storage capacity and high-speeds of such technologies), through the convergence of networking, management, and computing systems; this provides the basis for improved visibility, analytical capabilities, coordination, responsiveness, and collaboration, all of which supports decision making and planning, possibly reducing bullwhip effects [16]. RFID, another core enabler of IoT, also has the potential due to its ability to "track and trace" resources and products in real-time, enhancing responsiveness, demand fulfilment, product availability, quality, and flow, as well as enhanced inventory management, through control over product status (i.e., perishable item storage conditions) and movement throughout the supply and value chains, preventing stockout situations and increasing responsiveness to customer demands. Big Data, another IoT driver, is characterized by the facilitation of resource and innovation competency integration (i.e., SC innovation and product development) throughout the supply chain, leading to the generation of world-class production plans and effective order fulfilment management [16]. Figure 7.6 demonstrates the key impact of an Industry 4.0-based operational approach on supply chains.

3.2.2 Perspective of SC Risk Management and Resilience

The core components of SC agility, visibility and velocity, are also supported by Industry 4.0 technologies by enabling tracking and tracing, timely information

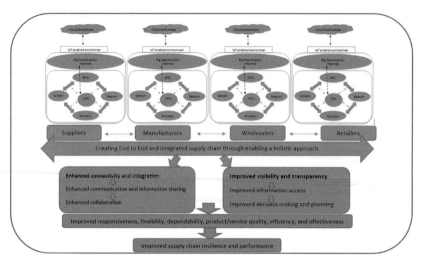

Figure 7.6: Industry 4.0-based supply network based on Fatorachian and Kazemi, 2021.

sharing, synchronized decisions, as well as flexibility and adaptability, decreasing the amount of time required to respond to and fully recover from SC disruptions, whilst also fostering sales performance and profitability [2, 7, 10, 15, 25]. Additionally, the concept of supply chain resilience, which can be thought of as the ability of a system to detect and defend against SC risks, has gained popularity in recent years, in order to protect firms and supply chains from unexpected disruptive events; these include proactive and reactive approaches to resistance and recovery efforts, such as supply chain reconfiguration, increased collaboration, resource sharing, connectivity, process flexibility, agility, responsiveness, redundancy, and visibility [2, 4, 7, 15, 16, 25]. Innovation in supply chain management generates positive risk management capabilities, leading to the creation of competitive advantage [63]. CPS enable SC resilience and risk management, through improved processes (and process reliability), proactive maintenance, and automation [16]. Although, collaboration can increase dependencies on SC members, it can also serve to bolster resilience via increased (real-time, secure) information sharing, enhanced data analytical capabilities, synchronized decision-making, resource allocation, knowledge management, aligned goals, and collaborative communication [2, 7, 25]. For instance, General Motors offers a series of best practices for monitoring SC risks in a comprehensive manner, via the utilization of a location-based intelligence system. This system enables the monitoring of an assortment of risks, which has aided GM in taking proactive measures to not only avoid, but be better prepared for, threats and disruptions (such as factory fires, forest fires, explosions, storms, floods, cyberattacks, strikes, and civil unrest) [47]. Other cutting-edge technologies such as Artificial intelligence (AI) techniques and blockchain can lead to development of robust and resilient supply chain models through improving response traceability [64].

3.2.3 SC Disruption Mitigation and Recovery Perspectives

The technologies associated with Industry 4.0 also have the potential to support robust mitigation and recovery strategies, that serve to improve SC resilience and ensure survival (throughout a recovery process that is ideally as short as possible) through swifter implementation, more flexible and efficient contracts, portfolio diversification (i.e. rapid product customization), increased trust, reliability, transparency, and enhanced collaboration, via improved information and knowledge generation, implementation, dissemination, and verification throughout the supply chain [2, 15, 25, 53, 59]. Mitigation strategies, according to Shao and Pan (2009), involve understanding the key players and are thus, greatly affected by collaboration, internal/ external integration, the ability to warn, and communication systems; this is addressed by Industry 4.0 technologies by fostering the development of effective communication and collaboration mechanisms, as well as facilitating information sharing, which leads to more effective purchasing, in addition to improved procurement and supplier relationship management (including supplier performance monitoring and auditing) [16, 29]. It has been proposed by many authors that Industry 4.0 technologies will serve an important long-term role in mitigating against disruptions with uncertain timings and varying levels of organizational impact; this increased supply chain resilience is the result of faster decision-making, enabled by real-time data (regarding SC capabilities/capacities, vulnerabilities), being shared throughout the system in an accurate, traceable, transparent (or visible), verifiable, timely manner [1, 6, 7, 11, 16, 25, 53]. For instance, organizations can make contingency plans through the application of scenario planning and simulation tools. Johnson & Johnson, by using live production rates and staffing level data, has been able to predict worst-case scenarios through mathematical and simulation tools/models, which has enhanced the firm's ability to plan interventions in advance (i.e., shipping method changes, shifting production to alternative sites). Furthermore, this system facilitates better planning of requirements, regarding input resources, by supply chain executives [47].

3.2.4 COVID-19/Pandemic Specific

The traceability enabled by the IoT, has great potential for use within the COVID-19 situation, as each individual step (i.e. when, where, and by whom the step was conducted) can be documented and accounted for throughout the supply chain, which closes product safety gaps, while enhancing trust among stakeholders [2, 10, 25, 53]. Additionally, IoT is a useful mitigation tool that reduces the need for physical contact, improved communication, as well as improved shortage detection, more accurate demand information, knowledge regarding storage conditions, and enhanced stock positions (via greater system control, product and process transparency, including distribution transparency , product monitoring, and sustainability), which, in turn, leads to increased productivity, enhanced product quality and reliability (by detecting performance variations/identifying problems via predictive maintenance), timely, proactive responses to market demands, improved decision-making, and thus, improved operational performance, throughout the supply chain [7, 10, 15, 16, 25].

Furthermore, the literature suggests that social distancing measures can be better managed by virtual reality and CPS technologies, and that online shopping can be mediated and better managed by IoT systems, as well as Big Data and Analytics; this is accomplished through insights into supply chain and consumer responses, that enable the generation of information relevant to forecasting, such as behavioural patterns, information regarding the most profitable customer segments, and frameworks describing correlation variables [6, 15, 16]. Big Data, a core component of IoT and CPS, has potential in developing warning and recovery capabilities in order to mitigate against pandemics, due to their ability to aid in understanding the spread of disease, consumer demands, transportation control, and recovery location selection; this data enables better decision making and planning, particularly as it relates to sourcing, inventory (and thus, warehousing) management, and shipment control, without increased costs [7, 16, 25].

Finally, through the application of cloud manufacturing models, companies can virtualize and encapsulate the input resources provided by suppliers as cloud services. When there is a disruption affecting the supply certain raw materials (required for production), the cloud manufacturing platform can aid in the quick identification of alternative suppliers [60].

3.2.5 Critical Commentary

Although, these technologies can be very beneficial on an organizational or supply chain level, it should be noted that job creation on a macro-scale during the recovery process will be paramount (due to the large number of layoffs experienced throughout COVID), which may clash with the Industry 4.0 technology implementation process, as job loss, or fears about job security are a major barrier (to the implementation of Industry 4.0) [6, 59]. Additionally, the application of Industry 4.0 (and its associated technologies) could increase disparities and inequalities between richer (more technically advanced) countries and poorer (less developed) countries [53].

There are also a number of difficulties/challenges associated with IoT implementation such as high levels of required training, skills, and expertise; data comprehension, analysis, collection, storage, and security (due to inadequate software security/authorization protocol, or lack of interfaces); high initial costs of implementation; required supply chain and business model changes (including governance changes); underdeveloped technological infrastructures (i.e. standardization, certification, and connectivity issues); lack of support for the digitalization of operations from various stakeholders (i.e. management, employees, supply chain members, customers, governments, etc.), which may be difficult to overcome successfully in the current environment [10, 15, 53]. Furthermore, in order to improve performance holistically, it is paramount to consider that the entire supply chain requires integration, not only with the business itself, but also the technological means through which the improvements previously described are enabled [16].

4. Conclusions and Recommendations

The past 12 months have been unprecedented for organizations all around the world due to the extent and quantity of supply chain disruptions caused by the COVID-19 pandemic. It has demonstrated the power of interconnected, digital supply networks to enable organizations to anticipate, sense, and respond to unexpected events and minimize their impacts. Hence, COVID-19 has resulted in firms increasing their expenditures into technological innovations that enhance the autonomy and agility of their supply chains. These are critical elements of supply chain resilience, due to their enhancement of the supply chain's ability to sense, adapt or respond to, and recover from, the negative consequences of expedient changes and disruptive events in a rapid fashion. The analysis of the effects of pandemic-type disruptions on supply chains and production systems indicates that the digitization of supply chains and business processes, and Industry 4.0 technology applications, are a significant contributor to controlling ripple effects and enhancing supply chain resilience. The firms that have successfully adopted innovative technologies associated with Industry 4.0 (such as Cyber Physical Systems) within their operations seem to better manage supply chain disruptions and effectively coordinate future recovery processes [64]. As such, the research suggests that more firms than ever are adopting technological innovations, to support the management of the supply chain. Many companies are now using technologies (i.e., Cyber-Physical Systems, Internet of Things, and Big Data Analytics) to help with supply chain mapping and analysis of supply chain disruptions with the primary reason behind uptake of these technologies being disruption caused by COVID-19 [65]. As discussed in this chapter, CPS and their enabling technologies have pervasive effects on SC resilience and risk management through enhancing the impact and effectiveness of supply chain disruption management strategies (mitigation and recovery strategies).

References

1. Graham, G., R. Handfield and L. Burns. Coronavirus, tariffs, trade wars and supply chain evolutionary design. International Journal of Operations and Production Management, (2020).
2. Lohmer, J., N. Bugert and R. Lasch. Analysis of resilience strategies and ripple effect in blockchain-coordinated supply chains: An agent-based simulation study. International Journal of Production Economics, 228 (2020): 107882.
3. Sarfraz, Z., A. Sarfraz, H.M. Iftikar and R. Akhund. Is COVID-19 pushing us to the Fifth Industrial Revolution (Society 5.0)? Pakistan Journal of Medical Sciences, 37(2) (2021).
4. Belhadi, A., S. Kamble, C.J.C. Jabbour, A. Gunasekaran, N.O. Ndubisi and M. Venkatesh. Manufacturing and service supply chain resilience to the COVID-19 outbreak: Lessons learned from the automobile and airline industries. Technological Forecasting and Social Change, 163 (2021): 120447.
5. Javaid, M., A. Haleem, R. Vaishya, S. Bahl, R. Suman and A. Vaish. Industry 4.0 technologies and their applications in fighting COVID-19 pandemic. Diabetes & Metabolic Syndrome: Clinical Research & Reviews, 14(4) (2020): 419–422.
6. Sarkis, J. Supply chain sustainability: Learning from the COVID-19 pandemic. International Journal of Operations & Production Management, (2020).
7. Yang, J., H. Xie, G. Yu and M. Liu. Antecedents and consequences of supply chain risk management capabilities: An investigation in the post-coronavirus crisis. International Journal of Production Research, (2020): 1–13.
8. Golan, M., L. Jernegan and I. Linkov. Trends and applications of resilience analytics in supply chain modeling: Systematic literature review in the context of the COVID-19 pandemic. Environment Systems and Decisions, 40(2) (2020): 222–243.
9. Ivanov, D. and A. Dolgui. Viability of intertwined supply networks: Extending the supply chain resilience angles towards survivability. A position paper motivated by COVID-19 outbreak. International Journal of Production Research, 58(10) (2020b): 2904–2915.

10. Končar, J., A. Grubor, R. Marić, S. Vučenović and G. Vukmirović. Setbacks to IoT implementation in the function of FMCG supply chain sustainability during COVID-19 pandemic. Sustainability, 12(18) (2020): 7391.

11. Kumar, M.S., R.D. Raut, V.S. Narwane and B.E. Narkhede. Applications of industry 4.0 to overcome the COVID-19 operational challenges. Diabetes & Metabolic Syndrome: Clinical Research & Reviews, 14(5) (2020): 1283–1289.

12. Mollenkopf, D., L. Ozanne and H. Stolze. A transformative supply chain response to COVID-19. Journal of Service Management (ahead-of-print), (2020).

13. Paul, S.K. and P. Chowdhury. A production recovery plan in manufacturing supply chains for a high-demand item during COVID-19. International Journal of Physical Distribution & Logistics Management, (2020).

14. Van Hoek, R.. Responding to COVID-19 Supply chain risks—Insights from supply chain change management, total cost of ownership and supplier segmentation theory. Logistics, 4(4) (2020): 23–41.

15. Czifra, G. and Z. Molnár. Covid-19 and Industry 4.0. Research Papers Faculty of Materials Science and Technology, Slovak University of Technology, 28(46) (2020): 36–45.

16. Fatorachian, H. and H. Kazemi. Impact of Industry 4.0 on supply chain performance. Production Planning & Control, 32(1) (2021): 63–81.

17. Kleindorfer, P.R. and G.H. Saad. Managing disruption risks in supply chains. Production and Operations Management, 14(1) (2005): 53–68.

18. Revilla, E. and M.J. Sáenz. Supply chain disruption management: Global convergence vs national specificity. Journal of Business Research, 67(6) (2014): 1123–1135.

19. Tang, C.S. Robust strategies for mitigating supply chain disruptions. International Journal of Logistics: Research and Applications, 9(1) (2006): 33–45.

20. FAOUN (Food and Agricultural Organization of the United Nations). COVID-19 and the risk to food supply chains: How to respond?.Food and Agricultural Organization of the United Nations, (2020): 1–7.

21. Galanakis, C. The Food Systems in the Era of the Coronavirus (COVID-19) Pandemic Crisis. Foods, 9(4) (2020): 523.

22. Blackhurst, J., C.W. Craighead, D. Elkins and R.B. Handfield. An empirically derived agenda of critical research issues for managing supply-chain disruptions. International Journal of Production Research, 43(19) (2005): 4067–4081.

23. Cappelli, A. and E. Cini. Will the COVID-19 pandemic make us reconsider the relevance of short food supply chains and local productions? Trends in Food Science & Technology, 99 (2020): 566–567.

24. Hong, P. and A. Kochar. Building resilient supply chains post-COVID-19. Supply Chain Management Review, (2020): 60–62.

25. Ivanov, D. and A. Dolgui. A digital supply chain twin for managing the disruption risks and resilience in the era of Industry 4.0. Production Planning & Control, (2020a): 1–14.

26. Manuj, I. and J.T. Mentzer. Global supply chain risk management. Journal of Business Logistics, 29(1) (2008a): 133–IX.

27. Manuj, I. and J.T. Mentzer. Global supply chain risk management strategies. International Journal of Physical Distribution & Logistics Management, 38(3) (2008b): 192–223.

28. Richey, R.G., J.B. Skipper and J.B. Hanna. Minimizing supply chain disruption risk through enhanced flexibility. International Journal of Physical Distribution & Logistics Management, (2009).

29. Shao, X.F. and Y. Pan. Supply chain collaboration and disruption mitigation capability. *In:* 2009 International Conference on Management and Service Science. IEEE, (2009): 1–5.

30. Talluri, S., T.J. Kull, H. Yildiz and J. Yoon. Assessing the efficiency of risk mitigation strategies in supply chains. Journal of Business Logistics, 34(4) (2013): 253–269.

31. Wang, X., P. Tiwari and X. Chen. Communicating supply chain risks and mitigation strategies: A comprehensive framework. Production Planning & Control, 28(13) (2017): 1023–1036.

32. Wu, Y., M. Dong, W. Tang and F.F. Chen. Performance analysis of serial supply chain networks considering system disruptions. Production Planning and Control, 21(8) (2010): 774–793.

33. Hobbs, J. Food supply chains during the COVID-19 pandemic. Canadian Journal of Agricultural Economics/Revue (Canadienned'agroeconomie), 68(2) (2020): 171–176.

34. Jangga, R., N.M. Ali, M. Ismail and N. Sahari. Effect of environmental uncertainty and supply chain flexibility towards supply chain innovation: An exploratory study. Procedia Economics and Finance, 31 (2015): 262–268.

35. Dolgui, A., D. Ivanov and B. Sokolov. Ripple effect in the supply chain: an analysis and recent literature. International Journal of Production Research, 56(1–2) (2018): 414–430. doi:10.1080/00207543.2017.1387680

36. Ivanov, D. and A. Dolgui. Ripple effect and supply chain disruption management: New trends and research directions. International Journal of Production Research, 59(1) (2021): 102–109.

37. Azad, N. and E. Hassini. Recovery strategies from major supply disruptions in single and multiple sourcing networks. European Journal of Operational Research, 275(2) (2019): 481–501.

38. Blackhurst, J., C.W. Craighead, M.J. Rungtusanatham and R.B. Handfield. The severity of supply chain disruptions: Design characteristics and mitigation capabilities. Decision Sciences, 38(1) (2007): 131–156.

39. Bode, C., S.M. Wagner, K.J. Petersen and L.M. Ellram. Understanding responses to supply chain disruptions: Insights from information processing and resource dependence perspectives. Academy of Management Journal, 54(4) (2011): 833–856.

40. Chopra, S. and M. Sodhi. Managing risk to avoid supply chain breakdown. Sloan Management Review, 46(1) (2004): 53–62.

41. Ivanov, D., A. Dolgui, B. Sokolov and M. Ivanova. Literature review on disruption recovery in the supply chain. International Journal of Production Research, 55(20) (2017): 6158–6174.

42. Ponomarov, S.Y. and M. Holcomb. Understanding the concept of supply chain resilience. The International Journal of Logistics Management, 20(1) (2009): 124–143.

43. Scheibe, K.P. and J. Blackhurst. Supply chain disruption propagation: A systemic risk and normal accident theory perspective. International Journal of Production Research, 56(1–2) (2018):43–59.

44. Wagner, A.M. and C. Bode. An empirical examination of supply chain performance along several dimension of risk. Journal of Business Logistics, 29(1) (2008): 307–325.
45. Hendricks, K.B. and V.R. Singhal. The effect of supply chain glitches on shareholder wealth. Journal of Operations Management, 21(5) (2003): 501–522.
46. Sawik, T. Two-period vs. multi-period model for supply chain disruption management. International Journal of Production Research, 57(14) (2018): 4502–4518.
47. Capgemini. Fast Forward: Rethinking supply chain resilience for a post-COVID-19 world [online]. Capgemini Research Institute, (2020). Last accessed 04 April 2021 at https://www.capgemini.com/wp-content/uploads/2020/11/Fast-forward_Report.pdf
48. Kerr, W. The COVID-19 pandemic and agriculture: Short- and long-run implications for international trade relations. Canadian Journal of Agricultural Economics/Revue (Canadienned'agroeconomie), 68(2) (2020): 225–229.
49. Ritchie, B. and C. Brindley. Supply chain risk management and performance: A guiding framework for future development. International Journal of Operations & Production Management, 27 (2007): 303–322.
50. Chang, W., A.E. Ellinger and J. Blackhurst. A contextual approach to supply chain risk mitigation. The International Journal of Logistics Management, (2015).
51. Ivanov, D., A. Pavlov, A. Dolgui, D. Pavlov and B. Sokolov. Disruption-driven supply chain (re)-planning and performance impact assessment with consideration of pro-active and recovery policies. Transportation Research Part E: Logistics and Transportation Review, 90 (2016b): 7–24.
52. Macdonald, J.R. and T.M. Corsi. Supply chain disruption management: Severe events, recovery and performance. Journal of Business Logistics, 34(4), (2013): 270–288.
53. Di Vaio, A., F. Boccia, L. Landriani and R. Palladino. Artificial intelligence in the agri-food system: Rethinking sustainable business models in the COVID-19 scenario. Sustainability, 12(12) (2020): 4851.
54. MarketlineFood Retail Companies Have Taken Innovative Steps to Survive During COVID-19. Food Retail. (2020): 1–14.
55. Reardon, T. and J. Swinnen. COVID-19 and resilience innovations in food supply chains. IFPRI book chapters, (2020): 132–136.
56. Sawik, T. Disruption mitigation and recovery in supply chains using portfolio approach. Omega, 84 (2019): 232–248.
57. Ivanov, D., A. Dolgui, B. Sokolov and M. Ivanova. Disruptions in supply chains and recovery policies: State-of-the art review. IFAC-PapersOnLine, 49(12) (2016a): 1436–1441.
58. Fatorachian, H. and H. Kazemi. A critical investigation of Industry 4.0 in manufacturing: Theoretical operationalisation framework. Production Planning and Control, 29(8) (2018): 633–644.
59. Acioli, C., A. Scavarda and A. Reis. Applying Industry 4.0 technologies in the COVID–19 sustainable chains. International Journal of Productivity and Performance Management, (2021).

60. Shen, W., C. Yang and L. Gao. Address business crisis caused by COVID-19 with collaborative intelligent manufacturing technologies. IET Collaborative Intelligent Manufacturing, 2(2) (2020): 96–99.

61. PWC. Supply chain and third party resilience during COVID-19 disruption [online]. PricewaterhouseCoopers (PwC) LLP. (2020). Last accessed 03 April 2021 at: https://www.pwc.com/jg/en/issues/covid-19/pwc-supply-chain-resilience.pdf

62. McKinsey Global Institute. Risk, resilience, and rebalancing in global value chains [online]. (2020). Last accessed 02 April 2021 at: https://www.mckinsey.com/~/media/McKinsey/Business%20Functions/Operations/Our%20Insights/Risk%20resilience%20and%20rebalancing%20in%20global%20value%20chains/Risk-resilience-and-rebalancing-in-global-value-chains-full-report-vH.pdf?shouldIndex=false

63. Kwak, D.W., Y.J. Seo and R. Mason. Investigating the relationship between supply chain innovation, risk management capabilities and competitive advantage in global supply chains. International Journal of Operations and Production Management, 38(1) (2018): 2–21.

64. Queiroz, M.M., D. Ivanov, A. Dolgui and S.F. Wamba. Impacts of epidemic outbreaks on supply chains: Mapping a research agenda amid the COVID-19 pandemic through a structured literature review. Annals of Operations Research, (2020): 1–38. https://link.springer.com/article/10.1007/s10479-020-03685-7

65. BCI. Supply Chain Resilience Report: COVID-19 has been a force for positive change in supply chain management; Supply Chain Resilience Report [online]. The Business Continuity Institute. (2021). Last accessed 04 April 2021 at: https://www.thebci.org/news/covid-19-has-been-a-force-for-positive-change-in-supply-chain-management.html

Part III

Solutions to Pandemic Challenges in Manufacturing Sector

Complex Adaptive Manufacturing System Concept as a Cyber-Physical Production System: Solutions to the Covid-19 Pandemic Challenges

Elvis Hozdić*, Sulejman Kendić and Zoran Jurković

1. Introduction

In the age of Information and Communication Technology (ICT) and the era of digitalization and cybernetics, where manufacturing companies are looking to adapt their manufacturing structures and systems according to the principles of the new industrial revolution known as Industry 4.0, Severe Acute Respiratory Syndrome Coronavirus Type 2 (SARS-CoV-2) has emerged as a current challenge for today's manufacturing companies on a global scale.

SARS-CoV-2 is a new virus with pronounced tropism on the epithelium of the human respiratory system. According to [1], SARS-CoV-2 is "the etiologic agent of the current rapidly growing outbreak of coronavirus disease (COVID-19)". It is extremely contagious and pervasive with a disruption of enzymatic processes in the human body. SARS-CoV-2 is transmitted by droplet infection, direct contact, contact with infected objects of further use, staying indoors, etc. This virus tends to spread rapidly, geographically from its initial epicentre, the city of Wuhan in Hubei Province, China, infecting individuals, families, groups, work teams, etc., and becoming a global pandemic with high mortality rates [2, 3]. The geographic distribution of the COVID-19 is shown in Fig. 8.1.

The World Health Organization (WHO) [4] declared SARS-CoV-2 as a pandemic and global health emergency in March 2020 [5]. According to [6], each infection leads to 5.7 new cases, and no person is immune unless prevention measures are followed. The number of new infections can be reduced by implementing preventive measures such as: hand washing, social distance, timely detection of infection, isolation of infected persons, and self-isolation of their close contacts.

---

*Corresponding author: elvis.hozdic@sckr.si

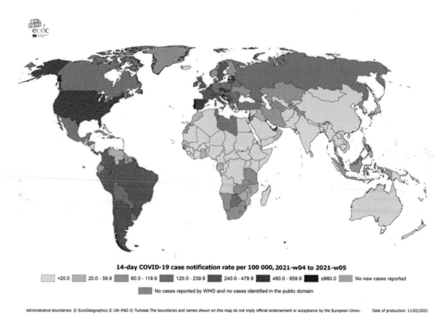

Figure 8.1: The geographic distribution of COVID-19: 14-day COVID-19 case notification rate per 100,000, 2021-w04 to 2021-w05 [4].

The pandemic nature of the SARS-CoV-2 virus causes many problems in the economy, education, work of production activities, tourism, transportation, etc., all of which were closed to avoid the spread of COVID-19. The SARS-CoV-2 pandemic has severely affected the global economy and businesses around the world [7].

The exponential spread of the SARS-CoV-2 pandemic across the globe forced countries to suddenly halt economic activities at the national level and stop economic exchanges between countries by closing borders [8].

UNCTAD* projected a decline in gross domestic product (GDP) of about 4.3 percent in 2020, with a global recovery of 4.1 percent expected in 2021 [9]. According to [9], "the developed economies are expected to be more affected in 2020 than developing countries, at -5.8 per cent and -2.1 per cent, respectively, and expect a weaker recovery in 2021, at +3.1 per cent compared with +5.7 per cent. Unlike the global financial crisis of 2008/09, developing countries are expected to experience negative growth in 2020, and developed economies are expected to experience a much deeper fall in output, at -3.4 per cent in 2009 compared with -5.8 per cent in 2020". The growth of world manufacturing is presented in Fig. 8.2.

According to the World Bank data, the economic growth rate of the world's top 10 economies over the past 5 years was presented in the paper [10]. The detailed statistical data over the last 5 years of real the GDP are presented in Fig. 8.3.

Figure 8.3 shows the reduction in the GDP of world's top 10 economic countries in 2020 due to the SARS-CoV-2 pandemic, other than India. Italy's GDP in 2020 was around -9.1, followed by France: -7.2, Germany: -7, United Kingdom: -6.5, Canada: -6.2, United States: -5.9, etc.

---

* UNCTAD – United Nations Conference on Trade and Development

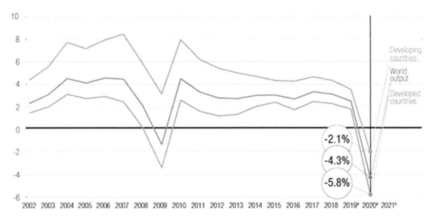

Source: UNCTAD (2020).
Note: Calculations for country aggregates are based on GDP at constant 2015 dollars
* Forecasts.

Figure 8.2: Trends in global economic growth [9].

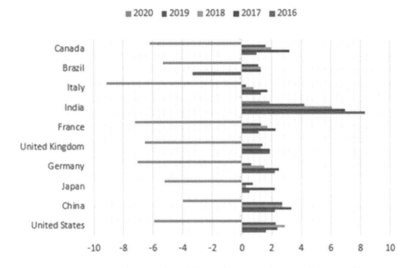

Figure 8.3: Annual GDP of world's top 10 economic countries, according to
the World Bank Data [10].

The SARS-CoV-2 has severely affected manufacturing industries in advanced industrialized countries such as China, USA and Germany. According to [9], "in the first quarter of 2020, global manufacturing output fell by almost 6 per cent compared to the same quarter of the previous year, as illustrated in Fig. 8.4. This was followed by a deeper decline in the second quarter of 2020 of more than 11 per cent. This was the biggest fall in world manufacturing output since the decline experienced in the global financial crisis of 2008/09, when output in the first quarter of 2009 fell by 14 per cent."

According to the literature review [8–9, 11–14], many companies face the following problems: (1) workers wear masks and keep a minimum distance from each

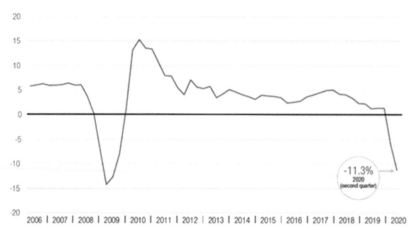

Source: United Nations Industrial Development Organization (2020).
Note: Year-on-year percentage change.

Figure 8.4: Growth in world manufacturing output [9].

other, (2) workers must be quarantined for several weeks, (3) demand for a product has shrunk, (4) demand for a product has advanced. As a result, future demand may disappear, (5) due to insufficient transportation capacity, products produced by a factory cannot be delivered to customers, etc. All these problems have affected the growth of global production output, as shown in Fig. 8.4.

From an industrial manufacturing perspective, manufacturing companies are faced with the rapid development of information and communication technologies (ICT) and the Internet (global opening and distribution with the aim of improving production) on the one hand, and the global SARS-CoV-2 pandemic (global closure) on the other. The fundamental question that arises from this context is: how to balance these two *"halves"*? The answer could undoubtedly be found in the basic principles propagated by the new industrial revolution – *Industry 4.0*. In this challenge, digital technologies, artificial intelligence and CPS play a key role.

A survey of digital technologies to combat the SARS-CoV-2 pandemic is presented in the paper [15]. Kumar et al. [15] discuss the various aspects of modern technologies used to combat COVID-19 crisis at different scales including medical imaging, disease tracking, outcome prediction, computational biology and drugs. In the paper [16], the authors present the major technologies used during the COVID-19 pandemic in the field of healthcare, education, work and daily life. The networked digital technologies used in the public health response to COVID-19 are presented in paper [17].

According to several authors [18–24], Industry 4.0 can be assumed as driven by the new scientific discoveries, enriched knowledge, new and better materials, and new technologies [25]. Based on the literature review, the most relevant core elements of Industry 4.0 are summarized, such as: Decentralization, connectivity, horizontal and vertical integration, collaborations, digitalization, cybernetization, smart machines and products, automation, etc. These elements are the key enablers of Industry 4.0.

In addition, novel organizational forms and innovative management principles of emergence, self-organization, learning, open innovation, collaboration, and networking of people and organizations will become the key elements of the next-generation manufacturing systems [25].

Under the influence of globalization, which brings many changes in all areas of life and especially in the area of industrial production, manufacturing companies are forced to adapt their manufacturing structures and processes to these changes and challenges in order to respond agilely and effectively to the complex demands of today's markets, which are increasingly global and less and less national [26].

Over time, different concepts of manufacturing systems and advanced automation technologies have been developed and implemented in industry, such as: automatic inspection [27], autonomous robots [28], ubiquitous manufacturing [29, 30], cloud manufacturing [31–33], etc. They were intended to respond to social conditions and market demands in the time in which they existed [34]. Changing social conditions and market requirements have repeatedly led to the need for changes in manufacturing structures.

Modern manufacturing companies must be aligned with sustainable, agile, connected, service-oriented, green, and social manufacturing practices, among others [35]. Due to the challenges of Industry 4.0 and recent developments in ICT, manufacturing companies today tend to structure their manufacturing systems in terms of cyber-physical systems (CPS) [34, 36, 37].

However, in order to develop and implement these principles, it is necessary to transform manufacturing systems from traditionally isolated, hierarchical structures to open and distributed, networked structures. The foundations for this transformation are the three central enablers of Industrie 4.0: connectivity, digitization and cybernetization [25].

Under the pressure of globalization and the exponential spread of the SARS-CoV-2 pandemic across the world, highly complex manufacturing systems are emerging. In such systems, the human factor plays a key role. In the paper [38] the author emphasizes the need to restructure the advanced manufacturing systems from the perspective of social factors.

This research addresses the question of how digital technologies and CPS can contribute to improved management, control and monitoring of production systems in the era of the global SARS-CoV-2 pandemic. The aim of this chapter is to model a complex adaptive manufacturing system (CAMS) in the form of a CPS. The paper first discusses the complex adaptive manufacturing systems and the problem of cyber-physical manufacturing systems. Then, the concept of CAMS in the form of CPS is introduced. Furthermore, the conceptual model and structure of CAMS as a cyber-physical production system (CPPS) [39] are presented.

2. Evolution of Manufacturing Systems

2.1 Traditional Manufacturing Systems

The term *"Manufacturing system"* was first introduced by M.E. Merchant [40]. Merchant introduced into manufacturing philosophy the systems approach as an important conceptual tool in the modeling and macro-level control of objects in manufacturing. Microscale modeling of the manufacturing system followed two directions: The first approach was proposed by J. Peklenik [41] and T. Sata [42]. The second approach was initiated by G. Spur [43]. The evolutionary development of the traditional manufacturing systems is described in more detail in the paper [38].

Today's manufacturing systems consist of many elements that are interconnected and attempt to achieve mutual communication and interaction in order to perform production activities [44].

It should be mentioned that there are also many advanced computerised devices and systems implemented in manufacturing systems, such as CNC machine tools, industrial robots, assembly systems, testing equipment, inspection equipment, sensor networks, control and computer networks, etc., which constitute cyber structures. All these elements are logically and/or physically interconnected and interact with each other and/or with the outside world, forming the new generation of advanced manufacturing systems [38].

According to [45], advanced manufacturing systems thrive in service systems, processes, equipment, automation, robots, measurement systems, advanced information processing, signal processing, etc. in manufacturing high-rise information systems in communication systems.

The development of new decentralized concepts of production systems is presented in the EU strategic document *"Factories of the Future"* [46].

A manufacturing system is a highly complex system that must be adaptively controlled at relevant levels by control commands of various kinds [47, 48]. Peklenik defines a factory as a complex adaptive manufacturing system (CAMS) and introduces three levels of organization: (1) the enterprise level (decision level), (2) the management level, and (3) the manufacturing level, see Fig. 8.5.

In the paper [48], Peklenik defined an elementary work system (EWS) as a basic building block of production systems. An EWS consists of a process, the process implementation device (PID) and a (human) *Subject*, see Fig. 8.6. The concept of EWS defines the base level of the production system.

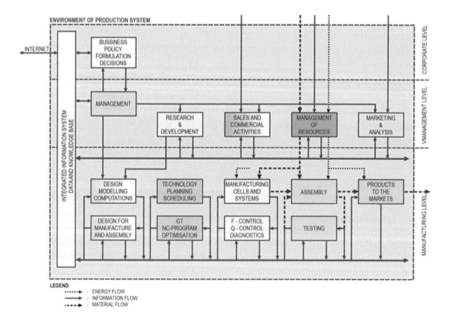

Figure 8.5: Factory as a complex multi-level system [47].

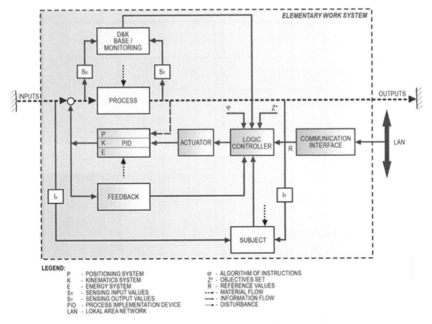

Figure 8.6: Elementary Work System (EWS) [48].

As the counterpart for representing EWS in the cyberspace Butala and Sluga introduced the virtual work system (VWS) in the paper [49]. The tandem of EWS and VWS form as a cyber-physical work system can be considered as an origin for developing building blocks of the future cyber-physical production systems (CPPS).

One question here is whether the EWS-VWS tandem is a self-sufficient form of production. Research [50] states that it lacks the management functionality to be an autonomous and self-sufficient building block of a production network or other network-based organizational forms, such as ubiquitous or cloud manufacturing systems. This realization has led to the concept of the Autonomous Manufacturing Work System (AWS) [50], which is an autonomous network node. The AWS encapsulates functionalities and competencies related to the management and operation of its core manufacturing processes and communication with the network, see Fig. 8.7. Physically, an AWS consists of manufacturing resources and the *Subjects* and can be considered as a sociotechnical system.

In the paper [51], Zupančič et al. propose a new participant in network manufacturing systems that can offer their service services in the form of different functionalities for each individual AWS. Such network participants are appointed Service Unit (SU). AWS and SU represent Manufacturing-oriented Service Networks (MOSeN) [51].

Today's manufacturing is an interconnected process involving multiple production units. Therefore, a comprehensive study of the manufacturing system is necessary. In order to focus on different problems, the whole manufacturing system is divided into hierarchical levels [52]. In the paper [52], five manufacturing levels are identified and scaled top-down: Production Network, Production Site, Production System, Machine and Process. According to [47–50, 52–54], the structural levels

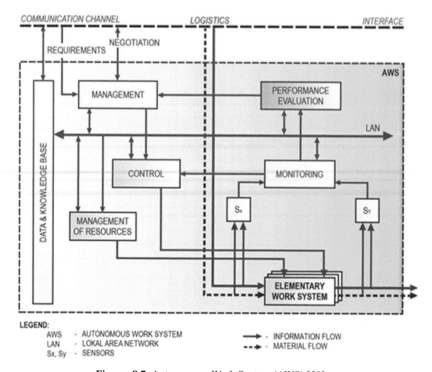

Figure. 8.7: Autonomous Work System (AWS) [50]..

and functional production structures in traditional production systems are shown in Fig. 8.8.

Network production systems (NPS) represent the network-based production systems that seek to take advantage of linkage and representation in the form of larger wholes. The importance of networks is that their building blocks maintain autonomous decisions and a competitive advantage is achieved through the coordination of the network. NPS is based on an application from the environment and is formed by highly competent partners, based on the need for a rapid response to any demand of the global market. With this type of network, production systems are considered as a new complex system [55]. These types of network organizations open new opportunities for competitiveness, innovation, agility, and adaptability in a production environment based on communication between partners and the exchange of information, knowledge, resources, and competencies based on mutual understanding, participation, and collaboration [56]. Productivity and robustness of the network production systems and production network, from the perspective of social networks, are described by the simulation study in the work of Putnik et al. [57].

Peklenik [58] emphasized that production networks, clusters and virtual enterprises based on cooperation are developed. According to [50], a production network provides a foundation for competitiveness, innovativeness, agility, and adaptability by enabling interconnected partners to (1) form long-term business coalitions, (2) develop mutual understanding and trust, (3) jointly respond to business opportunities, (4) achieve synergistic effects through cooperation, and (5) share information, knowledge, resources, competencies, and risks.

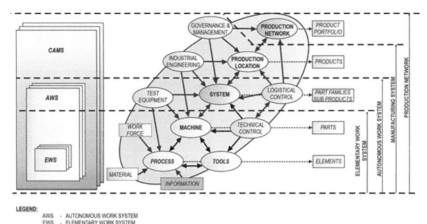

LEGEND:
AWS - AUTONOMOUS WORK SYSTEM
EWS - ELEMENTARY WORK SYSTEM
CAMS - COMPLEX ADAPTIVE MANUFACTURING SYSTEM

Figure 8.8: The manufacturing levels and the functional production structures in the traditional production systems, adapted to [52].

The interrelationships among the elements as well as their input variables at each level are mostly not as clearly defined in Fig. 8.8. Based on a review of the relevant literature in [26, 39], the vertical and horizontal integrations and connections between the elements of traditional manufacturing structures in the production environment are clearly illustrated and shown, see Fig. 8.9.

The EWS is horizontally integrated into a traditional organizational structure such as the Flexible Manufacturing System (FMS) and Dedicated Manufacturing Line (DML). The vertical connection of the operations and coordination & collaboration levels of the traditional manufacturing enterprise is provided by the communication connectivity of the systemic manufacturing structures (AWS and EWS). The vertical integration of the organizational manufacturing structure of the operational level with other organizational forms of the coordination and collaboration level is provided by the integration of FMS and DML in manufacturing departments and manufacturing plants.

AWS represents the systematic manufacturing structure of the middle part of the manufacturing enterprise or its coordination and collaboration level and enables the vertical connection of the EWS to several system manufacturing structures (e.g. manufacturing system) or the network manufacturing structures such as a manufacturing-oriented service network. AWS is horizontally integrated into the production plant/area and is horizontally connected to the network structure.

The CAMS as a basic element of the business level of traditional manufacturing enterprises enables horizontal integration into the organizational manufacturing structure of the ordered factory and horizontal connection of the enterprise to the network manufacturing structure of the said production network (PN).

Today's production system is a complex socio-technical-economic system that integrates production processes, equipment to carry out these processes and people, with the intention of transforming inputs of raw materials into products and their use or sale [38]. Such systems represent the new generation of advanced production systems in the form of cyber-physical systems.

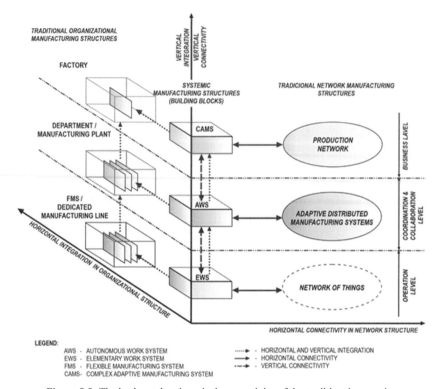

Figure 8.9: The horizontal and vertical connectivity of the traditional systemic manufacturing structures [26, 39].

2.2   From the Socio-Technical-Economic Systems Toward the Cyber-Physical Systems

It is well known that technical and social systems follow different laws. Technical systems follow the laws of natural sciences, while social systems follow the laws of sociology, social sciences and humanities. In a production system, two systems are interconnected due to the nature of processes, which requires mutual interactions. Thus, major improvements in the production system cannot be achieved by improving one system alone. Only through the joint development of the two systems can adequate results be expected [59].

The pursuit of such systems that could succeed and thrive in the global world involves meeting the needs of individual stakeholders beyond the level of achieving common goals and rapid responses to the constant changes (e.g., the global economic crisis, SARS-CoV-2 pandemic, etc.) that characterize today's manufacturing activities. For this reason, it is inevitable to develop and introduce new models of sociotechnical systems linked to modern production systems, based on advanced ICT and exploiting their potential [60].

In structuring the new sociotechnical systems, physical, cybertechnical, and social systems are brought together to achieve common goals, creating a space that takes on the characteristics of an intelligent environment. The role of the *Subject* in future production systems will undoubtedly influence the agility, efficiency, adaptability and robustness of such systems.

In the context of the fourth industrial revolution, the intensive digitalization and cybernetization of work is expected to automate most routine processes. Thus, the *Subject* will mainly perform creative, knowledge-based development processes (engineering) and management and decision-making processes that can be performed in real time and from anywhere thanks to intensive technological support. It is to be expected that the *Subject* will also function at the highest level, i.e. the management level itself. However, at this level it will be strongly supported by functions and support systems. These include defining the goals of the production system, monitoring and observing system behavior through analysis, diagnosis, forecasting, and visualization systems, and system monitoring of success indicators and other elements of business intelligence.

Based on the above, it can be concluded that digitalization or digital transformation is one of the key transformations in the modern world. Definitions of digitization and its role can be found in [61–63]. On this basis, Hozdić in [39], points out that "digitalization is the transfer of processes into the digital environment and their implementation through digital mechanisms". The functions performed in the digitized processes represent the digitized functions as shown in Fig. 8.10a.

Thus, according to [39], digitization enables the transformation of many information processes in production and is already intensive, but in addition to pure information processes, there are many other processes in production that cannot be digitized. These are material transformation processes (e.g. material handling processes, assembly processes, logistics processes, product testing processes, etc.). The physical elements (such as: machines and devices, actuators, sensors, as well as people or Subject, etc.) as well as computer elements (logical controls, digital processors, control programs, databases, etc.) are needed to carry out the processes. So, today's production systems consists of many physical and digital elements, with the digital component becoming more and more important and advanced, allowing the realization of advanced management, control and monitoring functions within the framework of the connection of the digital and physical worlds. This opens the way for the so-called cybernetization of functions in the field of manufacturing systems.

Based on the literature [47, 64], the author highlights the definition of the cybernation in [39]: "it is an advanced, computer-automated control, management, and monitoring of physical elements of the production system, which include: processes, machines and devices for process implementation and entities using the digital computer elements such as: logic controllers, digital processors, control programs, databases etc."

The functions performed in the cybernetic processes represent the cybernetic functions, as shown in Fig. 8.10b. The cybernetic functions are performed in the hybrid analog and digital worlds; their inputs and outputs are analog and digital. The digital mechanisms (e.g., algorithms, agents, expert systems, genetic algorithms, databases, etc.) and the physical analog mechanisms (e.g., process implementation devices, actuators, sensors, etc.) provide the implementation of the cybernetic functions.

Based on the previous definition of cybernetization, it can be concluded that such a transformation requires a vertical and horizontal integration of different environments, such as: the digital (cyber-environment), where digital elements exist, and the physical environment, where different machines and devices exist, and the social environment, where social elements (the *Subject*) exist.

This vision of convergence of social, cyber and physical elements in the next generation production systems dictates the development of the new concepts and

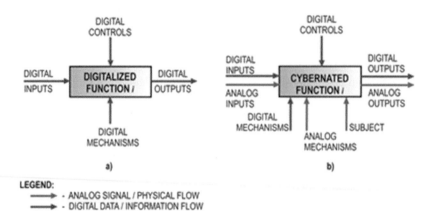

Figure 8.10: The functions in the field of the manufacturing: (a) Digitalized function, (b) Cybernated function [39].

models of the production systems [44]. One of the new concepts resulting from Industrie 4.0 is the so-called cyber-physical systems (CPS) [25].

2.3   Cyber-Physical Systems

Cyber-physical systems were first defined by Lee [65] as follows: "Cyber-physical systems (CPS) are integrations of computational and physical processes. Embedded computers and networks monitor and control of the physical processes, usually with feedback loops in which physical processes affect the computations and vice versa".

In the paper [66], Baheti and Gill CPS as transformative technologies for managing networked systems between their physical assets and computational capabilities. Proposed by Monostori [67]: "Cyber-physical systems (CPS) are systems of collaborating computational entities which are in intensive connection with the surrounding physical world and its on-going processes, providing and using, at the same time, data-accessing and data-processing services available on the internet". According to Leitão et al. [68] CPS constitutes a network of interacting cyber and physical elements aiming a common goal. The information flow between the cyber and the physical word is presented in Fig. 8.11.

Zhong et al. [70] presented a list of typical applications of CPS in various fields such as medicine and healthcare, biology, civil structures, autonomous vehicles, energy distribution and smart manufacturing. Jazdi [71] defined the main features of a CPS in the context of Industry 4.0 and presented the connection between a CPS, smart sensors, actuators and the cloud. Moreover, the characteristics of CPS along with those of Internet of Things (IoT), Internet of Service (IoS), Big Data and Cloud technology are outlined in the paper [72].

The potential and benefits of CPS to transform all aspects of industry sectors are enormous. Today, many industries have initiated projects in CPS [70].

2.4   Cyber-Physical Production Systems

Systemic combination of CPS and advanced manufacturing systems enables the structuring of the cyber-physical production systems (CPPS) [21, 73–75].

Monostori et al. [21] defines CPPS as a production system that uses CPS -related technology, including devices embedded in various equipment, to form a

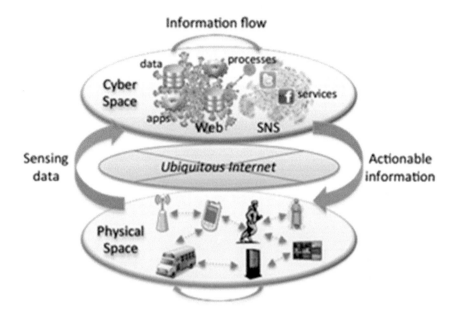

Figure 8.11: The flow of information between the physical and the cyber world [69].

concurrent network via continuous information processing and communication, and increase the flexibility and adaptability of the industrial production system in the case of a complicated production environment and changing demand, enhancing the personalized and highly efficient nature of modern industrial manufacturing.

CPPSs enable horizontal integration through value networks and vertical integration through networked manufacturing systems [74].

In the literature [20, 72, 76–79], several approaches toward the CPPS are presented.

In the paper [25], generic conceptual model of a cyber-physical production system (CPPS) is presented. A new approach for real-time management and control of CPPSs is presented in [25] and [80]. The concept of adaptive process control in manufacturing systems based on the integration of cyber and physical environments is presented in [44, 81]. Moreover, several new approaches to CPPS management and control are presented in [75, 82–85].

In the following, a model of a restructured complex adaptive manufacturing system in the form of a cyber-physical production system concept is presented.

3. Model of a Complex Adaptive Manufacturing System in the Form of a Cyber-Physical Production System

As mentioned earlier, the CAMS (a factory) is structured into three levels (the enterprise level, the management level, and the manufacturing level) [47]. To restructure the model CAMS, as proposed by Peklenik [47] according to the principles of CPS, the generic CPPS concept presented in [25] can be used. The developed reference model based on the CPPS concept is shown in Fig. 8.12.

The model consists of three elements: (1) the human *Subject* is part of the social system (SS) as a social element, (2) the cyber system (CS) as a cyber element, and (3) the elementary work system (EWS), elementary logistics system (ELS), and elementary service system (ESS) are part of the physical system (PS) as physical elements or physical work systems (PWS). Each of the elements exists in its own space: the subject in social space, the CS in cyberspace, and the PS in physical space. Connectivity between these elements, and thus between the different spaces, is enabled by the corresponding communication interfaces that also bridge the different spaces. Each element has the corresponding relationships with its specific environment: the subject with the social environment, the CS with the cyber environment, and the PS with the physical environment [25, 39].

The PWS structure is based on the Elementary Work System (EWS) structure developed by Peklenik [48]. Its core represents the process implemented on a process

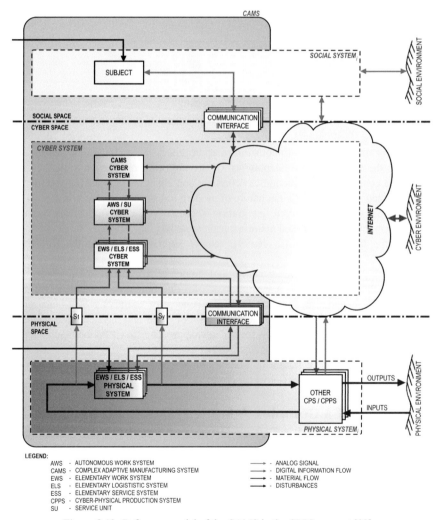

LEGEND:
AWS - AUTONOMOUS WORK SYSTEM
CAMS - COMPLEX ADAPTIVE MANUFACTURING SYSTEM
EWS - ELEMENTARY WORK SYSTEM
ELS - ELEMENTARY LOGISTISTIC SYSTEM
ESS - ELEMENTARY SERVICE SYSTEM
CPPS - CYBER-PHYSICAL PRODUCTION SYSTEM
SU   - SERVICE UNIT

⟶ - ANALOG SIGNAL
⟶ - DIGITAL INFORMATION FLOW
⟶ - MATERIAL FLOW
⟶ - DISTURBANCES

Figure 8.12: Reference model of the CAMS in the CPPS concept [39].

implementation device (e.g. machine tool) and controlled by a logical controller. The latter is connected to a network through a communication interface, which is used to download program code (e.g., NC code) to the controller and to communicate commands in the downstream direction and states as feedback [44]. An important part of the PWS is a monitoring system. It collects data from sensors that measure characteristic input and output parameters related to the process, PWS resources, workpieces, operation, and physical environment. The important difference between the EWS and the PWS is that in the latter, the *Subject* is moved from the physical space to the social space of the CPPS [25]. The structure of the PWS is shown in Fig. 8.13.

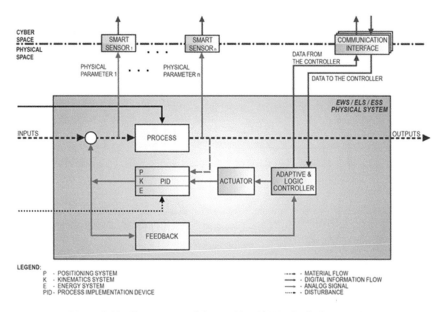

Figure 8.13: The structure of the EWS/ELS/ESS physical system [39].

The CS of CPPS [25, 38–39], is divided into three hierarchical levels: (1) operational level (EWS/ELS/ESS cyber system), (2) coordination and collaboration level (AWS/SU cyber system), and (3) business level (CAMS cyber system), see Fig. 8.14.

The EWS cyber system [25] enables (1) the interconnection of physical and social spaces in the EWS, (2) the digitization of functions (e.g., monitoring and control) and cybernetics and work processes in the EWS, (3) the development and implementation of new digitized functions in the EWS (e.g., self-organization, self-adaptation, self-diagnosis, self-learning, etc.), (4) the vertical interconnection of the EWS in the integrated work structure, and (5) the horizontal interconnection of the EWS in a network within the Internet of Things.

The AWS cyber system [25] enables (1) vertical interconnection with lower-level AWS cyber systems as well as higher-level cyber systems, (2) implementation of the digitized autonomous function in the AWS (resource management, scheduling, quality control, performance measurement, prognostics, self-learning, etc.), and

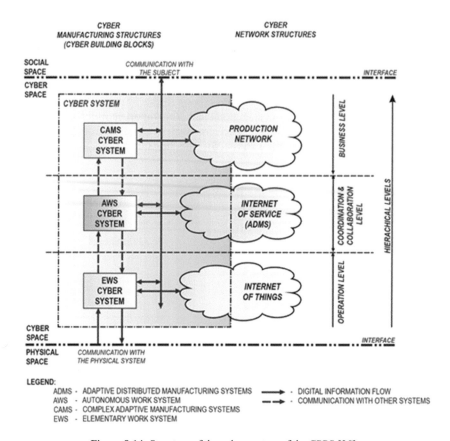

Figure 8.14: Structure of the cyber system of the CPPS [25].

(3) horizontal interconnection of the AWS with adaptive distributed manufacturing systems (ADMS) in the Internet of Services. The AWS cyber system is connected to the higher-level system through the coordination function, while it is connected to the lower-level systems (the EWS cyber systems) through the monitoring and control functions.

The structure of the EWS cyber system and the AWS cyber system is presented in the paper [25]. The partial reference model of the cyber system CAMS is shown in Fig. 8.15.

The cyber system CAMS, as shown in Fig. 8.15, enables (1) vertical connection with the lower-level AWS cyber systems and the EWS cyber system, (2) realization of functions such as sales, marketing, purchasing, project management, design, production planning, quality assurance, etc., and (3) horizontal connection of the CPPS in a production network or other networked forms [25].

The integration of cyber system elements could be realized by using various technologies such as Multi-Agent Systems (MAS), Service-Oriented Architecture (SOA), cloud computing, augmented reality, Big Data, machine-to-machine (M2M) communication and the like [74].

The management of manufacturing systems such as factories is a very challenging task due to their ever increasing complexity. It affects all actors in the

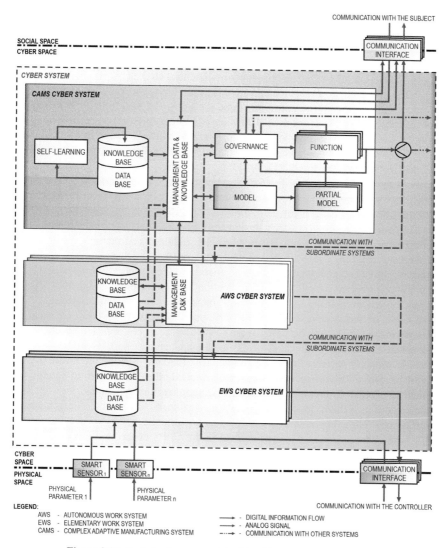

Figure 8.15: Partial reference model of the CAMS cyber system [25].

system and significantly influences the performance of the system. For this reason, the digitalization and cybernetization of this function could have several beneficial aspects [25].

Digitization of the inputs and outputs of functions, in the cyber system of the CAMS, enables a more advanced way of doing business. The main benefits of digitization will be demonstrated by: (1) higher agility and resilience of the system, (2) logical linkage between different functions, so that the output of one function is always a useful input for other functions, (3) real-time view of the whole production-business system of the company, (4) minimization of the space for human error in the realization of certain functions, (5) reduction of operating costs, etc. [38].

Through the governance function and the management data and knowledge base function, the CAMS cyber system is vertically connected to the AWS/SE cyber systems or EWS/ELS/ESS cyber systems. Such communication link enables the CAMS cyber system to retrieve information and data from and send management information to lower-level systems (e.g., tasks, production schedules, etc.).

The data and knowledge management function in the cyber system of the CAMS provides for the monitoring, processing and the storage of data from the lower levels of the cyber system. The processed data is stored in an integrative database of the cyber system CAMS. The generation of new information and knowledge from production data is enabled by the implementation of the self-learning function in the cyber system of the CAMS [39] (see Fig. 8.15).

At the business level of the CPPS cyber system, various processes take place, such as: Decision-making processes (operations management, project management, human resources management, etc.), transactional processes (procurement, payments, etc.), creative processes (research, design and planning of projects and systems, etc.), operational-market processes (sales planning, bidding, contracting, deal-making, complaint handling, etc.), technical-analytical processes (cost analysis, technical control, statistical quality analysis, etc.), general and legal processes (public relations, employee protection, environmental protection, fire protection, legal matters...), etc. From the processes listed, various business management functions are derived to meet the needs of the system environment (e.g., purchasing, sales, production, finance, human resources, etc.) or the needs of the CPPS itself (e.g., research and development, production planning, technical control, source management, etc.).

To properly perform its basic manufacturing function (making products), CAMS must interact with various external systems (outside the manufacturing enterprise), such as original equipment manufacturers, suppliers/supply chains, logistics and transportation systems, maintenance services, customers, buyers and sellers, financial institutions. These interactions are enabled by horizontal connections in cyber space.

The cyber system CAMS, as defined in the CPPS conceptual model [25], is a building block of network structures that are part of a broader PN structure, see Fig. 8.16. Through integration and involvement in the PN, the cyber system CAMS in the PN contributes to the competencies of the CPPS while adopting common policies, principles, goals and constraints.

The basic idea of the PN is conceived in the CPPS concept as the cooperative sharing of activities, exchange of information and also collaborative use of human, financial and technical resources to achieve a common goal and added value.

The networking of the cyber system CAMS with other PNs enables the creation of network structures such as a virtual business system or a virtual factory (VF). The participants in such networking structures gather around the original equipment manufacturer (OEM) [39]. The example of networking structures within the PN is shown in Fig. 8.16.

The required level of competencies is a basic condition for entry into CPPS or its cyber system of CAMS into VE. This condition is defined by the rules of admission to the PN. To participate in the PN, actors must have functional competences (knowledge and experience, technological equipment, etc.) and integration competences.

The resulting production network aims to respond to the complex market demand in terms of products, through a cooperative information link of the CPPS, which will be able to realize the process of development, production, distribution and service of the sophisticated product through the entire product life cycle.

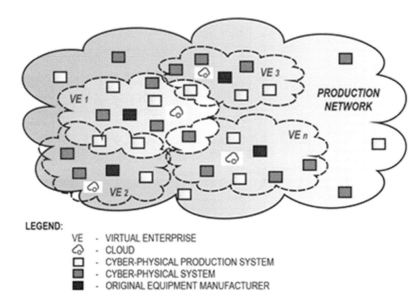

LEGEND:
VE   - VIRTUAL ENTERPRISE
  - CLOUD
  - CYBER-PHYSICAL PRODUCTION SYSTEM
  - CYBER-PHYSICAL SYSTEM
  - ORIGINAL EQUIPMENT MANUFACTURER

Figure 8.16: Model of the production network in the CPPS concept [39].

In the developed concept of CPPS [25, 39, 44], a new role of the Subject was defined. The Subject is located in its own space or the social space and is connected to other social systems as well as the cyber system, see Fig. 8.12.

The social space is a part of the social environment in which social networks and social systems exist, with the Subject as the basic element of such networks and systems. The social system is characterized by the social processes that take place within it. The Subject, as a basic element of such a system, establishes collaborative connections with other participants in the social space to perform business processes. In today's global world, the interactions within the social system do not only take place within the social space. Advanced ICT has enabled the relocation of interactions between participants to a cyber environment. From such an approach, the cyber-social network (CSN) is emerging, enabling a more advanced way of communicating and sharing knowledge and skills. The CSN is part of the broader concept of the Internet of People (IoP). The concept of IoP is presented in the paper [86]. The example of the CSN within the IoP is shown in Fig. 8.17.

The CSN provides a more advanced way to communicate and share knowledge and skills. The CSN and advanced ICT have enabled collaborative communication between Subjects as well as their agent structures that represent them in the cyber system. The collaborative communication of the Subject in the social system takes place through the social media (Facebook, Twitter, MS teams, etc.).

In the production domain, CSNs emerge at different management levels and are interwoven with the Internet of Things, the Internet of Services, product networks, service-oriented production networks, etc. The involvement of the Subject in the CSN and its connectivity with the elements of cyber systems is shown in Fig. 8.18.

At the operational level of the factory, the Subject is horizontally integrated into the operational CSN and connected to the EWS cyber system. The Subject communicates with the EWS cyber systems through the monitoring and identification

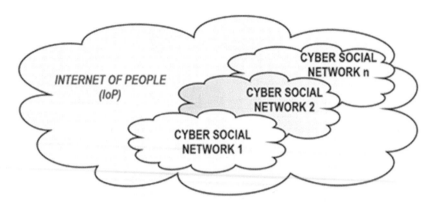

Figure 8.17: Model of the CSN in the CPPS concept.

function. At the operational level of the cyber system, the Subject's direct influence on the implementation of the EWS technological and management functions is minimized. All management and control activities can be left to the cyber elements present in the cyber EWS system.

At the coordination and collaboration level in a cyber system, there are collaborative relationships between the Subject and the system, as well as collaboration

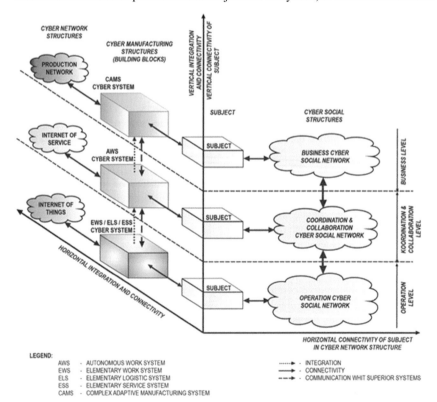

Figure 8.18: Integrating and connectivity of the *Subject* in the concept of the CPPS.

between the systems themselves. The role of the Subject at this level of the cyber system is more manageable. This means that the Subject provides the final decision-making (in case of conflict in decision-making of cyber-elements realizing functions in the cyber-system), defines algorithms for the behavior of cyber-elements (e.g., agents), sets goals, and observes, analyzes, and acts on the state of the entire AWS. The Subject communicates with the AWS cyber systems through the management and control functions. At this level of the factory, the Subject is horizontally integrated into the coordinating and collaborative CSN.

In the cyber-system CAMS the presence of the Subject is more pronounced through the function of governing. At this level, the Subject is extensively supported by functions from lower cyber subsystems (EWS cyber system, AWS cyber system) that allow it to control the system in real time and from anywhere. The Subject is a manager and controller in realizing certain functions at the business level of the cyber system. Through such a role, the Subject defines the goals of the production system, monitors and observes the behavior of the system through analysis, diagnosis, forecasting and visualization systems, and systematically monitors the success indicators of the entire production system. This allows it a high degree of real-time decision making, as well as communication, collaboration and coordination with other elements of the manufacturing system. At the business level of the factory, the Subject is horizontally integrated into the business cyber-social network, see Fig. 8.18.

The *Subject's* communication with the cyber elements (EWS cyber system, AWS cyber system, and CAMS cyber system) is enabled by the communication interface. The communication of the Subject with the cyber elements through the communication interface is shown in Fig. 8.19.

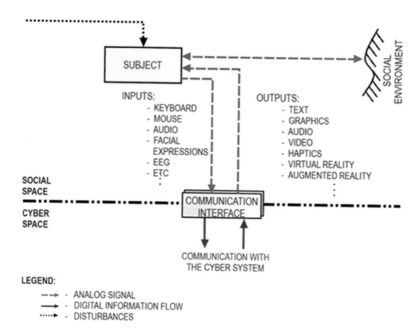

Figure 8.19: Connectivity and communication of the *Subject* in the CPPS concept [39].

The communication between the communication interface and the Subject is based on bidirectional analog communication. The communication from the Subject to the communication interface enables the transmission of commands from the Subject to the cyberspace (to the cyber elements such as EWS cyber system, AWS cyber system, and CAMS cyber system) through various inputs of the communication interface (e.g. keyboard, mouse, computer stick, sound, facial expressions, electroencephalography, etc.). Communication from the communication interface to the Subject occurs through outputs of the communication interface (e.g. text, graphics, audio, video, haptics, virtual reality, augmented reality, etc.).

The development and implementation of communication interfaces in CPPS concept is enabled by modern ICT and Internet. These communication interfaces between the Subject and the elements of the cyber system are based on human-machine interaction (HMI) and ensure non-contact communication of the Subject with the machine, remote work, monitoring, management and control of the manufacturing systems without geographical and time constraints. Some examples of communication interfaces for CPPS are presented in the papers [87–88].

4. Conclusion

This chapter reviews some of the research on cyber-physical manufacturing systems. The new model of a complex adaptive manufacturing system representing a factory is developed in the form of a cyber-physical system.

The developed CAMS model allows the integration of physical, cyber and social elements of the functional environment. The main advantage of the new model CAMS is that (1) the elements of the cyber system of the CPPS enable the management of production systems in real time, through the realization of the digitized and cybernetic functions of the CPPS, and (2) the connectivity of CAMS with other elements and systems through the production networks without geographical and temporal constraints.

The implementation of the CAMS concept based on the CPPS concept in the real industrial environment is a challenge for further research in the field of CPPS, thus contributing to the research towards Industry 4.0.

The implementation of the developed CAMS model is of particular importance during the SARS-CoV-2 pandemic. The developed CAMS model enables the management, control and monitoring of manufacturing systems in real time, by realizing the digitized and cybernetic functions of the CPPS. The developed model CAMS enables human-to-machine and inter-Subject communication without contact, which is particularly important from the point of view of epidemiological measures to prevent the spread of the SARS-CoV-2 pandemic.

By implementing this model of production systems, people (the Subjects) can very easily work from home and thus influence the spread of the SARS-CoV-2 pandemic. The physical contacts of the workers (the Subjects) in the production systems will be reduced to ensure a safe distance, thus reducing the probability of infection with the COVID-19 virus.

Acknowledgment

This work has been supported in part by the University of Rijeka under the project number [uniri-tehnic-18-100].

References

1. Li, Q., X. Guan, P. Wu, X. Wang, L. Zhou, Y. Tong, R. Ren, K.S.M. Leung, E.H.Y. Lau, J.Y. Wong, X. Xing, N. Xiang, Y. Wu, C. Li, Q. Chen, D. Li, T. Liu, J. Zhao, M. Liu, W. Tu, C. Chen, L. Jin, R. Yang, Q. Wang, S. Zhou, R. Wang, H. Liu, Y. Luo, Y. Liu, G. Shao, H. Li, Z. Tao, Y. Yang, Z. Deng, B. Liu, Z. Ma, Y. Zhang, G. Shi, T.T.Y. Lam, J.T. Wu, G.F. Gao, B.J. Cowling, B. Yang, G.M. Leung and Z. Feng. Early transmission dynamics in Wuhan, China, of novel Coronavirus – Infected Pneumonia. New England Journal of Medicine, 382(13) (2020): 1199–1207.
2. Bragazzi, N.L. Digital technologies-enabled smart manufacturing and Industry 4.0 in the post-COVID-19 era: Lessons learnt from a pandemic. International Journal of Environmental Research and Public Health, 17(13) (2020): 4785.
3. Zhu, N., D. Zhang, W. Wang, X. Li, B. Yang, J. Song, X. Zhao, B. Huang, W. Shi, R. Lu, P. Niu, F. Zhan, X. Ma, D. Wang, W. Xu, G. Wu, G.F. Gao and W. Tan. A novel Coronavirus from patients with Pneumonia in China, 2019. New England Journal of Medicine, 382(8) (2020): 727–733.
4. World Health Organization (WHO). Coronavirus disease (COVID-19) [online]. Available: https://www.who.int/emergencies/diseases/novel-coronavirus-2019/situation-reports, (2020).
5. Wang, L., Y. Wang, D. Ye and Q. Liu. Review of the 2019 novel coronavirus (SARS-CoV-2) based on current evidence. International Journal of Antimicrobial Agents, 55(6) (2020): 105948.
6. Sanche, S., Y.T. Lin, C. Xu, E. Romero-Severson, N. Hengartner and R. Ke. High contagiousness and rapid spread of severe acute respiratory syndrome Coronavirus 2. Emerging Infectious Diseases, 26(7) (2020): 1470–1477.
7. Cai, M. and J. Luo. Influence of COVID-19 on manufacturing industry and corresponding countermeasures from supply chain perspective. Journal of Shanghai Jiaotong University, 25(4) (2020): 409–416.
8. Tissir, S., S. El Fezazi and A. Cherrafi. Lean management and Industry 4.0 impact in COVID-19 pandemic era. Proceedings of the 5th NA International Conference on Industrial Engineering and Operations Management (IOEM2020), (2020): 3123–3129.
9. UNCTAD. Impact of the COVID-19 pandemic on trade and development: Transitioning to a new normal. Geneva, Switzerland (UNCTAD/OSG/2020/1), (2020).
10. Verma, P., A. Dumka, A. Bhardwaj, A. Ashok, M.C. Kestwal and P. Kumar. A statistical analysis of impact of COVID-19 on the global economy and stock index returns. SN Computer Science, 2(1) (2021): 27.
11. Chen, T. and C.W. Lin. Smart and automation technologies for ensuring the long-term operation of a factory amid the COVID-19 pandemic: An evolving fuzzy assessment approach. International Journal of Advanced Manufacturing Technology, 111(11–12) (December 2020): 3545–3558.
12. Kumar, A., S. Luthra, S.K. Mangla and Y. Kazançoğlu. COVID-19 impact on sustainable production and operations management. Sustainable Operations and Computers, 1 (2020): 1–7.
13. Harris, J.L., P. Sunley, E. Evenhuis, R. Martin, A. Pike and R. Harris. 2020. The Covid-19 crisis and manufacturing: How should national and local industrial

strategies respond? Local Economy: The Journal of the Local Economy Policy Unit, 35(4) (Jun 2020): 403–415.

14. Berchin, I.I. and J.B.S.O. de Andrade Guerra. GAIA 3.0: Effects of the Coronavirus Disease 2019 (COVID-19) outbreak on sustainable development and future perspectives. Research in Globalization, 2 (December 2020): 403–415.

15. Kumar, A., P.K. Gupta and A. Srivastava. A review of modern technologies for tackling COVID-19 pandemic. Diabetes & Metabolic Syndrome: Clinical Research & Reviews, 14(4) (Jul 2020): 569–573.

16. Vargo, D., L. Zhu, B. Benwell and Z. Yan. Digital technology use during COVID-19 pandemic: A rapid review. Human Behavior and Emerging Technologies. 3(1) (January 2021): 13–24.

17. Budd, J., B.S. Miller, E.M. Manning, V. Lampos, M. Zhuang, M. Edelstein, G. Rees, V.C. Emery, M.M. Stevens, N. Keegan, M.J. Short, D. Pillay, E. Manley, I.J. Cox, D. Heymann, A.M. Johnson and R.A. McKendry. Digital technologies in the public-health response to COVID-19. Nature Medicine, 26(8) (August 2020): 1183–1192.

18. Kegermann, H., W.D. Lukas and W. Wahlster. Industrie 4.0 – Mit dem Internet der Dinge auf dem Weg zur 4. Industriellen Revolution. Berlin: VDI Nachrichten, (2011).

19. Kegermann, H., W. Wahlster and H. Johannes. Recommendations for implementing the strategic initiative INDUSTRIE 4.0 Final report of the Industrie 4.0 Working Group. Frankfurt an Main, (2013).

20. Weyer, S., M. Schmitt, M. Ohmer and D. Gorecky. Towards Industry 4.0 – Standardization as the crucial challenge for highly modular, multi-vendor production systems. IFAC-PapersOnLine, 48(3) (2015): 579–584.

21. Monostori, L., B. Kádár, T. Bauernhansl, S. Kondoh, S. Kumara, G. Reinhart, O. Sauer, G. Schuh, W. Sihn, K. Ueda. Cyber-physical systems in manufacturing. CIRP Annals, 65(2) (2016): 621–641.

22. Dalenogare, L.S., G.B. Benitez, N.F. Ayala and A.G. Frank. The expected contribution of Industry 4.0 technologies for industrial performance. International Journal of Production Economics, 204 (October 2018): 383–394.

23. Frank, A.G., L.S. Dalenogare and N.F. Ayala. Industry 4.0 technologies: Implementation patterns in manufacturing companies. International Journal of Production Economics, 210 (April 2019): 15–26.

24. Alcácer, V. and V. Cruz-Machado. Scanning the Industry 4.0: A literature review on technologies for manufacturing systems. Engineering Science and Technology: An International Journal, 22(3) (June 2019): 899–919.

25. Hozdić, E., D. Kozjek and P. Butala. A cyber-physical approach to the management and control of manufacturing systems. Strojniški Vestnik – Journal of Mechanical Engineering, 66(1) (January 2020): 61–70.

26. Hozdić, E. Cybernetization of manufacturing systems. Proceedings of 13th International Scientific Conference Flexible Technologies (MMA2018), (September 2018): 79–82.

27. An, Z., Y. Wang, L. Zheng and X. Liu. Adaptive recognition of intelligent inspection system for cable brackets in multiple assembly scenes. The International Journal of Advanced Manufacturing Technology, 108(11–12) (June 2020): 3373–3389.

28. Huang, S., M. Ishikawa and Y. Yamakawa. A coarse-to-fine framework for accurate positioning under uncertainties—from autonomous robot to human-robot system. The International Journal of Advanced Manufacturing Technology, 108(9–10) (June 2020): 2929–2944.
29. Chen, T. and Y.C. Wang. An advanced IoT system for assisting ubiquitous manufacturing with 3D printing. The International Journal of Advanced Manufacturing Technology, 103(5–8) (August 2019): 1721–1733.
30. Lin, Y.C. and T. Chen. A ubiquitous manufacturing network system. Robotics and Computer Integrated Manufacturing, 45 (June 2017): 157–167.
31. Chen, T. and Y.C. Wang. Estimating simulation workload in cloud manufacturing using a classifying artificial neural network ensemble approach. Robotics and Computer Integrated Manufacturing, 38 (April 2016): 42–51.
32. Ghomi, E.J., A.M. Rahmani and N.N. Qader. Cloud manufacturing: Challenges, recent advances, open research issues, and future trends. The International Journal of Advanced Manufacturing Technology, 102(9–12) (February 2019): 3613–3639.
33. Ren, L., L. Zhang, L. Wang, F. Tao and X. Chai. Cloud manufacturing: Key characteristics and applications. International Journal of Computer Integrated Manufacturing, 30(6) (June 2017): 501–515.
34. Hozdić, E. Autonomous Work Systems in the Cyber-Physical Production Systems Concept. *In:* Karabegović, I. (ed.), New Technologies, Development and Application III. NT 2020. Lecture Notes in Networks and Systems, 128 (2020): 238–249. Springer, Cham.
35. Tao, F., Y. Cheng, L. Zhang and Y.C.A. Nee. Advanced manufacturing systems: Socialization characteristics and trends. Journal of Intelligent Manufacturing, 28(5) (February 2017): 1079–1094.
36. Gill, H. NSF perspective and status on cyber-physical systems. *In:* National Workshop on Cyber-physical Systems. Austin, TX, (2006).
37. Lee, E.A. and S.A. Seshia. Introduction to Embedded Systems: A Cyber-Physical Systems Approach. California, USA: Berkeley University of California, (2011).
38. Hozdić, E. Socio-Cyber-Physical Systems Alternative for Traditional Manufacturing Structures. *In:* Karabegović, I. (ed.). New Technologies, Development and Application II. NT 2019. Lecture Notes in Networks and Systems, 76 (2020): 15–24. Springer, Cham.
39. Hozdić, E. Model of Cyber-Physical Manufacturing Systems. Doctoral dissertation. Ljubljnaa, Slovenia: University of Ljubljana, Faculty of Mechanical Engineering, (2020).
40. Merchant, M.E. The Manufacturing System Concept in Production Engineering Research. CIRP Annals X, 2 (1962): 77.
41. Peklenik, J. Contribution to a correlation theory for the grinding process. Journal of Engineering for Industry, 86(2) (1964).
42. Sata, T. New identification methods for manufacturing processes. *In:* Advances in Manufacturing Systems, Research and Development. Pergamon Press, Oxford, (1971): 11–22.
43. Spur, G. Betrachtungen zur Optimierung des Fertigungs systems, Werkzeugmaschine. Werkstattstechnik, 57(9) (1976): 411–417.
44. Hozdić, E. and P. Butala. Concept of Socio-Cyber-Physical Work Systems for Industry 4.0. Technical Gazette, 27(2) (2020): 399–410.

45. High Level Group. High Level Group on Key Enabling Technologies. *In:* Thematic Report by the Working Team on Advanced Manufacturing System, European Commission, (2010).

46. Horizon 2020. The EU Framework Programme for Research and Innovation. *In:* Report of Pres. Barroso's Science and Technology Advisory Council (STAC): The Future of Europe is Science, October 2014, Brussels: European Union, (2014): 159.

47. Peklenik, J. Fertigungskybernetik, eine neue wissenschaftliche Dusziplin fur die Produktionstechnik. Berlin: Festvortrag anlasslich der Verleihung des Georg – Schlesinger Preises 1988 des Landes Berlin, (1988).

48. Peklenik, J. Complexity in Manufacturing Systems. CIRP Journal of Manufacturing Systems, 24 (1995): 17–25.

49. Butala, P. and A. Sluga. Dynamic structuring of distributed manufacturing systems. Advanced Engineering Informatics, 16(2) (April 2002): 127–133.

50. Butala, P. and A. Sluga. Autonomous work systems in manufacturing networks. CIRP Annals, 55(1) (January 2006): 521–524.

51. Zupančič, R., A. Sluga and P. Butala. A service network for the support of manufacturing operations. International Journal of Computer Integrated Manufacturing, 25(9) (March 2012): 790–803.

52. Wiendahl, H.P., P. Nyhuis and W. Hartmann. Should CIRP develop a Production Theory? Motivaton – Development Path – Framework. *In:* Sustainable Production and Logistics in Global Networks, Conference Proceedings of 43rd CIRP International Conference on Manufacturing Systems, (2010): 3–18.

53. Sluga, A., P. Butala and J. Peklenik. A conceptual framework for collaborative design and operations of manufacturing work systems. CIRP Annals, 54(1) January 2005): 437–440.

54. Wiendahl, H.P. and S. Lutz. Production in networks. CIRP Annals, 51(2) (2002): 573–586.

55. Westkämper, E. and V. Hummel. The Stuttgart enterprise model – Integrated engineering of strategic & operational functions. *In:* Manufacturing Systems. Proceedings of the CIRP Seminars on Manufacturing Systems, (2006): 89–93.

56. Zaletelj, V., A. Sluga and P. Butala. The B2MN approach to manufacturing network modeling. *In:* Proceedings of the 6th International Workshop on Emergent Synthesis IWES '06, (2006): 9–16.

57. Putnik, G., G. Škulj, R. Vrabič, L. Varela and P. Butala. 2015. Simulation study of large production network robustness in uncertain environment. CIRP Annals, 64 (2015): 439–442.

58. Peklenik, J. A new structure of an adaptable manufacturing system based on elementary work units and network integration. *In:* 7th Int. Conf. AMST 2005, Springer, (2005): 27–40.

59. Frei, F., M. Hugentobler and S. Schurman. Work Design for the Competent Organization. Praeger, Westport, CT, (1993).

60. Eason, K. Sociotechnical systems theory in the 21st Century: Another half-filled glass? *In:* D. Graves (ed.), Sense in Social Science: A Collection of Essays in Honour of Dr. Lisl Klein. (2008): 123–134.

61. Brennen, S. and D. Kreiss. Digitalization. *In:* The International Encyclopedia of Communication Theory and Philosophy, John Wiley & Sons, Inc. (2016).

62. Henriette, E., M. Feki and I. Boughzala. The Shape of Digital Transformation:

A Systematic Literature Review. In: Proc. 9th Mediterranean Conference on Information Systems (MCIS 2015), (2015): 1–13.

63. Parviainen, P., M. Tihinen, J. Kääriäinen and S. Teppola. Tackling the digitalization challenge: How to benefit from digitalization in practice. International Journal of Information Systems and Project Management, 5(1) (2017): 63–77.

64. Wiener, N. CYBERNETICS or control and communication in the animal and the machine. The Massachusetts Institute of Technology, Cambridge, MA, (1948).

65. Lee, E.A. Cyber Physical Systems: Design Challenges. *In:* International Symposium on Object/Component/Service-Oriented Real-Time Distributed Computing (ISORC), (2008): 363–369.

66. Baheti, R. and H. Gill. Cyber-physical systems. *In:* T. Samad and A.M. Annaswamy (eds.), The Impact of Control Technology. IEEE Control Systems Society, (2011): 161–166, available at www.ieeecss.org

67. Monostori, L. Cyber-physical production systems: Roots, expectations and R&D challenges. Procedia CIRP, 17 (2014): 9–13.

68. Leitão, P., A.W. Colombo and S. Karnouskos. Industrial automation based on cyber-physical systems technologies: Prototype implementations and challenges. Computer in Industry, 81 (September 2016): 11–25.

69. Eric, D.S., K.S. Kim, E. Subrahmanian, R. Lee, F.J. de Vaulx, Y. Murakami, K. Zettsu, R.D. Sriram. A vision of cyber-physical cloud computing for smart networked systems. NIST Interagency/Internal Report (NISTIR), National Institute of Standards and Technology, Gaithersburg, MD, (2013).

70. Zhong, R.Y., X. Xu, E. Klotz and S.T. Newman. Intelligent manufacturing in the context of Industry 4.0: A review. Engineering, 3(5) (October 2017): 616–630.

71. N. Jazdi. Cyber physical systems in the context of Industry 4.0. *In:* 2014 IEEE International Conference on Automation, Quality and Testing, Robotics, (May 2014): 1–4.

72. Wang, L., M. Törngren and M. Onori. 2015. Current status and advancement of cyber-physical systems in manufacturing. Journal of Manufacturing Systems, 37(2) (October 2015): 517–527.

73. Uhlemann, T.H.J., C. Lehmann and R. Steinhilper. The digital twin: Realizing the cyber-physical production system for Industry 4.0. Procedia CIRP, 61 (2017): 335–340.

74. Liu, Q., J. Chen, Y. Liao, E. Mueller, D. Jentsch, F. Boerner and M. She. An Application of Horizontal and Vertical Integration in Cyber-Physical Production Systems. *In:* 2015 International Conference on Cyber-Enabled Distributed Computing and Knowledge Discovery, (Sep. 2015): 110–113.

75. Jiang, Z., Y. Jin, E. Mingcheng and Q. Li. Distributed dynamic scheduling for cyber-physical production systems based on a multi-agent system. IEEE Access, 6 (2018): 1855–1869.

76. Lu, Y. Industry 4.0: A survey on technologies, applications and open research issues. Journal of Industrial Information Integration, 6 (June 2017): 1–10.

77. Tupa, J., J. Simota and F. Steiner. Aspects of Risk Management Implementation for Industry 4.0. Procedia Manufacturing, 11 (2017): 1223–1230.

78. Mourtzis, D., E. Vlachou and N. Milas. Industrial big data as a result of IoT adoption in manufacturing. Procedia CIRP, 55 (2016): 290–295.

79. Posada, J., C. Toro, I. Barandiaran, D. Oyarzun, D. Stricker, R. de Amicis, E.B. Pinto, P. Eisert, J. Döllner and I. Vallarino. Visual computing as a key enabling technology for Industrie 4.0 and Industrial Internet. IEEE Computer Graphics and Applications, 35(2) (March-April 2015): 26–40.

80. Hozdić, E. An ontology-based approach for production planning and control of cyber-physical production systems. *In:* I. Karabegović, A. Kovačević, L. Banjanović-Mehmedović and P. Dašić (eds.), Handbook of Research on Integrating Industry 4.0 in Business and Manufacturing. IGI Global, (2020): 274–300.

81. Hozdić, E. Integrating cyber and physical environments for adaptive process control in work systems. *In:* I. Karabegović, A. Kovačević, L. Banjanović-Mehmedović and P. Dašić, (eds.), Handbook of Research on Integrating Industry 4.0 in Business and Manufacturing. IGI Global, (2020): 164–191.

82. Schuhmacher, J. and V. Hummel. Decentralized control of logistic processes in cyber-physical production systems at the example of ESB logistics learning factory. Procedia CIRP, 54 (2016): 19–24.

83. Seitz, K.F. and P. Nyhuis. Cyber-physical production systems combined with logistic models – A learning factory concept for an improved production planning and control. Procedia CIRP, 32 (2015): 92–97.

84. Barenji, A.V., R.V. Barenji, D. Roudi and M. Hashemipour. A dynamic multi-agent-based scheduling approach for SMEs. The International Journal of Advanced Manufacturing Technology, 89 (2017): 3123–3137.

85. Meissner, H. and J.C. Aurich. Implications of cyber-physical production systems on integrated process planning and scheduling. Procedia Manufacturing, (2019): 28167–28173.

86. Conti, M. and A. Passarella. Internet of People (IoP) – An inter-disciplinary approach to networking in a human-centric NGI. European Commission, (2017).

87. Hozdić, E. and S. Kendić. Interfaces for cyber-physical production systems. International Journal of Mechanical Engineering and Automation, 2(3) (2015): 135–141.

88. Damiani, L., M. Demartini, G. Guizzi, R. Revetria and F. Tonelli. Augmented and virtual reality applications in industrial systems: A qualitative review towards the Industry 4.0 era. IFAC-PapersOnLine, 51(11) (2018): 624–630.

Major Advancements of Industry 4.0 to Overcome Challenges in Manufacturing during the COVID-19 Pandemic

Mohd Javaid*, Abid Haleem and Rajiv Suman

1. Introduction

With growing levels of customization, Industry 4.0 is pushing faster and more versatile production. In the age of Industry 4.0, supply chains are quicker, more flexible, and more open. In conjunction with Big Data analytics, the combination of pervasive sensors and networking ensures that manufacturers will have complete visibility of their incoming products, knowing each shipment's exact location and condition during the COVID-19 pandemic. Automated handling ensures that items are selected and put in the correct position. Thus, taken to an extreme, as a seamless production method, a single part should be able to move from serial processes to produce a single part as quickly and efficiently as multiple parts can be produced [1, 2].

New manufacturing technology, such as additive manufacturing, can manufacture polymer and metal parts consistently and repeatably. The performance of 3D printing equipment has improved dramatically in recent years. Thus, to provide a versatile means of producing spares or replacement parts, 3D printers have escaped the confines of conventional prototyping roles. In this way, manufacturers may eliminate the need for warehousing favouring on-demand manufacturing of such products in or near their facilities, thus increasing the supply chain's flexibility [3, 4].

The management of industrial machinery is being changed by digitalization. Sensors, software, and networking allow machine manufacturers, such as drivers and motors, to determine the output of their goods in situ under specific after-care packages, helping the customer prevent downtime by detecting issues before they occur. IoT-enabled devices also contribute to developing new business models where the end-user leases a service or solution efficiently rather than purchasing a computer,

*Corresponding author: mjavaid@jmi.ac.in

thereby eliminating high upfront capital costs. This provides a digitally integrated network of physical devices that enable communication and data sharing over the internet. These intelligent devices can range from smartphones, household devices, cars and buildings. Industrial IoT is an internet-of-things subset, which incorporates different sensors, software and electronics into industrial machinery and systems to collect data on their conditions and performance in real-time [5–7].

While the introduction of new technologies is still difficult, most factories already have a range of systems which makes this process more difficult. These processes tend to be slightly static, and even the more significant part of an organization will consciously oppose change. It creates an environment where most industrial firms are grappling with adopting innovative strategies and technical adaptation during the COVID-19 pandemic. In the area of emerging technologies, Industry 4.0 applies to a variety of transformative developments. Today, worldwide manufacturers link machines to the cloud as the first step towards Industry 4.0 and build personalized models of their industry IoT [8, 9].

In the past, much manual labor was involved in the inventory monitoring process. However, the stock's manual monitoring may be a challenge since hospitals buy a range of goods and store several things for site procedures. Big Data applies to large and complex IoT computer data sets. These data sets are collected through many clouds, business and website software, computers, sensors, cameras and more in various formats and protocols during the COVID-19 pandemic. Data from production equipment equipped with ERP, CRM and MES systems sensors and databases are a wide range of forms to be considered within the manufacturing sector.

2. Effects of COVID-19 on the Manufacturing Field

New technologies have made linking suppliers to a wide range of service providers worldwide simpler than ever. As COVID-19 continued to take hold and countries followed lockdown at different levels, many conventional ties between supply and demand were disrupted. Many factories did not secure the supplies they needed to run and had to quickly find substitute vendors, based in the industry and their suppliers' position and many a time, they failed. Fortunately, for provider's exploration, interactive platforms exist. Digital technologies allow the rapid detection of contingency supplies and new solutions if accessible via web portals or software incorporated in business resource planning solutions [10, 11].

Although several industries have been affected by the COVID-19 pandemic. Industry 4.0 applications accelerated the process of product creation by encouraging team members to work remotely. However, the teams do not have to be in a shared room to perform main activities that undertake product innovations between software and ensure efficient conversion of CAD files into algorithms that automatically track design. In comparison, cloud computing solutions will efficiently ensure that the latest information is exchanged and exchanged with all required team members. In addition to the apparent advantages of productivity, the health benefits, of course, are also evident.

The COVID-19 pandemic creates incidents: some workers have been ill and have posed big production problems. Digital task lists and work routers will make sure a program stays on track and components remain listed. The overall lack of real-time visibility into various production processes is one of the main challenges facing manufacturers. It will not be until a product is complete that producers who do not use automated solutions to track multiple processing phases will know that a problem existed with a component of a system that could be fixed in the previous era. The introduction of a detailed feedback loop will solve various problems. Manufacturers may use machine learning and specialized algorithms to pull data from computers rapidly and efficiently in real-time to enable shop managers' detection and correction of possible problems [12, 13].

During the COVID-19 pandemic, it was necessary to restrict peoples ability to touch, and producers wanted to ensure activities went smoothly while ensuring social distancing between employees. The mechanization or outsourcing of workshop processes can be tackled gradually, and a remote monitoring system can be introduced. Mechanizing more activities ensures fewer employees meet each other and but reduces human jobs. A remote monitoring system helps administrators monitor processes from anywhere so that operators do not have to be there personally to make sure they operate properly. The staff will be secure, and the risks of a break-out are minimized significantly with limited interaction between teams [14–16].

The pandemic has, in many ways, influenced not just how producers perform but also how their investments, especially digital technologies, are valued. For many, COVID-19 has expanded the need for resources that enable today's reality to work. However, what counts will strongly rely on an operator's specific operating climate and goals. The pandemic has checked the sophistication of the industry 4.0 trend. As COVID-19 spread across the world, it allows teams to run simultaneously, if not quicker, to have real-time information about anything, from manufacturers to the factory floor.

In the post-COVID-19 environment, digital transitions across industries and geographies have been accelerating, with companies and individuals taking advantage of emerging technology within a comprehensive system. In this crucial time, which led to debates on the next boundaries of industrial technology, the manufacturing industry is highly dependent on the critical workforce at the shop floor and vulnerable to fluctuations in supply chains. Industry 4.0 is composed of communication technology, advanced research, robotics, and advanced production, and well before the COVID-19, it was gathering traction, allowing enterprises to change industry to create more value. In the sense of global pandemics that cause people to escape in person communication with each other; however, the value of Industry 4.0 technology has become much clearer. The coronavirus is changing digital game rules for business. It also revealed the vulnerability of today's implementation and created a higher standard for performance. The pandemic improved the ideals of industry 4.0. Besides, the transition to the next normal post-COVID-19 changed the meaning [17–19].

Over the past decade, a series has been widely implemented favouring creative development strategies, such as IoT, artificial intelligence, machine intelligence, 3D printing and robotics. With the opportunity to connect and communicate this to the R&D or the Engineering department at any point in producing and using a product, suppliers can enhance the design, minimize the expense, and gain better consumer loyalty. Sophisticated production capability and collaboration in the digital supply chain will allow companies to improve the view of shop floors, recognize bottlenecks in processes, and handle operations more flexibly. It, in turn, encourages intelligent factory capabilities, where static assembly lines are converted into versatile production cells allowing a shift from mass production to mass adaptation. Corporations are mindful that inspiring workers is vital for long-term sustainability. Any time factories need humans, regardless of how far technology goes. Also, new tasks and operations will be generated as the pace of automation rises. Solutions in information management may require higher support levels. Operators fill unautomated functions, complete dynamic assignments, and make intuitive choices [20, 21].

COVID-19 interruption was an external factor, where many who have digitalized their operations, and integrated Industry 4.0 technology into their organizational plans were better able to handle disruptions. They will also revive the after-pandemic in the best possible way. Businesses show the value proposition by developments in Industry 4.0 technological applications and digital business models. It also revealed the vulnerability of today's implementation and created a higher standard for performance. The pandemic improved the ideals of industry 4.0. Agility and organizational stability have emerged as main competitive goals over expanded efficiency and cost-reduction, which was, for the most part, the primary target. The goals of Industry 4.0 are also illustrated by technology that enables remote work and teamwork, with more than half of the respondents employed in projects in that field. Technologies that promote coordination and visibility across the supply chain representing the need for volatile and interrupted supply networks to be managed [22, 23].

Digital innovations are all feasible today through more agile manufacturing processes, higher efficiency, and creative business models. However, the future of innovation has much greater potential with advanced technologies to provide the industries with new opportunities to meet consumer needs and expectations during the COVID-19 pandemic. Digitalization across the industry is taking shape at an impressive rate, with the COVID-19 pandemic stopping the traditional global business ecosystem. It offers digital leaders the opportunity to discover and implement innovative digital policies to promote digital transformation throughout the organization. Even where the initial impact of COVID-19 has begun to diminish, serious dislocations appear to remain an event for some time, with leaders under constant pressure. However, before the pandemic, volatility became a slogan among supply chain and manufacturing leaders. Industry owners exploits Industry 4.0 solutions, implements nerve cantering approaches or control tower approaches to improve the end-to-end transparency of supply chain and quick tracking automation programs because of COVID-19 employee shortages and travel limits.

3. Major Benefits of Industry 4.0 Technologies

New industrial applications for artificial intelligence, cloud computing, connective Things, big data analytics, quantum computing, 3D printing, cyber-physical systems and many other technologies have been developed rapidly in succession. The fourth Industrial Revolution is going on, in which factories or manufacturing units are becoming more flexible with customer-based production by using big data analysis, software, sensors, continuous connectivity and monitoring for new business models. In the manufacturing sector, Industry 4.0 is proving itself a key factor for need-based production. A good example of digitization of the Supply Chain is Intelligent Lots, in which products and pallets are categorized by smart information that encourages the acceptance of the concept of Just in Time in manufacturing. These kinds of technological adaptation, the information about inventory, location, temperature, machines, and production can be easily monitored and can be the base for a newer technical adaptation like smart picking of products, components or raw material [24–26]. The health/performance of each industrial network's components' health/ performance can be monitored centrally via sensors, software, and wired or wireless connectivity at any time. Industry 4.0 technologies are used for:

- Real-time production optimization in the manufacturing environment
- Continuous re-calibration of outputs
- Ensures optimal performance of each element involved
- Industrial assets will always be working to maximum efficiency

With varying customer requirements, the manufacturing units are trying to mold them as per requirements for better responsiveness. For this kind of flexible manufacturing system, companies can adopt an IoT enabled platform for better reactiveness which enables a company with:

- Continual production
- Routing flexibility
- Reduced in-process breakdowns

In this way, a particular product can be made through various routes or by continuous operations on several machines. If job shop activities can be employed for route flexibility, hierarchical models allow dynamic simulation for various production activities. In this way, the virtue of any company's adaptability towards flexible manufacturing increases with maximum utilization of its assets. Machine flexibility is the main focused area for implementing Industry 4.0 to adopt its methodologies with decentralized manufacturing and autonomous production, making flexibility part of machines more exciting from the research point of view [27–29]. These are widely used in the production line's rapid realignment that connects industrial networks and automation by employing standard interfaces and smart infrastructure. These kinds of systems include:

- High-quality sensors interfaced with ethernet
- Quick fit communication cables for robotic arms
- Dynamic manufacturing lines
- Faster and intuitive maintenance

Several components or equipment working together converts an industrial/ manufacturing unit into a intricate ecosystem that runs for a particular response. That makes each component of this mechanical ecosystem working towards the clear visible importance of all operational processes. Internet of Things is providing such flexibility of real-time monitoring from anywhere in the world. Any individual asset/ unit can be easily monitored for its performance through a tablet or computer by just plugging in this networked system.

4. Industry 4.0 for Manufacturing

By implementing physical production and operations, together with intelligent digital technology such as machine learning and big data, Industry 4.0 creates a more integrated and a more connected ecosystem for manufacturing and supply chain management organizations. This industrial automation provides a manufacturing infrastructure that allows machines to track and accumulate real-time insights through networking and sensors to help industries develop and make independent decisions. It is becoming important to provide digital technology that allows remote work and teamwork and removes the need for non-critical workers' to leave their homes. More sophisticated systems, such as machine learning/artificial intelligence algorithms and wearable devices, contribute to the fundamental touch and position tracing of smartphone apps and video conferencing applications and help sustain secure business distances as development begins again. Supervisors can then remotely and in real-time track factory output [30, 31].

Wearable devices can improve remote maintenance assistance, for example, when operators need off-site assistance due to travel limitations. This improves the availability of computers by reducing downtime. Automated equipment management and process control systems will improve the continuity of operations. These systems will also further refine running equipment and process parameters, improve equipment for reduced cycle times, and improve productivity, output, energy, and flow, a particularly enticing prospect for continuous process industries that continuously track and optimize process parameters.

Digital innovations will go one step forward in quality control in addition to optimizing day-to-day activities. Automated production management and quality control can be achieved with predictive algorithms, which can alleviate worker availability restrictions while increasing the accuracy and quality control threshold in industries. A remote logistics control towers can create a live view of success from loading in the factory to loading in the distribution points at all outbound logistics levels. These techniques combined with automated fleet administration, path planning and carrier analysis will improve transport asset uptime while improving service, management, and resource allocation. These adjustments will collectively improve organizational flexibility in crisis management [32, 33].

Warehouses provide numerous automation opportunities. This includes shuttle systems, automatic inventory storage and recuperation systems, smart cabinets, smart pick robots and cobots, automated and smart sorting, filtering, and packaging systems, and stock inspection drones. A digital twin will lead to optimum storage operations to establish a digital duplication of the warehouse to interpret various digital technology effects. Other Industry 4.0 technologies will also support warehousing workers, including software for improved realism to make it much faster and more reliable to order multiple orders and exoskeletons to prevent accidents sustained by the repetitive handling of heavy materials [34, 35].

This degree of instability caused by the pandemic has never been seen before in the global supply chain. Some factories ceased production, and many saw a large decrease in demand, and others saw a major rise in demand. This crisis somehow influences each maker, and this poses an existential challenge for many. Industry 4.0 was a very significant field for various manufacturers until the recession. It was an interesting subject and was perceived by many as a constructive and forward-looking topic.

5. Major Advancements of Industry 4.0 during COVID-19

During COVID-19, Industry 4.0 innovations started to significantly affect manufacturers' transitions around the world. Today, a whole new standard of value has been taken on by solutions like IoT, AI, analytics, and automation. The pandemic has tremendously expedited companies' push to change online. Advances such as IT and Organizational Technology (OT) convergence brought together data that could drive productivity and creativity. The value of fully integrated, robotic workflows was born from the new technology.

Since more businesses depend on these innovations to maintain their activities, previous digital transformation problems have been questioned. Cloud storage helps businesses extend and contract IT technology on a cost-effective basis, which was crucial to the crisis's growth of needs. The pandemic showed that 5G is necessary to allow industry 4.0 to be transformed and new usage cases and the market need for reliable wireless networking developed. Health officials attempted with Big Data and Big Data Modeling to grasp the pandemic. These cases were monitored, diseases tracked, and models dispersed in different towns, regions, and nations [36–38].

AI can better understand the history of infection and to attempt to forecast overburdening in COVID-19 cases to help hospital authorities navigate system demand. Besides that, it is used to clean and manage contactless deliveries. Artificial intelligence was behind the scenes to help find new ways to interact with consumers and partners, simplify company operations or optimize online orders. AI is learning from experience to change in the future. The rise in AI dependency will lead to a more sophisticated artificial intelligence. The advantage for producers is numerous with the utilization of Industry 4.0 since intelligent productive processes are increased. As data is fed into AI-driven solutions, the continuous tracking of equipment and systems is also accompanied by optimizing properties and stocks. The AI solution learns and interprets data trends and related effects in such a digital shop floor, contributing over time to increasing fault forecasts, protection, and productivity. Besides, producers have the visibility to ramp up or down production and minimize downtime [39, 40].

AI is, however, the most powerful way to help forecast the future if there is a historical archive to benefit from and use. It is difficult to see how consensus on AI-based forecasts can be more readily formed right now. The prevailing complexity in terms of demand planning argues that roles can be best performed to increase the visibility of inventories and profits. To resolve the pandemic's issues, certain firms have made their catalogues easier and reduced uncertainty.

As social distance remains necessary, autonomous interactive apps and chatbots can allow companies to communicate with consumers while reducing the direct encounters between individuals. Automation is going to play an even bigger role in development. For machinery and control systems, we foresee more robots being used. Remote setup, control, diagnostics and troubleshooting, and servicing, repair, and operations will include sensors, IoT-based modules, and VR applications. An intensified emphasis will be on securing all endpoints that directly access the organization's properties and data and software on company servers and in the cloud. Robust architecture, installation, incorporation of supply chain tools, sensors, network, and device stack, monitoring and assurance services will be stressed [41, 42].

The opportunity to assess people's wellbeing is a barrier to economic reopening. Wearables and mobile health-application IoT devices such as exercise/health-tracking have already gained broad acceptance. These will also be mainstreamed along with remote-controlled infrared thermal and laser scanners, biometric health sensors and screening tools to allow doctors to remotely monitor the health and, where possible, to administer early therapies and treatments. Big data & AI will help improve network planning efficiencies, forecast demand, build intelligent storage centers, optimize distribution times and cut costs. For cooperation with both consumers and collaborators, AI-enabled chatbots can be used.

The present crisis and recent wrinkles such as the emergence of Homework and telehealth have also stressed the need for quicker remote interactions. For uses such as virtual identity, remote training, and educational courses, 5G technology is instrumental. Connectivity is a core component of Industry 4.0 and 5G, allowing bandwidth of the next stage, higher throughput, low latency, and more efficient communication [6]. This changes our way of working and shopping; the recession often threatens traditional business models. Many enterprises, such as e-commerce, drone-based shipping, remote workforces training and joint innovation plans, aim to initiate or extend digital and contactless business models to move forward [42, 43].

Thus, to adapt to the situation, firms with scaled-up cases from business 4.0 before COVID-19 were best equipped to use them. Technologies can use this as a model for many scenarios during the pandemic to brace themselves for the unexpected closure of production facilities or raw material supply shortages. The pandemic has also prompted businesses to re-evaluate their digital innovations' success, as industry 4.0 innovations become important for early adopters in their crisis response.

6. Improvement of the Design Process using Industry 4.0

Improvement in the design process enhanced manufacturers to achieve efficient result during the COVID-19 pandemic. With a specifically defined input design brief, the designer and developer may explore all potential solution configurations using an AI algorithms, commonly referred to as a generative design program. The algorithms can then be evaluated with the aid of a machine learning suite of solutions. The test process offers more information about which ideas/design choices have not been made. It allows for future progress before an ideal solution is achieved.

The entire Industry 4.0 configuration is protected by artificial intelligence. AI algorithms also improve the manufacturing supply chain, making them react faster to changes in the market and predicting them during the COVID-19 pandemic. The sophistication with which industrial automation uses artificial intelligence demands that manufacturers' partner with experts to develop custom solutions. Although several businesses continue to deny the effect of Industry 4.0 or fail to find the expertise to incorporate this for their particular implementations better, many others are now introducing amendments and planning for a future in which smart machines boost their business [44, 45].

When new input is introduced, a linked supply chain may be modified and adapted. A linked device will proactively tune to this truth and amend production goals through a weather delay linking a shipment. Robotics are now more inexpensive and open to applications of all sizes and for types of organizations. Autonomous robots can quickly and reliably assist suppliers, from choosing goods in a factory to making them ready to ship. The Internet of Things represented by embedded devices is a core component of industry 4.0.

7. The Flow of Data and Information through Industry 4.0 Technologies

To ingest vast data flows obtained by IoT, the use of sensors and computers is useful. Such large data pools will be virtually difficult for a human operator to contextualize, making it important for machines to do so. Mixed reality also plays a significant part in Industry 4.0. Big businesses are now issuing mixed-reality products to increase productivity and smart decisions making through the improved connectivity and visualization of contextualized data. Much of the progressive work performed by human operators has been carried out by robotics, analysis, and machine learning algorithms. It ensures higher and more effective developments all day, mainly by human operators' control and repair processes. Industry 4.0 not only makes manufacturing systems more effective and of greater efficiency, but it also makes possible predictive and reactive repairs and improvements, resulting in reduced downtime and lower capital costs over time. Closer communication across the whole supply chain is feasible with more connectivity, mutual data, and improved insights, leading to performance, optimization, and creativity across the whole production field for the longer term [46, 47].

Digital development requires using an interactive, computer-based framework composed of modelling, analytics, and various cooperation methods to concurrently established concepts of products and manufacturing processes. The new technology developments in business are industry 4.0, where robotics, data sharing, cyber physics, the Internet of Things, Cloud, Big Data, and semantic computing are involved. Industry 4.0 is expected to be the backbone for convergence across corporate borders with physical objects, human actors, smart devices, product lines, and systems to enable smart companies better manufacture targets using emerging technology and inventions during the COVID-19 pandemic. Industry 4.0 is meant to shift the entire output equation by delivering more consistency without losing efficiency, cost, and speed.

8. Industry 4.0 for Addressing Major Challenges

Industry 4.0 addresses major challenges such as capital and energy management and city development, and population transition. It makes the whole value network of the output to be continued in production, productivity improvements and coordinated cost control. Because the sector needs trained employees, this intelligent help takes on the entire repetitive job, allowing the qualified workers to concentrate on innovative, value-added enterprise and enhance the professional and work-life balance. Digital to physical processes enable producers to adapt quickly to numerous changes arising from changing demand, inventory, and unforeseen machinery failures [48, 49].

Smart factories are closely integrated organizations that can communicate and change their output with various networks. Technologies can gather knowledge about all activities, including intralogistics, warehousing, prototyping, manufacture, distribution and distribution of services downstream. Both development and processing activities of products are synchronized and aligned with the life cycles of products. New synergies between commodity and manufacturing processes arise. The launch of IoT opened the doors to several efficiency enhancements by full regulation. IoT migrated to the manufacturing field from our homes and workplaces, which is IoT, and is a crucial factor in the change in the automotive sector and has by far saw the most investment toward a future.

IoT sensors gather composite inventory data from different phases of a product cycle and other syndicated data. This data includes the whole composition of raw materials, temperature and operating conditions, waste, shipping impacts and more concerning finished goods. The IoT device will also provide the consumer feeling details about the usage as it is used in the final product. Both these inputs can be evaluated later to recognize and address quality problems that result in a substantial change. With the Industrial Internet of Things, big data analyses are effectively feasible [50, 51].

By using IoT sensors for goods and packaging, suppliers can obtain useful insights into how different consumers use them. Intelligent methods of monitoring the component's degradation during transport, the temperature, path and other factors in the atmosphere can be used. In essence, this provides information that can restructure products and packaging to enhance consumer service and often even packaging costs. It enables supervisors and plant managers to monitor the factory units from a distance and benefit from process automation and optimization. This makes the daily work seamlessly simplified.

Industry 4.0 is a standardized framework, which uses the cyber approach in industrial goods and services and uses digital communication. It is usually incorporated into the Smart Factory, a transversal mechanism irrespective of the business sector that produces fully automated and interactive industrial development through which equipment, people and instruments collaborate through an intelligent management system. Cost reductions are quickly considered to reduce resource consumption and remove downtimes representing reduced commodity prices. In comparison, current manufacturing inefficiencies have accelerated, cost optimization steps have been insufficient, and lean production ideals have been applied genuinely.

9. Automation Using Industry 4.0 Technologies

Industry 4.0 technologies provides benefit to industries, warehouse staff and minimize the errors and accidents. Lockdown policies have obliged corporations, companies, and industry to locate some of their products, modify the way they purchase and distribute their products, digitally make operations virtual, and increase digital penetration rates for remote operations [52, 53].

Automation and robotics have been instrumental in expanding the floor and ensuring sufficient space for workers during the COVID-19 pandemic. The industry has seen many new development methods to be able to act. The principle of personalization, for example, has been strong since the pandemic. Though it is still important for some markets, such as business computing and networking, it is not as important as we first thought to customers. Additive manufacturing has been excellent for quickly prototyping tools, fixtures, and spare parts. But the promise that additive manufacturing could help customized production. Something else that has been incredibly helpful is simulating the employee view, especially during the pandemic. This process helps businesses understand the factory and how people utilize equipment, ensuring ergonomic design while promoting safety and efficiency and keeping employees at a 'social distance' in a pandemic environment.

10. Industry 4.0 for Supply Chain during COVID-19

The coronavirus pandemic has revealed many challenges of the supply chain, and unprepared corporations are ratcheting up. Many people have recorded delays, especially because regional and national lockdowns make things complicated. Shipment companies have released service suspension notifications in the countries involved, but there has been a continued slowdown, while respective sender and recipient countries have not stopped sending and receiving. Technology that improves the visibility of the supply chain can enable customers to withstand pandemics and possible difficulties. In future, technologies from Industry 4.0 can be used to store vital data from our health system that can be used for another related COVID-19 pandemic. Specialists, doctors, are all impacted by COVID-19 and other concurrent pandemics or epidemics are about to welcome this growth. It can be used to automate all surgical supplies, software, and processes. To establish an intelligent healthcare infrastructure, the medical sector can grow further and respond to new technologies [54, 55].

Companies may also review departmental or shift-level data, keep up to date with overall efficacy or focus on new systems well against shifts. Industry 4.0 businesses should also apply automation to help them solve COVID-19 challenges. Real-time platforms may include scarcity warnings or demand changes to notify businesses of potential disasters. Industrial robotics can maximize efficiency, streamline processes, and operate continuously. Both these advantages are highly appealing as corporations rebound. Robots may grow into key components of corporate adoption. Some countries have surpassed their coronavirus's worst outbreak, but labour shortages are still there, and infected individuals need to self-quarantine. Companies may want to cautiously explore robotic opportunities and wait for outcomes before they intensify. There are several ways in which manufacturers can use modern and proven emerging technologies in practice to work securely through the pandemic while pursuing efficient, profitable, and reliable operations in the long term.

11. Industry 4.0 Applications in Manufacturing during the Pandemic of COVID-19

Industry 4.0 has wide-ranging applications in the field of manufacturing. It is used to increase operating performance, rationalize demand forecasts, break down data silos, carry out predictive maintenance, and provides protection and immersive training for staff during the COVID-19 pandemic. Industry 4.0 enhanced its applications for the in-depth analysis, floor data sensors, intelligent warehouses, simulated modifications and inventory and assets tracking. Industry 4.0 innovations enable producers to connect the distance between what were once independent systems to a more visible and consistent perspective of the whole enterprise. Industry 4.0's goal is dramatically improved quality, performance and self-managing manufacturing processes in which workers, machinery, facilities, distribution networks, and working-in-process sections interact actively and cooperate COVID-19 pandemic. The main priority is to attain low-cost mass manufacturing efficiencies by using embedded processing and communications. Manufacturing and distribution systems are intelligently interconnected across business borders and offer a more effective and scalable, lean output environment in real-time [56–59]. This makes it easier to create intelligent supply chains that span any step of the product's life cycle, from the innovative product design to generate, manufacture, use and maintain to recycle. In this way, the environment will adapt and consistently improve to its customer's needs, from product concept to recycling. The significant applications of Industry 4.0 in manufacturing during the COVID-19 pandemic are discussed in Table 9.1.

Table 9.1: Industry 4.0 applications in manufacturing during the pandemic of COVID-19

S. No	Applications	Description	References
1	Appropriate Production planning	• Industry 4.0 technologies are used for appropriate planning regarding ongoing production, logistics planning, supply planning and demand forecasting during the COVID-19 pandemic. • AI is used for autonomous planning and effectively optimize the entire value chain. • Technologies used in Industry 4.0 enable remote work and collaboration, which helps maintain safe distancing to follow the major requirement of the COVID-19 pandemic.	[60–62]
2	Remote monitoring and controlling	• As a primary means of detecting and removing bottlenecks and reducing waste, Industry 4.0 technologies can be used for remote monitoring and controlling. • The combination of sensors and wireless networking is used to track industrial equipment of all kinds in real-time, with machine learning-powered data analytics used to detect patterns and anomalies during the COVID-19 pandemic. • Industry 4.0 technologies provide instant access to the right information, which is presented efficiently. • It ensures that workers can perform higher quality work in less time, with lesser errors.	[63, 64]
3	Improve the performance of manufacturing	• These digital technologies are used to improve the performance of manufacturing by reducing errors. • The data is digitally collected, which can help supervise and remotely monitor manufacturing industries' performance during the COVID-19 pandemic. • These technologies enhance remote assistance using virtual reality and help to improve overall efficiency by reducing maintenance downtime.	[65, 66]
4	Proper data analysis	• Computer model learning and data visualization can support processes of data analysis. • Machine learning methods are commonly used for processing large data sets using	[67, 68]

		a powerful computational algorithm; this creates an infrastructure needed for more efficient storage and management of such data. • Cloud computing provides a medium for remote servers to store and process massive quantities of data during the COVID-19 pandemic.	
5	Enhance the quality management system	• These technologies are used to improve the entire manufacturing operation, which enhances the quality management system. • Inspection and quality control process after manufacturing can take place automatically. • This also creates automatic management systems in warehouses during the COVID-19 pandemic.	[69, 70]
6	Perform a variety of tasks	• In smart factory settings, lightweight, space-saving robots that can work alongside humans without a protective cage provide new versatility levels. • Equipped with a suite of sophisticated motion, vision and positioning sensors, these collaborative robots will perform a variety of tedious and boring tasks easily during the COVID-19 pandemic.	[70, 71]
7	Tracking of devices	• Digitalization gives manufacturers the ability to track more than just the output of devices. Such an approach offers a more detailed way of allocating costs within an enterprise, and therefore an opportunity to enhance cost calculations and overall financial efficiency.	[72, 73]
8	Flexible computing services	• Cloud computing provides solutions that required heavy computing power to be implemented. • Cloud computing's ability to deliver flexible computing services and space allows market intelligence to be gained by businesses using big data analysis to consolidate and streamline production and business activities during the pandemic.	[73, 74]
9	Manufacturing data compilation	• Big Data is a compilation of data within and outside the business from conventional and modern sources. • Data from networks is now gathered all around the world using this technology. Industry 4.0's transformation will transform how businesses and solutions operate together, making smarter, more intelligent decisions during the COVID-19 pandemic.	[75, 76]

(Contd.)

Table 9.1: (*Contd.*)

S. No	Applications	Description	References
		• The Smart Factory model offers a seamless link between individual production stages, from design phases to on-the-ground actuators. • Technologies will enhance processes by way of self-optimization shortly applications can adapt themselves to the transport profile and autonomous network context.	
10	Monitoring of machines	• Cyber-physical networks are device, network, and physical operation integrations during the COVID-19 pandemic; they use the system to understand behaviours to monitor machines and networks' outcome and control physical systems through feedback loops. • It reflects on the incorporation of machines and applications into devices and provides a relationship between the cyber-physical networks, human beings and intelligent factories that interact through IoT. • This helps production partners to exchange information easily, without mistakes.	[77, 78]
11	Interconnection of the entire manufacturing system	• This automation involves the interconnection of systems, accountability of information and technological support for decentralized decisions. • This will allow the autonomous and independent development of joined-up systems which can cooperate. • The system will contribute to problem-solving and monitoring and thus improve efficiency during COVID-19 pandemic.	[79, 80]
12	Automated communication system	• Industry 4.0 is a standardized framework using a cyber solution for consumer goods and services and automated communications. Commonly related to the Smart Factory idea, a cross-cutting mechanism makes manufacturing productions fully integrated and interconnected, independent of the business sector: machines, people, and equipment communicate for a smart management system and interact together. The effect of digitization transforms the manufacturing system day after day and makes it much more dynamic. Industry 4.0 technologies provide greater flexibility to reach the markets is now necessary, and individual clients must be made more dynamic during the COVID-19 pandemic.	[81–83]

13	Physical development using computers	• These fourth technological revolutions have been brought on by the development of physical inventions using computers. • These new technologies approaches are used to store and use knowledge for effective decision-making. • The advancement of digitization, including Cloud and remote computing, IoT, smart computers, AI and machine learning, is represented by industry 4.0. • Effective development companies need to operate together with the numerous individuals, facilities and procedures that form their supply chain. • Industry 4.0 allows companies to make more efficient and successful during COVID-19 pandemic. This represents a big advantage and increases the productivity of firms.	[84–86]
14	Enhanced development methods	• Industry 4.0's ultimate aim is to enhance development methods. This is the only way to navigate the independent processes so well known for streamlining activities within the landscape of Industry 4.0. • There have been several new innovations in the automotive sector in recent years. Industry 4.0 is just the latest advancement in this sector. It has the power to shift the whole tide of the industry as a full-length and cohesive set of innovations during COVID-19 pandemic. • It develops a reality in standard automation, and factories are more sophisticated than ever before.	[87, 88]
15	Digitization across organizations	• Digitalization across industries is taking shape at an impressive pace when the COVID-19 pandemic stops the traditional global corporate ecosystem. • This has provided digital leaders with unique opportunities to discover and implement innovative digital strategies that drive digital transformation throughout their organizations. • Industry leaders exploit solutions in industry 4.0, implementing new approaches to increasing transparency through the end-to-end supply chain and quick-tracking automation programs because of COVID-19 employee shortages and travel restrictions.	[89, 90]
16	Perform wide varieties of operations	• Industry 4.0 seeks to accumulate significant volumes of data across a wide variety of operations.	[91, 92]

Table 9.1: (*Contd.*)

S. No	Applications	Description	References
		• In the manufacturing context, the production planning program is the secret to using the data gathered and converting it into an operational output that feeds the linked supply chain. • Sensors can read calculation proprieties to avoid loss, track levels, and improve efficiencies to construct an intelligent facility during the COVID-19 pandemic. • Excellent tests in extreme environments and climates extend the sensor scope of different kinds of systems and processes.	
17	Predictive maintenance	• The key aim of predictive maintenance is to anticipate the next malfunction of a component/machine/system, then alert staff to the introduction of focused maintenance procedures to deter failure and has extensive applications in maintaining the future factories. • Robotics has become more stable in manufacturing, and AI can play a key role in ensuring human capital protection and allowing robots further accountability to further refine processes based on data from the manufacturing floor in real-time.	[93, 94]
18	Better connectivity	• Connectivity becomes more relevant as the number of smart devices and the number of data collected, processed and stored increase. Companies would all require their data to be shareable and compatible between the company and third-party stakeholders to improve operational standards. • The data generated by sensors and IoT-driven systems are much too large to be processed by humans during COVID-19 pandemic. • The algorithms of AI and machine learning will make or make suggestions for data and flag irregularities.	[95, 96]
19	Decision-making processes	• The decision-making process is then quicker, and the final result is high quality and effective. The development process is accelerated as the component is aware of its specification. Industry 4.0 produces and fosters resilience in the method. • As the production unit can accommodate new items and experiments in design, there is some improvement in the ongoing process during COVID-19 pandemic.	[97, 98]

		• The assembly line in Industry 4.0 allows a better view of product and process architecture. Industry 4.0 gives suppliers detailed knowledge and response to help satisfy their consumers.	
20	Digital solutions	• Today, digital solutions make it possible to adapt industrial operations, increase productivity, and develop innovative business models. However, the future of innovation offers an even greater potential, with cutting-edge technologies, which creates new opportunities for the industry to meet customer needs and expectations during the COVID-19 pandemic.	[99, 100]
21	Business in profitable sectors	• The demand for certain goods is growing for a few businesses, while whole factories' activities had stopped due to coronavirus's shutdown. Companies now explore in detail how Industry 4.0 technologies will help them return to a profitable sector. • The intelligent technological acquisition strategies and solutions appear the most realistic to improve and cope with an enterprise's future. • Industry 4.0 seeks to develop existing innovation platforms and manufacturing processes through new technologies.	[100, 101]
22	Extracting real-time information	• Industry 4.0 is having advanced manufacturing technology to extract real-time information and make accurate decisions in real-time. Decisions based on obsolete knowledge are one of the most common pitfalls. • Flexible interfaces become increasingly necessary, whether from an internal source or collaborating with a partner. Effective time data must quickly meet the right decision-makers to make informed decisions quickly during the COVID-19 pandemic. Good decisions are taken based on existing knowledge.	[102, 103]
23	Tracking of devices	• Digitalization gives manufacturers the ability to track more than just the output of devices. Such an approach offers a more detailed way of allocating costs within an enterprise, and therefore an opportunity to enhance cost calculations and overall financial efficiency.	[104, 105]

12. Discussion

Although robots have been used for decades in construction, Industry 4.0 has resurrected this technology. A new breed of autonomous robots has arisen with advanced technologies capable of executing complex and responsive tasks. This can identify, interpret, and act on the information they obtain from their surroundings and cooperate and learn from individuals, assisted by state-of-the-art tools and sensors. Advances of power and data storage in information processing has also led to new cases for several items. A development-friendly climate made prohibitively costly innovations affordable and scalable. Many of Industry 4.0 definitions favour unique developments in technology. The development of business cases for technologies such as artificial intelligence, big data, and the integration of the internet of things, omnivorous Internet connectivity, 3D printing and cyber-physical systems. Several analysts argued that Industry 4.0 is better interpreted as a change in the technology-to-work relationship. Here, advanced technology leads into a new era because relations between workers and factory-level machinery change fundamentally.

Innovations in industry 4.0 that encompass mobile computing to cloud computing have experienced extensive growth in the last decade and now are ready as inter-connected production networks that are usable on a commercial basis Industry 4.0 technologies. It contains the cornerstone for access data in real-time that can contribute to new lean efficiency levels for the sector. It is used in several ways and encloses many innovations in its centre.

A key example of this technological evolution is autonomous mobile robots (AMRs). AMR gives industrial centres greater stability and improved performance. The simulated copies of existing installations, procedures, and application can be generated through these software technologies. Such decisions will then be checked robustly to allow decentralized and cost-efficient decisions. This can be generated in the real world and connected over the internet to allow cyber-physical systems to collaborate, interact and build a combined mechanism of real-time data sharing and automation for industry 4.0. These virtual copies can be used to generate data in the real world. The digitalization and linking of systems to sophisticated analytical technologies allows workers to gain more information, carry out experiments, creativity and decide in Real-Time to keep their output going smoothly. Suppliers will see where they are defective and where they can procure inventory through a digital supply chain. Automation is also a fantastic example: High-speed cameras will predict whether a line is beginning to wear down or whether you need to fix a particular segment.

The most urgent problem for manufacturing is preparing for modern labour requirements, safeguarding employee welfare, introducing social separation steps to avoid worker loss, and preserving high levels of efficiency to deter transmission to the workplace. Wearable devices to control compliance with social distance and dangerous physical interactions can incorporate solutions for this issue, AI-based risk-analysis software to predict communication scenarios. This technology enables remote cooperation with non-critical employees. However, process management and automation of plant and factory logistics are also directions in which certain businesses will minimize the decreased labour force's impact. Solutions that need current technical infrastructure will be taken up less often in this period. However, these apps' growth is rising as more and more businesses are becoming less dependent on humans. Meanwhile, the adoptions rates of technologies such as cryptocurrency, nanotechnology and innovative end-to-end automatic processes that require substantial investment lack additional solutions as a matter of urgency and minimize long-term reimbursement cycles.

13. Future Scope

As companies understand that digital processes are needed for business stability in crisis times, the future of Industry 4.0 looks bright. Industry players using digital technologies now are more likely to pass and have been willing to continue their activities without losing productivity uninhibited by new circumstances. Companies will concentrate their resources and finances on the most urgent technology for survival in the short term. However, on a long-term basis, without the restrictions on cash conservation currently put, corporations will continue to invest in digital technologies that allow them to turn their businesses radically for increased competitiveness down the value chain.

In the future, the innovations associated with the Fourth Industrial Revolution deliver powerful and reliable ways of coping with COVID-19 pandemic speed, scale and impact, ranging from artificial intelligence for medical detection to mobile devices for data processing and touch monitoring. Innovations are now promising to control the pandemic better and deal with it. AI and mobile technology have data collecting tools to help track connections, control symptoms and avoid outbreaks and vulnerabilities. In rapid diagnostics, therapeutics, tracking and monitoring, the development of modern types of personal protective equipment and vaccinations, innovative material and nanotechnologies also play a critical role.

14. Conclusion

Although the Covid-19 pandemic has given manufacturers an entirely new variety of problems, the introduction of Industry 4.0 technologies will solve many of those challenges. Those producers who profit from digital solutions are better placed than those who do not. They will emerge from this difficult moment in an enviable role by retaining the capacity to travel as rapidly as before the pandemic and, in turn, finding opportunities to maximize productivity. Industry 4.0 technologies gather a wide variety of data that can be used by computational software to enhance performance and efficiency. Analytics are being utilized on various occasions, like predictive maintenance in real-time, which lets factories prevent output interruptions from factory unplanned equipment faults, which directly increases a properties' efficiency. Industry 4.0 uses the term cyber-physical systems which consists of physical entities, such as computer-based algorithm processes managed or tracked. Industry 4.0 businesses will use automation also to help them deal with COVID-19 problems. Efficient platforms can provide alerts on shortages or demand changes and provide companies with warnings to mitigate potential disasters. Furthermore, and while businesses restart, there is the possibility of catching the infection. Many company leaders will make software and wearables to monitor connections and help them maintain people secure and minimize risks during COVID-19 pandemic.

References

1. Narayanamurthy, G. and G. Tortorella. Impact of COVID-19 Outbreak on Employee Performance – Moderating Role of Industry 4.0 Base Technologies. International Journal of Production Economics, 108075.
2. Abdel-Basset, M., V. Chang and N.A. Nabeeh. An intelligent framework using disruptive technologies for COVID-19 analysis. Technological Forecasting and Social Change, 163 (2021): 120431.
3. Sarfraz, Z., A. Sarfraz, H.M. Iftikar and R. Akhund. Is COVID-19 pushing us to the Fifth Industrial Revolution (Society 5.0)? Pakistan Journal of Medical Sciences, 37(2) (2021).
4. Sharma, R., A. Shishodia, S. Kamble, A. Gunasekaran and A. Belhadi. Agriculture supply chain risks and COVID-19: Mitigation strategies and implications for the practitioners. International Journal of Logistics Research and Applications, (2020): 1–27.
5. Czifra, G. and Z. Molnár. Covid-19 and Industry 4.0. Research Papers Faculty of Materials Science and Technology Slovak University of Technology, 28(46) (2020): 36–45.
6. Vaishya, R., A. Haleem, A. Vaish and M. Javaid. Emerging technologies to combat the COVID-19 Pandemic. Journal of Clinical and Experimental Hepatology, 10(4) (2020): 409–411.
7. Hopkins, J.L. An investigation into emerging Industry 4.0 technologies as drivers of supply chain innovation in Australia. Computers in Industry, 125 (2021): 103323.
8. Ilmi, Z., D.C. Darma and M. Azis. Independence in learning, education management, and Industry 4.0: Habitat Indonesia during COVID-19. Journal of Anthropology of Sport and Physical Education, 4(4) (2020): 63–66.
9. Galanakis, C.M., M. Rizou, T.M. Aldawoud, I. Ucak and N.J. Rowan. Innovations and technology disruptions in the food sector within the COVID-19 Pandemic and post-lockdown era. Trends in Food Science & Technology, (2021).
10. Galanakis, C. M. The food systems in the era of the coronavirus (COVID-19) pandemic crisis. Foods, 9(4) (2020): 523.
11. Sarkis, J. Supply chain sustainability: Learning from the COVID-19 Pandemic. International Journal of Operations & Production Management, (2020).
12. Akpan, I.J., E.A.P. Udoh and B. Adebisi. Small business awareness and adoption of state-of-the-art technologies in emerging and developing markets, and lessons from the COVID-19 Pandemic. Journal of Small Business & Entrepreneurship, 1–18.
13. Swayamsiddha, S. and C. Mohanty. Application of cognitive Internet of Medical Things for COVID-19 Pandemic. Diabetes & Metabolic Syndrome: Clinical Research & Reviews, (2020).
14. Verawardina, U., L. Asnur, A.L. Lubis, Y. Hendriyani, D. Ramadhani, I.P. Dewi and T. Sriwahyuni. Reviewing online learning facing the COVID-19 outbreak. Talent Development & Excellence, 12 (2020).
15. Haleem, A., M. Javaid, R. Vaishya and S.G. Deshmukh. Areas of academic research with the impact of COVID-19. The American Journal of Emergency Medicine, 38(7) (2020): 1524–1526.

16. Belhadi, A., S. Kamble, C.J.C. Jabbour, A. Gunasekaran, N.O. Ndubisi and M. Venkatesh. Manufacturing and service supply chain resilience to the COVID-19 outbreak: Lessons learned from the automobile and airline industries. Technological Forecasting and Social Change, 163 (2021): 120447.
17. Kumar, R., R.K. Singh and Y.K. Dwivedi. Application of Industry 4.0 technologies in SMEs for ethical and sustainable operations: Analysis of challenges. Journal of Cleaner Production, 275 (2020): 124063.
18. Sarkis, J., M.J. Cohen, P. Dewick and P. Schröder. A brave new world: Lessons from the COVID-19 Pandemic for transitioning to sustainable supply and production. Resources, Conservation, and Recycling, (2020).
19. Kumar, A., S. Luthra, S.K. Mangla and Y. Kazançoğlu. COVID-19 impact on sustainable production and operations management. Sustainable Operations and Computers, 1, 1–7.
20. Shen, W., C. Yang and L. Gao. Address business crisis caused by COVID-19 with collaborative intelligent manufacturing technologies. IET Collaborative Intelligent Manufacturing, 2(2) (2020): 96–99.
21. Bahl, S., M. Javaid, A.K. Bagha, R.P. Singh, A. Haleem, R. Vaishya and R. Suman. Biosensors applications in fighting COVID-19 Pandemic. Apollo Medicine, 17(3), (2020): 221.
22. Siriwardhana, Y., C. De Alwis, G. Gür, M. Ylianttila and M. Liyanage. The fight against the COVID-19 Pandemic with 5G technologies. IEEE Engineering Management Review, 48(3) (2020): 72–84.
23. Çalık, A. Key enablers assessment to implement Industry 4.0 technologies in the future for the Turkish Manufacturing Sector. *In:* Handbook of Research on Sustaining SMEs and Entrepreneurial Innovation in the Post-COVID-19 Era, IGI Global, (2021): 243–265.
24. Ashima, R., A. Haleem, S. Bahl, M. Javaid, S.K. Mahla and S. Singh. Automation and manufacturing of smart materials in Additive Manufacturing technologies using Internet of Things towards the adoption of Industry 4.0. Materials Today: Proceedings, (2021).
25. Javaid, M., A. Haleem, R. Vaishya, S. Bahl, R. Suman and A. Vaish. Industry 4.0 technologies and their applications in fighting COVID-19 pandemic. Diabetes & Metabolic Syndrome: Clinical Research & Reviews, 14(4) (2020): 419–422.
26. Acioli, C., A. Scavarda and A. Reis. Applying Industry 4.0 technologies in the COVID–19 sustainable chains. International Journal of Productivity and Performance Management, (2021).
27. Kumar, M.S., R.D. Raut, V.S. Narwane and B.E. Narkhede. Applications of Industry 4.0 to overcome the COVID-19 operational challenges. Diabetes & Metabolic Syndrome: Clinical Research & Reviews, 14(5) (2020): 1283–1289.
28. Ammar, M., A. Haleem, M. Javaid, R. Walia and S. Bahl. Improving material quality management and manufacturing organisations system through Industry 4.0 technologies. Materials Today: Proceedings, (2021).
29. Acevedo-Flores, J., J. Morillo and C. Neyra-Rivera. Industry 4.0 Technologies in the Control of Covid-19 in Peru. *In:* The International Conference on Advances in Emerging Trends and Technologies, Springer, Cham, (October 2020): 275–289).
30. Lu, Y. Industry 4.0: A survey on technologies, applications and open research issues. Journal of Industrial Information Integration, 6, (2017): 1–10.

31. Ratnasingam, J., A. Khoo, N. Jegathesan, L.C. Wei, H. Abd Latib, G. Thanasegaran and M.A. Amir. How are small and medium enterprises in Malaysia's furniture industry coping with COVID-19 Pandemic? Early evidences from a survey and recommendations for policymakers. BioResources, 15(3) (2020): 5951–5964.

32. Ivanov, D. and A. Dolgui. A digital supply chain twin for managing the disruption risks and resilience in the era of Industry 4.0. Production Planning & Control, (2020): 1–14.

33. Sharma, A., S. Bahl, A.K. Bagha, M. Javaid, D.K. Shukla and A. Haleem. Multi-agent system applications to fight COVID-19 Pandemic. Apollo Medicine, 17(5) (2020): 41.

34. Akkaya, B. Leadership 5.0 in Industry 4.0: Leadership in perspective of organisational agility. *In:* Managing Operations throughout Global Supply Chains. IGI Global, (2019): 136–158.

35. Khan, I.H. and M. Javaid. Automated COVID-19 emergency response using modern technologies. Apollo Medicine, 17(5) (2020): 58.

36. Chauhan, A., S.K. Jakhar and C. Chauhan. The interplay of circular economy with Industry 4.0 enabled smart city drivers of healthcare waste disposal. Journal of Cleaner Production, 279 (2021): 123854.

37. Javaid, M. and I.H. Khan. Internet of Things (IoT) enabled healthcare helps to take the challenges of COVID-19 Pandemic. Journal of Oral Biology and Craniofacial Research.

38. Freund, L. and S. Al-Majeed. The Industry 4.0 Knowledge & Technology Framework. PalArch's Journal of Archaeology of Egypt/Egyptology, 17(9) (2020): 6321–6339.

39. Almeida, F., J.D. Santos and J.A. Monteiro. The challenges and opportunities in the digitalization of companies in a post-COVID-19 world. IEEE Engineering Management Review, 48(3) (2020): 97–103.

40. Quinn, L.M., M.J. Davies and M. Hadjiconstantinou. Virtual consultations and the role of technology during the COVID-19 Pandemic for people with type 2 diabetes: The UK perspective. Journal of Medical Internet Research, 22(8) (2020): e21609.

41. Masood, T. and P. Sonntag. Industry 4.0: Adoption challenges and benefits for SMEs. Computers in Industry, 121 (2020): 103261.

42. Sharma, A., S. Bahl, A.K. Bagha, M. Javaid, D.K. Shukla and A. Haleem. Blockchain technology and its applications to combat COVID-19 pandemic. Research on Biomedical Engineering, (2020): 1–8.

43. Sajid, S., A. Haleem, S. Bahl, M. Javaid, T. Goyal and M. Mittal. Data science applications for predictive maintenance and materials science in context to Industry 4.0. Materials Today: Proceedings, (2021).

44. Lee, S.M. and S. Trimi. Convergence innovation in the digital age and in the COVID-19 pandemic crisis. Journal of Business Research, 123 (2021): 14–22.

45. Okorie, O., R. Subramoniam, F. Charnley, J. Patsavellas, D. Widdifield and K. Salonitis. Manufacturing in the time of COVID-19: An assessment of barriers and enablers. IEEE Engineering Management Review, 48(3) (2020): 167–175.

46. van Hoek, R., B. Gibson and M. Johnson. Talent management for a post-COVID-19 supply chain—The critical role for managers. Journal of Business Logistics, (2020).

47. Choong, Y.Y.C., H.W. Tan, D.C. Patel, W.T.N. Choong, C.H. Chen, H.Y.

Low and C.K. Chua. The global rise of 3D printing during the COVID-19 Pandemic. Nature Reviews Materials, 5(9) (2020): 637–639.

48. Bosman, L., N. Hartman and J. Sutherland. How manufacturing firm characteristics can influence decision making for investing in Industry 4.0 technologies. Journal of Manufacturing Technology Management, (2019).

49. Bonilla-Enriquez, G. and S.O. Caballero-Morales. The opportunities of Industry 4.0 in the post-COVID-19 era. The International Journal of Business Management and Technology, 4(3) (2020): 243–247.

50. Ndiaye, M., S.S. Oyewobi, A.M. Abu-Mahfouz, G.P. Hancke, A.M. Kurien and K. Djouani. IoT in the wake of COVID-19: A survey on contributions, challenges and evolution. IEEE Access, 8 (2020): 186821–186839.

51. Gupta, D., S. Bhatt, M. Gupta and A.S. Tosun. Future smart connected communities to fight covid-19 outbreak. Internet of Things, 13 (2021): 100342.

52. Kamal, M.M. The triple-edged sword of COVID-19: Understanding the use of digital technologies and the impact of productive, disruptive, and destructive nature of the Pandemic. Information Systems Management, 37(4) (2020): 310–317.

53. Haleem, A. and M. Javaid. Additive manufacturing applications in Industry 4.0: A review. Journal of Industrial Integration and Management, 4(04) (2019): 1930001.

54. Wuest, T., A. Kusiak, T. Dai and S.R. Tayur. Impact of COVID-19 on manufacturing and supply networks—The case for AI-inspired digital transformation. Available at SSRN 3593540, (2020).

55. Joshi, A.M., U.P. Shukla and S.P. Mohanty. Smart healthcare for diabetes during COVID-19. IEEE Consumer Electronics Magazine, 10(1) (2020): 66–71.

56. Ivanov, D. and A. Dolgui. Viability of intertwined supply networks: Extending the supply chain resilience angles towards survivability. A position paper motivated by COVID-19 outbreak. International Journal of Production Research, 58(10) (2020): 2904–2915.

57. Narula, S., A. Kumar, S. Prakash, M. Dwivedy, H. Puppala and V. Talwar. Modeling and analysis of challenges for Industry 4.0 implementation in the medical device industry to post COVID-19 scenario. International Journal of Supply and Operations Management, (2021).

58. Stankov, U. and U. Gretzel. Tourism 4.0 technologies and tourist experiences: A human-centered design perspective. Information Technology & Tourism, 22(3) (2020): 477–488.

59. Verma, P., V. Kumar, P.C. Bhatt, V.A. Kumar Drave, S.C. Hsu, K.K. Lai and V. Pal. Industry 4.0 in emerging economies: Technological and societal challenges for sustainability. In: Applications and Challenges of Maintenance and Safety Engineering in Industry 4.0. IGI Global, (2020): 31–48.

60. Khurshid, A. Applying blockchain technology to address the crisis of trust during the COVID-19 Pandemic. JMIR Medical Informatics, 8(9) (2020): e20477.

61. Wang, J., J. Shen, D. Ye, X. Yan, Y. Zhang, W. Yang and L. Pan. Disinfection technology of hospital wastes and wastewater: Suggestions for disinfection strategy during coronavirus disease 2019 (COVID-19) pandemic in China. Environmental Pollution, (2020): 114665.

62. Yin, S., N. Zhang and H. Dong. Preventing COVID-19 from the perspective of industrial information integration: Evaluation and continuous improvement of

information networks for sustainable epidemic prevention. Journal of Industrial Information Integration, 19 (2020): 100157.

63. Reong, S., H.M. Wee, Y.L. Hsiao and C.Y. Whah. Industry 4.0 approaches for supply chains facing COVID-19: A brief literature review. *In:* International Conference on Intelligent Computing & Optimization, Springer, Cham, (December 2020): 1242–1251.

64. Queiroz, M.M., D. Ivanov, A. Dolgui and S.F. Wamba. Impacts of epidemic outbreaks on supply chains: Mapping a research agenda amid the COVID-19 Pandemic through a structured literature review. Annals of Operations Research, (2020): 1–38.

65. Lăzăroiu, G., J. Horak and K. Valaskova. Scaring ourselves to death in the time of COVID-19: Pandemic awareness, virus anxiety, and contagious fear. Linguistic and Philosophical Investigations, 19 (2020): 114–120.

66. Lee, J., B. Bagheri and H.A. Kao. A cyber-physical systems architecture for Industry 4.0-based manufacturing systems. Manufacturing Letters, 3 (2015): 18–23.

67. Coatney, K. and M. Poliak. Cognitive decision-making algorithms, Internet of Things smart devices, and sustainable organizational performance in Industry 4.0-based manufacturing systems. Journal of Self-Governance and Management Economics, 8(4) (2020): 9–18.

68. Bayram, M., S. Springer, C.K. Garvey and V. Özdemir. COVID-19 digital health innovation policy: A portal to alternative futures in the making. Omics: A Journal of Integrative Biology, 24(8) (2020): 460–469.

69. Ardito, L., A.M. Petruzzelli, U. Panniello and A.C. Garavelli. Towards Industry 4.0: Mapping digital technologies for supply chain management-marketing integration. Business Process Management Journal, (2020).

70. Ivanov, D., C.S. Tang, A. Dolgui, D. Battini and A. Das. Researchers' perspectives on Industry 4.0: Multi-disciplinary analysis and opportunities for operations management. International Journal of Production Research, (2020): 1–24.

71. Ye, Q., J. Zhou and H. Wu. Using information technology to manage the COVID-19 Pandemic: Development of a technical framework based on practical experience in China. JMIR Medical Informatics, 8(6) (2020): e19515.

72. Chen, T. and C.W. Lin. Smart and automation technologies for ensuring the long-term operation of a factory amid the COVID-19 Pandemic: An evolving fuzzy assessment approach. The International Journal of Advanced Manufacturing Technology, 111(11) (2020): 3545–3558.

73. Juergensen, J., J. Guimón and R. Narula. European SMEs amidst the COVID-19 crisis: Assessing impact and policy responses. Journal of Industrial and Business Economics, 47(3) (2020): 499–510.

74. Teräs, M., J. Suoranta, H. Teräs and M. Curcher. Post-Covid-19 education and education technology 'solutionism': A seller's market. Postdigital Science and Education, 2(3) (2020): 863–878.

75. O'Dowd, K., K.M. Nair, P. Forouzandeh, S. Mathew, J. Grant, R. Moran and S.C. Pillai. Face masks and respirators in the fight against the COVID-19 Pandemic: A review of current materials, advances and future perspectives. Materials, 13(15) (2020): 3363.

76. Fields, Z., Z.M. Abdullah, A.N. Musisi and N.K. Mitchley. Using collective creativity and Industry 4.0 technology to reduce the negative impact of a

pandemic on entrepreneurs. *In:* Handbook of Research on Using Global Collective Intelligence and Creativity to Solve Wicked Problems. IGI Global, (2021): 133–155.

77. Rommer, D., J. Majerova and V. Machova. Repeated COVID-19 pandemic-related media consumption: Minimising sharing of nonsensical misinformation through health literacy and critical thinking. Linguistic and Philosophical Investigations, 19 (2020): 107–113.

78. Díaz-Chao, Á., P. Ficapal-Cusí and J. Torrent-Sellens. Environmental assets, Industry 4.0 technologies and firm performance in Spain: A dynamic capabilities path to reward sustainability. Journal of Cleaner Production, 281 (2021): 125264.

79. Ng, H.S. Opportunities, challenges, and solutions for industry 4.0. *In:* Business Management and Communication Perspectives in Industry 4.0. IGI Global, (2020): 32–51.

80. Ye, J. The role of health technology and informatics in a global public health emergency: Practices and implications from the COVID-19 Pandemic. JMIR Medical Informatics, 8(7) (2020): e19866.

81. Chowdhury, M.T., A. Sarkar, S.K. Paul and M.A. Moktadir. A case study on strategies to deal with the impacts of COVID-19 Pandemic in the food and beverage industry. Operations Management Research, (2020): 1–13.

82. Savić, D. COVID-19 and work from home: Digital transformation of the workforce. Grey Journal (TGJ), 16(2) (2020): 101–104.

83. Singh, S., R. Kumar, R. Panchal and M.K. Tiwari. Impact of COVID-19 on logistics systems and disruptions in the food supply chain. International Journal of Production Research, (2020): 1–16.

84. Golinelli, D., E. Boetto, G. Carullo, A.G. Nuzzolese, M.P. Landini and M.P. Fantini. Adoption of digital technologies in health care during the COVID-19 Pandemic: Systematic review of early scientific literature. Journal of Medical Internet Research, 22(11) (2020): e22280.

85. Larrañeta, E., J. Dominguez-Robles and D.A. Lamprou. Additive manufacturing can assist in the fight against COVID-19 and other pandemics and impact on the global supply chain. 3D Printing and Additive Manufacturing, 7(3) (2020): 100–103.

86. Hofmann, E. and M. Rüsch. Industry 4.0 and the current status as well as future prospects on logistics. Computers in Industry, 89 (2017): 23–34.

87. Shao, X.F., W. Liu, Y. Li, H.R. Chaudhry and X.G. Yue. Multistage implementation framework for smart supply chain management under Industry 4.0. Technological Forecasting and Social Change, 162 (2021): 120354.

88. Mubarik, M.S., N. Naghavi, M. Mubarik, S. Kusi-Sarpong, S.A. Khan, S.I. Zaman and S.H.A. Kazmi. Resilience and cleaner production in Industry 4.0: Role of supply chain mapping and visibility. Journal of Cleaner Production, 292 (2021): 126058.

89. Petracca, F., O. Ciani, M. Cucciniello and R. Tarricone. Harnessing digital health technologies during and after the COVID-19 Pandemic: Context matters. Journal of Medical Internet Research, 22(12) (2020): e21815.

90. Hizam-Hanafiah, M. and M. Soomro. The situation of technology companies in Industry 4.0 and the open innovation. Journal of Open Innovation: Technology, Market, and Complexity, 7(1) (2021): 34.

91. Rahardja, U., S. Sudaryono, N.P.L., Santoso, A. Faturahman and Q. Aini. Covid-19: Digital signature impact on higher education motivation performance. International Journal of Artificial Intelligence Research, 4(1) (2020): 65–74.

92. Allam, Z., G. Dey and D.S. Jones. Artificial intelligence (AI) provided early detection of the coronavirus (COVID-19) in China and will influence future Urban health policy internationally. AI, 1(2) (2020): 156–165.

93. Alwashmi, M.F. The use of digital health in the detection and management of COVID-19. International Journal of Environmental Research and Public Health, 17(8) (2020): 2906.

94. Attaran, M. 3D printing role in filling the critical gap in the medical supply chain during COVID-19 Pandemic. American Journal of Industrial and Business Management, 10(05) (2020): 988.

95. Sahal, R., J.G. Breslin and M.I. Ali. Big data and stream processing platforms for Industry 4.0 requirements mapping for a predictive maintenance use case. Journal of Manufacturing Systems, 54 (2020): 138–151.

96. Tarifa-Fernández, J. Sustainable implications of Industry 4.0. *In:* Responsible, Sustainable, and Globally Aware Management in the Fourth Industrial Revolution. IGI Global, (2019): 29-53.

97. Butt, J. Exploring the interrelationship between additive manufacturing and Industry 4.0. Designs, 4(2) (2020): 13.

98. Prasad, D.K., M. Rao, D.R. Vaidya and B. Muralidhar. Organisational climate, opportunities, challenges and psychological wellbeing of the remote working employees during COVID-19 Pandemic: A general linear model approach with reference to information technology industry in Hyderabad. International Journal of Advanced Research in Engineering and Technology (IJARET), 11(4) (2020).

99. Alan, H. COVID-19 Pandemic and digitalization of service organizations: A Trademark Approach. Electronic Turkish Studies, 15(6) (2020).

100. Azizaha, Y.N., M.K. Rijalb, U.N.R. Rumainurc, S.A. Pranajayae, Z. Ngiuf, A. Mufidg and D.H. Maui. Transformational or transactional leadership style: Which affects work satisfaction and performance of Islamic University Lecturers during COVID-19 Pandemic. Systematic Reviews in Pharmacy, 11(7) (2020): 577–588.

101. Di Vaio, A., F. Boccia, L. Landriani and R. Palladino. Artificial intelligence in the agri-food system: Rethinking sustainable business models in the COVID-19 scenario. Sustainability, 12(12) (2020): 4851.

102. Zimmerling, A. and X. Chen. Innovation and possible long-term impact driven by COVID-19: Manufacturing, personal protective equipment and digital technologies. Technology in Society, 65 (2021): 101541.

103. Fernández-Caramés, T.M. and P. Fraga-Lamas. Use case based blended teaching of IIoT Cybersecurity in the Industry 4.0 era. Applied Sciences, 10(16) (2020): 5607.

104. Chamola, V., V. Hassija, V. Gupta and M. Guizani. A comprehensive review of the COVID-19 Pandemic and the role of IoT, drones, AI, blockchain, and 5G in managing its impact. IEEE Access, 8 (2020): 90225-90265.

105. Elavarasan, R.M. and R. Pugazhendhi. Restructured society and environment: A review on potential technological strategies to control the COVID-19 Pandemic. Science of the Total Environment, 725 (2020): 138858.

Implementation of Cyber Physical Systems in Additive Manufacturing to Sustain Covid-19 Pandemic

Shrushti Maheshwari, Ashish Siddharth and Zafar Alam*

1. Introduction

The global medical emergency of the novel Coronavirus was first identified in December 2019, in Wuhan, China [1]. Since then, it has rapidly spread its tentacles throughout the world and was declared a pandemic by WHO by March 11th, 2020 [2]. The virus is referred to as SARS-CoV-2, and the disease it transmits is called COVID-19. The SARS-CoV-2 virus causes severe acute respiratory issues and spreads through aerosols and droplets, direct or indirect contact with a contaminated surface, in which the virus may remain up to 72 hours [3]. Therefore, to control the drastic exponential growth of this sudden outbreak, extensive precautions and restrictions were implemented worldwide. This resulted in the scarcity of workforce, the requirement of social distancing, and logistic issues all converging to create enormous disruptions in the manufacturing processes and supply chains globally. On the other hand, the demand for medical accessories like masks, ventilators valves, face shields, ear savers, nasopharyngeal swabs, etc., soared. During such an unprecedented critical situation, the global production system needed to lean towards decentralized manufacturing and a high level of customizability for precise needs.

Owing to attributes like rapid manufacturing, detailed design customization, lower lead times, agile supply chains, complex design freedom, digital and decentralized manufacturing, additive manufacturing (AM) is being utilized to mitigate the supply-demand gap. Additive manufacturing enables a shorter supply chain by eliminating various physical supply chains in traditional manufacturing. The additive manufacturing processes consist of interlacing the cyber processes and virtual supply chain with the physical manufacturing processes, making it a cyber-physical system. This provides AM flexibility to customize the supply chain leading to freedom on-site, on-demand manufacturing. However, increased interconnectivity

---

*Corresponding author: zafar@iitism.ac.in

and the interdependency of the cyber and physical components expose AM process to cyber attacks. Therefore, it becomes necessary to examine every aspect of the AM processes thoroughly.

2. Additive Manufacturing

Additive manufacturing is a process of creating a three-dimensional object by laying down successive layers of materials at a predetermined speed and layer thickness of materials which may be biomaterials, metals, ceramics, plastics, concrete, or other adhesive materials. Unlike subtractive manufacturing processes, it fabricates parts by adding material layer-by-layer as per requirement. This leads to precise manufacturing at an affordable price. Figure 10.1 describes generic steps of AM process.

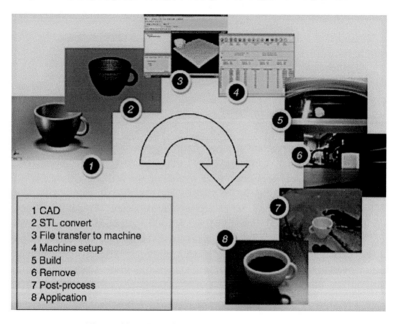

1 CAD
2 STL convert
3 File transfer to machine
4 Machine setup
5 Build
6 Remove
7 Post-process
8 Application

Figure 10.1: Generic steps for the AM process [4].

2.1   Additive Manufacturing Techniques for Covid-19 Combat Products

Several techniques have been developed over time, leading to the increased diversity of materials, shortening of lead times, fabrication of customer or patient-specific parts. However, when it comes to the application of AM parts in the medical domain, extra attentiveness should be taken. Materials used for fabricating medical parts should be biocompatible, non-toxic, and compatible with current AM techniques. Few standard AM techniques are described.

2.1.1 Fused Deposition Modeling (FDM)

Fused deposition modeling or fused filament fabrication (FFF) is an extrusion-based process and was first developed by Stratasys, USA [5]. In this process, materials are feed into the system in the form of the filament. The filament is then heated to a semi-molten state before extrusion. Then the filament moves between the rollers to propagate the semi-molten extrude further. A temperature-controlled extruder then oozes out the filament material. The forced-out extrudate is deposited onto a platform in a layer-by-layer manner. After finishing one layer the platform gets lowered further and then the next layer gets deposited. According to requirements,a single nozzle or multiple nozzles is used. When printing an intricate design, the support material is required, which is removed post-fabrication via various post-processing techniques available. Figure 10.2 schematically describes the working of the FDM process.

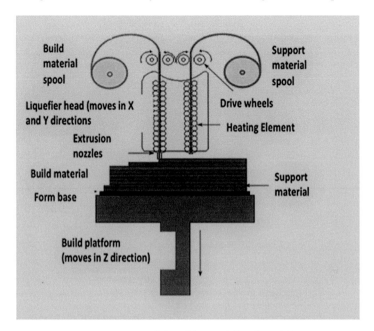

Figure 10.2: Fused deposition modeling (FDM) [6].

2.1.2 Stereolithography (SLA)

Stereolithography works on the principle of creating solid parts using selective solidification of liquid photopolymer resin with a UV laser. In a photopolymer vat, a UV laser traces a cross-section in a layer based on the CAD model's information. The UV laser is precisely controlled to draft a 2D predetermined contour of the object to be made. The laser cures or hardens the resin, thus forming a skinny sliced solid layer. The part under construction rests on a platform dipped in a vat of resin, as shown in Fig. 10.3. The platform is then lowered, and again the next slice or layer is created. This process is repeated until the complete object is formed. Post-processing or post-curing is done to remove the support structures.

2.1.3 Selective Laser Sintering (SLS)

Selective laser sintering belongs to the powder bed fusion-based additive manufacturing process, which uses a laser beam for selective sintering. In SLS, the powder of material to be printed is spread on a build platform at an elevated temperature but below the melting point or glass transition temperature. CO_2 lasers then selectively sinter and fuse the powder according to the contour shape of the layer being printed. The surrounding powder remains loose and serves as a support to the consequent layer,eliminating the need to provide secondary support. Infrared heaters are kept above the bed temperature and above the feed cartridges to pre-heat the powder in the feed cartridges. This, along with preheating of the bed, effectively reduces laser power requirements [4]. Once the layer is formed,the bed is lowered by layer thickness, and power is fed again. The exact process is repeated till the complete product is created. Figure 10.4 schematically describes the SLS process.

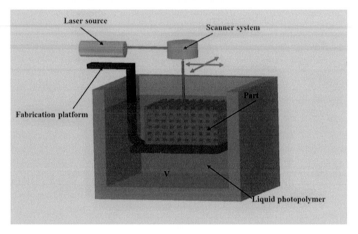

Figure 10.3: Stereolithography (SLA) [7].

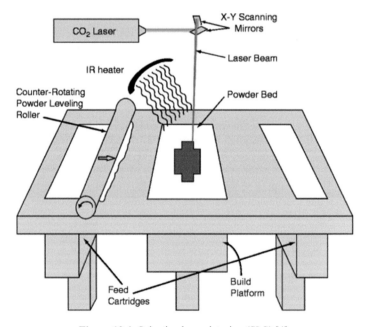

Figure 10.4: Selective laser sintering (SLS) [4].

2.1.4 Multi Jet Fusion (MJF)

Multi-jet fusion is a copyrighted technology of Hewlett-Packard (HP) [8]. Similar to SLS, it also comes under the class of powder bed fusion additive manufacturing. However, in contrast to SLS where laser power is used as a heat source, MJF utilizes an arrangement of infrared lamps as the primary heat source. An ink or fusion agent is mixed with the powder (as shown in Fig. 10.5) using an inkjet nozzle to increase the absorbtivity of the infrared light used. In some cases, a water-based agent is sprayed over the contour of part edges to improve resolution [9].

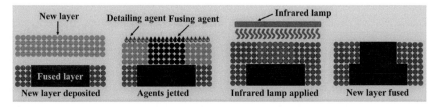

Figure 10.5: Multi jet fusion (MJF) [9].

2.2 Products Manufactured by AM Techniques to Help Combat COVID-19

This section focuses on discussing the manufacturing processes used to attain products such as face masks, ventilator parts, etc., which play a crucial role in fighting back the challenges faced during the COVID-19 pandemic. The next part of this section also includes the information from the survey (Table 10.1) done to gain knowledge about the materials used by the manufacturers during the production of the respective item(s).

2.2.1 Face Mask

A surgical mask covering an individual's mouth and nose serves as a physical obstruction amid the covered part and its surroundings and thereby protecting the user from airborne contaminants, particulate materials, and fluid. The FDA sets distinguished definitions and standards for all the different types of face masks to avoid any kind of potential health hazards during COVID-19 [10]. N95 masks can filter at least 95% of airborne particles larger than 0.3 μm even though the COVID-19 virus particle size is under 0.16 μm [11]. The massive surge in the need of face masks during the COVID-19 pandemic lead to an acute shortage of face masks. Having the potential in printing layer structured, better fitting masks 3D printing became a feasible option in masks' mass production. Czech Technical University (CTU) printed a face mask prototype using HP's MultiJet Fusion 3D printer. Upon further design improvement, the prototype RP95-M mask qualified the standard of providing FFP3 protection against the coronavirus [12].

    A nonprofit digital platform named Maker Mask designed a respiratory face mask using 3D printing techniques and shared its design in the public domain after getting approval from the US National Institute of Health(NIH) [13]. Collaborating with their networks worldwide, they gathered 1000 makers and produced around 1,00,000 masks through additive manufacturing by June 2020. Masks were cost-effective as well as reusable by changing the filter. Due to the prolonged use of masks by health care workers and others, ear savers or mask extenders were suggested to release the ears' pressure. Glowforge [14], a 3D laser printer (cutter) manufacturer, has assembled its user base of makers and manufacturers to produce millions of ear savers. Face Mask Fitters are used ensure a perfect fit or to arrange the face mask accordingly to the shape of a person's face. Bellus3D manufactures plastic frames using 3D printing, according to the user's personalization, to improve the seal of surgical or similar face masks. A user-specific design is created using face scan software for improving the fitting of surgical masks and for minimizing air escape around the edges of the fitter [15].

2.2.2 Face Shield

Face shields consist of a clear visor or transparent plastic sheet attached to a frame or headband and an elastic retainer protecting the user from sprays and splashes. Face shields are considered class I medical devices by the FDA [16]. WHO suggested using face shields as a substitute for masks in case of a shortage of masks.

Prusa Research has designed and 3D printed a face shield named Prusa PRO, which met the standards of EN 166:2001 for protection against drops and sprays (protection class 3) [17]. The design was made open source so that a global shortage could be replenished to some extent. In the face of a critical shortage of protective equipment for frontline health workers, Open Works has launched a collaborative project to 3D print face shields. With over 80,000 face shields in production and more than 3400 volunteers on board,3D crowd UK is a massive effort to deliver PPE to frontline staff in the UK [18]. Further, the SLA3D printing technique was used to create a hollow frame for the assembly of face shields with an additional benefit of external airflow aiding in the visor's defogging and obstructing the flow of ambient air [19]. BCN3D (Barcelona-based 3D printing company) came forward in designing, prototyping, and producing face shields using Polyethylene Terephthalate Glycol (PET-G) due to its high chemical resistance. They used FDM to manufacture reusable face shields as pieces that could be thoroughly disinfected repeatedly without getting damaged [20]. Stratasys, the leading manufacturer of face shields, has released all the design files in the public domain. It also facilitated 100,000 face shields to hospitals within one month. This effort was made in collaboration with Minnesota Dunwoody College of Technology using 100 dedicated teams around the world and with the use of additive manufacturing techniques [21].

Airwolf3D, a 3D printing company in California, released design files for 3D printing face shields and produced guidelines for using ABS (Acrylonitrile Butadiene Styrene) as a printing material for parts of the face shields and their further assemblage with plastic shields [22]. Nexa3D, a 3D printer manufacturer in California, came forward to mitigate the shortage of PPE. They initiated a facility for mass production of two different designs based 3D printed face shields [23].

2.2.3 Nasopharyngeal Swab

Measuring, managing, modelling, and controlling the widespread spread of Covid-19 requires proper and timely testing of the suspected person. Testing requires specimens from the upper respiratory tract, which is done using a skinny and long nasopharyngeal swab. It consists of a long thin, flexible rod-shaped stick with short synthetic fibers attached to its head. It should be noted that the swab should not contain calcium alginate, which can kill Coronavirus [24]. It has been considered an FDA class I medical device [25].

Cox and Koepsell [26] created swabs using Formlabs Form 2 and Form 3B SLA 3D printers. Clinical tests observed that the efficiency of 3D printed nasopharyngeal swab was equivalent to commercially available synthetic swab. A California-based company Forecast 3D a GKN Powder Metallurgy company, partnered with Abiogenix, Fathom, and HP, produced nasopharyngeal (NP) swabs for use in COVID-19 test kits. The ability to collect adequate viral fluid, patient sensitivity comfort, and breakpoint reliability was evaluated in clinical tests for the nasopharyngeal Abiogenix spiral swab design chosen from over 150 designs [27].

Formlabs, a Boston-based 3D printing company, teamed up with USF Health, Northwell Health, and Tampa General Hospital in the United States. The collaboration aimed to design, create, and test NP swabs for printing on Formlabs 3D printers [28]. Arnold et al. [29] created a swab with an open lattice design that could be made with the DLP method. The model was put to the test, and the findings were found to be 90% accurate when using commercial swabs as the gold standard, indicating that the design is acceptable for the test.

2.2.4 Ventilator Parts

Ventilators are the mechanical support system that provides breathable oxygen to aligning patients. A ventilator aids a patient by blowing oxygen at a prescribed pressure and prescribed humidity during inhalation difficulties. A ventilator rhythmically pushes a stream of oxygen to inflate the lungs. The severe lack of ventilators was visible during the Covid pandemic. In some cases, the doctor had to choose between seriously ill patients based on their severity. Italian company Isinnova was one of the first companies to design 3D printed ventilator valves. It enabled hospitals to make use of already available snorkelling masks as oxygen masks [30]. Roboze printed a T connector which enabled the hospital to connect a single ventilator to 2 patients [31]. Ferrari, a sports car maker, also printed and circulated respiratory valves used in ventilators [32]. Materialise is a Belgium company specializing in 3D printed equipment; they 3d printed a valve that can hold together a non-invasive mask, a filter, and a PEEP valve [33].

Table 10.1: Summary of AM processes used for manufacturing products to help combat Covid-19

S. No	Printing techniques	Material used	Product printed
1	FDM	PETG, ABS, PLA, TPV	Face shield, Ear savers, Mask fitters, Surgery mask, safety goggles, Hand-free Handle, valves
2	SLS	PLA/PETG	Face shields, Safety goggles, Half face masks, Nasopharyngeal swabs, valves.
3	SLA	PLA, ABS, Resins	Nasopharyngeal swabs, safety-goggles
4	MJF	PA12	Half-face masks, hand-free door openers

3. Cyber-Physical Systems

Cyber-Physical Systems (CPS) are multidimensional engineered systems where physical systems or processes are augmented with cyber components. Both act as heterogeneous components that have a seamless and tight integration between them. In other words, CPS can be defined as "physical and engineered systems whose operations are monitored, controlled, coordinated, and integrated by a computing and communicating core" [34]. In CPS, integration of 3C's known as communication, control, and commutation provides monitoring, real-time sensing, and information feedback. The basic concept of cyber-physical systems is described in Fig. 10.6. The transfer of information from physical to cyber components takes place with sensors and other data acquisition devices. Information is then processed and analyzed using proper data processing and modelling techniques to reach a suitable output or insights, implemented in the physical system using actuators and other devices.

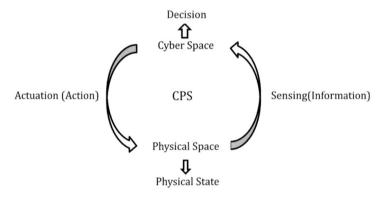

Figure 10.6: Basic concept of cyber-physical system.

3.1   Cyber-Physical Systems in Manufacturing

With improved intelligent mechanisms and better algorithms, the link between the computational and physical world will improve. Consequently, drastic improvements will occur in autonomy (smart machines and devices), functionality, reliability, and efficiency of cyber-physical systems. Monostori et al. introduced the concept of a cyber-physical system in the production domain [35]. Lee et al. [36] proposed 5 level CPS structure for the implementation of CPS in the manufacturing domain. Figure 10.7 methodically describes CPS architecture for the manufacturing processes.

Tao et al. [37] proposed a computing- and service-oriented manufacturing model. Further, the concept, architecture, and core enabling technologies, and typical cloud-based manufacturing characteristics were discussed. Four typical cloud-based manufacturing service platforms, i.e., public, private, community, and hybrid platforms, are introduced. A ten-layer architecture for cloud-based manufacturing is hierarchically presented in Fig. 10.8.

Liu et al. [38] developed a scalable and service-oriented layered architecture of the cyber-physical manufacturing cloud (CPMC) and a virtualization method of manufacturing resources. The conceptual model of CPMC is described in Fig. 10.9, where manufacturers and customers are connected via cloud services.

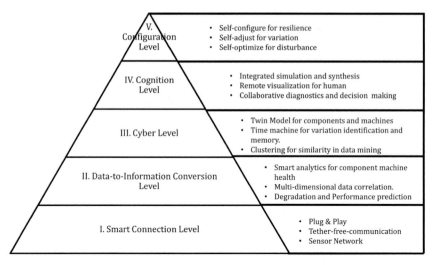

Figure 10.7: CPS architecture for manufacturing processes [36].

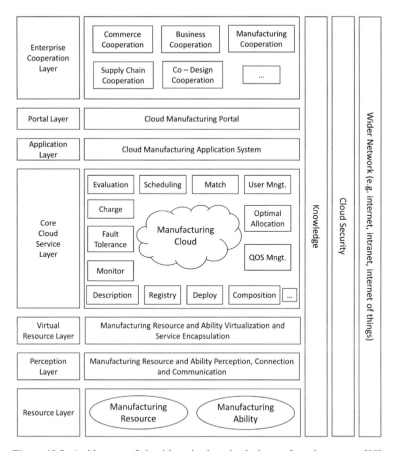

Figure 10.8: Architecture of cloud-based cyber-physical manufacturing system [37].

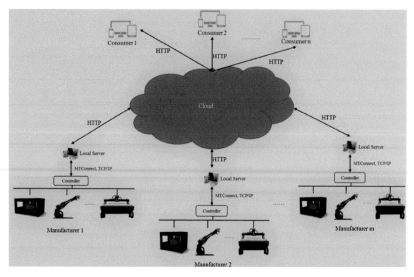

Fig 10.9: The conceptual model of CPMC [38].

4. AM – A Cyber-Physical System (CPS) during Covid-19 Pandemic

It has been widely observed that during the COVID-19 emergency, there was a massive disruption in the supply chain leading to a shortage of materials, workforce, and other resources. This disruption has led to the need to augment manufacturers, suppliers, and customers at a single platform where the needs, demands, and availability of the resources can be mapped globally to opt for suitable options or processes. Implementation of CPS in additive manufacturing leads to decentralization of manufacturing, i.e., the freedom to manufacture what one wants, where one wants,and when one wants. From the literature review, it has been evident that there arose various scenarios in additive manufacturing during COVID-19 pandemic where there was a need to import or supply design files, to virtually access 3D printers, or robust interaction between cyber and physical processes. To thoroughly analyze the functioning, the interdependency of the two components: physical process and cyber components, it is necessary to study each scenario separately. Since it is a complex structure with numerous individuals involved at different stages, it becomes necessary to establish the boundary of responsibility for product safety and authenticity. Therefore, an effort has been made to identify the role and responsibility of different actors. Different models based on the implementation of AM in various scenarios have been discussed in the following section. Based on these analyses and the current global necessity, a new model's basic idea has been presented.

4.1 Supply Chain Models

4.1.1 Model 1

Considering additive manufacturing during the COVID-19 situation, there were multiple cases where raw materials (ABS (Acrylonitrile Butadiene Styrene), PLA,

Polyethylene Terephthalate Glycol (PET-G)) for printing various medical entities like masks, face shields, PPE kit, parts of ventilators, etc. were to be supplied to the manufacturer who owns the 3D printer. Design files were either purchased or imported from designers or various free repositories like NIH 3D Print Exchange [39], Thingiverse [40], GrabCAD [41], MyMiniFactory [42], and others.

Design files are to be supplied with proper instruction such as surface finish, dimensional tolerances, etc. This scenario is discussed in Fig. 10.10, where station 2 is the manufacturing unit. Raw materials are procured from a manufacturer at different stations involving physical chain logistics. Design files are imported from designers or free online repositories (considered station 3) following a cyber or virtual supply chain. In this case, responsibility for the quality of the product lies in the manufacturer's hand solely. Interaction of the virtual supply chain with the physical supply chain makes this cyber-embedded AM a cyber-physical system.

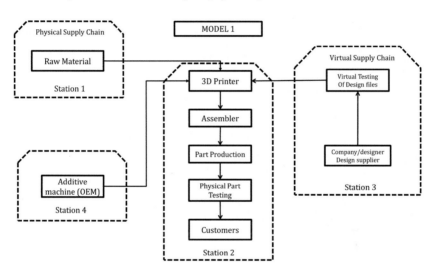

Figure 10.10: Model 1.

4.1.2 Model 2

There were several cases where due to the shortage of machines, raw materials, or other resources, several companies/individuals outsourced necessary parts. Skilled CAD designers, design analysts, and 3D printing professionals may develop CAD models from scratch or download them from online repositories. The design was supplied through a virtual or cyber supply chain. Parts were printed as per the 3D printing instruction and design provided by the parent company.

In this case, the product's quality lies both on the parent company and the 3D printing contractor. If the product does not perform its intended function, the 3D printing instructions will be investigated for accuracy, and the processes of the 3D printing contractor that printed the part will be investigated to check if the instructions to print the product were followed correctly. After printing, testing and validating the product, it is shipped back to the parent company. It is then assembled, checked, and following the physical supply chain, and it reaches the customers. This model, in

Fig. 10.11, where station 2 is the central manufacturing unit, and the printing services are outsourced to station 1. This model differs from model 1 based on the main product. In this model, virtual location of design suppliers can be considered primary IPs, and due to the unavailability of printing resources or other constraints, the printing of part is outsourced. For example, various universities and schools outsourced their design files to be printed to other companies where resources were available during COVID-19. There were various organizations, start-ups, etc., that provided 3D printing services. For example, 3D Crowd UK [18] established a network where one could get, volunteer, or supply 3D printing services. This model comprises intricate interlacing of cyber as well as physical components making it a cyber-physical system.

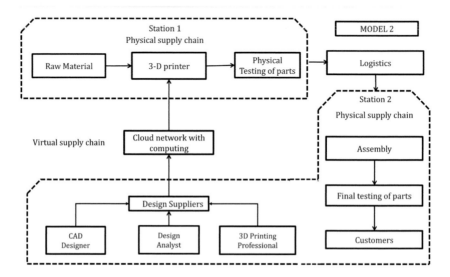

Figure 10.11: Model 2.

4.1.3 Model 3

This model deals with the scenarios where due to the sudden disruption of the supply chain, lack of manpower, or to follow social distancing norms, it was necessary for a trained professional to remotely access and monitor a 3-D printer. Although this model is still in its infancy, however advent in technologies like the IIoT (industrial internet of things) will lead to a firm and secure connection which will rapidly increase usage of this model. The most incredible benefit of IIoT is that it dramatically improve operating efficiency. In IIoT technology, sensors and actuators are attached to physical devices that can be monitored and operated remotely. This model, as described in Fig. 10.12, includes an operator at a different station that remotely accesses the 3D printer available at a different station. One such example of this scenario concerning additive manufacturing is using the KUKA robot for manufacturing 3D parts [43]. During Covid, the KUKA robot has been used in various universities and industries by programming it as a 3D printer. The operator can remotely access the KUKA robot using IoT and access its services, thus maintaining social distancing with the physical system and human resources.

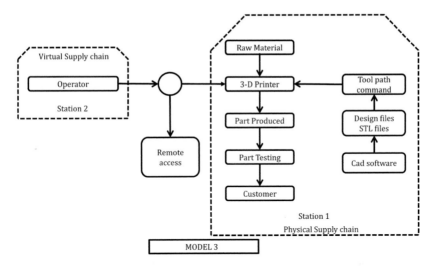

Figure 10.12: Model 3.

4.1.4 Proposed Model

It has been well established that to withstand COVID-19 or any such medical emergency arriving in the future, the manufacturing domain and supply chain need diversification and decentralization. After examining the existing models and the requirements of the manufacturing system in such times, an idea of a new model has been proposed in this section. This model is in its basic form and requires further study and analysis. The model is an integration of CPS-based AM with cloud manufacturing and thereby forming a robust, decentralized system where services and products can be customized according to the needs and demands of customers or situations. It aims at bringing manufacturing facilities, manufacturing software, customers, suppliers, manufacturers, design suppliers all under a common shared secure platform so that on-demand, on-site, sustainable production with real-time data sharing and monitoring can take place. The proposed model is described schematically in Fig. 10.13. A feedback loop is established, which gathers information from the existing customers about the product, its authenticity, and its performance which helps in determining the performance of the products. Based on this data, the process can be iterated effectively. The various stations have been defined which works independently as well as can be interconnected according to the need. Station 1 deals with customer's demand and supply along with the monitoring logistics involved during the entire process via the indent management system. Station 2 supplies customizable CAD models, design files according to consumer's demands. Station 3 serves as a 3D printer rental provider. Station 4 supplies printing services like slicing software. An operator is connected to terminal 6, where a local, as well as a remote operator, can monitor the entire process.

One such example of cloud-based design collaboration and coordination is witnessed in the project of reconstruction of the Afsluitdijk. This 32-kilometer dam protects a large portion of the Netherlands from the Wadden Sea and regulates the water level in Lake IJsselmeer, Holland's biggest lake. This scheme's sheer scale means that over 500 architects, civil engineers, and contractors are all collaborating throughout the design and pre-construction phases from different geographic locations. This

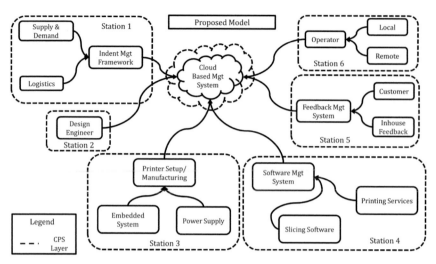

Figure 10.13: Proposed model.

requires a common cloud-based online platform for designers, planners, contractors to access, share, store, amend and work on designs and models based on real-time data and the latest information. For this purpose, Autodesk's BIM 360 Model Coordination platform was used. This cloud-based platform connects AEC teams, helping them to execute on design intent and deliver high-quality constructible models on a single platform [44]. This helps the team to coordinate, run automated clash detection, extract real-time data for design coordination, ensuring simultaneous working for all departments and thereby speeding up the complete process.

The proposed model (Fig. 10.13) follows a similar concept as the example stated above, i.e., every segment starting from customers, designers, manufacturer, supplier, and logistics are intricately connected. This ensures every member and segment involved is updated simultaneously with the latest information or the iteration proposed. If there is any feedback or query raised by any of the members, then actions can be incorporated immediately, leading to stage-wise iteration.

Being a cyber-physical system, each segment is vulnerable to different attacks. Therefore, security in this model needs to be incorporated individually in every segment. According to the vulnerabilities of each segment, suitable security layers can be established within the organization itself or can be outsourced.

5. Current Risks, Threats, and Security Methods

AM being a CPS (cyber-physical system), has an intricate interlacing of cyber and physical components. With the increased interactions between cyber and physical components in the AM system, susceptibility to cyber-attacks, threats, intellectual property thefts, data exfiltration, counterfeit production increases. Due to the constant connection between the physical parts produced and cyber components, attacks and threats in the cyber components directly affect the quality, authenticity of the part printed. And when this product is used in medical emergencies like COVID-19, where the quality and legitimacy of the product unswervingly affect human lives, it becomes indispensable to have a firmly monitored, secure, reliable AM system. Henceforth, it becomes a necessity to identify potential attacks and threats, manage and monitor the vulnerability of the system. In this section, we identify current threats and attacks in the virtual as well as physical components in the existing supply chain models. Attacks on the entire AM process are hierarchically shown in Fig. 10.14.

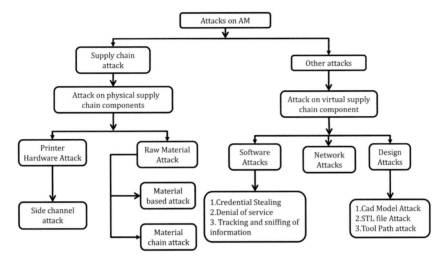

Figure 10.14: Attacks on AM.

5.1 Supply Chain Attacks

It includes attacks on physical and virtual components of the supply chain as well as intermediate cyber-to-physical and cyber-to-cyber- attacks on the logistics of the supply chain. To analyze the security aspects and form a robust, safe automated AM process, it is required to scrutinize vulnerabilities in every stage of the supply chain. Since the security and authenticity of the physical products (raw material, printed parts, etc.) are co-dependent on virtual components (design files, network, software, etc.), it is crucial to study cyber-threats and risks of existing models as well. Potential attacks on each of the above-mentioned models are discussed in this section. Models along with components prone to different attacks are shown in Figs 10.15, 10.16, and 10.17.

5.1.1 Attacks on Physical Supply Chain

(a) **Printer attacks:** One of the cyber-attacks on the AM system is in the physical-cyber domain known as side-channel attacks. The consequences of this attack includes Intellectual Property (IP) theft and leakage of confidential trade data. Though IP theft is common in the cyber-to-cyber domain but could also be done via information obtained from the physical domain. For example, by extracting information from side channels of the physical domain like power supply, acoustics, electromagnetic emissions, etc., secret keys can be stolen from the systems performing cryptographic computations and connected to these channels [45]. One such example is the extraction of information from exploiting sounds emitted during Fused Deposition-based 3D printing. An attacker may access the

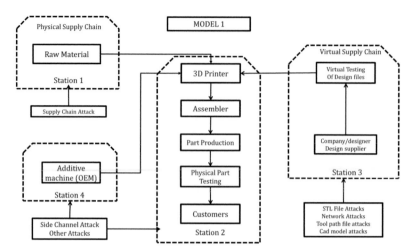

Figure 10.15: Attacks on model 1.

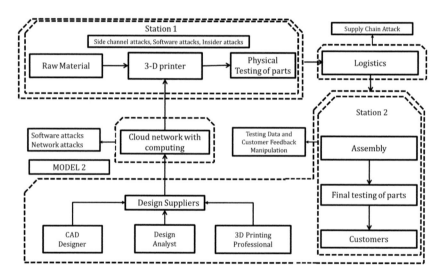

Figure 10.16: Attacks on model 2.

information of cyber domain data (G-codes) from the physical domain (sound from the 3D printer)as described further in Fig. 10.18 [46].

(b) **Raw material attacks:** The quality of raw materials can be compromised either by attacking the physical supply chain or by directly attacking the material itself. By attacking the logistics of the supply chain time of arrival of the product can be delayed, thereby delaying the entire process. Therefore, various monitoring systems such as indent management systems in e-procurement of material should be used, where material could be monitored at various stages starting right from the ordering till its arrival. Additionally, the quality of material can also be hindered by exploiting the feedstock settings, manipulating the feed material, or other material storing parameters like temperature, humidity, etc.

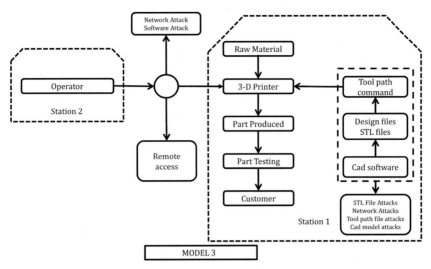

Figure 10.17: Attacks on model 3.

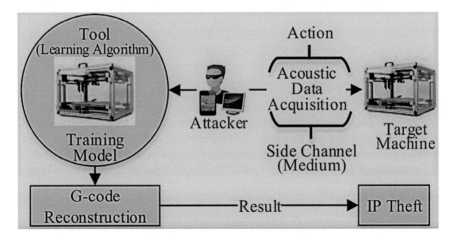

Figure 10.18: Acoustic side-channel attack model [46].

5.1.2 Attacks on Virtual Supply Chain

5.1.2.1 Design Attacks

(a) **Attacks on the CAD model:** The building of the CAD model is the first step in the designing process of the AM supply chain. It contains all the necessary information about the geometric data of the part to be printed. Intentions behind these attacks include stealing or corrupting the file. Any undetected damage to the CAD model transmits to .STL/.AMF file then further to tool command file, thereby propagating through entire supply chain leading to the printing of defected part/product. Therefore, to increase odds in detecting attacks, it is suggested to use revision management in PLM software [47]. These files serve as valuable IPs for many of the companies/suppliers. Therefore, distortion or loss of these files leads to huge loss and can lead to unauthorized reverse engineered production of the stolen part. For example, ESET's research showed that a worm ACAD/Medre.A was designed to steal and corrupt AutoCAD drawings [48].

(b) **Attacks on the STL/AMF files:** After the completion of the CAD model, it is then converted into an STL/AMF file. These are considered a de facto standard for almost every AM process. STL file contains only geometric details of the CAD model in the form of triangular facets. Each facet comprises three vertices along with an outward normal. Compared to the CAD model, it contains less information which makes it less prone to reverse engineering. However, these can be easily manipulated due to their lesser complexity. Further, since a single STL file can be used in different printers, it becomes more vulnerable to attacks and has severe implications on all the products formed using a defective STL file. Sturm et al. [47] studied the various potential attacks on STL files and their further implications. Void creation, scaling disruption, indents/protrusions creation, corruption/illegal encryption are significant threats to an STL file. These attacks can have severe repercussions on the part to be manufactured. Therefore, proper security measures are required.

(c) **Attacks on toolpath files:** STL files contain the details of the model, which is converted further into layers. Further, the toolpath is created from these layers. The toolpath file contains the instructions for the controllers to move nozzles, power, coordinate axes, extrusion rate, feed input, etc. An attack on these files includes alteration of tool path [49], exploitation in printing location, pattern, and timing leading to excess material at some position and scarcity of material at other, damage to tool and machine.

5.1.2.2 Software Attacks

Software threats or attacks can be classified into two categories: Malicious and Non-malicious. Malicious attacks are intentional and are designed to steal information, data, passwords, corrupt files, etc. These are malicious software(malware) and can attack the system in the form of computer viruses, Trojans, worms. Some of this malware are even designed to provide remote access to the attacker. For example, a Trojan horse: In the case of AM a CPS, this can lead to unauthorized access of machines, digital files, IPs to an attacker, denial of service leading to severe implications for the quality as well as the authenticity of the final physical product. Therefore, proper encryption, information hiding, and security are required.

5.2   Security Solutions

In this section, various security solutions have been discussed for the CPS implemented additive manufacturing. These solutions could help in preventing existing threats and risks already discussed in the previous section. In addition to traditional system integrity, authenticity and confidentiality are equally important. When a part comes out of additive manufacture, it must be the exact desired part, without substitution or tampering. Besides, the associated files must be vigorously protected from disclosure.

5.2.1 Trusted Protection Module (TPM)

Trusted Protection Module (TPM) is a chip-based microcontroller that securely stores encryption keys, certificates, passwords, and other artifacts. It functions on the authentication and attestation/encryption process. When an additive manufacturing system is fastened with TPM, an encryption key pair is provided where the private key never leaves the equipment. When the part file is attested under the relating public key, it must be unattested on this particular printer, and just if this present printer's product has not been undermined. A distant attacker cannot acquire a duplicate of the decoding private key, and in this way, cannot decrypt the required additive file. Essentially, a section document can be endorsed by a private key in the TPM, and when approved by the relating public key, the authenticity is ensured by the system's hardware [50].

5.2.2 Cyclic Redundancy Error

CRC or Cyclic Redundancy Check is a method of detecting accidental changes/errors in the .STL file. CRC uses Generator Polynomial, which is available on both sender and receiver sides. Encrypted data or a key is generated from Generator Polynomial. This helps in the continuous checking of the .STL file against file manipulation and duplication. The modulo-2 binary division is used to divide binary data by the key and store the remainder of the division. Again on the receiver end same algorithm is performed, and if the remainder is zero, then it is confirmed that the file received is complete and error-free.

5.2.3 Checksum

The checksum is an error detection technique that can be used in AM virtual supply chain to identify whether an error has occurred or not in the .STL or CAD file that has been transmitted via the network. It does not take into account the number of error bits and the type of error. This is a block code method where a checksum is created based on the data values in the data blocks to be transmitted using some algorithm and appended to the data. When the receiver gets this data, a new checksum is calculated and compared with the existing checksum. A non-match indicates an error.

5.2.4 Hashing Algorithm

Hashing is a procedure regularly utilized in security to guarantee the legitimacy of a file. The file is run into the hashing function, which produces a line of the character called a hash. The hash is then posted alongside the record. At the point when a client downloads a file, they can run it through the equivalent hashing capacity and contrast the next hash and the posted hash. On the off chance that the two hashes match, the file can be thought to be indistinguishable from the first. What makes hashes viable is their capacity to change over a considerable document into an exact string that can be effortlessly shared. Any slight change in the record creates an enormous change in the hash. The basic adding of a solitary character to a book document will change the hash that is produced. At the elementary level, hashes can be (and are) utilized to guarantee that the .STL record received has not been altered. While this builds security, it adds some extra work to the interaction. Moreover, a record might be assaulted after it has been received and hashed or before it was hashed regardless. This issue could be tended to a limited extent by including the hash work at the hour of document creation, inside the CAD programming itself, and producing a hash work at the last advance all the while, where the .STL record is stacked into the printer programming to be changed over to a tool path [47, 51].

5.2.5 Quick Response Code

The virtual supply chain in AM poses various challenges when it comes to security and authenticity of the part produced. Quick response (QR) code presents diverse opportunities to encrypt files, gain control and protect unauthorized production of parts. Chen et al. [52] presented the possibility of exploiting the layer-by-layer process of AM for inserting an identification code inside the 3D printed part. This could be designed without negotiating mechanical properties. Further, to obfuscate code, it could be segmented into innumerous fractions, each at a different location and position. This leads to a single correct viewing orientation. However, the size of these embedded codes can be reduced. As machine learning emerges, a new possibility of using microstructure's natural features as product authentication can be explored [53].

5.3 Emerging Security Solutions

5.3.1 Digital Twinning

Digital twins are virtual representations or digital replicas of a manufacturing system or supply chain or any service containing all necessary conditions and properties of the system. In additive manufacturing, the digital twin can be used to not only monitor the process but also aids in determining potential cyber-attacks. Digital twinning of AM is still in its infancy, owning to hurdles like the requirement of the vast amount of data to properly train the model to obtain accurate results. Data can be collected from experiments, sensors, numerical simulation, etc. Collection and classification of big data require the implementation of cloud computation with the cyber-physical system (CPS) in AM. To date, AM lacks in proper convergence of virtual and physical space leading to fragmented, stale, improper data collection. Mandolla et al. [54] proposed a digital twin for additive manufacturing in the aircraft industry through the exploitation of Blockchain solutions (shown in Fig. 10.19).

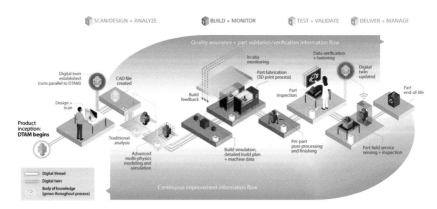

Figure 10.19: The digital thread for AM [48].

6. Conclusion

This study provides a detailed analysis of AM as a CPS and its implementation in mitigating the demand-supply gap that arose due to massive disruption in the global supply chain by the COVID-19 pandemic. Supply chain models currently used were discussed, and also a basic idea of a new model was presented. Risk and cyber threats were analyzed on these models, and security solutions to existing problems were provided. It has been observed that the ability of AM to achieve a high level of customization according to needs, decentralized manufacturing and its agile supply chain made it a vital manufacturing technique. Post covid, it is expected to have a shorter and more fragmented supply chain. This can be achieved with the further digitalization of AM process and better integration of its cyber and physical components. These changes will result in different manufacturing processes with more partnerships in an open AM ecosystem and cloud-integrated AM. However, with the increase in the cyber-physical system, concerns about the security and authenticity of products arise. Proper safety measures and protocols should be defined against cyber threats and attacks.

References

1. Zhu, N., D. Zhang, W. Wang, X. Li, B. Yang, J. Song, X. Zhao and W. Tan. A novel coronavirus from patients with pneumonia in China, 2019. New England Journal of Medicine (2020).
2. World Health Organization WHO Director-General's opening remarks at the media briefing on COVID-19, 11 March 2020 (2020): https://www.who.int/dg/speeches/detail/who-director-general-s-opening-remarks-at-the-media-briefing-on-covid-19-11-march-2020
3. Wesemann, C., S. Pieralli, T. Fretwurst, J. Nold, K. Nelson, R. Schmelzeisen, E. Hellwig and B.C. Spies. 3-D printed protective equipment during COVID-19 pandemic. Materials, 13(8): (2020): 1997.
4. Gibson, I., D. Rosen, B. Stucker and M. Khorasani. Additive Manufacturing Technologies. Vol. 17, p. 195. New York: Springer, (2014).
5. Stratasys, Fused deposition modelling. http://www.stratasys.com [accessed on 22.03.2021]
6. Mobaraki, M., M. Ghaffari, A. Yazdanpanah, Y. Luo and D.K. Mills. Bioinks and bioprinting: A focused review. Bioprinting, 18 (2020): e00080.
7. Wang, X., M. Jiang, Z. Zhou, J. Gou and D. Hui. 3D printing of polymer matrix composites: A review and prospective. Composites Part B: Engineering, 110 (2017): 442–458.
8. O'Connor, H.J., A.N. Dickson and D.P. Dowling. Evaluation of the mechanical performance of polymer parts fabricated using a production scale multi jet fusion printing process. Additive Manufacturing, 22 (2018): 381–387.
9. Cai, C., W.S. Tey, J. Chen, W. Zhu, X. Liu, T. Liu, L. Zhao and K. Zhou. Comparative study on 3D printing of polyamide 12 by selective laser sintering and multi jet fusion. Journal of Materials Processing Technology, 288 (2021): 116882.
10. Tareq, M.S., T. Rahman, M. Hossain and P. Dorrington. Additive manufacturing and the COVID-19 challenges: An in-depth study. Journal of Manufacturing Systems, (2021).
11. Ishack, S. and S.R. Lipner. Applications of 3D printing technology to address COVID-19-related supply shortages. The American Journal of Medicine, 133(7) (2020): 771–773.

12. Czech Technical University. CIIRC CTU Develops Own Prototype of CIIRC RP95 Respirator/Half Mask. https://www.ciirc.cvut.cz/covid/ [accessed 21.03.2021].
13. Maker Mask. https://www.makermask.com/ [accessed 22.03.2021].
14. Glowforge.Ear savers: https://meet.glowforge.com/earsavers/ [accessed 19.03.2021].
15. Longhitano, G.A., G.B. Nunes, G. Candido and J.V.L. da Silva. The role of 3D printing during COVID-19 pandemic: A review. Progress in Additive Manufacturing, (2020): 1–19.
16. Bellus3d:Mask-fitter: https://www.bellus3d.com/solutions/mask-fitter/ [accessed 24.03.2021].
17. Prusa 3D. 3D printed face shields for medics and professionals: https://www.prusa3d.com/covid19/ [accessed 18.03.2021].
18. 3D Crowd UK. https://www.3dcrowd.org.uk/ [accessed 16.03.2021].
19. Maracaja, L., D. Blitz, D.L. Maracaja and C.A. Walker. How 3D printing can prevent spread of COVID-19 among healthcare professionals during times of critical shortage of protective personal equipment. Journal of Cardiothoracic and Vascular Anesthesia, 34(10) (2020): 2847–2849.
20. BCN3D Technology. 3D printing at BCN3D to change the face of the global Covid-19 pandemic. https://www.bcn3d.com/here-to-help-3d-printing-to-change-the-covid-19-pandemic/ [accessed 16.03.2021].
21. Stratasys. Stratasys Responds to COVID-19 with 3D Printed Face Shields & Testing Swabs. https://www.stratasys.com/covid-19 [accessed 22.03.2021].
22. Evolusi 3D. EVOLUSI 3D Fight COVID-19: https://www.evolusi3d.com/evolusi-3d-fight-covid-19.html/ [accessed 17.03.2021].
23. Nexa 3D. 3D Printing Leader Nexa3D Launches Service to Deliver NexaShield PPE to Frontline Healthcare and Other Mission Critical Workers. https://nexa3d.com/3d-printing-leader-nexa3d-launches-service-to-deliver-nexashield-ppe-to-frontline-healthcare-and-other-mission-critical-workers/ [accessed 09.03.2021].
24. Coronavirus (COVID-19) and Medical Devices. https://www.fda.gov/medical-devices/emergency-situations-medical-devices/coronavirus-covid-19-and-medical-devices [accessed 03.03.2021].
25. Centers for Disease Control and Prevention (CDC). Information for Laboratories about Coronavirus (COVID-19). Interim Guidelines for Clinical Specimens for COVID-19 | CDC [accessed 03.03.2021].
26. Cox, J.L. and S.A. Koepsell. 3D-printing to address COVID-19 testing supply shortages, Laboratory Medicine, 51(4) (July 2020): e45–e46, https://doi.org/10.1093/labmed/lmaa031.
27. Forecast 3D now producing nasopharyngeal swabs for COVID-19 test kits. https://www.gknpm.com/en/news-and-media/news-releases/2020/forecast-3d-now-producing-nasopharyngeal-swabs-for-covid-19-test-kits/ [accessed 21.03.2021].
28. Formlabs: 3D printed test swabs for COVID-19. https://formlabs.com/covid-19-response/covid-test-swabs/ [accessed 16.03.2021].
29. Arnold, F.W., G. Grant, P.F. Bressoud, S.P. Furmanek, D. Chung, N. Sbaih, D. Karmali, M. Cahill and G. Pantalos. A comparison efficacy study of commercial nasopharyngeal swabs versus a novel 3D printed swab for the detection of SARS-CoV-2. The University of Louisville Journal of Respiratory Infections, 4(1) (2020): 41.

30. Isinnova. Easy-Covid19 ENG. https://www.isinnova.it/easy-covid19-eng/ [accessed 17.03.2021].
31. COVID-19 Emergency: The value of collaboration: COVID-19, the value of collaboration and sharing (roboze.com) [accessed 19.03.2021].
32. Ferrari Corporate. Ferrari continues its efforts to fight the Covid-19 pandemic. https://corporate.ferrari.com/en/ferrari-continues-its-efforts-fight-covid-19-pandemic [accessed 21.03.2021].
33. Materialise. 3D-Printed Non-Invasive PEEP Masks Aim to Alleviate Ventilator Shortage. https://www.materialise.com/en/node/7056 [accessed 14.03.2021].
34. Rajkumar R., I. Lee, L. Sha and J. Stankovic. Cyber-physical systems: The next computing revolution. Proceedings of the Design Automation Conference 2010, Anheim, CA, US, (2011): 731–736.
35. Monostori, L. Cyber-physical production systems: Roots, expectations and R&D challenges. Procedia Cirp, 17 (2014): 9–13.
36. Lee, J., B. Bagheri and H.A. Kao. A cyber-physical systems architecture for industry 4.0-based manufacturing systems. Manufacturing Letters, 3 (2015): 18–23.
37. Tao, F., L. Zhang, V.C. Venkatesh, Y. Luo and Y. Cheng. Cloud manufacturing: A computing and service-oriented manufacturing model. Proceedings of the Institution of Mechanical Engineers, Part B: Journal of Engineering Manufacture, 225(10) (2011): 1969–1976.
38. Liu, X.F., M.R. Shahriar, S.N. Al Sunny, M.C. Leu and L. Hu. Cyber-physical manufacturing cloud: Architecture, virtualization, communication, and testbed. Journal of Manufacturing Systems, 43 (2017): 352–364.
39. COVID-19 Response | NIH 3D Print Exchange. https://3dprint.nih.gov/collections/covid-19-response (2020) [accessed 22.03.2021].
40. Thingiverse—Digital Designs for Physical Objects. https://www.thingiverse.com/(2020) [accessed 23.03.2021].
41. GrabCAD Community Library. https://grabcad.com/library. (2020) [accessed 23.03.2021].
42. MyMiniFactory|100,000+ 3D Print Files & Models (2020) Guaranteed. https://www.myminifactory.com/ [accessed 19.03.2021].
43. KUKA Robots Print Protective Equipment in Northern Italy. https://ifr.org/case-studies/industrial-robots/with-3d-printing-against-the-coronavirus [accessed 09.03.2021].
44. Weatherproof Infrastructure: Reinforcing the Largest Dike in the Netherlands with BIM. https://construction.autodesk.com/customers/afsluitdijk-case-study/ [accessed 08.03.2021].
45. Standaert, F.X., T.G. Malkin and M. Yung. A unified framework for the analysis of side-channel key recovery attacks. *In:* Annual International Conference on the Theory and Applications of Cryptographic Techniques, pp. 443–461. Springer, Berlin, Heidelberg, (2009).
46. Al Faruque, M.A., S.R. Chhetri, A. Canedo and J. Wan. Acoustic side-channel attacks on additive manufacturing systems. *In:* 2016 ACM/IEEE 7th International Conference on Cyber-Physical Systems (ICCPS) IEEE, (April 2016): 1–10.
47. Sturm, L.D., C.B. Williams, J.A. Camelio, J. White and R. Parker. Cyber-physical vulnerabilities in additive manufacturing systems: A case study attack

on the STL file with human subjects. Journal of Manufacturing Systems, 44, (2017): 154–164.

48. Deloitte. https://www2.deloitte.com/xe/en/insights/focus/3d-opportunity/3d-printing-digital-thread-in-manufacturing.html [accessed 08.03.2021].

49. Zeltmann, S.E., N. Gupta, N.G. Tsoutsos, M. Maniatakos, J. Rajendran and R. Karri. Manufacturing and security challenges in 3D printing. Jom, 68(7) (2016): 1872–1881.

50. Safford, D.R. and M. Wiseman. Hardware rooted trust for additive manufacturing. IEEE Access, 7 (2019): 79211–79215.

51. Trouton, S., M. Vitale and J. Killmeyer. 3D opportunity for blockchain: Additive manufacturing links the digital thread, (2016).

52. Chen, F., Y. Luo, N.G. Tsoutsos, M. Maniatakos, K. Shahin and N. Gupta. Embedding tracking codes in additive manufactured parts for product authentication. Advanced Engineering Materials, 21(4) (2019): 1800495.

53. Gupta, N., A. Tiwari, S.T. Bukkapatnam and R. Karri. Additive manufacturing cyber-physical system: Supply chain cyber security and risks. IEEE Access, 8 (2020): 47322–47333.

54. Mandolla, C., A.M. Petruzzelli, G. Percoco and A. Urbinati. Building a digital twin for additive manufacturing through the exploitation of blockchain: A case analysis of the aircraft industry. Computers in Industry, 109 (2019): 134–152.

Part IV
Frameworks and Perspectives

Intelligent Cyber-Physical Production System Framework for Industry 4.0 Realization

Jitin Malhotra and Sunil Jha*

1. Introduction

The manufacturing industry is a significant contributor to the economy of any country, and without this sector, the overall development of a country is in a challenging state. The challenging times of the COVID-19 pandemic made us realize the importance of this industry and there arose the need of making manufacturing systems resilient enough to tackle such situations. The outbreak which presumably started from Wuhan, China in 2019 spread around the globe at an exponential rate and potentially derailed the world economy. In fact, considering just the situation of G7 countries which are the worst affected countries, they contribute 65% of world manufacturing, 60% of GDP and 41% of manufacturing exports. The manufacturing sector is likely to get a triple-hit affect due to supply disruptions, supply chain contagions, and demand disruptions during this difficult situation [1].

As the correct estimations of full effects of the COVID-19 pandemic's effects cannot be made, assurance of long-term operations of factories has taken a critical toll because of it. Further current needs coincide with the digitalization needs i.e., demand of fully customized and personalized products [2, 3], manufactured products with sophisticated designs [4], more service-accustomed manufacturing [5, 6], energy needs [7], and a demand of higher quality products with minimum costs [8, 9], to mention a few. As rightly depicted by Tao et al. in the pre pandemic situations, the trend is shifting towards something termed as **TQCSEFK** (faster **T**ime-to-market, maintaining highest **Q**uality, with the lowest **C**ost, providing best **S**ervice to customers, retaining **E**nvironment cleaner, providing greater **F**lexibility, and highest **K**nowledge), and is very well applicable in the situations like the pandemic as well [10].

Considering the challenges posed above and with advancements in information and communication technologies (ICT), a term Cyber-Physical Systems (CPS) was

---

*Corresponding author: suniljha@mech.iitd.ac.in

Nomenclature

CPS	Cyber-Physical Systems
CPPS	Cyber-Physical Production Systems
CNC	Computer Numerically Controlled
AI	Artificial Intelligence
IoT	Internet of Things
IIOT	Industrial Internet of Things
AMMS	Advanced Micromachining System
AGV	Automated Guided Vehicle
IPC	Industrial PC
CAD	Computer-Aided Design
AWS	Amazon Web Services
ML	Machine Learning
EDM	Electric Discharge Machining
RAMI	Reference Architectural Model Industries
IIRA	Industrial Internet Reference Architecture
SIRI	Smart Industry Readiness Index
AR	Augmented Reality
VR	Virtual Reality
MR	Mixed Reality
CCD	Charged Coupled Device
RPi	Raspberry Pi
SaaS	Software as a Service
PdM	Predictive Maintenance

introduced by the National Science Foundation in the US in 2006, which states the merger of cyber parts to physical world entities, stating that it appears to be a solution [11]. In this highly competitive and dynamic market, manufacturing companies want to secure their positions and further improve their competitiveness. Thus, they are working towards developing and integrating complex production networks having a more flexible and resilient nature [12, 13]. Also, when these highly data-intensive, automated cyber-physical systems are added to production facilities, it makes them smarter, and a special term is created for such systems called Cyber-Physical Production Systems (CPPS) [14, 15, 16]. This chapter focuses on such systems which have the capability to tackle the challenges posed by pandemic like situations.

Thinking about CPPS entities, there is a requirement of standards, architectures/ frameworks for transitioning the current facilities to a more adaptable and smarter systems which are Industry 4.0 compliant. Few researchers in academia have presented some architectures like Lee et al. [17] proposed a unified 5C level architecture for CPS; Zhang et al. [18] presented an add-on CPS for existing machining centres; Liu and Xu [19] proposed architecture for cyber-physical machine tool centred CPPS. Even some consortiums are established worldwide for the promotion of fourth industrial revolution in pre-pandemic times which if realized in current circumstances will definitely give a boost to the manufacturing sector [20–23].

In addition to core CPPS its related technologies like big-data [24], Industrial Internet of Things (IIOT) [25], cloud computing [26], etc. can also play a role in transitioning to a smart factory environment. After carefully analyzing the literature, a key finding was that case-based architectures have been proposed by many researchers previously, but they lack a detailed physical implementation. Further, the requirements of Industry 4.0 i.e., manufacturing systems to be more flexible, reliable, scalable, adaptable, autonomous, with the ability to shorten manufacturing time and costs and fulfil heterogenous needs of customers 24×7 are very well required in COVID-19 like situations also. These systems should be interlinked, interconnected, have the ability to interact, and integrated from top to bottom of the manufacturing pyramid. So, a framework called Intelligent Cyber-Physical Production System (i-CPPS) is proposed in the current chapter, to fulfil the needs of the manufacturing sector in COVID-19 situations and can be applied on both new and legacy production systems.

The main contributions of this research are:

a. Identifying and listing technical requirements for a CPPS framework, which mostly stands relevant in COVID-19 situations.
b. Proposing an Intelligent Cyber-Physical Production System (i-CPPS) framework, connecting all elements of a manufacturing enterprise from the smallest manufacturing entity to the cloud platform.
c. Step by step implementation of i-CPPS framework covering all the building blocks with a detailed prototype usecase implementation flow in a smart factory scenario.
d. Three brief application areas in times of COVID-19 situation where i-CPPS framework can come in handy during the realization phase.

The rest of the chapter is organized as follows:

Section 2 puts forward research questions related to a smart factory considering the currently available literature on CPPS architectures and related terms with a special emphasis on implementations done till now. This section further lists the requirements of a CPPS framework which needs to be considered in defining and implementing any CPS framework for manufacturing.

Section 3 introduces a four-level Intelligent Cyber-Physical Production System (i-CPPS) framework. It elaborates the architectural layout and various technological functions available at each level. Detailed steps for implementing i-CPPS framework in a factory environment are given.

Section 4 provides a prototype use case implementation flow in a smart factory environment starting from a customer query to final product delivery based on i-CPPS framework. This section also presents 3 brief application areas in COVID-19 pandemic situation which can be realized using proposed framework.

Section 5 concludes the work with a discussion on how the requirements listed in Section 2 are covered in proposed the i-CPPS framework and provide future directions on how to promote an i-CPPS framework and inspire the research community and industry personnel to implement it with ease.

2. Literature Review

The current section presents a literature review which is available in the domain of CPS and its related terms with a focus on manufacturing. Authors have tried to create a comprehensive conceptual view of what needs to be called a smart production facility and tried looking for some concrete industrial implementations, but with no luck. Some research questions are formulated during the creation of this holistic view of a smart production facility,and it's assumed by answering these questions, a comprehensive list of requirements for a CPPS framework can be formulated. The authors do not claim the requirement list to be exhaustive, but they are a very good starting point for what to expect from an Industry 4.0 compliant facility and points to a prominent direction for achieving the goals of smart manufacturing. Research Questions (RQ) are listed as follows:

RQ 1:   What are Cyber-Physical Systems?
RQ 2:   What are Cyber-Physical Production Systems?
RQ 3:   What are the key features of Cyber-Physical Production Systems?
RQ 4:   On what parameters, do the production facilities need to be assessed so as to be called smart production systems?
RQ 5:   What about the legacy production facilities, will they be also supportable under these smart production systems?
RQ 6:   What industry standards are available for a smart factory?
RQ 7:   How will the data generated inside the factories be utilized in the creation of smart factories?
RQ 8:   What cyber-security measures need to be taken inside a smart production facility?
RQ 9:   What are the steps to create a smart production facility?
RQ 10: How Cyber-Physical Production Systems can tackle COVID-19 pandemic like situations?

The questions above are answered by considering the CPS based works available in literature in the manufacturing sector. This exercise also helps in listing out requisite requirements of a Cyber-Physical Production System framework which can guide in the creation of new production facilities or upgrading the legacy production facilities. A complete CPPS framework is further proposed by authors in Section 3 considering the requirements (**R1, R2, R3** . . . etc.) mentioned in the current section with a detailed description of prototype implementation flow of this framework and brief applications in Section 4. So, let us start from question 1:

RQ 1: What are Cyber-Physical Systems?

CPS origin is linked to embedded systems [27], and researchers define them as a conglomeration of computing entities to physical systems, to perform specified tasks. In-fact these embedded devices are tightly integrated with physical entities to embed intelligence to them. These low-power devices have the capabilities to sense, analyze, control, and actuate the physical entities in real-time.

The CPS are next generation engineered systems which have capabilities ranging from self-awareness, self-prediction, self-comparison, self-organization, and self-maintenance [28]. CPS has in its applications in domains like manufacturing [11, 15–22, 29], transportation [30–33], healthcare [33–36], robotics [37–39], agriculture [40–43], energy [44–47], to name a few.

RQ 2: What are Cyber-Physical Production Systems?

The Cyber-Physical Production Systems (CPPS) are defined as a collection of smart, autonomous,and co-operative entities and systems that are networked across all levels of production, i.e., starting from individual machines and going up to cover whole factories with a deep integration to various business-related functions [16]. For creating such smart systems, there is a need of a framework which can guide the industry personnel to create new manufacturing facilities or upgrade the existing one into an Industry 4.0 compliant facility.

The extent of CPPS is across the full production facility, but such smartness cannot be achieved without knowing what to achieve from a smart production facility. So, there is a need to define some objectives, like a goal to optimize the energy consumption in the production facility or to trigger a warning by analyzing the high vibrations in machine sensory data which can schedule a predictive maintenance so as the unexpected production down-time can be reduced,all of these will fully justify the needs of a CPPS. These smart systems will have intelligent software modules with some predefined and universally applicable goals irrespective of a type of smart entity like energy optimization goal or a waste reduction goal, and these entities have hard-coded these software modules into them,but some of them will be programmed based on the needs of the application by the AI based algorithms running in the smart production facility like monitoring the tool wear so as to maintain necessary surface roughness for a machined part [48]. For declaring and realizing these definitive goals, the AI and machine learning will surely play a significant role and neural network-based smart models need to be defined. Also, the goals need to be defined individually as well as collectively in the CPPS chain. So, this gives us the first requirement of a CPPS framework:

R1:   Definitive achievable goals defined individually for each CPPS element and collectively for the CPPS chain

Various international organizations have proposed reference architectures to implement these CPPS like Reference Architectural Model Industries 4.0 (RAMI 4.0) [20] proposed in Germany, which unites 3 significant domains of engineering, depicted in a three-dimensional form. This model is based on the 6 layers smart grid architecture, and its first dimension covers the main blocks of an organization from businesses to assets stacked vertically, second covers the hierarchy levels in an organization, i.e., from a product, field device to a connected world of a large number of devices. The third dimension is the life cycle of the products, as all the layers and levels are considered along a product lifecycle. Another popular model is Industrial Internet Reference Architecture (IIRA) as proposed by Industrial Internet Consortium [21], which is like RAMI 4.0 and consists of three axes architecture in which Z-axis has various viewpoints about the product and company. The X-axis depicts all stages of the lifecycle of the product, starting from idea conceiving to its disposal. And the third axis covers various sectors, so some specific concerns of each domain are taken into consideration. One more reference architecture is the Smart Manufacturing Ecosystem [22] by NIST, USA. This is designed around the manufacturing pyramid and consists of 3 dimensions, i.e., the life cycle of a product, the lifecycle of a production facility, and the business function. In this architecture, everything revolves around the manufacturing pyramid and it covers from field level devices to the enterprise levels. Few more reference architectures are also proposed by various countries like Intelligent Manufacturing System Architecture [23] proposed by China, Industrial Value Chain Reference Architecture [49], by Japan. The reference architectures proposed are still in their infancy states and mostly conceptual, which make it a little bit more difficult for industries to implement them.

Further reviewing the works of the academic community, a famous 5C architecture by Lee et al. [17] exists, which focusses on the Industry 4.0 based manufacturing unit. This architecture defines 5 levels in which a guideline is given on how the cognition in manufacturing is achievable. Its focus is more on providing cognitive functions to CPS. Its lowest level initiates the data acquisition in the physical world and reaches a level of cognition at the top level where the systems can work autonomously and have self-awareness and self-configuration like features. Liu and Xu [19] proposed a new generation cyber-physical machine tool called machine tool 4.0 which integrates machine tool, machining processes, computation and networks utilizing the embedded devices and completes the feedback loops in a CPPS. Liu and Jiang [29] proposed architecture for intelligent manufacturing in the shop floor having an interconnection of hardware devices, data acquisition, processing, visualization, and knowledge acquisition and learning module.

Reviewing the above works from academia and industry, it was quite evident that some kind of consciousness (intelligence) needs to be imparted to the physical systems so as to make them smart and work in an autonomous manner [17, 28]. The consciousness can be imparted to these machines by hardware as well as software means such as installing more sensors on them (hardware means),or by deploying AI based predictions and decision-making models on them, or by providing feedback loops in the systems, which leads to our second requirement of a CPPS framework:

R2:   The CPPS framework should make physical components enough capable to self-configure, self-aware, self-predict, self-optimize, and self-protect themselves by embedding intelligence in them, so as they are usable in multiple domains with heterogeneous communication environments

RQ 3: What are the key features of Cyber-Physical Production Systems?
The Cyber-Physical Production Systems are defined in the *RQ 2* in quite a detail, now let us dive deep into features of these smart production systems. There is a need of CPPS to have a connected nature so that the data and information can flow in a smooth manner, but a major concern of current production systems are the proprietary interfaces [50] for data communication with automation hardware like Profinet in case of Siemens hardware or Ethernet I/P in Allen Bradley hardware. This creates a major bottleneck as the interoperability and interconnection is not so efficient among these proprietary protocols and also the total cost of ownership is quite high [51], so MT Connect [52] and OPC-UA [53] like open-source standards for industrial data communication come into the picture which can play a significant role in getting over

this barrier. The CPPS element should support a well-defined, universally accepted, and interoperable standards for communication to individual components defined in the CPPS chain. CPPS components having external interoperability provides flexibility and customizations in the system by utilizing standard interfaces. This gives us our third requirement of a CPPS framework:

R3: A well-defined, universally accepted, and interoperable standardized interfaces throughout the CPPS chain

Talking further about the features of these CPPS elements as rightly depicted by researchers in [9, 11, 16], these systems should have the flexibility and scalability so as the heterogenous elements can be connected in an efficient manner. The CPPS framework defined should be capable enough to scale up or down for numerous applications with varying sizes and complexity. It should support heterogeneous cyber-physical components, users, complex applications, and a variety of data traffic volumes to achieve a common manufacturing goal. So, in an ideal situation, the same facility is competent enough to produce a complicated part and a simple part in varying batch size based on the needs. And to achieve all of this, the modular configuration plays a big role [50]. The framework should focus on the modularity of systems having smart components working on standardized interfaces with predefined characteristics. The system configuration can be changed in real time based on product requirements giving more flexibility and reliability to the production system. This leads to fourth requirement of a CPPS framework:

R4: A sense of scalability and flexibility across the CPPS structure with modular and reliable elements throughout the CPPS chain

The elements of CPPS framework should demonstrate a sense of modularity and reliability in the domains of inter and intra device communication, services, applications, and big-data managing capabilities to meet the system requirements of Industry 4.0 compliant systems. Also, the system should be resilient enough to thwart unwanted external and internal changes in the system [11]. So, to have such modularity, the CPPS elements should have component definitions which help them to establish a link to various components with a wide range of functions connected across the CPPS chain, based on the needs of the applications and goals [50]. Component's discovery and detailed characteristics should be well defined in a definition library, so that plug and play functionality can be achieved [16]. This gives us our fifth requirement of a CPPS framework:

R5: Unambiguous component definitions of each element throughout the CPPS chain

RQ 4: On what parameters, do the production facilities need to be assessed so as to be called smart production systems?

Although the reference architectures are the traditional way to assess any facility for their smartness, however there is a good initiative by the Singapore Economic Development Board (EDB) in collaboration with top technology companies, consultancy firms, and experts from industry and academic, where they launched a Smart Industry Readiness Index (SIRI) with an Assessment Matrix in November 2017 to help manufacturers measure their readiness towards the Industry 4.0 needs

[54]. This index has three major building blocks which are Technology, Process, and Organization. These building blocks further have 8 pillars of the index, which are the crucial areas, and the companies must have their eyes on to achieve the goal of becoming smart industries. These pillars can be mapped onto 16 dimensions which are the assessment areas for a company and can help them in evaluating their facilities as per Industry 4.0 readiness. Each dimension further has 6 bands along which evaluation can be done. It also has a prioritization matrix for industries to focus on the key areas to improve in order to get maximum benefits. This index could be a good way to start the assessment of any industry and even the architectures or frameworks defined for the manufacturing sector could derive some key points and features from it for assessments, which are currently missing.

RQ 5: What about the legacy production facilities, will they be also supportable under these smart production systems?

The CPS with its related technologies could help in taking a step forward in the direction of innovation and act as the carriers to transition from Industry 3.0 to Industry 4.0. But one of the concern of manufacturers and factory owners is about the brownfield installations and how will these technologies be deployed in them for benefits? Very little work has been reported in literature about this concern e.g., Zhang et al. [18] proposes an add-on CPS architecture for existing machine tool by. It is a 3-layer architecture in which a machine tool is made smart by adding some additional sensors to it, acquiring and processing data from them and further storing it in the cloud. This work further complements a brief implementation on few systems in the lab environment. Similarly, there is talk about legacy systems of Industry 3.0 to Industry 4.0 [55] and about migration of current components to be supportable under Industry 4.0 trends [56]. Considering this concern, the architecture should support legacy components available in the chain to achieve more from it as this would be one of the cost-effective solutions instead of straight away replacing them by new components and systems. One of the solutions could be to design specialized embedded components for these older physical systems which can act as a bridge considering the security aspects, make them capable enough to get connected on open standards in an efficient way which will further accelerate them towards Industry 4.0. This gives us our sixth requirement of a CPPS framework:

R6:   Support for legacy components and systems in CPPS chain considering both hardware and software terms for efficient control in a secured manner

RQ 6: What industry standards are available for a smart factory?

As the fourth industrial revolution is still in its infancy, worldwide many organizations are working towards a development of standards. As stated earlier in answer to *RQ 2* about the reference architectures, the organizations are trying to modify the currently available standards so that they can be adapted according to the Industry 4.0 needs. As described by Trappey et al. [57], where they have divided the full production systems in 4 major layers, and along each layer various components and systems are categorized which further list available standards for each of them. The first layer is the perception layer which covers the physical systems having sensors and actuators, second is the transmission layer which focusses on communication methods and its related protocols. Third layer is the computation layer which covers the cyber part of the CPPS i.e., hardware, software, algorithms, cloud platforms, etc., which embeds the consciousness into the physical systems. Last is the application layer, which collects the data from previous layers and acts as a bridge between the customers and provides all business-related functions available to customers and organizations. The standards and regulations are available for the basic components in an individualized manner, but it is not available for a complete system, so there is a need that either these standards be adapted for needs of Industry 4.0 or they can be defined from scratch. In a similar way few countries like Australia [58] and Germany [59]are also working towards defining the standards for various components and systems which can ease the transition of the manufacturing sector towards a more smart and intelligent future. So, this gives us our seventh requirement of a CPPS framework.

R7: The CPPS elements compliance with necessary regulations and standards laid for product quality, environmental safety, human safety or related to any function present in the full product life cycle

RQ 7: How the data generated inside the factories will be utilized in the creation of smart factories?

Communication and Data are the key ingredients of smartness [17]. In absence of any,the requisite smartness cannot be achieved as predicted or imagined under the regime of Industry 4.0. The communication is well described above and covered under the requirement **R3**, so now it is time to discuss the data. Tapping of a large pool of data most popularly termed big data is not possible, if a medium/path to access it is absent or the CPS technologies are not utilized properly,but if everything is done right it will majorly be contributing to the customer centric products, achieve a definitive goal of optimized production facilities with less wastage and a huge financial savings [60].The big data has five major challenges termed as 5 V's of big data: volume, variety, veracity, velocity, and value [61]. So, the CPPS framework defined should have some way to tackle these 5V challenges to get the most out of the enormous data generated in the factories. Starting from the first two V's of big data i.e.,Volume and Variety: these two are directly linked to the capabilities of physical systems. Every physical system is generating the data but to capture them fully there is a need to modify the hardware and software terms. Data captured is just not from the traditional system but is captured from various heterogenous sources available in the factory and even humans are its contributors. Heterogeneity leads to uneven data formats and vary from system to system, but to properly get the value out of it, data needs to be in a proper structure, where the software can play a huge role by properly formatting the data during acquisition itself. The next challenge comes in managing and the storage of this big data, so as real time interfacing and decision making can be done. This leads to our eighth requirement of a CPPS framework:

R8: The CPPS elements should capture structured or unstructured data from various distributed systems, manage them and store them in a neutral format for accessibility purposes

The third and fourth V are the Veracity and Velocity, as the initial challenge of data capture is linked to capabilities of both the hardware and software. Now the huge data once acquired needs to be processed and meaningful insights are required out of them, but the reliability of data or the authenticity of the data needs to be verified as the smart algorithms would take decisions based on them. If the input data is incorrect the output will be incorrect also, which poses a challenge of verifying the data in real time and which is also streamed in large quantities continuously into the software modules. To tackle the data veracity issue, the software modules can be configured to utilise the data from simulations, historical data or even from a similar physical system which needs to be done in real time but mostly would be limited by the computing capabilities of the systems installed [60]. Even Velocity challenge depends on the capabilities of the physical system at the acquisition end, transfer capabilities and then analyzing in real time. Also, the velocity challenge varies from application-to-application basis, some data may be changing in microseconds but others may not be changing even for days. This leads to our ninth requirement of a CPPS framework:

R9: The CPPS framework should have a mechanism to check data authenticity and cater to the needs of customers considering the capabilities of software and hardware modules

Last V is the Value which focuses on getting the benefits from the heterogeneous data acquired and analyzed with help from smart algorithms. Once the data is properly processed and analyzed only then is the data presentable across various platforms based on the needs. This value is the key factor and helps in optimizing the manufacturing systems. All the applications and decisions will focus on this aspect whether related to design, planning, tracking, manufacturing, quality control or scheduling maintenance activities [62]. This leads to our tenth requirement of a CPPS framework:

R10: Meaningful inferences and informative plots from processed ubiquitous raw data

Tao et al. [62] explained the smart manufacturing scenarios and application in a data driven environment. Importance of data is described briefly by authors in starting from the first industrial revolution to the future of big data-based manufacturing. They also explained the role of data in the complete product life cycle and proposed a data driven smart manufacturing framework. The applications of data are not only limited to four pillars of product life cycle i.e., design, plan manufacture and recycle but also covers the other major task in the industry like the predictive maintenance scheduling, tracking material and distribution in an optimized way based on real time situations, real time quality control tasks, to name a few. Also, in [24], authors presented a big data-based analytics platform with two very good actual applications in a real time machining task. Some more applications like this one [63], where a controller tuning is done with the help of big data in a CNC machine, also [64] where a quality control application is implemented based on big data. Looking at the smart future in fourth industrial revolution, data will play an eminent role in achieving the smartness.

RQ 8: What cyber-security measures need to be taken inside a smart production facility?

The traditional IT systems have various security measures and standards defined from a very long time. But with the emergence of smart production systems that have IT technologies connected to the physical production systems, all of which were till now disconnected from the outside world, poses a new and serious threat to these physical systems [65]. Although mostly problems related to cyber-security would have solutions inspired from the traditional IT systems. Even then there would be few challenges which currently seem an issue in physical systems in comparison to traditional IT systems like as defined by authors in [66] the secure development lifecycle with timely low-cost and reliable patches in terms of hardware and software, assessment of various attack detection and security models, data security in terms of manufacturing processes and internal data. Also, as described by Chhetri et al. [67], there is a need of confidentiality, integrity, and availability in product life cycle stages i.e., design, prototyping, ordering, industrial processing, sales, and in maintenance. They also described various trends in these stages. Although much work has not been done by academia and industry in this domain, it surely needs to be a part of the smart production systems. This leads to our eleventh requirement of a CPPS framework.

R11: **The CPPS framework should have provisions to maintain security of all CPPS elements, communication networks and the data streams in CPPS chain at utmost priority**

RQ 9: What are the steps to create a smart production facility?

The previous 8 questions mostly cover the various perspectives of the smart production facilities and define what a smart production could be, but now the main question arises, how to implement it? During the literature review, the authors find that minimal literature is available on examples or prototype implementation of various proposed CPS, CPPS frameworks or even architecture proposed for various interlink technologies like IOT [68, 69], IIOT [70–74], cloud computing [5, 6, 10, 26], FOG computing [75–78], EDGE computing [79–81], big data [24, 63, 64, 82–84], and smart factory [85–88], etc. Also, a literature review on Industry 4.0 by Kamble et al. [89] also states the fact to prove that work done on Industry 4.0 and its related technologies are conceptual works: 47%, case studies: 27%, simulation work: 10%, experimental work: 7.5%, survey: 6%, and prototype: 2.5%. The actual prototype implementation is mere 2.5%, so there is very major gap in the implementation of CPS, CPPS and manufacturing focussed frameworks in the real world. So, there is no step-by-step implementation available till now, but authors have made an attempt in the current work to fill this gap with an Intelligent Cyber-Physical Production System (i-CPPS) framework for the Industry 4.0 environment having a special focus on steps detailing its implementation and an actual prototype implementation in forthcoming sections.

RQ 10: How Cyber-Physical Production Systems can tackle COVID-19 pandemic situations?

The COVID-19 pandemic is an unexpected, unwanted, and difficult situation for almost all industries in world, whether it's the manufacturing or tourism or the education sector. But manufacturing being the critical industry of any country and without it the economy cannot sustain this and with this pandemic is affected the most as everything comes to standstill in a lockdown condition. High risks and the high mortality rate of COVID-19 further created more challenging issues like the disruptions of supplies, demand-side shocks, transportation problems, production disruptions, and distorted demand patterns. The anomalies that affected the market and ramped up the production of some products like masks, PPE kits, sanitizers, gloves, ventilators, oximeters, etc., whereas on the other side reduced the operations in some industries like aircraft manufacturing, automobile manufacturing, etc. These challenges emerging out from the COVID-19 pandemic further arose the need for production facilities to be more robust, flexible, interconnected, reconfigurable and resilient to tackle such dynamic situations. Here the CPS with its related technologies can play bigger role not just in handling the situations but also improving them by providing consciousness to machine tools and to make them smarter. All four blocks of product life cycle i.e., design, manufacture, maintenance and recycle will benefit from these systems as the digitalization trend will open doors for a smarter and collaborative platform which can work with humans, behave like humans, and learn from them. Let's take an example for shortage of ventilators which arose during this pandemic and manufacturing sectors were not capable to ramp up their production in such a short duration amid the restrictions posed due to COVID-19, but by implying the technologies from Industry 4.0 cloud and considering a modular, flexible, reconfigurable, network oriented, data intensive product approach helped in manufacturing and fulfil the needs of ventilator. Similarly, other health care needs like PPE kits, masks, gloves, nasal swabs, sanitizers, etc. were also manufactured by implying the approach of cyber-physical systems in manufacturing sector. Also, Section 4.3 presents three application areas which can be a realized by help from CPS and its related technologies and can create production facilities smarter.

3. Intelligent Cyber-Physical Production System (i-CPPS) Framework

Section 2 reviews the needs and expectations of CPS in production systems, CPS frameworks proposed till now for production systems, presented the critical requirements for a CPPS framework, and concluded with a need of a CPS framework for a production system with detailed implementation steps. This section in conjunction with Section 4 fulfils this gap with an Intelligent Cyber-Physical Production System (i-CPPS) framework which is applicable to a single smallest manufacturing entity capable of performing manufacturing tasks independently and to multiple manufacturing entities working in a collaborated manner forming a factory. It shows the way to impart intelligence in each manufacturing entity, connects them to the cloud platforms with a capability of intra and inter-enterprise communication to realize the goals of smart manufacturing.

The hierarchical architecture of i-CPPS is presented in a four-layer structure in this section, as shown in Fig. 11.1. All four levels have their individual role to play in this framework and they share a progressive and interdependent relationship amongst them to achieve higher levels of autonomy. The first level is termed unit level and is a vital constituent of this architecture. Here the intelligence is added to physical systems, to make them smart and autonomous. Also, the data is captured from heterogeneous sources, pre-processed in real time on EDGE devices, critical decisions are made autonomously, and transferred to the upper level. The second is shop-floor level, which constitutes a group of unit level entities working in collaboration. A FOG cluster analyses the pre-processed data using AI/ML algorithms and develop AI models for deployment at unit level. It is also responsible for regularly updating the digital twins. The third level is factory level, which combines various shopfloors and acts as a complete service and management platform inside a factory. This level takes care of the needs of the previous two levels in terms of resources, inventory, raw materials, energy needs, etc. Topmost is the cyber level, which provides a platform to serve the needs of various enterprises and customers. It handles the big data generated by individual factories, keeps a copy of it, analyses it, processes it using AI algorithms,

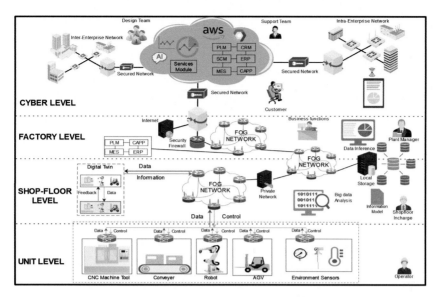

Figure 11.1: Hierarchical architecture of i-CPPS framework.

and provides key control actions for the factories while taking human experts in a loop.

3.1 Unit Level

Unit level comprises a minimal manufacturing entity capable of performing defined manufacturing-related functions in a standalone manner. Each unit level entity contains hardware components and software modules which are packaged to form these smart systems. The key elements of unit level are detailed in Fig. 11.2. The first element is the physical entity which is a group of components like motors, linear actuators, drives, mechanical grippers, spindles, etc. assembled in a specific fashion to form unit level smart entities like CNC machining centres, robots, conveyors, AGV, to name a few.

The second element is a continuous stream of data, generated and acquired out of these physical entities and through external sensors like temperature sensors, vibration sensors, optical sensors, cameras, etc. Physical entities are the primary source of data, like in a CNC machining centre, position data, rotatory/linear speeds data, voltages and current across various smaller modules and systems. This element plays a crucial role in interfacing the state of the physical entity, helps in updating the digital twins and comes handy in maintenance and disposal related activities.

The third element is the EDGE device, which is an embedded hardware connected on top of physical entities. It acts as a computing part which is added to these physical components for making the physical entity smart by embedding intelligence into them. This device is capable enough to run AI/ML models for real-time analysis, common fault detection, and alert generation purposes. EDGE device has least latency rates, usually in the range of micro-seconds, so as critical decisions can betaken in real-time. It also provides the heterogeneous network connecting capabilities to these physical entities for establishing communication with other unit level devices and connect to the upper levels.

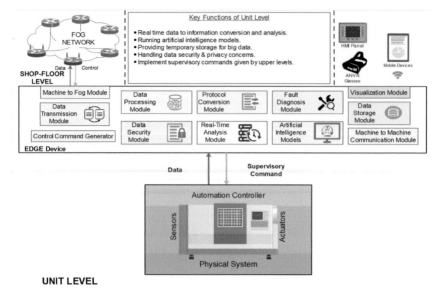

Figure 11.2: Unit level of i-CPPS framework.

These three elements are the core constituents of unit level. They are combined to realize the goals of smart manufacturing by efficiently utilizing the resources provided to each of physical systems, implementing data acquisition, data transfer, and analysis by AI models at EDGE, as well as realize control commands generated by upper levels. The roles of humans at this level are usually in the form of operators for these unit level smart entities for monitoring and maintenance purposes utilizing the HMI panels or augmented/virtual reality-based glasses.

3.2   Shop-floor Level

When multiple unit level devices are grouped and tend to work in collaboration for achieving a manufacturing goal this forms the second level of i-CPPS framework termed as the shop-floor level, as shown in Fig. 11.3. Various unit level smart entities interact, inter-operate, interconnect, and communicate in such a way to realize the targets of smart manufacturing. Flexibility, which is one of the critical components of the fourth industrial revolution, is realized by this level.

The key element of this level is a FOG network, which is a cluster of computing modules, storage modules, data processing modules, service modules, etc. and is available at both shop-floor and factory levels. Using this cluster network, the first task for this level is to create information models for individual unit level devices. Information models constitute two components static and dynamic. The static component has data like manufacturer details, entity specifications, manuals, CAD drawings, characteristics data, storage instructions, historical product life cycle data, shipping data, assembly instructions, etc. The dynamic component is the real-time data generated out of unit level smart entities.

On the combination of static and dynamic data components, the digital twins of the unit level entities come into existence, which is one of the key elements of Industry 4.0 requirements. These twins help in developing AI/ML models for deployment at

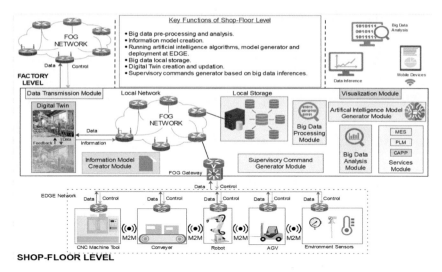

Figure 11.3: Shop-floor level of i-CPPS framework.

EDGE and play a vital role in the production and business-related functions and making decisions at upper levels. Also, it utilizes various manufacturing software as a service like MES, PLM, CAPP, etc. at this level. Shop-floor level first simulates the production digitally and then assigns individual tasks to unit level devices based on their availability, criticality of the job, and nature of the job, with corresponding initial parameters provided as feedback from digital twins.

Shop-floor level assists the factory level in addressing the challenges of achieving operational excellence by providing necessary data in a required format and implementing the supervisory commands generated by factory level. AI/ML plays a bigger role in the smooth execution of tasks at this level. The latency among the data flow varies based on the task like a safety-related task for human or unit entity runs in near real-time, but a maintenance scheduling task may run in microseconds or seconds brackets. Humans play a crucial role as the shop floor managers, commissioning smart entities, and in scheduling, maintenance-related activities utilizing the large dashboard-based interfaces and AR/VR/MR technologies.

3.3 Factory Level

The third level of i-CPPS framework is factory level which integrates multiple shopfloors, and business functions like logistics, inventory, maintenance, etc. inside a factory, as shown in Fig. 11.4. This level's prime responsibility is to manufacture the products as demanded by users with required specifications and quantity,package them and ship them. Factory level addresses the challenges of optimizing the technology to make a manufacturing organization risk free and safer, and achieves the goals of operational excellence and establishes a closed loop between the planning, execution, and control functions to optimize production and business-related operations.

For realizing these goals, the FOG network plays a key role. It has a lot more software modules connected in addition to the shop-floor level's modules like the logistics management module, inventory management module, energy analysis module, maintenance module, etc. The FOG plays a crucial role in providing

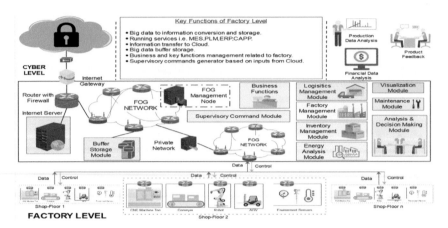

Figure 11.4: Factory level of i-CPPS framework.

communication links inside and outside of the factory. It also has a management node which handles all the data traffic inside the factory, makes various services available to the shop-floor and cyber level considering the cyber-security and privacy needs. The data transmission and flow at this level varies based on the criticality of the task i.e., if communicating with the logistics team or the finance team, the data flow rate can be kept in seconds, but if communicating to the shop floor, it needs to be in microseconds. The humans play a significant role as the factory or plant in-charge, which can take critical decisions regarding production and business-related matters. Also, there are teams which take care of the maintenance of entities at unit level and shop-floor levels, manage logistics, financial, inventory, resources, etc. They all work together to optimize the production and efficiently utilize the resources.

3.4   Cyber Level

The Cyber level is the topmost level of i-CPPS framework and is an application focussed layer in this framework. This level is a computing model having the capabilities to provide an on-demand access through networks to a shared pool of fully configurable computing resources, i.e., servers, data storage, applications, and services as shown in Fig. 11.5. These resources can be accessed as and when required and can be released when not in use.

    This level plays a crucial role throughout the product's life cycle, starting from customer queries to their disposals. Its role does not end with the products but also plays a prominent role in the efficient utilization of resources, machines, and humans in an organization. In addition to hosting services as required in various phases of the product life cycle, it manages data and knowledge bases which helps in creating machine learning and artificial intelligence models for various smart applications. This platform provides seamless integration and efficient collaboration via a web or a smart mobile application for customers, manufacturers, vendors in the supply chain, logistic vendors, service and support personnel's and disposal collection vendors for smoothing the production process.

    The cyber level connects directly to each factory in a secured manner, and the information is acquired for analysis, creating a knowledge database and models, and

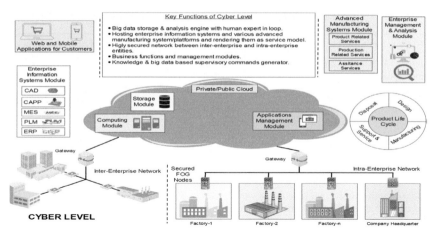

Figure 11.5: Cyber level of i-CPPS framework

informative visualizations are generated for critical business decision making. This level also provides the skeleton of digital twins to factories and continually updates them in its record for future needs based on the processed real-time data from factories.

The cyber level offers advanced manufacturing system modules which are designed for product-related, production-related, or assistance services-related tasks. Similarly, the factories as a service can also be utilized based on the demands of certain products; maintenance can be triggered based on predictive models and maintenance personnel can be utilized as service based on needs. This level further promotes knowledge-intensive manufacturing by inter-connecting distributed resources and capabilities which have a pool of multidisciplinary knowledge. This service's model helps in achieving flexibility in manufacturing, which is a key element of smart manufacturing. Also, for fulfilling the needs of Industry 4.0 with a requirement of a batch size of one, this platform plays a crucial role in establishing the i-CPPS framework and advance towards a social manufacturing period where the public can also take part in various stages of the product lifecycle and fully customize the products as per their needs. As all the data from factories are available in the Cloud, the customers can track their products in real-time and can even utilize the AR/VR/MR based techniques to view the manufacturing in real-time.

3.5 Relevance of Requirements in i-CPPS Framework

The requirements listed in Section 2 gives the direction to define a CPPS framework, and the same has been taken care of in the proposed i-CPPS framework as shown in Table 11.1. The requirements are non-exhaustive but at-least if they are covered in a single implementation, it would be a significant progress towards the goals of Industry 4.0. Also, the fulfilment of requirements is the task of the complete CPPS chain, it may be satisfied by a single level or multiple levels could satisfy it.

4. i-CPPS Framework Implementation

In this section, the Intelligent Cyber-Physical Production System Framework implementing steps are detailed as taken at each level with their required softwares

Table 11.1: Relevance of requirements in i-CPPS framework

RequirementsLevels	Unit	Shopfloor	Factory	Cyber
R1: Definitive achievable objectives defined individually for each CPPS element and collectively for the CPPS chain.	✓	✓	✓	✓
R2: The CPPS framework should make physical components enough capable to self-configure, self-aware, self-predict, self-optimize, and self-protect themselves by embedding intelligence in them, so as they are usable in multiple domains with heterogeneous communication environments.	✓	✓		
R3: A well-defined, universally accepted, and interoperable standardized interfaces throughout the CPPS chain.	✓	✓	✓	
R4: A sense of scalability and flexibility across the CPPS structure with modular and reliable elements throughout the CPPS chain.	✓	✓		
R5: Unambiguous component definitions of each element throughout the CPPS chain.	✓	✓	✓	
R6: Support for legacy components and systems in CPPS chain considering both hardware and software terms for efficient control in a secured manner.	✓			
R7: The CPPS elements compliance with necessary regulations and standards laid for product quality, environmental safety, human safety or related to any function present in the full product life cycle.		✓	✓	
R8: The CPPS elements should capture structured or unstructured data from various distributed systems, manage them and store them in a neutral format for accessibility purposes	✓	✓		
R9: The CPPS framework should have a mechanism to check data authenticity and cater to the needs of customers considering the capabilities of software and hardware modules.	✓			
R10: Meaningful inferences and informative plots from processed ubiquitous raw data.	✓	✓	✓	✓
R11: The CPPS framework should have provisions to maintain security of all CPPS elements, communication networks and the data streams in CPPS chain at utmost priority	✓	✓	✓	✓

modules and hardware components. Section 4.1 details the building blocks of current i-CPPS implementation, starting from unit level to the cyber level, considering the requirements listed in Section 2. For the unit level, a CNC micro-machining centre was chosen. Further for the shopfloor and factory level, a FOG network was developed on the MATLAB Production Server [90]. It has connectivity to locally hosted databases and the Google Firebase platform with Google Cloud Storage [91] for data storage purposes. In the Cyber level, a website was hosted, which had connectivity to Google Cloud Storage using Firebase SDK [92]. Section 4.2 showcases a prototype implementation scenario of a smart factory after combining all individual building blocks mentioned in Section 4.1, making it Industry 4.0 compatible based on the i-CPPS framework.

4.1 Building Blocks of i-CPPS Framework Transition

This section talks about the individual building blocks formed for an i-CPPS framework implementation, right from unit level to the cloud level. The purpose of this section is to provide intricate details of each block within this framework and help researchers and industry people to take it as a reference point for i-CPPS implementation.

4.1.1 Description of Physical Entity: Unit Level

Advanced Micromachining System (AMMS) is a fully automated five axes CNC machining centre which was conceptualized, designed, manufactured, and assembled in-house. The experimental setup of AMMS is shown in Fig. 11.6. The motion control, process control and measurement software are all integrated in a single GUI. This machining centre is capable of performing five different machining processes, i.e., micro-milling, micro-laser beam machining, micro-EDM, micro-grinding, and micro-drilling, with in-situ measurement facilities, i.e., an optical sensor for roughness measurement, a microscope for in-process image capturing and measurement facility, a 6 axes dynamometer for force and torque measurement, and an energy meter all integrated into a single machine. Specifications of this machining centre are given below in Table 11.2. For the current implementation, the micro-milling process is chosen in a 3 axes configuration with other machining heads and axes locked safely. Figure 11.7 shows the architecture of AMMS implemented at the unit and shopfloor level as per i-CPPS framework.

Table 11.2: Specifications of AMMS

- Machine dimensions: 1200 mm × 900 mm × 2000 mm
- Five axes system with individual travel limits:
  - X: 300 mm
  - Y: 300 mm
  - Z: 150 mm
  - A: +60° to –60° (limit by software)
  - C: 0° to 360°
- Work volume: 50 mm × 50 mm × 50 mm
- 5 axes CNC functionality achieved by a customized motion controller.
- Intel i7 processor-based IPC system with windows operating system and 15-inch multitouch screen.
- Machining processes: μ-milling, μ-drilling, μ-grinding, μ-EDM, μ-laser.
- In-situ roughness measurement using an optical sensor.
- 6 axes HBM force and torque measurement.
- Microscope with CCD camera.
- Energy meter.

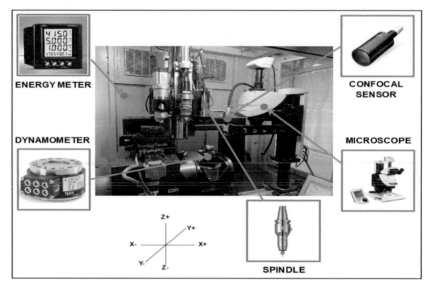

Figure 11.6: Experimental setup of AMMS.

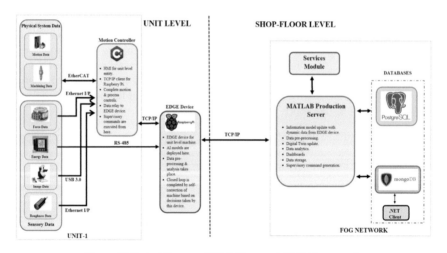

Figure 11.7: Architecture of AMMS as per i-CPPS framework.

4.1.2 Configuring Data Acquisition Process: Unit Level

This sub-section contains details about configuring machining process data, motion control data and sensor data. Table 11.3 lists all the heterogeneous data variables acquired and processed. As mentioned in Section 4.1.1, the micro-milling process is chosen for implementation, so its three main machining parameters, i.e., Spindle Speed, Feed, Depth of Cut are to be selected before machining. These three parameters are selected based on RSM based optimum machining parameter selection algorithm [93] considering the energy requirements, required surface roughness value and the tools remaining useful lifetime [94–96].

Table 11.3: List of data variables captured

- Machining Process Data
  - Spindle Speed (S)
  - Feed (F)
  - Depth of Cut (D)
- Motion Control Data
  - Commanded Position_X (Xcp)
  - Actual Position_X (Xap)
  - Commanded Position_Y (Ycp)
  - Actual Position_Y (Yap)
  - Commanded Position_Z (Zcp)
  - Actual Position_Z (Zap)
  - Commanded Velocity_X (Xcv)
  - Actual Velocity_X (Xav)
  - Commanded Velocity_Y (Ycv)
  - Actual Velocity_Y (Yav)
  - Commanded Velocity_Z (Zcv)
  - Actual Velocity_Z (Zav)
  - Commanded Acceleration_X (Xca)
  - Actual Acceleration_X (Xaa)
  - Commanded Acceleration_Y (Yca)
  - Actual Acceleration_Y (Yaa)
  - Commanded Acceleration_Z (Zca)
  - Actual Acceleration_Z (Zaa)
- Sensor Data (Raw)
  - Force_X (Fx)
  - Force_Y (Fy)
  - Force_Z (Fz)
  - Torque_X (Tx)
  - Torque_Y (Ty)
  - Torque_Z (Tz)
  - Ra (R)
  - Img (I)
  - Energy (E)

Motion control parameters include the axes variables, i.e., commanded position, actual position, commanded velocity, actual velocity, commanded acceleration, actual acceleration for all three axes and is captured at a frequency of 1000 Hz. In AMMS, cutting force and torque data is available through the HBM six axes dynamometer and surface roughness values from Micro-Epsilon confocal sensor over ethernet I/P, available in a CSV file. The microscope images are also available over USB, which are transferred to the database after the end of every machining cycle. Further, an energy meter for measuring the machine's power and current consumption is connected over RS-485 to the EDGE device and is pushing data to the database at a frequency of 1000 Hz. The acquisition frequency is pre-selected before data acquisition, and some pre-processing is done before storing it in a database. The pre-processing algorithms are developed in MATLAB and are elaborated in Section 4.1.5.

4.1.3 EDGE Device: Unit Level

A Raspberry Pi 3 Model B+ is chosen as an EDGE device. This embedded hardware runs a Raspbian operating system with AI models deployed on it. The RPi was connected to AMMS over TCP/IP. It captures data from an energy meter sampled at 1000 Hz over RS-485 protocol. This device then further keeps an eye over all the data before passing it to the local database, and the AI/ML models specific to abnormality detection are deployed on it using the MATLAB SIMULINK support packages and MATLAB Coder for Raspberry Pi [97].

A simple model was created for the energy prediction of the machine considering the machining parameters; current tool wear state and target surface roughness value as done in [98]. This model predicts the energy consumption based on the previous knowledge of the machining done on AMMS at various machining parameters with variable tool wear states and surface roughness value achieved. It was created at the shopfloor level, as stated in Section 4.1.7 utilizing the pre-processing algorithms stated in Section 4.1.5.

4.1.4 FOG Network: Shop-floor Level & Factory Level

A cluster of the database, computing modules and service modules, when combined forms the FOG network. The backbone of FOG is MATLAB Production Server [90] which is an application server that manages the complete FOG network efficiently. This server connects to unit-level devices in the downward direction and the cyber level in an upward direction. Figure 11.8 shows a screenshot of MATLAB Production Server configured in a Windows PC at the shopfloor level. On the left panel, it is visible, that a local server is configured, and an instance named 'pser1' is running. Also, a Redis database for caching is configured. Further, there are few applications/ models configured in the production server for pre-processing data, detection, and predictions tasks.

The first element of FOG is the database, here, 2 local database servers are configured one is a NoSQL database (MongoDB) for storing all the static data, and other is a relational database (PostgreSQL) for storing all dynamic data like machining data, motion data and sensor data. The MongoDB stores all the static information (as described in Section 4.1.6) through a .Net based app and provides data to the

Figure 11.8: MATLAB Production Server running at Shop-Floor Level.

information model as and when required. The PostgreSQL gets its data after pre-processing algorithms (deployed in production server) pre-process it and find key features which converts raw data to information. In addition to storing the data locally, the pre-processed data is pushed to the cloud from the FOG network. For this Google Firebase is used, which is a NoSQL database and stores only the information helpful for creating the skeleton of digital twins and for displaying on dashboards at various managerial levels in an organization.

In addition to the database, there are computing capabilities of the FOG cluster, which are used to create various AI models and trains them based on the data captured at unit-level. The AI/ML models are created and trained in MATLAB using the Deep Learning and Machine Learning toolboxes [99, 100]. These models are deployed in the production server, and the EDGE devices accesses these updated models as clients for making predictions and detection works. These models also play a crucial role in the creation of digital twins.

A service module for software like CAPP, CAM, etc. is also running at the shop-floor level. Here, as per the user requirement, the CAD model of the part to be manufactured is passed to Mastercam2020 software [101]. A custom post processor was developed for AMMS, and G&M codes are generated for the product to be machined with an efficient tool path planning. Currently, this step is done manually, but it can be configured automatically once the SaaS feature is available for this software.

A management module acts as the managerial module in the FOG network, while having complete control over the FOG network and mostly resides at the factory level. Usually, this module is an IT module which defines the access levels for personal working at each level in a factory, for example an operator has access to machines assigned to him/her and only can access them. Also, it can be reassigned based on the needs of the production. Similarly, a plant head has access to all data flowing in the FOG network and is usually presented to him via dashboards. This module is further tasked with scheduling maintenance tasks, placing orders for raw material, scheduling shipping tasks, etc. It also takes care of cyber-security perspectives of the FOG network, for which SSL based authentication and secured HTTPS can be configured in Production Server.

4.1.5 Data Pre-Processing Algorithms: Unit Level and Shop-Floor Level

Various pre-processing algorithms for selecting time and frequency domain features [102] are implemented in MATLAB, before writing data to the database. Table 11.4 shows a list of time and frequency domain features. The machining parameters were chosen based on parameter selection algorithm (Section 4.1.7) and remain static for a machining cycle, so they are directly pushed to the database. Further, the data from motion control is also pushed to the database and are mostly used for various predictions, and abnormality detection applications like commanded position and actual position variation beyond a tolerance range, or calculating RUL for components like machining tools, linear ball-screw based slides, etc. For various measurement data like force data and energy data, critical time-frequency domain features are selected based on RSM based algorithms [93]. Algorithms for performing these pre-processing are all programmed in the MATLAB and are deployed on EDGE device. These features further play a key role in AI/ML modelling. The surface roughness value is calculated based on a custom algorithm [103], which calculates roughness (R_a) value

Table 11.4: List of time and frequency domain features

Domain	Feature name	Mathematical equation
Statistics	RMS	$x_{\text{rms}} = \sqrt{\dfrac{1}{n}\sum_{i=1}^{n} x_i^2}$
	Variance	$x_{\text{var}} = \dfrac{1}{n}\sum_{i=1}^{n}(x-\bar{x})^2$
	Maximum	$x_{\text{max}} = \max(x)$
	Skewness	$x_{\text{skew}} = E\left[\left(\dfrac{x-\mu}{\sigma}\right)^3\right]$
	Kurtosis	$x_{\text{kurt}} = E\left[\left(\dfrac{x-\mu}{\sigma}\right)^4\right]$
	Peak-to-Peak	$x_{\text{p-p}} = \max(x) - \min(x)$
Frequency	Spectral Skewness	$f_{\text{skew}} = \sum_{i=1}^{k}\left(\dfrac{f_i-\bar{f}}{\sigma}\right)^3 S(f_i)$
	Spectral Kurtosis	$f_{\text{kurt}} = \sum_{i=1}^{k}\left(\dfrac{f_i-\bar{f}}{\sigma}\right)^4 S(f_i)$
Time-Frequency	Wavelet Energy	$E_{\text{wt}} = \sum_{i=1}^{N} wt_{\varphi}^2(i)/N$

from the confocal data. Also, tool wear is calculated from the images captured on the microscope, currently in a manual manner and then pushed to the database.

4.1.6 Information Model: Shop-Floor Level

There are two data components static data and dynamic data. When these 2 components are combined, they form an information model which plays a crucial role inthe development of digital twins. It also reveals the capabilities of a machining centre and helps in maintenance related tasks.

In the current implementation, the static data is added to MongoDB using a custom Net based apprunning on the FOG network at a shop-floor level which stores all non-changing data like CAD models, manufacturing details, purchase details, etc. in different document format like jpeg images, pdf documents, word documents, etc. in a network drive. A database was created for each shopfloor inside the factory, as shown in Fig. 11.9. The first database configured is 'shop-floor1' with a collection of unit level entities in it and the current implementation focuses on a collection titled 'AMMS', which has various components and modules and each of them is added as a document to this collection. Here, only components relevant to the micro-milling

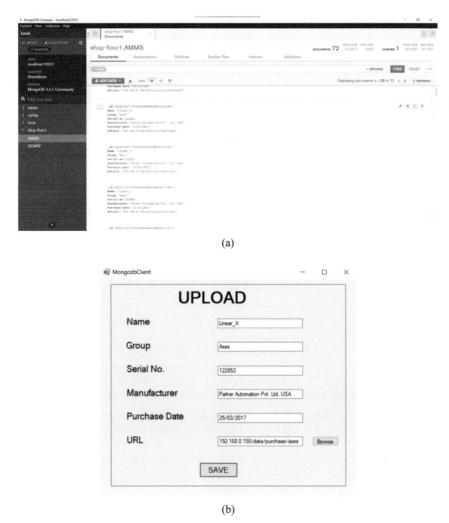

(a)

(b)

Figure 11.9: Screenshot of (a) MongoDB database, (b) .NET app running at shop-floor level.

process are added. A static id is automatically generated for each document by MongoDB, and it can be used as a reference to get details about the module. Also, each component in the collection is given a QR code with the details shown in Table 11.5. This .Net app also acts as an inventory management system for the components.

The dynamic data from each component is added to the PostgreSQL database after applying pre-processing algorithms as defined in Section 4.1.5. Here, this dynamic data is pushed in a column format for all three types of data, i.e., motion data, process data, and sensor data. In the process data table, the process parameters selected based on parameter selection algorithm running in Production Server are directly pushed to the database. Motion data is critical in various detection and prediction tasks, so the variables are sent to the database without any processing. The sensor data is a

Table 11.5: List of data variables stored in database

Variable	Details
id	Unique id generated automatically for each component by MongoDB.
Name	Name of the component.
Group	Group name for classification like axes, measurement, etc.
Serial No.	The serial number of components.
Manufacturer	Manufacturer of the component.
Purchase Date	Purchase date of the component.
Details	A URL link to network storage where all manuals, troubleshooting guides, bills, purchase orders, and complete details for each component is stored based on the groups.

significant constituent of dynamic data, and pre-processing is required before pushing the data. Important critical features from the raw data are pushed to the database as listed in Table 11.4, so as efficiently as the information can be retained instead of whole raw data. This data also plays a crucial role in digital twin creation tasks. Screenshot of the administrator page of PostgreSQL database as running locally is shown in Fig. 11.10. This database has six tables as can be seen in the left panel for heterogeneous data. Also, a list of variables under each table is listed in Table 11.6.

Table 11.6: List of data variables stored in the database

S. No.	Table	Variable
1.	Machining_process_data	Spindle_speed, Feed, Depth_of_cut.
2.	Motion_control_data	Xcp, Ycp, Zcp, Xap, Yap, Zap, Xcv, Ycv, Zcv, Xav, Yav, Zav, Xca, Yca, Zca, Xaa, Yaa, Zaa.
3.	Force	Fx, Fy, Fz, RMSx, RMSy, RMSz, MAXx, MAXy, MAXz, MINx, MINy, MINz.
4.	Energy	raw, MAX, MIN, RMS, VAR, SKEW, KURTOSIS, peaktopeak, spectral_skew, spectral_kurtosis.
5.	Torque	Tx, Ty, Tz, RMSx, RMSy, RMSz, MAXx, MAXy, MAXz, MINx, MINy, MINz.
6.	Roughness	raw, MAX, MIN, RMS, VAR, SKEW, KURTOSIS, peaktopeak, spectral_skew, spectral_kurtosis.

4.1.7 AI/ML Model Creator: Shop-Floor Level

The AI/ML model is designed in MATLAB using the Deep Network Designer App [104], which has some standard pre-train models, and these models can be customized based on applications, or new models can be created from scratch with basic building blocks. Further, there are Neural Net Clustering [105], Fitting [106], Pattern Recognition [107], and Time Series [108] apps in MATLAB for training models based on application type. Once a model is created, it needs to be updated based on the new data which is continuously generated, so a training algorithm is deployed in the Production Server which re-trains the model if the model performance significantly degrades. These models are further available for EDGE devices for prediction and detection works.

Figure 11.10 Screenshot of PostgreSQL database running at Shop-Floor Level.

Here, an anomaly detection model was created and deployed for detecting the tool breakage during the ongoing machining; this model is trained on previous machining data and is depicted in Algorithm 1 below. Also, a parameter selection algorithm, based on previous machining knowledge, considering minimum energy requirements, and required surface roughness value is deployed as a model in the Production Server. This algorithm helps in setting the optimum machining parameters considering the needs as referenced from [93]. The step-by-step implementation for algorithms is as below:

Algorithm 1: Tool Breakage Detection:

Step 1: Read sensor data from energy meter and dynamometer.

Step 2: Read the NC code currently running.

Step 3: If motion command is given for the machining tool, then compare the air cutting value of voltage from energy meter with present voltage values.

Step 4: If the difference between present voltage values and air cutting is more than 0.20 V, then the tool is either broken or is not touching the workpiece value. (Here 0.20 V is chosen based on previous experimental data.)

Step 5: Issue a warning for the tool, not in touch and stop the machine.

Algorithm 2: Optimum Parameter Selection:

Step 1: Input required surface roughness value from the customer.

Step 2: Input last tool wear value, last spindle speed, feed and depth of cut assigned.

Step 3: Evaluate the optimum parameter based on the following equation from reference [93], considering the roughness tolerance range of ± 5%, low power consumption and low tool wear values.

$$L_n(R_a) = -3.87 - 0.094A + 0.73B + 0.27C + 0.043BC + 0.087AC + 0.41B^2 + 0.32C^2 \qquad [93]$$

Here A is spindle speed, B is feed, and C is depth of cut.

Step 4: Set the spindle speed, assign feed and depth of cut to a variable to be used during generating part program.

4.1.8 Dashboards: Shop-Floor Level, Factory Level and Cyber Level

For the creation of dashboards at various levels of i-CPPS framework, Tableau Professional version is used. Tableau has direct connectivity to the MATLAB Production Server, so no additional code required [109]. Various kind of dashboards are created based on the access level, and relevance of data to the concerned humans, like the dashboard for the maintenance personal state, the running status and machine down status, but the factory manager has access to all the data on his dashboard and is concerned more about the production and its relevant data. Figure 11.11 shows a dashboard for the shopfloor manager with the overall equipment efficiency, number of parts produced, machine status and current job details. It is a simple dashboard designed for a shopfloor manager running locally and connected to the Production Server for prototyping purposes. This implementation is based on a web data connector type of implementation with the Production Server, and currently, no data is transferred back from Tableau to the Production Server but can be done in the external service interface option in the Production Server.

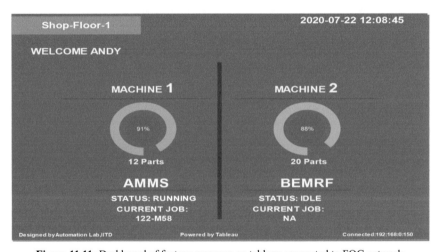

Figure 11.11: Dashboard of factory manager on tableau connected to FOG network.

4.1.9 Mobile/Web App: Cyber Level

A website was created for demonstration purposes as shown in Fig. 11.12. This website has a standard e-commerce type of interface. It has a provision to place an order for custom products, for which users need to upload a CAD model of the part with required specifications to be manufactured. The website is connected to the Google Firebase platform [92] and furthermore to the Google Cloud Storage [91] to get all the information entered by the customer. The CAD file with the required specification is stored in the Google cloud storage using the Google Firebase SDK [92]. After analyzing the CAD file and specifications, a human generates a quotation for the query. On order confirmation, the CAD file and product specifications are available for the factory to download. The factory downloads the files using a .NET

Figure 11.12: Web interface for customers.

based web application running in the factory level and communicates it further to the MATLAB Production Server, which comes into action and starts its manufacturing-related tasks.

4.2   Prototype Use-Case Implementation Flow of a Smart Factory:

A prototype implementation flow of i-CPPS framework in a manufacturing organization is presented by combining building blocks as stated in Section 4.1. The implementation is depicted in a way to show the functions happening at each level of the i-CPPS framework. It starts with an order query by a customer at the cyber level and ends with the shipping of the product to the customer at the factory level. This prototype scenario combines all the steps in the previous section and showcases a transition towards the smart and intelligent organization.

Figure 11.13 shows the complete prototype scenario with the data flow shown by the sequence numbers on it. Here, a customer queries for a custom product by uploading a CAD file and required specifications (step 1). Then the cyber level in smart factory analyses the CAD and provides a required price quotation with the estimated delivery time (step 2). If the customer agrees with the price quote and places order(step 3), a confirmation with the expected delivery time is communicated back (step 4). In the backend, it is the Google Firebase platform through which the data is stored in the Google Cloud Storage using Firebase SDK (step 5). Also, the CAD and specifications are shared with the factory using Firebase SDK and .NET web app client running at the factory level (step 6).

Once the .NET app receives required files from Google Firebase, it further shares the same to the Production Server which is the backbone of FOG network (step 7). All the specifications and CAD drawings are stored in a network drive hosted at the factory level (step 8). Based on product requirements, this server checks for the inventory (step 9) and on confirmation (step 10) further calls the parameter selection algorithm (step 11), which provides three main machining parameters, i.e., Spindle Speed, Feed, Depth of Cut (step 12). Next, a CAM service is called (step 13), which generates a part program for the CAD given by the customer and stores it in a network drive at the shop-floor level (step 14). The parameters and G&M codes are further passed onto the unit level device via an EDGE device (step 15). Machining starts once the raw material and G&M codes are loaded in the physical entity (step 16),

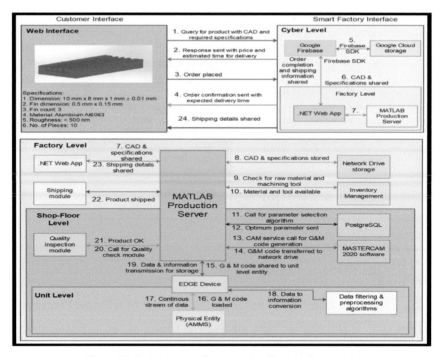

Figure 11.13: Implementation scenario of i-CPPS framework.

and a continuous stream of data is generated (step 17). This data is filtered and pre-processed (step 18) using models/algorithms running in Production Server and data is stored to PostgreSQL database running locally (step 19). The FOG further calls the quality inspection module (step 20), which checks whether the part produced is as per the given specifications. If the part is okay (step 21), then the shipping module is called which packages the product and ships it to the customer (step 22), and the shipping details are shared with the customer using the web interface (step 23, 24).

This prototype implementation shows the full cycle of the i-CPPS framework and makes the factory a smart factory by utilizing the digitalization trend. Also, all the data captured is stored and analyzed, which further contributes to improving the data filtering and processing algorithms/models and better analysis purposes.

4.3   Applications of i-CPPS Framework

This section briefly presents few applications of the i-CPPS framework in a production environment showcasing its advantages and its potential capabilities. Although these applications are developed for achieving the goals of Industry 4.0 but are also relevant in a pandemic like situation and further strengthen the needs of digitalization. Few factors which need to be considered during the current pandemic situation are the implementation of effective and safe methods to prevent the spread of COVID-19. These factors include use of methods acceptable to workers and are easy for them to adopt and putting a check on production cost because of the extensive cost rise in the purchase of miscellaneous items such as sanitizers, PPE kits, masks for operators at the shopfloor. The overall worker safety is of utmost at priority, but the production should not be hampered, and costs need to be kept at a minimum level. The applications briefed here can only be possible by successful and efficient implementation of CPS in production facilities.

4.3.1 Predictive Maintenance (PdM)

This application is one of the critical applications concerning the health of systems and its sub-systems at the unit level of i-CPPS framework. Although this term is not new and in industry environment,human operators do these tasks based on their experiences. The main requirements of PdM in a fully autonomous production scenario are connectivity, interoperability, information availability, and decision-making capabilities as listed in [110]. These all requirements are fulfilled in the proposed i-CPPS framework as all the data is available at EDGE devices and in the FOG network, with AI modelling capabilities at shop-floor level. One application of PdM is tool wear prediction in machining, which is directly related to product quality and production efficiency. If tool wear prediction is done well in advance and compensatory steps are taken such as choosing optimized machining parameters, then the production quality can be controlled, production efficiency can be optimized, and the tools are used till their actual life and wastage can be reduced, etc. Also, this application is much more relevant in a pandemic like situation as maintenance scheduling can be done based on health data, tool orders can be placed based on production requirements in advance, production facilities can be more optimized, critical jobs can be scheduled based on health status data, etc.

4.3.2 Remote Machine Control and Monitoring

This application lays emphasis on controlling the unit level entities in a remote fashion as done in [111], here through OPC UA, where a robot is controlled remotely. This application in terms of COVID-19 requirements plays a significant role as the entities are controlled by operators without touching them, it can be done either through a voice-based control or gesture-based control or through mobile applications which provide the human operators access to machine tools based on their authority. This application does have some challenges like connectivity problems, technical glitches, security aspects which can be tackled and mostly have already been tackled in the i-CPPS framework presented in previous section. The unit level devices are connected to FOG network which can control them and provides a path to control them, also the MATLAB Production Server has an SSL based authentication and secured HTTPS which covers the security aspects and lastly a web-based app or mobile app can be easily connected to Firebase SDK and Google Cloud which based on requirements can provide a secure access to machine tools. Also, if an operator is available in the factory and in front of a unit device, it can communicate with the help of Bluetooth or Wi-Fi through EDGE devices.

4.3.3 Self-Awareness Capabilities in Physical Systems

One of the key elements of Industry 4.0 is to impart consciousness to physical entities, so as to make them aware about themselves. This awareness makes them smarter and further pushes them to think and take decisions in an autonomous way. This consciousness can only be imparted by implying technologies present under an Industry 4.0 cloud with a tight integration of software modules and hardware systems.

AI and the deep learning algorithms surely will play a deeper role in achieving it and the neural network models need to be running on these physical elements and they need to process the data coming from various sources like sensors, motion systems, environment, human inputs, etc. One example of these bigger applications could be the self-repair capability, the physical entity can diagnose the fault in the servo motors, or by inspecting the product surface roughness can get to know itself that there is an issue that needs addressing. For example for surface quality, either a finishing tool is required to be changed if it has reached the end of its life or if optimized machining parameters are to be used. These capabilities can reduce the need of a human operator for inspection purposes thereby directly reducing the health risks of COVID-19. Also, as the connectivity is a key element of cyber-physical systems, and in cases where machine is not able to troubleshoot itself at first place, it can call for help by sending text messages or e-mails to the persons in charge or event to domain experts. This ultimately reduces the need of domain experts amid the travel restrictions of COVID-19 and mitigating the exposure risk. As this application will also include digital twin which forms a digital replica of the physical system and tries troubleshooting in a simulated environment before replicating the same in real time.

5. Discussions and Conclusion

The COVID-19 pandemic has a large impact on the manufacturing sector across the world. But the long-term operation of factories in a safe manner is a need in these difficult times. The CPS and its related technologies can be a solution to tackle such situations. The current chapter has proposed an Intelligent Cyber-Physical Production System framework for manufacturing facilities to transition towards the goal of Industry 4.0 and is complemented by the detailed prototype use-case implementation. The implementation is followed by three applications which are helpful in the COVID-19 pandemic situation. This framework's key highlights include detailed steps with focus on individual building blocks of i-CPPS framework.

The requirements listed in Section 2 are addressed and implemented in Section 4. Starting from the query and manufacturing of a custom part with delegation of work to specific smart unit level entities and even check for the necessary raw materials and tools pointing towards a goal-oriented manufacturing which is what the requirement **R1** is. Also, the deployment of smart algorithms of tool wear detection and optimum parameter selection satisfies the **R2** as of making the CPPS elements self-aware and self-optimize. The various protocols utilized in the implementation ranging from Ethernet I/P to EtherCAT and even RS-485 shows the interconnection and interoperability in the framework focussing on **R3**. Further due to interoperability and the modular nature of the CPPS elements addition and deletion of elements is quite easy and the same was tested by addition of vibrations sensors to the CNC machine, partially fulfilling the requirement **R4**. Section 4.1.6 shows the information models implemented at shop-floor level which focuses on the component definitions, so as they can be utilized in various applications and the decision-making tasks like scheduling maintenance related tasks satisfying the **R5**. Looking at the data flowing in the current implementation and as elaborated in Sections 4.1.2–4.1.8, the data acquisition, structuring, processing, and smart AI/ML model-based inferencing was done with dashboards to show the results covering the requirements **R8**, **R9**, and **R10**. Also, the FOG cluster takes care of the security perspectives in current implementation like a TLS/SSL based encryption and certificate/token-based authentication methods for various elements and databases connected to it and data flows through it in a secured manner fulfilling the needs of requirement **R11**.

This work is targeted to contribute towards the goal of the Smart Manufacturing/ Industry 4.0 by implementing an architecture which can help in the transition to an Industry 4.0 compliant organization. After working with the implementation of i-CPPS framework on a single machining centre, it is understood that this framework is fully scalable, and the primary step would be more or less same for all unit level devices whether it is a robot or a conveyor. The information models would come in handy for judging the capabilities of the factories and real-time data, and AI based modelling would further help in almost all phases of the product life cycle, not just for the products manufactured, even for these unit level devices also. One more important aspect of current implementation is that all the software and hardware modules used are industrial compliant systems, enabling manufacturers to utilize this work as a base for transition of their own industries to a smart Industry 4.0 compliance industry. This framework contributes to a smarter and digitized future.

Considering the danger of COVID-19 it is still uncertain when the production facilities will be able to work at their maximum capacities in an efficient manner. But this i-CPPS framework has shown some light that the digitalization trend can help in tackling these difficult times with ease. Although the COVID-19 pandemic will be over, but the lasting effects it will leave behind can be managed by this digital trend of transition manufacturing industries towards a bright future where batch size one production will be possible at minimal costs with the least wastage.

References

1. Baldwin, R. and B.W.D. Mauro. Economics in the time of COVID-19: A new eBook. VOX CEPR Policy Portal, (2020).
2. Wu, D., D.W. Rosen, L. Wang and D. Schaefer. Cloud-based design and manufacturing: A new paradigm in digital manufacturing and design innovation. Computer-Aided Design, 59 (2015): 1–14.
3. Tao, F., Y. Cheng, L. Zhang and A.Y.C. Nee. Advanced manufacturing systems: Socialization characteristics and trends. Journal of Intelligent Manufacturing, 28(5) (2017): 1079–1094.
4. Tao, F., L. Zhang and A.Y.C. Nee. A review of the application of grid technology in manufacturing. International Journal of Production Research, 49(13) (2011): 4119–4155.
5. Xu, X. From cloud computing to cloud manufacturing. Robotics and Computer-integrated Manufacturing, 28(1) (2012): 75–86.
6. Ren, L. L. Zhang, L. Wang, F. Tao and X. Chai. Cloud manufacturing: Key characteristics and applications. International Journal of Computer Integrated Manufacturing, 30(6) (2017): 501–515.
7. Challenges Facing the Manufacturing Industry and Taking the First Steps toward the Revitalization of Manufacturing. Association for Manufacturing Excellence, USA (accessed 10 April 2021). https://www.ame.org/sites/default/

files/AME_Whitepaper_Challenges%20Facing%20Industry%202011-02-24%20FINAL.pdf. (2011).

8. Wu, D., M.J. Greer, D.W. Rosen and D. Schaefer. Cloud manufacturing: Drivers, current status and future trends. *In:* International Manufacturing Science and Engineering Conference, American Society of Mechanical Engineers, 55461 (2013): V002T02A003.

9. Putnik, G., A. Sluga, H. ElMaraghy, R. Teti, Y. Koren, T. Tolio and B. Hon. Scalability in manufacturing systems design and operation: State-of-the-art and future developments roadmap. CIRP Annals, 62(2) (2013): 751–774.

10. Tao, F., Y. Cheng, L.D. Xu, L. Zhang and B.H. Li. CCIoT-CMfg: Cloud computing and internet of things-based cloud manufacturing service system. IEEE Transactions on Industrial Informatics, 10(2) (2014): 1435–1442.

11. Gunes, V., S. Peter, T. Givargis and F. Vahid. A survey on concepts, applications and challenges in cyber-physical systems. KSII Transactions on Internet & Information Systems, 8(12) (2014).

12. Study: Present and future of technical maintenance. Bearing Point, Germany. (accessed on 10 April 2021). https://www.bearingpoint.com/de-de/unser-erfolg/insights/gegenwart-und-zukunft-der-technischen-instandhaltung/ (in German), (2015).

13. Schreiber, M., K. Vernickel, C. Richter and G. Reinhart. Integrated production and maintenance planning in cyber-physical production systems. Procedia CIRP, 79 (2019): 534–539.

14. Smart Maintenance for Smart Factories. Acatech-National Academy of Science and Engineering, Germany (accessed on 10 April 2021). https://www.acatech.de/wp-content/uploads/2018/03/acatech_POSITION_KF_EN_Smart_Maintenance_final.pdf. (2015)

15. Monostori, L., B. Kádár, T. Bauernhansl, S. Kondoh, S. Kumara, G. Reinhart, O. Sauer, G. Schuh, W. Sihn and K. Ueda. Cyber-physical systems in manufacturing. Cirp Annals, 65(2) (2016): 621–641.

16. Monostori, L. Cyber-physical production systems: Roots, expectations and R&D challenges. Procedia Cirp, 17 (2014): 9–13.

17. Lee, J., B. Bagheri and H-A. Kao. A cyber-physical systems architecture for industry 4.0-based manufacturing systems. Manufacturing Letters, 3 (2015): 18–23.

18. Zhang, C., P. Jiang, K. Cheng, X.W. Xu and Y. Ma. Configuration design of the add-on cyber-physical system with CNC machine tools and its application perspectives. Procedia Cirp, 56 (2016): 360–365.

19. Liu, C. and X. Xu. Cyber-physical machine tool – The era of machine tool 4.0. Procedia Cirp, 63 (2017): 70–75.

20. Sharpe, R., K. Van Lopik, A. Neal, P. Goodall, P.P. Conway and A.A. West. An industrial evaluation of an Industry 4.0 reference architecture demonstrating the need for the inclusion of security and human components. Computers in Industry, 108 (2019): 37–44.

21. The Industrial Internet of Things Volume G1: Reference Architecture. Industrial Internet Consortium, USA (accessed on 10 April 2021). https://www.iiconsortium.org/IIC_PUB_G1_V1.80_2017-01-31.pdf. (2017).

22. Current Standards Landscape for Smart Manufacturing Systems. NIST, USA (2016) (accessed on 10 April 2021). https://nvlpubs.nist.gov/nistpubs/ir/2016/NIST.IR.8107.pdf

23. Wei, S., J. Hu, Y. Cheng, Y. Ma and Y. Yu. The essential elements of intelligent manufacturing system architecture. *In:* 2017 13th IEEE Conference on Automation Science and Engineering (CASE), IEEE, (2017): 1006–1011.

24. Woo, J., S-J. Shin, W. Seo and P. Meilanitasari. Developing a big data analytics platform for manufacturing systems: Architecture, method and implementation. The International Journal of Advanced Manufacturing Technology, 99(9) (2018): 2193–2217.

25. Modoni, G.E., A. Trombetta, M. Veniero, M. Sacco and D. Mourtzis. An event-driven integrative framework enabling information notification among manufacturing resources. International Journal of Computer Integrated Manufacturing, 32(3) (2019): 241–252.

26. Lu, Y. and X. Xu. Cloud-based manufacturing equipment and big data analytics to enable on-demand manufacturing services. Robotics and Computer-Integrated Manufacturing, 57 (2019): 92–102.

27. Component Specific Machining Center Configuration by the Use of Additional Cyber-physical Modules. BaZMod Consortium, Germany (accessed on 10 April 2021). http://www.bazmod.de/ (2016) (in German).

28. Bagheri, B., S. Yang, H.-A. Kao and J. Lee. Cyber-physical systems architecture for self-aware machines in industry 4.0 environment. IFAC-PapersOnLine 48(3) (2015): 1622–1627.

29. Liu, C. and P. Jiang. A cyber-physical system architecture in shop floor for intelligent manufacturing. Procedia Cirp, 56 (2016): 372–377.

30. Cook, W., A. Driscoll and B. Tenbergen. Airborne CPS: A simulator for functional dependencies in cyber physical systems: A traffic collision avoidance system implementation. *In:* 2018 4th International Workshop on Requirements Engineering for Self-Adaptive, Collaborative, and Cyber Physical Systems (RESACS), IEEE, (2018): 32–35.

31. Vierhauser, M., J. Cleland-Huang, S. Bayley, T. Krismayer, R. Rabiser and P. Grünbacher. Monitoring CPS at runtime – A case study in the UAV domain. *In:* 2018 44th Euromicro Conference on Software Engineering and Advanced Applications (SEAA), IEEE, (2018): 73–80.

32. Qu, F., F-Y. Wang and L. Yang. Intelligent transportation spaces: Vehicles, traffic, communications, and beyond. IEEE Communications Magazine, 48(11) (2010): 136–142.

33. Baheti, R. and H. Gill. Cyber-physical systems. *In:* Impact Control Technology, IEEE Control Systems Society, IEEE, (2011): 161–166.

34. Kim, K-D. and P.R. Kumar. Cyber–physical systems: A perspective at the centennial. Proceedings of the IEEE, 100(Special Centennial Issue) (2012): 1287–1308.

35. Lee, I. and O. Sokolsky. Medical cyber physical systems. *In:* Design Automation Conference, IEEE, (2010): 743–748.

36. Arney, D., S. Fischmeister, J.M. Goldman, I. Lee and R. Trausmuth. Plug-and-play for medical devices: Experiences from a case study. Biomedical Instrumentation & Technology, 43(4) (2019): 313–317.

37. Chibani, A., Y. Amirat, S. Mohammed, E. Matson, N. Hagita and M. Barreto. Ubiquitous robotics: Recent challenges and future trends. Robotics and Autonomous Systems, 61(11) (2013): 1162–1172.

38. Dimitrov, V., V. Jagtap, M. Wills, J. Skorinko and T. Padır. A cyber physical

system testbed for assistive robotics technologies in the home. *In:* 2015 International Conference on Advanced Robotics (ICAR), IEEE, (2015): 323–328.

39. Mikusz, M. and A. Csiszar. CPS platform approach to industrial robots: State of the practice, potentials, future research directions. *In:* PACIS, (2015): 176.

40. Saad, A. and A. Gamatié. Water management in agriculture: A survey on current challenges and technological solutions. IEEE Access, 8 (2020): 38082–38097.

41. Liu, R., Y. Zhang, Y. Ge, W. Hu and B. Sha. Precision regulation model of water and fertilizer for alfalfa based on agriculture cyber-physical system. IEEE Access, 8 (2020): 38501–38516.

42. Rad, C.-R., O. Hancu, I.-A. Takacs and G. Olteanu. Smart monitoring of potato crop: A cyber-physical system architecture model in the field of precision agriculture. Agriculture and Agricultural Science Procedia, 6 (2015): 73–79.

43. Tang, S., Q. Zhu, X. Zhou, S. Liu and M. Wu. A conception of digital agriculture. *In:* IEEE International Geoscience and Remote Sensing Symposium, IEEE, 5 (2002): 3026–3028.

44. Taneja, J., R. Katz and D. Culler. Defining CPS challenges in a sustainable electricity grid. *In:* 2012 IEEE/ACM Third International Conference on Cyber-Physical Systems, IEEE, (2012): 119–128.

45. Zhou, X., Z. Yang, M. Ni, H. Lin, M. Li and Y. Tang. Analysis of the impact of combined information-physical-failure on distribution network CPS. IEEE Access, 8 (2020): 44140–44152.

46. Bermejo, J.F., J.F.G. Fernández, A.J.G. López, F.O. Polo, A.C. Márquez and V.G.-P. Díaz. A CPS for condition based maintenance based on a multi-agent system for failure modes prediction in grid connected PV systems. *In:* Value Based and Intelligent Asset Management, (2020): 165–185. Springer, Cham.

47. Rodrigues, F., C. Cardeira, J.M.F. Calado and R. Melício. Family houses energy consumption forecast tools for smart grid management. *In:* CONTROLO 2016, (2017): 691–699. Springer, Cham.

48. Lins, R.G., P.R.M. de Araujo and M. Corazzim. In-process machine vision monitoring of tool wear for cyber-physical production systems. Robotics and Computer-integrated Manufacturing, 61 (2020): 101859.

49. Industrial Value Chain Reference Architecture (IVRA). Industrial Value Chain Initiative, (2016) (accessed on 10 April 2021). https://iv-i.org/docs/doc_161208_Industrial_Value_Chain_Reference_Architecture.pdf.

50. Ribeiro, L. Cyber-physical production systems' design challenges. *In:* 2017 IEEE 26th International Symposium on Industrial Electronics (ISIE), IEEE, (2017): 1189–1194.

51. Garcia, M.V., E. Irisarri, F. Pérez, E. Estévez and M. Marcos. OPC-UA communications integration using a CPPS architecture. *In:* 2016 IEEE Ecuador Technical Chapters Meeting (ETCM), IEEE, (2016): 1-6.

52. https://www.mtconnect.org (accessed on 10 April 2021).

53. https://opcfoundation.org/about/opc-technologies/opc-ua (accessed on 10 April 2021).

54. The Singapore Smart Industry Readiness Index. Singapore Economic Development Board, Singapore (accessed on 10 April 2021). https://www.edb.gov.sg/en/news-and-events/news/advanced-manufacturing-release.html., (2019)

55. Zakoldaev, D.A., A.V. Shukalov and I.O. Zharinov. From Industry 3.0 to Industry 4.0: Production modernization and creation of innovative digital companies. *In:* IOP Conference Series: Materials Science and Engineering, 560(1) (2019): 012206. IOP Publishing.

56. Rosendahl, R., N. Schmidt, A. Lüder and D. Ryashentseva. Industry 4.0 value networks in legacy systems. *In:* 2015 IEEE 20th Conference on Emerging Technologies & Factory Automation (ETFA), IEEE, (2015): 1–4.

57. Trappey, A.J.C., C.V. Trappey, U.H. Govindarajan, A.C. Chuang and J.J. Sun. A review of essential standards and patent landscapes for the Internet of Things: A key enabler for Industry 4.0. Advanced Engineering Informatics, 33 (2017): 208–229.

58. https://i4amf.aigroup.com.au/streams/standards-guidelines/ (accessed on 10 April 2021).

59. http://i40.semantic-interoperability.org/index.html#about (accessed on 10 April 2021).

60. Shao, G., S-J. Shin and S. Jain. Data analytics using simulation for smart manufacturing. *In:* Proceedings of the Winter Simulation Conference 2014, IEEE, (2014): 2192–2203.

61. Yin, S. and O. Kaynak. Big data for modern industry: Challenges and trends [point of view]. Proceedings of the IEEE, 103(2) (2015): 143–146.

62. Tao, F., Q. Qi, A. Liu and A. Kusiak. Data-driven smart manufacturing. Journal of Manufacturing Systems, 48 (2018): 157–169.

63. Chang, W-Y. and S.-J. Wu. Big data analysis of a mini three-axis CNC machine tool based on the tuning operation of controller parameters. The International Journal of Advanced Manufacturing Technology, 99(5) (2018): 1077–1083.

64. Fahmideh, M. and G. Beydoun. Big data analytics architecture design—An application in manufacturing systems. Computers & Industrial Engineering, 128 (2019): 948–963.

65. Pereira, T., L. Barreto and A. Amaral. Network and information security challenges within Industry 4.0 paradigm. Procedia Manufacturing, 13 (2017): 1253–1260.

66. Kieseberg, P. and E. Weippl. Security challenges in cyber-physical production systems. *In:* International Conference on Software Quality, (2018): 3-16. Springer, Cham.

67. Chhetri, S.R., N. Rashid, S. Faezi and M.A.A. Faruque. Security trends and advances in manufacturing systems in the era of industry 4.0. *In:* 2017 IEEE/ACM International Conference on Computer-Aided Design (ICCAD), IEEE, (2017): 1039–1046.

68. Atzori, L., A. Iera and G. Morabito. The internet of things: A survey. Computer Networks, 54(15) (2010): 2787–2805.

69. Internet of Things in 2020 Roadmap for the Future. Infso D.4 Networked Enterprise and Rfid Infso G.2 Micro and Nanosystems in Co-Operation with the Working Group Rfid of the Etp EPoss (accessed on 10 April 2021). https://docbox.etsi.org/erm/Open/CERP%2020080609-10/Internet-of-Things_in_2020_EC-EPoSS_Workshop_Report_2008_v1-1.pdf,(2008).

70. Gilchrist, Alasdair. Industry 4.0: The industrial internet of things. Apress, 2016.

71. Alexopoulos, K., S. Koukas, N. Boli and D. Mourtzis. Architecture and

development of an Industrial Internet of Things framework for realizing services in Industrial Product Service Systems. Procedia CIRP, 72 (2018): 880–885.

72. Liao, Y., E. de Freitas, R. Loures and F. Deschamps. Industrial Internet of Things: A systematic literature review and insights. IEEE Internet of Things Journal, 5(6) (2018): 4515–4525.

73. Jeschke, S., C. Brecher, T. Meisen, D. Özdemir and T. Eschert. Industrial internet of things and cyber manufacturing systems. *In:* Industrial Internet of Things, (2017): 3–19. Springer, Cham.

74. Boyes, H., B. Hallaq, J. Cunningham and T. Watson. The industrial internet of things (IIoT): An analysis framework. Computers in Industry, 101 (2018): 1–12.

75. Zhou, Z., J. Hu, Q. Liu, P. Lou, J. Yan and W. Li. Fog computing-based cyber-physical machine tool system. IEEE Access, 6 (2018): 44580–44590.

76. O'donovan, P., C. Gallagher, K. Bruton and D.T.J. O'Sullivan. A fog computing industrial cyber-physical system for embedded low-latency machine learning Industry 4.0 applications. Manufacturing Letters, 15 (2018): 139–142.

77. Wu, D., S. Liu, L. Zhang, J. Terpenny, R.X. Gao, T. Kurfess and J.A. Guzzo. A fog computing-based framework for process monitoring and prognosis in cyber-manufacturing. Journal of Manufacturing Systems, 43 (2017): 25–34.

78. de Brito, M.S., S. Hoque, R. Steinke, A. Willner and T. Magedanz. Application of the fog computing paradigm to smart factories and cyber-physical systems. Transactions on Emerging Telecommunications Technologies, 29(4) (2018): e3184.

79. Qi, Q. and F. Tao. A smart manufacturing service system based on edge computing, fog computing, and cloud computing. IEEE Access, 7 (2019): 86769–86777.

80. Yu, W., F. Liang, X. He, W.G. Hatcher, C. Lu, J. Lin and X. Yang. A survey on the edge computing for the Internet of Things. IEEE Access, 6 (2017): 6900–6919.

81. Shi, W., J. Cao, Q. Zhang, Y. Li and L. Xu. Edge computing: Vision and challenges. IEEE Internet of Things Journal, 3(5) (2016): 637–646.

82. Xu, L.D. and L. Duan. Big data for cyber physical systems in industry 4.0: A survey. Enterprise Information Systems, 13(2) (2019): 148–169.

83. Gokalp, M.O., K. Kayabay, M.A. Akyol, P.E. Eren and A. Koçyiğit. Big data for industry 4.0: A conceptual framework. *In:* 2016 International Conference on Computational Science and Computational Intelligence (CSCI), IEEE, (2016): 431–434.

84. Wang, L. and G. Wang. Big data in cyber-physical systems, digital manufacturing and industry 4.0. International Journal of Engineering and Manufacturing (IJEM), 6(4) (2016): 1–8.

85. Chen, B., J. Wan, L. Shu, P. Li, M. Mukherjee and B. Yin. Smart factory of industry 4.0: Key technologies, application case, and challenges. IEEE Access, 6 (2017): 6505–6519.

86. White Paper: Factory of the future. International Electrotechnical Commission, Geneva (accessed on 10 April 2021). https://www.iec.ch/whitepaper/ futurefactory/ (2015).

87. Bergweiler, S. Smart factory systems – Fostering cloud-based manufacturing based on self-monitoring cyber-physical systems. Development, 2 (2016): 3.

88. Yoon, S.C., J. Um, S.-H. Suh, I. Stroud and J.-S. Yoon. Smart Factory Information Service Bus (SIBUS) for manufacturing application: Requirement, architecture and implementation. Journal of Intelligent Manufacturing, 30(1) (2019): 363–382.

89. Kamble, S.S., A. Gunasekaran and S.A. Gawankar. Sustainable Industry 4.0 framework: A systematic literature review identifying the current trends and future perspectives. Process Safety and Environmental Protection, 117 (2018): 408–425.

90. https://www.mathworks.com/products/matlab-production-server.html (accessed on 10 April 2021).

91. https://cloud.google.com (accessed on 10 April 2021).

92. https://firebase.google.com/docs/storage/gcp-integration (accessed on 10 April 2021).

93. Natarajan, U., P.R. Periyanan and S.H. Yang. Multiple-response optimization for micro-endmilling process using response surface methodology. The International Journal of Advanced Manufacturing Technology, 56(1–4) (2011): 177–185.

94. He, Yan, Pengcheng Wu, Yufeng Li, Yulin Wang, Fei Tao and Yan Wang. A generic energy prediction model of machine tools using deep learning algorithms. Applied Energy, 275 (2020): 115402.

95. Li, H., W. Wang, Z. Li, L. Dong and Q. Li. A novel approach for predicting tool remaining useful life using limited data. Mechanical Systems and Signal Processing, 143 (2020): 106832.

96. Wu, J., K. Hu, Y. Cheng, H. Zhu, X. Shao and Y. Wang. Data-driven remaining useful life prediction via multiple sensor signals and deep long short-term memory neural network. ISA Transactions, 97 (2020): 241–250.

97. https://www.mathworks.com/hardware-support/raspberry-pi-matlab.html (accessed on 10 April 2021).

98. Shao, H., H.L. Wang and X.M. Zhao. A cutting power model for tool wear monitoring in milling. International Journal of Machine Tools and Manufacture, 44(14) (2004): 1503–1509.

99. https://www.mathworks.com/products/deep-learning.html (accessed on 10 April 2021).

100. https://www.mathworks.com/products/statistics.html (accessed on 10 April 2021).

101. https://www.mastercam.com/ (accessed on 10 April 2021).

102. Cai, W., W. Zhang, X. Hu and Y. Liu. A hybrid information model based on long short-term memory network for tool condition monitoring. Journal of Intelligent Manufacturing, 31(6) (2020): 1497–1510.

103. Iqbal, F. and S. Jha. Closed loop ball end magnetorheological finishing using in-situ roughness metrology. Experimental Techniques, 42(6) (2018): 659–669.

104. https://www.mathworks.com/help/deeplearning/ref/deepnetworkdesigner-app.html (accessed on 10 April 2021).

105. https://www.mathworks.com/help/deeplearning/ref/neuralnetclustering-app.html (accessed on 10 April 2021).

106. https://www.mathworks.com/help/deeplearning/ref/neuralnetfitting-app.html (accessed on 10 April 2021).

107. https://www.mathworks.com/help/deeplearning/ref/neuralnetpattern recognition-app.html (accessed on 10 April 2021).
108. https://www.mathworks.com/help/deeplearning/ref/neuralnettimeseries-app.html (accessed on 10 April 2021).
109. https://www.mathworks.com/products/reference-architectures/tableau.html (accessed on 10 April 2021).
110. Meesublak, K. and T. Klinsukont. A cyber-physical system approach for predictive maintenance. *In:* 2020 IEEE International Conference on Smart Internet of Things (SmartIoT), IEEE, (2020): 337–341.
111. Ayatollahi, I., B. Kittl, F. Pauker and M. Hackhofer. Prototype OPC UA server for remote control of machine tools. *In:* Proceedings of International Conference on Innovative Technologies, (2013): 73–76.

Online Education during the COVID-19 Pandemic: An Indian Perspective for Better Planning

Abhishek Bhatnagar* and Nomesh B. Bolia

1. Introduction

Coronavirus disease (COVID-19) started in the month of December 2019 and spread to different parts of the world within the next few weeks. The rate of transmission of the disease was high enough that it caused the governments of different countries to put restrictions on public activities that included a full or partial lockdown of the services. India was put under full lockdown on March 25, 2020 and certain restrictions on the movement of goods and people started even before the full lockdown was imposed in the country. Schools and colleges were shut down early in March and students were advised to leave the campuses (of Higher Educational Institutions, (HEI's)) in order to avoid the risk of virus spread. This initiated the online mode of delivering the lectures/instructions to the students in schools and HEI's [1]. The chapter contains a literature review on the types of online learning systems, challenges faced in online learning and associated barriers. After the literature survey, it lists out some problems faced specifically in the Indian context and certain ways to overcome these challenges and barriers.

2. Literature Review

The literature review has been classified into four broad parts, namely, (i) Online Education systems and its types, (ii) Characteristics of online education systems, (iii) Challenges and barriers in the online education systems and (iv) Impact of the COVID pandemic on education systems.

2.1 Online Education Systems

Education systems can be broadly divided into two parts (i) where the students and

*Corresponding author: abhishekjmi11@gmail.com, mez158446@iitd.ac.in

teachers physically attend the school/college and lectures are delivered through a direct contact between the students and teachers and (ii) where students have access to the content through the use of Information and Communication Technology (ICT) tools [2]. The second mode of education delivery is known as online education [3]. Further, this can be classified in terms of the requirement of an internet connection (live classes/synchronous) or recorded classes (asynchronous) where the content is uploaded and can be viewed later upon the availability of the internet connection and convenience [1, 3]. In the online education setting, the content is created by the faculty who teaches a given course [4], the delivery is enabled through an online platform where students and teachers can interact with each other (synchronous), that is, two way communication in case of live classes or one way communication in case of recorded lectures (asynchronous) [5, 6]. Paulsen [5] discusses two models of online education, a simplistic model, named jigsaw model of online education and a more complex version called the hub model. The four main components of online education are Content Creation Tools (CCT), Learning Management Systems (LMS), Student Management Systems (SMS) and Accounting Systems (AS). In the Jigsaw model, these four systems interact CCT with LMS, LMS with SMS and SMS with AS [7]. The hub model is the more realistic model but a complex one to cater to a large number of students and faculty. In this model, Student Management Systems (SMS) takes the central stage (hub) and the other systems interact with it. This, is in addition to the four components, and also has the Prospective System, Logistics System and the Customer Relationship Management System.

2.2   Characteristics of Online Education Systems

Online learning systems can offer flexibility in terms of the delivery of content in a variety of ways using videos, presentation slides, boards etc. [1, 3, 8, 9]. These can be useful for students who prefer learning through visual tools. Furthermore, a teacher can cater to a large number of students at a particular time. The lectures can be accessed at a later stage by the students in asynchronous mode [8]. Further, this is cost efficient and eliminates transportation costs and can be accessed from any location with internet connectivity [10, 11]. These can be accessed through a variety of devices such as mobile phones, tablets, laptops and desktop [12].

Though the online system of education has several advantages, however, it offers certain disadvantages and several barriers to its actual implementation. The disadvantages of the online system of education are an increase in screen time for students that can cause potential health hazards for them, including being lazy and lethargic as they do not travel to school [13]. It can cause monotony and isolation for the students, as they are away from their peers [14]. Teachers need to be properly equipped with the required hardware and have proper training to use the teaching software [4]. For the synchronous mode of learning, this would require proper internet connectivity [15]. Further, personal cognition is another issue where each learner has a different way of learning. A student can find it tough to adapt to online learning which involves less interaction between teacher and learner as compared to a physical classroom setting [4, 9, 14]. One of the major disadvantages of online based systems is the difficulty in assessments as compared to a physical classroom [11]. Also, an online system may hinder the social and holistic development of an individual.

2.3 Challenges and Barriers in the Online Education Systems

While there are advantages of the online system, there are many barriers to its implementations within a short span of time for both the teachers and students [16–18]. The barriers/issues can be classified in terms of (i) those faced by the faculty, (ii) those faced by the students and (iii) those faced by facilitators. Also, these can be classified in terms of (i) technological barriers, (ii) infrastructural barriers, (iii) pedagogical and assessment barriers and (iv) interpersonal and social barriers.

For the faculty, the online system of education brings about a pedagogical challenge on how to create good quality content that can be delivered to the students without monotony and boredom [16]. However, with an increased number of platforms available with different features, it becomes difficult to decide on a suitable platform for delivering a particular type of topic in a course. This requires teachers to be well versed with multiple platforms. Further, there is an absence of eye to eye contact between the teacher and students as there would be in a physical classroom, hence, it becomes difficult for the teacher to get an appropriate feedback from the students of their understanding of the lesson [1]. Additionally, the evaluation part becomes difficult since students have different levels of connectivity, it is tough to maintain a consistent scheme of assessment [11, 16].

For the students, the main challenge is to cope up with a large amount of screen time that can potentially cause boredom due to much less interaction with the teachers and classmates. Since, different teachers prefer to use a dissimilar mode of ways, the students need to be equipped with the relevant software in their devices and should be able to use them. However, this is a challenge in India particularly in the case of school education in rural settings due to the digital illiteracy of the parents. Further, time management in online assessments is an issue where the students have to write on paper and then click a photo/scan and upload on the respective online system. Usage of a variety of devices/gadgets with variable camera quality is also a challenge. Also, there is a mismatch in the marks obtained and the actual calibre of the students due to malpractices owing to limited proctoring of assessments.

For the facilitators, scheduling of the lectures is a major concern to ensure a seamless learning process for the students. Further, they need to ensure availability of the hardware for the teachers and students [17] and to train the teachers on certain aspects of technology and software packages for delivering lectures.

2.4 Impact of the COVID Pandemic on the Education Systems

The COVID-19 pandemic has impacted the way industries used to function. Since the lockdown has been imposed in different parts of the world, the education systems have shifted in an online mode more due to the need of the hour rather than by choice. Some recent practices to deal with sudden shift to online mode of education have been identified through few pieces of recently published literature on online education. Kimmel et al. [19] entails the development of multiple kinds of material for a topic based on providing a better learning of the subject so that the videos are not too long and monotonous. Further, students should be encouraged to take notes during the entire online class to keep themselves involved and grasp the concepts better.

Yucesoy-Ozkan et al. [20] describe the situation in Turkey, a country that has limited internet connectivity for its population, and provided free internet data access to the students. It further, used TV channels to provide educational content for the students. However, TV does not have an interactive feature which is a disadvantage as it creates monotony. Further, they conducted live lectures through a centralized portal in addition to the use of platforms like Zoom, Google Meet, Skype etc. Also, a centralized database of the worksheets and files were uploaded. However, strict evaluation practices were not followed in schools. The higher education institutions also shifted to live online classes as well as related materials.

A study carried in Spanish schools and universities highlighted that students enjoyed online learning in terms of the content, however, missed the social aspects of face to face learning [21].

A study carried in Bhutan revealed positive experiences while using google classroom. However, enabling google classroom was a challenge due to the digital divide in Bhutan. This effort was mandated centrally by the Ministry of Education [22].

3. Online Education Delivery in the Indian Context

India is a vast country with varied demographics and socio-economic backgrounds. A traditional classroom system of education is mostly followed in the country, and there is a high level of familiarity with physical classroom teaching and learning process. Additionally, many families live in a single room housing, which creates disturbances and makes it harder for the students to concentrate. Several households have far fewer the number of devices required for learning than the actual number of children who require these devices.

However, a sudden shift to the online system without leaving time for any preparations and training has resulted in certain barriers. We divide the barriers to online learning specific to the Indian context and the sudden shift to online system for schools as well as for Higher Educational Institutions. The barriers in the online

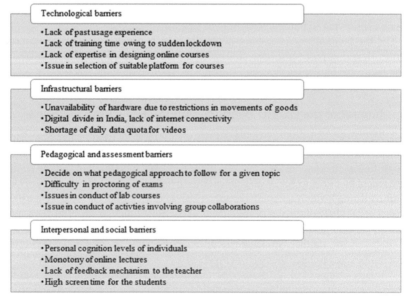

Figure 12.1: Barriers to online education and due to sudden shift to online education.

system of education especially during a pandemic time have been divided based on the literature survey and discussions with faculty and students, which can be divided into the following broad and sub-categories in Fig. 12.1.

4. Solutions to these Challenges in the Indian Context

While there are many challenges due to the sudden shift to the online mode of education in India, these can be better planned through the appropriate use of technology. The hardware challenges need to be overcome initially to facilitate the use of technology. In a rural setting, distribution of the hardware to individuals is very difficult due to the consideration of cost, as well as the difficulty on reaching remote areas due to movement restrictions [23]. For such areas, small learning centres can be facilitated with appropriate social distancing measures where large televisions/projectors can be installed and classes of different grades scheduled at different times for those without hardware availability. These can be optimally done by using mathematical models in public sector domains [24, 25] such as facility location models and assignment models [26] to assign students to these locations and scheduling models to schedule the lectures. These are appropriate at the school level since most of the students are locals and have same language preference. However, such setups are not cost friendly in the cases of lesser demand, as in the case of higher education where students have gone home and each area does not cater to a large number of students for a given course. In such a case, distribution of individual devices mostly facilitated by their institutions is a better option and relevant software can be customized based on the needs. This hardware distribution can be done optimally through the Vehicle Routing Problem (VRP). An online portal can be developed such that requirements of specific locations can be captured and relevant hardware need is taken care of. The schema is shown in Fig. 12.2.

India is a country that has a large number of languages and dialects which makes it very tough for designing course content in all regional languages in a short span of time, especially in the case of school education. Further, different education boards have different content and its associated pedagogy that needs to be converted into effective online teaching learning material. Here, different boards can decide on a pre-specified curriculum and materials be made in main languages and further be translated using appropriate technologies and language processing softwares as in Fig. 12.3.

To overcome the monotony of the online lectures, it should be ensured that blended learning happens which is a combination of videos, slides, games to engage students, online assignments to encourage collaboration that can be done through platforms like Google Classrooms [7]. School children are younger in age and not tech savvy, hence, proper training of parents to use the relevant tools should be provided. These tools should be easy to use and be provided in multiple languages to cater to parents with different backgrounds [23]. A totally online education may not be desirable for ever (after pandemic times), however, in the current scenario, there is a scope to evolve and engage in new practices. In emergencies, such prior planning and a totally online mode of education will work. Apart from that, a hybrid system which uses the best of both in-person interaction between teachers and peers, and, online tools will deliver the best results.

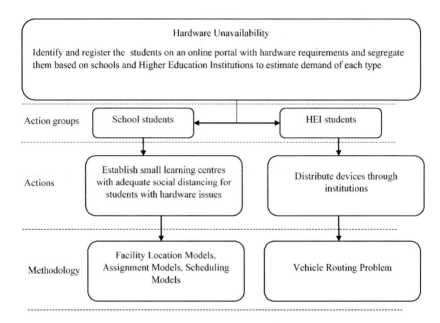

Figure 12.2: Tackling hardware unavailability issues.

Figure 12.3: Content creation in local languages

Once the situation normalizes, the teaching mode should be blended in order to utilize the latest technology as well as physical classes. This will help people with different cognition levels to understand the content better. Also, the material developed can be further refined and utilized for a better teaching learning processes. Additionally, animations to show the functioning of equipment for lab courses can be useful, however, they can seldom replace the actual laboratory experience for the students that gives an hands-on opportunity for learning. For example, certain branches of engineering like Computer Science has comparatively fewer issues being taught online as much of the content can be covered online, however, core engineering branches that require laboratory equipment and field data find an online system difficult and it also hampers the research ecosystem in these branches.

5. Conclusion

This chapter presented the characteristics of online education which has been a reality amongst schools and Higher Education Institutions as a result of the COVID-19 pandemic. Few studies/practices related to the transitions to online education were presented in the chapter and barriers related to the Indian context were reported. A solution framework for the Indian context was offered. Mathematical Modelling along with language processing tools can be useful for better decision making and the delivering of these lectures. A concept of blended learning can be implemented in the future with contents suitable for online and offline learnings be identified and developed accordingly.

References

1. Karyala, P. and S. Kamat, Online education in India – the good, the bad and the ugly! (2021).
2. Lee, J.W. Online support service quality, online learning acceptance, and student satisfaction. Internet High. Educ., 13(4) (2010): 277–283.
3. Doyumğaç, I., A. Tanhan and M.S. Kiymaz. Understanding the most important facilitators and barriers for online education during COVID-19 through online photovoice methodology. Int. J. High. Educ., 10(1) (2020) 166.
4. Lloyd, S.A., M.M. Byrne and T.S. Mccoy. Faculty-perceived barriers of online education. J. Online Learn. Teach., 8(1) (2012): 1–12.
5. Paulsen, M.F. Online education systems: Discussion and definition of terms. Online J. Distance Learn. Adm. 5(3) (2002): 1–8.
6. Peimani, N. and H. Kamalipour. Online education and the Covid-19 outbreak: A case study of online teaching during lockdown. Educ. Sci., 11(2) (2021): 1–16.
7. Chang, W. and V. Benson. Jigsaw teaching method for collaboration on cloud platforms. Innov. Educ. Teach. Int., (2020): 1–13.
8. Chen, T., L. Peng, B. Jing, C. Wu, J. Yang and G. Cong. The impact of the COVID-19 pandemic on user experience with online education platforms in China. Sustain., 12(18) (2020): 1–31.
9. Berge, Z.L. Barriers to Online Teaching in Post-Secondary Institutions: Can Policy Changes Fix It? (1996).
10. C.C. of Aurora. PROGRAMS & CLASSES [Online]. Available: https://www.ccaurora.edu/programs-classes/online-learning/benefits-online-education, (2021).
11. Kumar, D. Pros and Cons of Online Education, (2010).
12. Kamali, A. and L. Kianmehr. The paradox of online education: Images, perceptions, and interests. US-China Educ. Rev. A, 5(9) (2015): 591–601.
13. Gautam, P. Advantages and disadvantages of online learning [Online]. Available: https://elearningindustry.com/advantages-and-disadvantages-online-learning, (2021).
14. Pappas, B.C. Top 8 eLearning barriers that inhibit online learners engagement with eLearning content [Online]. Available: https://elearningindustry.com/top-elearning-barriers-that-inhibit-online-learners-engagement-elearning-content (2021).
15. Singh, D.K. 10 barriers to overcome for growth of online education in India [Online]. Available: https://coursewareworld.com/online-learning-in-india-and-its-barriers/ (2021).
16. Joshi, A. and M. Vinay. Impact of coronavirus pandemic on the Indian education sector: Perspectives of teachers on online teaching and assessments. Interact. Technol. Smart Educ., (2020).

17. Onyema, E.M., Impact of Coronavirus pandemic on education. J. Educ. Pract., 11(13) (2020): 108–121.
18. Korkmaz, G. and C. Toraman. Are we ready for the post-COVID-19 educational practice? An investigation into what educators think as to online learning. Int. J. Technol. Educ. Sci., 4(4) (2020): 293–309.
19. Kimmel, H.S., J.D. Carpinelli, G.T. Spak and R.H. Rockland. A methodology for retaining student learning during the pandemic, in educational practices during the COVID-19 viral outbreak. International Perspectives, (2020): 17–34.
20. Yucesoy-Ozkan, S., F. Kaya, E. Gulboy, D.E. Altun and N. Oncul. General and special education practices during the Covid-19 viral outbreak in Turkey. International Perspectives, (2020): 35–78.
21. Alba-Linero, C., S.-N. Moral-Sanchez and P. Gutierrez-Castillo. Impact of Covid-19 on education in a Spanish University: What should we change? in Educational Practices during the COVID-19 viral outbreak. International Perspectives, (2020): 97–122.
22. Kado, K., N. Dem and S. Yonten. Effectiveness of Google classroom as an online learning management system in the wake of Covid-19 in Bhutan: Students' perceptions, in educational practices during the COVID-19 viral outbreak. International Perspectives, (2020): 137–158.
23. Malik, A. Over 80% parents in 5 states say digital schooling failed during lockdown. Study, (2021).
24. Gupta, M. and N.B. Bolia. Efficiency measurement of Indian high courts using DEA: A policy perspective. J. Policy Model., 42(6) (2020): 1372–1393.
25. Bhatnagar, A. and N.B. Bolia. Analysis of school performance in Delhi, India using Decision Tree Algorithm. *In:* Proceedings of the International Conference on Industrial Engineering and Operations Management Dubai, UAE, March 10-12 (2020): 569–570.
26. Bhatnagar, A. and N.B. Bolia. Improved governance of Indian school system through school consolidation. J. Policy Model., 41(6) (2019): 1160–1178.

Part V
Use cases of Solutions to Pandemic Challenges

The Future Workplace: A Symbiotic System of Systems Environment

Alistair McConnell, Daniel Mitchell, Karen Donaldson, Sam Harper, Jamie Blanche, Theodore Lim, David Flynn and Adam Stokes*

1. Current State of the Energy Sector in the United Kingdom

The United Kingdom (UK) generated 119.3TWh of renewable energy in 2019 an increase of 8.5% on 2018, meaning that 36.9% of the UK's energy supply came from renewables. In the first quarter of 2020 alone, 47% of electricity generated came from renewables [1] and by 2050 the goal is for 100% of it to be from renewable sources. A recent analysis showed that the UK was placed to be able to deploy over 40GW of offshore wind generation by 2030 [2].

In the UK the predominant mode of production of renewable energy is through wind, both from onshore and Offshore wind farms [3]. However, the UK still relies on oil, gas and nuclear power to fully sustain its electrical demands [4]. The entire energy sector still requires humans to aid in energy generation, whether this is operating machinery on an Oil Rig in the North Sea, and monitoring systems in a control room for an Offshore Turbine or nuclear power plant.

Humans are typically required for performing inspection and monitoring operations as well as interventions when required. These jobs are considered to be located in extreme environments such as areas of extreme weather [5], potential Hydrogen Sulphide build up [6, 7] and high-pressure equipment blowouts [8] to name but a few. All these issues and dangers still exist but there is now the COVID-19 pandemic to also consider.

All regions of the world have been affected by the COVID-19 pandemic, the main transmission of the virus appears to be airborne and while maintaining one's safety is possible outside the risk is considerably greater when the environment is enclosed/confined [9]. Offices and factories have proven ideal breeding grounds for COVID-19 outbreaks [10, 11] showing the chance of the virus spreading indoors an increase in comparison to outdoors and this even extends to multiple floors and entire

*Corresponding author: adam.stokes@ed.ac.uk

buildings dependent on the air conditioning systems used. For this reason, the vast majority of countries affected by the pandemic are either in or have used one form or another of lockdown [12].

Lockdowns or stay at home regulations require workers where possible to as the name suggests to stay at home and work from there, this limits the possibility of viral spread and has reduced the overall CO_2 emissions [13] however the amount of power used domestically has increased [14].

The question is how can these new dangers of a pandemic and the past dangers of the extreme environments be mitigated using cyber-physical systems? A Symbiotic System of Systems Approach (SSOSA) via bidirectional communications can ensure the knowledge transfer across system elements to enhance the connectivity between robotics, infrastructure, and environmental systems.

2. Trends in Industrial Asset Management

As industry can be asset-heavy, the implementation of asset management can be viewed as an essential part of the effectual and efficient operation of an industrial organization. These asset-heavy industries can encounter over-capacity and low investment returns, therefore it is crucial for these organizations to implement a management system that allows for a continual life cycle, optimal operation and general equipment effectiveness through a complete asset management strategy [15]. It is necessary to identify what assets an organization has and to monitor and regularly inspect their current condition in order to effectively maintain them [16].

The term industrial asset management is used to describe any systematic process that maintains an asset throughout its lifecycle, through continuous planning and controlling, with the aim of maximising the reliability, lifetime, safety and value of assets whilst minimising costs [17].

Asset management is implemented through strategic policies that not only maintain assets but includes any actions that are required following any form of failure. These policies should align with the objectives and asset purpose of an organization, to achieve a steady operation to meet these objectives whilst maintaining a desired level of quality [18].

An established, optimized asset management strategy should be a detailed and thorough overview of an organization's assets with consideration to any existing management objectives and performance targets. It should include a detailed risk management directory outlining current asset conditions with any historical and predicted deterioration and mechanical failures. Additionally, it should account for all financial and resources capabilities as well as constraints.

The International Organizations for Standardization (ISO) have produced an overview of asset management along with asset management systems. These standards identify common asset management procedures that are applicable for implementation across a broad range of organizations, asset types and cultures [19].

Asset management ought to consist of some defined key principles and attributes to be successful [19].

- Primarily, the asset management approach should be holistic rather than compartmentalized and identify risks with their associated costs and/or benefits (risk-based).

- Additionally, it should be systematic and be a repeatable, consistent, and methodical approach (systematic).
- And it should establish the ideal value of performance and cost over an assets life cycle (optimal).
- It should also consider how the asset may change and thus perform in the future to guarantee that there is sufficient provision made for any future requirements of the asset (sustainable).
- Whilst recognizing that, to ensure success that the combination of attributes and all interdependencies are vital to this success (integrated).

For these principles to be successfully implemented there are a few essential aspects that should be considered. The organization should have good leadership and be working with a clear direction. The staff should be competent, have cross-functional coordination and commitment to the systematic process of asset management.

The ISO of asset management further explains that asset management required a coherent direction from management and actioning and implementation by knowledgeable and experienced employees. The ISO of asset management explains that lead management should show evidence of how they plan and commit to the execution and development of the organization's asset management structure and how they will continually improve its effectiveness. This involves selecting people responsible for the assets and the asset system to ensure that it delivers all the outlined requirements of the asset management policies objectives and strategies.

If a there is no articulated direction and outlined priorities, then the management of assets becomes very difficult and it is at risk of becoming inefficient and ineffective, which wastes resources, time, and money. Therefore, the ISO have outlined several enablers that are important for effective asset management and have a substantial impact on the efficiency and effectiveness on an asset management system. These enablers are described as: (i) structure, authority and responsibilities; (ii) outsourcing of asset management activities; (iii) training, awareness and competence; (iv) communication, participation and consultation; (v) asset management system documentation; (vi) information management; (vii) risk management; (viii) legal and other requirements; (ix) management of change [19]. It is evident that these enablers and key principles require and rely on continual human involvement and actions.

The global, ongoing, COVID-19 (coronavirus) pandemic was declared as a Public Health Emergency of International concern, by the World Health Organization (WHO) in January 2020. Later in March 2020, it was declared as a global pandemic. Prevention methods were put into place by each country's government to reduce the spread of the virus and to bring some level of overall protection to the population. These prevention methods included the wearing of facemasks, avoiding going out in public, social distancing as well as being advised to work (remotely) from home as a replacement for going to your place of work.

The COVID-19 pandemic, when it occurred, was an unexpected and unprecedented situation. Throughout the world, companies and organizations had to adapt and conform to the new restrictions and repercussions that came with the situation, which brought unique challenges with it. One of these challenges was managing their assets, as with employees working from home it is difficult to remain in control and consistent with the company's assets.

The challenges that occur with people working remotely are, largely, due to two different concerns. One being that with company employees requiring equipment to work at home, then a company can find it difficult to keep, literal track of their assets due to an increase in employee use of company devices. As to where these assets, such as laptops or software licences, are and who is operating them and in what capacity which can lead to assets being lost or becoming unaccounted for. Secondly, with employees not being able to frequently, if at all, work on site at a company there is increased risk linked with an absence of systematic asset management being conducted due to the necessity for human involvement. Consequently, the global pandemic has, further, pushed companies and organizations to reassess how they implement their asset management systems and how their employees can work effectively whilst working remotely [20–22].

Therefore, despite these standardizations and guidelines several industrial organizations have not optimized the operations and performances of their assets, especially in situations of exceptional and unanticipated circumstances [23, 24]. Industrial organizations can be challenged with insufficient and inaccurate maintenance procedures and money loss or interruptions to production due to unplanned outages and downtimes. Therefore, industrial processes are presently undergoing a digital transformation which is creating with it a new generation of intelligent, automated asset management solutions.

The world is continually making technological advances which can often mean that industrial companies can find themselves without a mature asset management strategy, due to insufficient data, which inevitably can lead to several challenges. However, these technological advances intelligence have also provided large amounts of asset data which has proven beneficial to asset management [25].

Industry 4.0, frequently designated the fourth industrial revolution or the Internet of Things (IoT), and was first developed in 2011 with the aim of maximising the productivity and efficiency in industry. The overall concept of Industry 4.0 is to connect the physical and virtual world together to solve various issues and problems in industry [26]. This is achieved using the internet and with the application of cyber-physical systems in an industrial production to achieve the Internet of services and the internet of things (IoT) [27]. IoT allows health monitoring of assets in real-time through automated data collection, which is analysed by algorithms for predictive maintenance (PdM).

Two other methods of maintenance are preventive and reactive, where the asset monitoring is conducted as cycle based or a run-to-failure respectively. One of the most effective ways to avoid failure of an asset is to plan for regular maintenance to reduce the risk of the asset's failure probability increasing. However, the probability of failure that is associated with the age of the asset, only accounts for a small percentage of total assets owned by an organization. Furthermore, the remaining percentage of the assets will fail at irregular and random intervals. This makes preventive maintenance an inappropriate approach for this particular group of assets as it is likely that they could deteriorate and/or fail between the times scheduled for maintenance. In addition to this, reactive maintenance can be costly for critical assets as this will involve the interruption of production and thus there will be a lost revenue associated with this.

Historically, the application of predictive maintenance was fragile and expensive, as it involved the creation of custom programming software which allowed several systems to interface with each other to obtain data and deliver reports or warnings. However, any changes in this integration could cause the application to break.

Industrial Internet of Things (IIoT) platforms have made the development and support of predictive maintenance simpler.

As industrial markets are asset-intensive it is evident why asset management, reactive and predictive, and the general optimization of assets is significant to industries such as oil, gas, and manufacturing. Therefore, a particular priority of Industry 4.0 is the optimization of the management and tracking of assets. Further, Asset Performance Management (APM) 4.0 enables organizations to go beyond merely understanding their asset structure but to develop their asset usage in a much more comprehensive way. The main technological enablers of Intelligent Asset Management (IAM) are cloud computing, Internet of things, big data management and cyber security. IAM systems combines asset management with digitization to provide effective and optimized asset management through exceptional knowledge exchanges and management [28].

Asset management can be significantly enhanced through the development of digital technologies, e.g. Artificial Intelligence (AI) and Digital Twins (DT). As we have seen, data is crucial to effective asset management. This data can be classified into two different categories, reference and operational data which can be explained as data that informs us about everything concerning asset components, functioning and its configuration and data that can provide a real-time status, environmental data and maintenance history respectively. The combination of these data sets is referred to as a DT. Through a combination of these digital technologies, it is possible to conduct predictive or prescriptive maintenance and to link current asset management systems with those for process control.

An organization that has an IoT network are able to use smart assets that can transmit real-time data on the current condition of an asset to a central control centre, from which the key performance indicators (KPIs) can be calculated from the gathered data through the use of machine learning algorithms and AI. This automated data analysis can identify any trends and irregularities in the data to optimize and prioritize a schedule of required maintenance [29].

It was discussed earlier that maintenance practices can be separated into different categories, namely, preventive, conditional and reactive. Through the IIoT, two further categories have evolved, predictive and prescriptive maintenance strategies. Prescriptive maintenance is a multi-variate model that utilizes various equipment and process data to identify and resolve or repair an issue, which is especially valuable in diagnostic situations where advanced or specialized knowledge or skills are required. Predictive maintenance that utilizes machine learning or individual algorithms specific to pieces of equipment for automated and multivariant data collection, this can be particularly useful in situations where a critical asset will encounter unexpected downtime which can have a substantial impact on an organization.

Sensorization is the terminology used to describe the use and integration of numerous sensors on a machine or device. Sensors are an effective and economical method for measuring and monitoring various variables such as temperature and vibration, therefore, sensors can enable equipment to detect any issues through an automated process.

The implementation of Industry 4.0 can be achieved, in part, through sensorization However, before this can occur it is necessary for any existing operations to be digitized to allow for real-time detection of faults and problems. Real-time monitoring allows for immediate action should a fault or problem occur, eliminating any delays which can prove to be costly to an organization. Additionally, real-time monitoring produces a data bank of useful and informative information regarding an asset that can in turn be used to optimize its operations.

Currently, asset monitoring is heavily human dependent. Sensorization removes the requirement of human monitoring which can, on occasions, lead to improper practice or insufficient detailing. By removing human reliance from asset monitoring this can allow for resources to be used in other critical areas as well as permitting, as mentioned, auto-detection of issues and the following required actions.

Due to the dangerous nature of the environment that requires sensorization, Robotics and Autonomous Systems (RAS) are becoming the go to method for sensor placement. They are not only being used for placing sensors but for independent inspection, monitoring and maintenance of any area required. The predominant use of robotics in the offshore sector has been in the form of Remote Operated Vehicles (ROVs) [30] and Autonomous Underwater Vehicles (AUVs) [31]. A comprehensive review of the recent developments in robotics for the Oil and Gas (O&G) sector has been published by Bogue [32].

These inspection methods can only be used periodically as they are expensive to deploy as all require trained operators and ships to launch from. Although providing essential information, they do not offer any form of real-time monitoring.

The potential for fire or explosion on any offshore platforms can be considered one of the most dangerous scenarios [33], and for this reason, any potential robot that has to operate in this area, would need to adhere to the ATEX directive 2014/34/EU in the European Union, the DSEAR in Britain or obtain IECEx certification for outside the EU and USA regions. A method of mitigating the danger of electronic ignition is to remove the electronics and replace them with an integrated fluidic logic circuit [34]. Fluidic logic circuits are at fundamental stage of research and have therefore not been deployed in the field to fully test them but have seen a recent uptick in research development [35–38].

A trend in the field of robotics is the increased integration or entire migration away from hard rigid robotic components traditionally used towards the use of soft flexible systems. Soft robotic systems can be both safer for humans to be close to due to their compliance [39] but they can also be a lower risk to the overall working environment since if there is a collision the robot should just deform around the object and thus not damage the structure. Soft robots have been used in the field for marine life sampling [40] and recent developments have allowed them to dive to the depths required for deep-sea foundation monitoring [41]. A comprehensive review of area of soft robotics for marine environments has been created by Aracri et al. [42].

RAS are certified as safe upon their purchase from a manufacturer. However, from this point onwards, there is no current method to verify that a robot is safe and certified as fully operational for deployment. A future enabler in the trustworthy deployment of RAS and AI includes the servitization of these assets. This is defined as the requirement to inspect a robotic platform to ensure that the platform is certified as operationally reliable, safe and has the ability to function fully. The service procedure should be set out by the manufacturer and regulated by a governing body. The service schedule recommends specific checks and replacement parts including actuators and sensors at certain intervals based on a reliability model of the component. As Cyber-Physical Systems (CPS) are deployed in more remote scenarios, for example, deployed further from the shoreline in the offshore sector, an increasing requirement is to ensure the reliability of these assets for Beyond Visual Line of Sight (BVLOS) operations. This includes the reliability of robotics which can utilize run-time reliability ontologies and infrastructure which employs effective asset management procedures.

For the use of any RAS assets an operator would typically begin to learn how to control a robot through a simulator and once experienced on that system they would be training in-situ on the robots themselves. Once given operational control the operator would normally view a control panel and a view from any onboard camera on a computer screen. This view can be limiting for the operator and as asset inspection and maintenance has progressed and band width for robotic systems have increased the use of Virtual Reality (VR), Augmented Reality (AR) and mixed reality (MR) have also begun to be used. VR has seen an increasing use for robotic operational training [43, 44] while the use of AR and MR is increasing in usage when the robot is being controlled [45, 46].

It can be seen that even before the pandemic there was a shift to using sensorization, RAS, VR and AR, the restrictions placed upon workers for travel and office work has accelerated the uptake and investment in the trends which augment remote work. The next section explains the current asset management methodologies that are used in the energy industry and how they are developing to incorporate an increase in CPS.

3. Asset Management Methodologies

The energy industry requires a continuous year-round cycle of maintenance which requires the permanent presence of a Condition and Performance Monitoring (CPM) system [47]. The CPM systems are designed to maximize production uptime and asset availability. CPM systems react to the asset managers need to continuously demonstrate 'fitness for service' and improve the understanding of an assets condition. This supports the decision-making process for de-rating, process optimization and scheduling for remedial action and maintenance. There is also an objective of providing evidence-based knowledge to support the extension of components Remaining Useful Life (RUL) where this justification ties with brown fields.

Technological advancements have enabled oil and gas deployments to expand into deep and ultra-deep waters [48, 49] however, this presents challenges due to more hazardous weather conditions and increasing distance to the shoreline. It is therefore essential to improve an understanding of the numerous potential issues related with deployment and operation in unfamiliar environments and accept full answerability for the subsequent economic consequences. Subsea well system interventions and repairs become increasingly expensive due to longer delays because of availability and mobilization durations for the required intervention vessels. These costs increase alongside the distance from a fault to the shoreline.

Short- and long-term success and efficiency of the management of inspection, maintenance and repair activities directly affect Key Performance Indicators (KPI) including:

1. **Availability:** How many assets are ready for operation?
2. **Reliability:** Maintenance should be the first priority to ensure reliability. This has been considered a key objective in subsea operations conducted by the O&G sector.
3. **Life Cycle Costs:** Neglected maintenance results in more expensive remedial action as failing equipment needs to be replaced which reduces the life cycle

costs of the equipment and increases costs. Scheduled maintenance should instead be optimized where the cost requirements for the life cycle of the asset must be considered as the failures per equipment per time of operation.

4. **Safety:** Assets should have the capability to perform safely and must follow set safety standards. The safety parameters must be designed for all types of assets. A measurement should be created to measure the safety parameter per asset per maintenance level and repair. An asset is only available as fully operational if this measurement is 0%.

5. **Asset Management Satisfaction:** A direct impact on the asset manager satisfaction will be achieved from an effective maintenance which has been performed to high quality and will last a long duration. The asset manager is affected by the status monitoring and maintenance of the equipment.

One method that is being used to maximize the Remaining Useful Life (RUL) of assets and maintain peak system-level effectiveness, is that a myriad of industries have been transitioning from traditional reactive condition-based monitoring and maintenance systems to a predictive maintenance model. This transition is essential to gain a Return on Investment (ROI) and reach performance targets. To manage KPIs more effectively and provide support for asset managers with a systematic work process for successfully managing technical risk and uncertainties, this section presents a knowledge representation framework for end-to-end intelligent asset maintenance systems and processes. This work also presents the groundwork in developing a maintenance knowledge-based model describing the O&G environments and similar industrial scenarios.

3.1   Maintenance Processes in the Oil and Gas Industry

Complex industrial assets including floating production, storage, and offloading (FPSO) vessels, underwater wells and pipelines require maintenance which is often an intricate and critical task. Maintenance activities include techniques such as on-condition monitoring and predictive maintenance. Different types of maintenance outlining the flow of actions for each are displayed in Fig. 13.1 [50].

Standard maintenance is typically performed with respect to time. This usually relates to safety-critical items, including valves and Emergency Shut Down (ESD) systems. During this period, maintenance regimes and records for all assets must be kept and stored efficiently. This can be a time-consuming task unless a modern well system control and data gathering system is available and in place. There is also the problem that assets can deteriorate just as rapidly if they are being unused as compared to operational every day; the items which deteriorate will vary for each case. Condition monitoring is completed by examining the operation of the equipment and changing components or parts of the equipment shows signs of wear beyond pre-set limits. On-board monitoring usually does the inspection where the data is stored and then downloaded for the maintenance facility. Predictive maintenance systems are focused on the analysis of current equipment states with the objective to expose emerging problems which will prevent catastrophic failure via device maintenance. The aim of predictive maintenance is to detect smaller problems which require smaller remedial action rather than large failures. Predictive maintenance can allow for the modification of system parameters, replacement or tuning of components and drives down expenses for equipment upkeep as faults and failures increase the downtime of an asset and can damage devices severely.

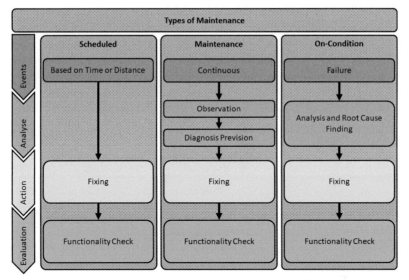

Figure 13.1: Types of maintenance and their succession of events [51].

Predictive maintenance regimes require access to the condition of assets to both look at data and the knowledge which can be obtained from the data. Reasoning algorithms within embedded decision-making agents can optimize the long-term management of heterogeneous assets and allow for a rapid response to events by autonomously coupling resource capabilities with alerts in real-time.

A challenge represented in CPM is that these applications are mono domain, targeting only systems (i.e. flowlines or control systems). Therefore, it often isolates the platforms and restricts the potential of multiple coordinated actions between adaptive collaborative systems.

In typical information flows, the main use of the data acquisition systems is to collect information from the sensor data. In order to embed tools which can support decision making and interoperability, it is required that these systems have the capability to deal with and understand the highly complex and dynamic environments they are installed in. Decision support tools are therefore constricted to the quality and scope of the information available.

Shared knowledge representation is therefore required to give them the required common situational awareness. Knowledge from two sources can provide this information: the domain knowledge retrieved by the expert and the inferred knowledge from the processed sensor data. For these two examples, it is essential for the data to be stored, accessed, and shared efficiently via deliberative agents in near to run time.

3.2   Data Flow in Maintenance Processes

Maintenance processes depend on comprehensive and timely delivery of information from embedded data gathering systems to the persons performing the required operations. This enables for the integration of maintenance related information from multiple sources into an automated maintenance system in order to give appropriate maintenance support. The variety of data contributes to the maintenance process and is represented in the data flow illustrated in Fig. 13.2 which represents the typical life cycle of maintenance activities [50].

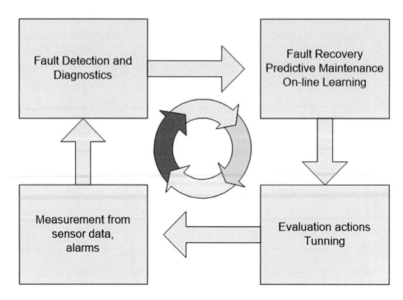

Figure 13.2: Flow diagram of maintenance processes [51].

When observing the maintenance environment, knowledge is produced by interactions among systems, system observers, obstacles, engineering objects and instruments. Complex system interactions must be forwarded into infrastructural layers established on the knowledge of a system, which must be dedicated to human and data communications. For the environment which requires a large amount of problem solving, their collective vocabularies must be associated with the communication crossing the layers. The synthesis of this information would impact on the knowledge technologies employed for solving engineering problems encountered within the maintenance domain.

3.3   Knowledge-based System for Maintenance Domain

Maintenance, as with any other engineering process, is the human effort to alter or facilitate an environment to become more suitable or responsive to perceived human requirements. Many different physical outputs are created as a result; define, design, develop or maintain a system. A wide range of personnel are involved in engineering; engineers, managers and others who produce artefacts. The majority of knowledge about a system is created from a combination of human observations, designs and experiments as a result. This includes ensuring that a system and the relevant personnel, all know what they know and when they need to know it; resulting in mutualistic and commensalistic symbiosis. With a computing perspective, knowledge management must be implemented. This must encapsulate its meta-systems in whichever forms to show how knowledge is grounded from a level of engineering to the level of business organization that managed the engineering processes.

Logical extensions can be made to integrate information in knowledge-based systems. Therefore, the concept of knowledge is presented within this chapter with attention to each details as this is considered a driving element of intelligent maintenance systems. This commences with the basic definition of the knowledge-based system where this task is abstract and extends to the maintenance domain for O&G. The knowledge-based system will be constructed with a number of different layers to represent different aspects of the systems as maintenance activities.

A key objective which is presented in this chapter is to establish a knowledge-based system for the maintenance domain with coherence of the interaction between infrastructure and data, objects, humans, systems, devices and communications to achieve or solve problems. This also includes software tools and all support systems including computers, web and data networks.

For a coherent infrastructure all the involved interactions, and some aspects and system concepts need to be considered before establishing the main requirements for the maintenance of a knowledge-based system.

- Models can be created in a wide range of domains—this includes a range of viable alternatives. The most effective solution almost always depends on the possible extensions and applications.
- The development of a knowledge-based system is an iterative process.
- Concepts in the system should be close to objects (physical or logical) and relationships in the domain of interest, e.g., asset maintenance domain. These are most likely to be nouns (objects) or verbs (relationships) in sentences that describe the domain.

Going into further detail, the implementation of a knowledge-based system and how detailed or general the system will be designed to be will guide many of the decisions for the model. Among a number of options, some aspects can be determined or designed to work more effectively for the projected task, be more intuitive, more extensible and with increased maintainability. Furthermore, the knowledge-based system facilitates a model of reality of the world where the concepts within the system must reflect this reality. Once the first version of the system is defined, it can then be evaluated and debugged by imposing it on an application or for problem solving methods or by discussion with experts in the field. This would then result in the initial model then being revised and improved where an iterative process of design continues throughout the entire lifecycle of a knowledge-based system.

3.4 Model for Predictive Maintenance

As discussed previously, predictive maintenance for assets in the O&G environment is a knowledge-intensive task which tends to be performed or supervised by human experts. The primary objective of the predictive maintenance processes is to improve equipment reliability by identifying problems before they cause failure and further damage which will render it as a catastrophic failure and increase the lifecycle costs of the asset. The secondary objective is to provide advanced warning of developing problems before the equipment fails catastrophically during operations in production. In order to avoid an unexpected breakdown of the system, its goal is to predict when and what maintenance actions are required. Figure 13.3 illustrates all the inputs and outputs which should be considered in the intelligent maintenance process of a system for the realization of predictive maintenance.

Embedded tools and annotated sensor data serves as an input for the prediction and diagnostic task to produce optimum fault detection. Diagnostic and prediction outputs serve as an input to the planning task involving sub-tasks such as fault recovery and on-line learning. For constructing a model, Fig. 13.3 describes the array of tasks

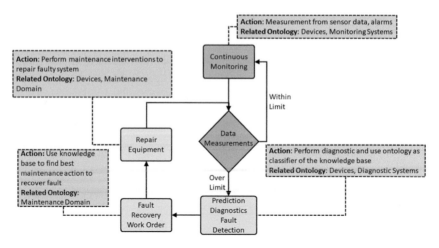

Figure 13.3: Inputs and outputs involved in predictive maintenance [51].

and their breakdown into subtasks which are required. If a list of input/output roles are in place to serve as knowledge roles is created where the most important elements can be created by different knowledge types. These knowledge types include domain, concepts, relations or rules and are described as follows:

- **Parameter:** A calculated or measured quantity whose value can detect abnormal behaviour.
- **Source:** An element that can be observed or detected.
- **Symptom:** A negative source.
- **Norm:** Expected values of a parameter for normal condition.
- **Discrepancy:** A quantified difference to the norm.
- **Fault:** Cause of symptom.
- **Location:** Where a symptom or fault is found.
- **Action:** An activity to eliminate a fault or to improve situation.

The knowledge roles could represent the meta-concepts in the knowledge-based system and could be expressed in the relational task-domain (fault detection – well system). This can be observed as in Fig.13.3 due to the several domain knowledge models (i.e. ontologies [52, 53]) which can be constructed for the scenario of maintenance in the O&G environment. The models could be created for the wells where domain models could encapsulate the maintenance activities, fault detection and diagnostics. These domain models represent the knowledge of the domain independently of their own use. However, the application of predictive maintenance as a knowledge-based system will employ existing domain models using relations and concepts from these models to optimize knowledge transfer.

The domain models are where the data is collected, distributed and measured. The reports are then circulated where groups can participate and communicate with each other. Data in a physics-based infrastructure cannot be explained merely as a consequence of a differing coherence of an assertion. They depend on where the sensors are situated, where the data is channelled, who makes the assertion, how the data is stored and filtered and what methods are used to understand and explain the observed phenomenon. Therefore, the knowledge-based system is systematically constrained by the physics-based infrastructure. The prior knowledge for the model design must be closely inherent to understandings of the physical systems as well as practical experience of the systems. Therefore, the knowledge-based system is systematically constrained by the physics based infrastructure. The priori knowledge for the model design must be closely inherent to the understanding of physical systems alongside the practical experience of the systems. A process which completes problem solving for a given application can be supported by 'content' from the priori system information. Another interactive layer is human-oriented.

For example, the maintenance of an engine, used to be a traditional event where an engineer would answer a repair-call with the parts and tools required to fix the issue. It now includes how to detect the first sign of a developing problem from the engine before it reaches a failure. Engineers can analyze the failure of equipment and utilize forecasting to assess the chance of failure of the same equipment failing in the same asset or other units, or proceed with data gathering, data clustering, testing, fault or defect diagnosis, planning spare parts, making recommendations, reporting major factors affecting a systems life, all in a technical and timely manner. All layers are meaningful and usable only when a system observer participates in a particular communication. Whether a maintenance engineer can exploit in an elliptical or anaphoric resolution is dependent on the role that the engineer has most recently played in the communication in the physics-based infrastructure.

The domain model is a description of the real-world things of interest and consists of a set of conceptual classes, their associations and attributes modelled with knowledge-based class descriptions. In the O&G example, the domain model consists of faults which can be described by a failure event. Furthermore, condition monitoring methodologies are employed to trigger predictive action when failure states are predicted. Predictive maintenance actions can be classified as a subclass of a proactive maintenance type similar to a scheduled maintenance action. The possibility of a fault can be reduced due to proactive maintenance. In case of a failure state, reactive maintenance action, or on-condition, restores the system state to normal. Reactive and proactive maintenance actions are subclasses of maintenance actions. All these concepts related to the asset maintenance domain are presented in Fig. 13.4, where it can represent the initial knowledge model to anchor the collaborative approach in the knowledge model design.

The Maintenance Type I the key concept of this model. A fault triggers the Maintenance Type depending on the nature of the problem (Existing Fault or Incipient Fault) the maintenance type is classified into two different and disjoint Corrective Maintenance or Predictive Maintenance. Associated to each Maintenance Type individual, there is a Work Order, which lists the variety of Maintenance Activity that are necessary to recover or repair the fault. In other words, the model deals with both the forecastable faults and some faults which are unknown or exceptional in their evolution. This trigger different classifications of responses. The main relationships associating these concepts are:

- Fault Requires Maintenance Type
- Maintenance Type has Work Order
- Work Order has First Maintenance Activity
- Maintenance Activity has Next Maintenance Activity

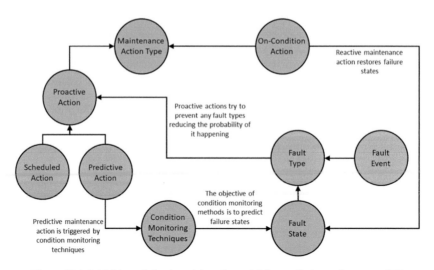

Figure 13.4: Initial knowledge-based domain model for predictive maintenance [51].

Feedback can be taken from several participants in the collaborative design process of the knowledge-based model. The sub-classification of the maintenance actions to proactive and on-condition is unnecessary. These options can be represented as instances of the maintenance action class. Furthermore, the maintenance schedule could be linked to the respective maintenance actions.

The primary aim of condition monitoring techniques is to predict the failure state, but the method could not trigger any maintenance action. Failures can be prevented by the maintenance action where the condition monitoring is associated with a number of limited failures. Also, each failure state could not be associated with a condition monitoring method.

In viewing Fig. 13.4, doubts could be made about the differences between the failure state and failure event. A fault is a possibility for or an existence of a failure event or state. However, an event is a state change of a system. This enables an event to be described with the resulting state or a state with the causing event. Events of interest that affect assets in the O&G domain in the shape of a Failure Mode and Effective Analysis (FMEA) can be seen in Table 13.1.

3.5   System Architecture

A number of different layers should be included in the construction of the knowledge-based system. The layers are used to represent different aspects of the system, for information integrating for intelligent monitoring, which is established on a multi-tier architecture and a common terminology. A view of the architecture for information integration is displayed in Fig.13.5. From the ground up, there is an abstraction and aggregation process in place, which abstracts from the low-level, proprietary information to higher-level information. This is enhanced by the semantics which are embedded in the knowledge-based model.

Table 13.1: Characteristics of events and effects considered in the knowledge-based model [51]

Event	Effect duration	Event duration	Occurrence
Fatigue	Dynamic, Vibration	Continuous	Continuous
Excessive loading	Static, Quasi-static, Dynamic	Short or continuous	Sudden
Shock loading	Vibration	Quick	Sudden
Force monitoring	Static, Quasi-static, Dynamic	Change, Drift	Continuous
Shape monitoring	Static	Long	Regular
Third party interference	Dynamic, Vibration	Quick, Change	Sudden
Fluid properties	Static, Quasi-static, Dynamic	Change	Sudden
Leak	Dynamic, Vibration	Change	Sudden

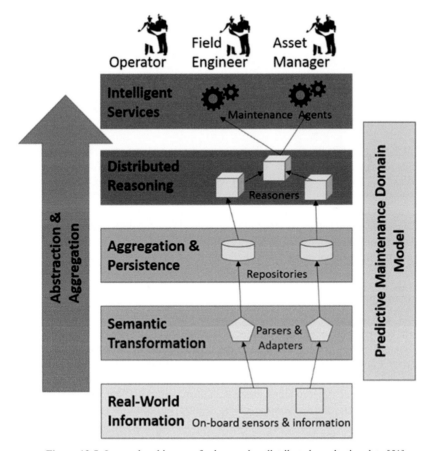

Figure 13.5: Layered architecture for integrating distributed monitoring data [51].

- **Real-World Information:** Real-world data is accessible via the lower level. This is gathered from sensors or the digital version which is stored in databases (for example in some databases of the stakeholder, in geo information systems, or on the internet). The predominant challenge for data acquisition and later integration on this layer is heterogeneity.
- **Semantic Transformation:** The second layer is where the software parsers and adapters are situated. These transform real-world data into a common language. The output of the different software parsers and adapters are kept in distributed repositories. Consistent descriptions between the predictive maintenance domain model and the semantics of the generated data (relations and properties of referenced objects) are important.
- **Aggregation and Persistence:** Repositories, databases and distributed information are integrated within this layer.
- **Predictive Maintenance Domain Model:** This layer represents an XML-based data model which uses description logics for stipulating the terminology of the predictive maintenance domain as well as the O&G domain.
- **Distributed Reasoning** [54]: This layer comprises of reasoners. This can be described as a software-based inference engine which interprets and analyses information by deriving additional data by employing descriptive logic.
- **Intelligent Services:** The top layer consists of services and maintenance agents (software agents) which can collaborate autonomously with each other to analyse certain fault scenarios. This supports corresponding decision-making tasks (for example predictive maintenance: a maintenance working order for an asset-based on symptom analysis).

4. Offshore Energy Case Study

One of the largest EPSRC funded UK based academic and industry collaboration for robotics in extreme environments is the UK Robotics and Artificial Intelligence Hub for Offshore Robotics for Certification of Assets (ORCA Hub). The ORCA Hub is a four year, multi-organization project with the primary goal to use teams of robots and Autonomous Intelligent Systems (AIS) on remote energy platforms to facilitate cost-effective, secure and enhanced efficient operational practices [46]. The ORCA Hub is a collaboration between leading industrial companies with academic institutions. The creation of a fully autonomous offshore platform, being governed and inspected from the mainland is the ultimate goal of the ORCA Hub, as it would allow for a reduction in the number of workers in hazardous environments. The idealized system created in the ORCA Hub is comprised of the remote energy platform, related assets, monitoring systems, and the heterogeneous robotic systems (aerial, surface, and marine robots) required to ensure the platforms continuous autonomous functionality.

To achieve the ORCA Hub's goal of autonomous offshore infrastructure a host of different robotic and sensors systems are required to be able to operate independently and in conjunction with each other and humans. There are multiple different areas that are required to be sensorized for accurate monitoring on an offshore energy platform. For example, on a wind turbine the blades require inspection for corrosion, water ingress and internal damage, the internal monopile, housing and nacelle require an array of sensors monitoring for different environmental measurands such as structural vibration, machine vibration, weld strain, humidity, pressure and temperature, the underwater foundation of the turbine requires inspection for scour, corrosion in the foundation and damage to the outlet pipes.

To monitor the different areas of an offshore platform there needs to be a combination of permanently deployed sensors and other inspection methods that can be used periodically and when required. The Limpet sensor [55, 56] is a multi-sensor platform created to be deployed by humans or robots wherever it is required. Each Limpet contains a temperature, vibration, strain, humidity, pressure, and light sensor as well as the ability to have custom sensors plugged into it. They offer multiple communication modalities such as infrared, Lo-Ra, Wi-Fi and acoustic. Robot Operating System (ROS) is integrated into each Limpet allowing for data transfer between the robots used in the ORCA Hub. For inspection of wind turbine blades and insulated areas a Frequency-Modulated Continuous-Wave (FMCW) has been developed [57]. To inspect metallic sections an Electromagnetic-acoustic transducers (EMAT) sensor has been developed and deployed [58].

How to deploy and these sensors in extreme environments is a key part of ORCA Hub mission and there are multiple robots being used. For terrestrial requirements, the Husky a wheeled robot developed by Clearpath Robotics [59] and the ANYmalC a quadruped robot developed by ANYbotics [60] have been used. Quadruped robots can be used to overcome obstacles that regular tracked or wheeled robots cannot achieve such as stairs or uneven terrain [61]. Aerial inspections are conducted via drones [62]. To conduct aerial operations different anchoring and perching methods [63], mobile polymer repair systems [64] as well as multiple flying morphologies [65] that could allow a drone to also perform an underwater inspection [66] were developed. Underwater inspection comes from a range of different AUV's such as the Falcon [67] and BlueROV2 [68].

To both accurately show where all the sensors and robots are located in an industrial site a DT [69] can be implemented. A DT will show a digital replica of the industrial site and can be both used for accurate simulation before robots are deployed and as real-time displays of the data being gathered by the different systems functioning at that point.

Another key and often overlooked element of implementing robotic systems into remote areas is how they will interact with the humans operating them both remotely and potentially in the field, this area is known as Human-Robot Interaction (HRI). Within the ORCA Hub the MIRIAM (Multimodal Intelligent inteRactIon for Autonomous systeMs) [70] system was created as a way for operators to query their robotics in real-time and using natural language. Work was required on how natural language could be used to command robots and to understand the information they are feeding back to the operators. Trust between human and robots is essential when it comes to performing complex and dangerous tasks [71, 72]. The primary method is through the use of natural language interactions to allow for the robot's decisions to be made in a transparent and understandable manner.

While the operation of a robot remote should not demand a large degree of physical exertion there can be a greater mental strain placed on the operator. With this strain in mind researchers have also developed ways of eye-tracking [73] and cognitive load [74, 75] that can be combined with the remote operating system to create a safer working environment.

With such a broad range of robotic and sensors systems being developed to be deployed together and to function for long periods of time with minimal to no human interaction the entire robotic ecology/system needs to be carefully designed and managed. The method proposed to efficiently and effectively do this is through the creation of a Symbiotic System of Systems Approach (SSOSA).

4.1   Design of the Symbiotic System of Systems

An assessment of the top-down challenges of Robotics and AI (RAI) and Operations and Maintenance (O&M) allows for a digital architecture which enhances the symbiosis to be created, which includes planning, functional, safety and operational necessities to ensure foresight and resilient autonomous missions. The inclusion of a SSOSA results in the creation of a symbiotic ecosystem across people, robotic platforms, infrastructure, environment, and systems.

Smart environments, CPS, robotic platforms and humans are all elements included within Symbiotic RAI relationships and are able to cooperate when performing tasks [76]. Mutualism, commensalism and parasitism are the three most fundamental forms of symbiosis. Parasitism is defined as a relationship where only the parasitic component benefits, while the host component is harmed. Interactions between one element, resulting in one being unaffected while the other benefits, is defined as commensalism. Mutualism defines a relationship where both elements benefit [77, 78].

Key barriers inhibiting the commercialization of autonomous systems include operational resilience and safety compliance in BVLOS robotics, where impediments in the development and deployment of state-of-the-art RAS were identified due to the limitations in interaction between Cooperation, Collaboration and Corroboration (C^3). This includes the interaction with human, environment, infrastructure and autonomous systems. These three interactions are based on inter-intra (internal and external) goals and laws, for instance the envelope of a mission which has been predefined. In the design of a SSOSA, C^3 results in collaborative governance to ensure the resilience of an autonomous mission, increases safety and creates a hyper enabled overview for the human operator. This accelerates the future ability to methodically characterize trusted relationships, especially as robots become resident systems and humans operate remotely.

As inspired by nature, data (information) interactions and awareness of the system are regulated by guidelines to ensure reliable communications. The SSOSA and the created Symbiotic Digital Architecture (SDA) generates an upgraded environment and model for hyper-enabled safety and operational requirements alongside knowledge distribution/sharing in autonomously operated functions and isolated robotic operators. Collaborative governance can be reached via the implementation of an ontology which is driven by AI on a RAS to monitor the resilience of the vehicle in real-time, in conjunction with edge analytics for an improvement in holistic transparency/visibility for a system. This offers a continued tactical viewpoint of a remote resource, ensuring safety governance is always at the front and centre of a mission.

In our roadmap, we define two steps in the advancement towards trusted autonomy, self-certification, and symbiosis across robotic, infrastructure and environmental systems. These paradigms signify increasing tiers of mission resilience and safety, allowing for an acceleration in effective servitization to ensure alignment of the conditions required for a progressively automated seaward ecosystem. This chapter focuses on the first tier – *"Adapt and Survive"* with our next objective our roadmap aimed at the second tier – *"Adapt and Thrive"*.

1ˢᵗTier – Adapt and Survive: An autonomous mission or operation with a mission envelope that is predefined. The architecture of the system can assess: any effects of the variables within a situation from the infrastructure,robot reliability, environment and operator interactions; collaborating and distributing data and information with a remote operator; negating unknown and known risks to the safety and reliability of the CPS and its mission. Commensalism and mutualism are achieved to ensure survivability of a CPS and the completion of the objectives of a mission without violating safety governance [79].

2ⁿᵈTier – Adapt and Thrive: An enhancement of the standards outlined in the first tier with the addition of utilizing a distribution map of knowledge which has the ability to recommend options for an observer on updated priorities of the multi-objective mission. This incorporates the RAS evaluating unanticipated variables, their outcomes and creating solutions for optimization of a mission. This develops the symbiotic relationship further where CPS are at the forefront. Resource sharing via a DT which has minimal elements of parasitic capabilities can make sure a CPS thrives however, in no way to the detriment of another RAS [79].

The SDA and SSOSA have been initially developed for the needs of the offshore renewable energy sector however, the intent is for a broader facilitation for resident and BVLOS RAS via shared operational and resilience requirements. Innovative information flows between crucial front-end systems and decision assistance across robot, isolated/remote operator and infrastructure created via a digital synthetic environment with bidirectional interaction (C^3).

4.2   Symbiotic Interactions and C³ Governance

Symbiotic relationships and interactions include formal and informal interactions that operate alongside collaborative governance. Augmented learning processes,trusted autonomy,decision-making, and problem-solving are critical in the integration of RAS/I and human interaction that results in human-robot systems. Multiple types of technologies enable symbiosis between a human and robot depending on the conditions of the function. Natural language, mouse-based or gesture interaction for MR is included within these elements of symbiotic interaction [80]. Typically, only a single element of symbiosis is captured by these technologies as illustrated within Fig. 13.6 (Previous Autonomous Systems); cooperation, collaboration, or corroboration. The SSOSA further develops the symbiotic interactions across systems to achieve collaborative governance.

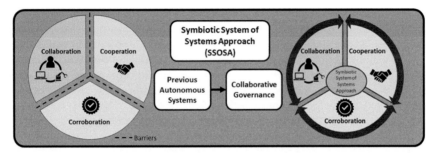

Figure 13.6: Diagram highlighting the barriers in the current state-of-the-art and the route to collaborative governance via a SSOSA.

The interrelationships between the host and symbiont represents the symbiotic interactions. We define a symbiont as a system that requires an interaction between another system's elements. The symbiont tends to depend on the host resources for it to operate effectively [81]. Rudimental symbiotic interactions are represented in Table 13.2. When a positive outcome is reached by both symbiont and host, mutualism exists in the relationship. The interaction between a robot and human can be included under this definition as the human benefits from the RAS completing objectives and the host benefits as the operator has the interaction capability to advise on the CPS operations. A commensalistic relationship is achieved when the host is unaffected and symbiont obtains a positive result. An example includes improving human efficiency via an AI bot, yet receiving no benefits in return. When the symbiont benefits at the expense of the host, the symbiont is classed as a parasite. When there is a mix of new and legacy systems the interactions between technologies could be observed as parasitic due to resource competition with the host, e.g., power drain. An example of this includes if a robotic platform (symbiont) had the capability to connect and steal charge from another robotic platform (host) for the symbiont power supply to accomplish its mission. This could detriment the mission envelope of the host as it would have a reduced battery for the completion of task. Intra-inter processes and collaborations will always generate symbiotic competition for resources. The problem we propose includes: to what degree do the decisions made become detrimental to an objective or mission? For example, a human operator may have time limitations on the completion of a project which uses a RAS. If the RAS acquires a fault, depending on the system, the human operator could override the ontology to continue the mission at the detriment of the robotic platform. Therefore, the human becomes a parasite to the system. However, automation via the development of ontologies can reduce this effect to ensure beneficial symbiotic relationships and ensure predetermined rules and regulations are followed.

Table 13.2: Fitness outcomes and symbiotic typology [79, 82]

Type of interaction	Fitness outcome	
	Symbiont	**Host**
Mutualism	Positive	Positive
Commensalism	Positive	Neutral
Parasitic	Positive	Negative

The ability to control a system remotely is defined as teleoperation. This enables a human to collaborate with a robot and can be achieved via line of sight or remotely via real-time information on a computer display. The mutualistic relationship via these types of technologies, where visualization supports the observer to improve the functionality of the robot, benefits both aspects of the paired connection. Increased levels of autonomy enable RAS to produce run-time maps of the operational environment from LiDAR sensors for path planning, where MR devices can be implemented to provide novel methods to visualize RAS and CPS [83–85].

Cooperation is often achieved via speech recognition technology which allows human operators to interact with CPS, often employed by sectors, which deal with increasingly large volumes of data [86, 87]. An information transaction hub of data can be created by the employing a DT which can virtualize and control assets for remote monitoring, interaction, and navigation. This is a form of commensalism due to the human benefitting from the relationship across the systems. The cloud computing infrastructure handles the computational burden from speech processing, leading to no effect on the performance of the robot or autonomous system, whilst augmenting the ability of the operator. Devices can be controlled with no physical inputs via the implementation of 'call out' instructions. To ensure seamless integration of 'call out' instructions, it is paramount that they are designed to be intuitive to the operation and operator, however, it is difficult for all commands to be voice-based [88].

Continuous missions typically use input systems such as standard controllers due to the operations and motions to new locations, which are not determined in the mission plan, this is the reason why voice commands are less prominent. However, voice commands which allow the robotic system to autonomously move to a directory of predetermined locations (e.g. "home" or "generator") are effective solutions [89]. Software accessibility is improved via Speech recognition, a control method only surpassed only by touch-based interactions for speed of operation for senior users [89]. Allowing for a twin to be accessible on more devices (other than a standard desktop) such as virtual reality headsets which have zero physical inputs, allowing for on-site operations to be performed.

MR devices, including the Microsoft HoloLens, operate as a cooperative technology using gesticulation via a user interface. Design standards are yet to be fully created for this technology, however, the HoloLens offers pre-created gestures within its functionality. Gestures including an 'air tap' and 'dragging' allows for interaction via sliders and option controls within in the 3D environment, in addition to the capability to reposition on-screen elements. A distinctive feature these devices offer is the capacity to visualize the environment with the virtual robot positioned within, evaluating the space for safe robot operation. The processing load is on the HoloLens, which has a devoted processor and is represented as commensalistic collaboration. The gestures create benefit to the ability of the operator to interact, whilst not being negative to the functionality of the RAS. The operation of the HoloLens is displayed in Fig. 13.7, demonstrating interaction with a model by accessing the outcomes from the DT of an offshore asset without having an influence on the functionality of the wind farm array [90].

Undesirable and unforeseen events are minimized by ensuring operators have the ability to interact with a DT simulation [91]. The comparison and accuracy of outcomes in the digital environment compared to the deployed asset establishes corroboration. Integrating this methodology with resilient and different modes from input systems protects and maintains trust in the application. The combination of collaboration and corroboration is accomplished in the DT as the remote operator may terminate the operation of a CPS when completing any objectives during a mission in run-time. Actionable information ensures that an operational overview is always available via the DT. Mutualistic and commensalistic relationships are achieved between the symbiont (operator) and host (robotic platform) to ensure there is resilience to the mission envelope and performance of the CPS. Twins date back to the 1960sin the simulations of the National Aeronautics and Space Administration (NASA) Apollo 13 mission. A physical analogue of the command module was designed to steer the malfunctioning mission on its return to earth following a crucial system failure on the vessel [92]. Recently, improvements in newly available and easy access to hardware have facilitated extensive use of DTs to observe and run simulations to attain outcomes, possibilities and incorporate training sector-wide [93–97].

Figure 13.7: Spectator view from a HoloLens where the user is utilizing the HoloLens to interact with a model of an offshore wind farm and examine the effects on the windows [14].

We discover a bottleneck in the current trajectory of robotic integration of systems defined under symbiotic envelopes. Present systems, as discussed previously in this section, are restricted to reaching a single aspect of either collaboration, corroboration or cooperation. To further advance symbiotic relations, it is vital that the combination and communication between C^3 is achieved in collaborative governance between infrastructure, people, autonomous systems and environment.

Additional instances of symbiotic interactions are clustered into the following groups and presented in Table 13.3. A human collaborator can be considered as a symbiotic relationship and comprises of a relationship between a person and RAS. This adds additional safety characteristics for a robot to maintain distance from humans or to allow robots to work in a shared workspace. Another partnership achieved includes multi-platform, which can include the symbiosis between the coordination of robots or robotic swarms during a mission. The Internet of Things (IoT) allows infrastructural sensors to be paired alongside DTs of buildings and includes overview and control of climates, access areas and associated autonomous systems. Asset integrity is an active area of development for use alongside DTs and enables fault detection via structural health monitoring sensors to be displayed in the synthetic environment and may also provide systems diagnoses to an operator. The application of a SSOSA gives the opportunity to define and include multifaceted architectures and processes within the systems engineering society.

Table 13.3: Examples of symbiotic relationships [79]

Symbiotic relationship	References
Human Collaborator	[98–102]
Multi-Platform	[101, 103–105]
Infrastructural Sensors	[106–108]
Asset Integrity Inspection	[109–111]
System of Systems	[112–114]

4.3   Symbiotic Digital Architecture to Enhance Resilience and Safety Compliance

Ensuring the safety of any RAS represents a specific challenge faced by human operators. Although many standards are considered as safe by legislators for robotic systems; safety criteria, including ISO 61508 and domain-specific standards including ISO 15066 (collaborative robots), ISO 10218 (industrial robots), or RTCA DO-178B/C (aerospace), and even ethical aspects (BS8611), none of which consider fully autonomous systems capable of handling important decisions which are critical to safety.

Within this subsection, the limits of the present system of system approaches and symbiotic systems are highlighted. A SSOSA consists of a variety of widely recognized symbiotic interactions, with the inclusion of the author's specific innovative relationships, which further develop the state-of-the-art symbiosis and are presented within the sliced portions shown in Fig. 13.2. The advancement of DTs has fuelled the advancement of different symbiotic relationships. A DT allows a human operator to C^3 interactively with the synthetic environment and real-world platform as represented in Slice A. Majority of symbiotic system methods are widely recognized as multi-platform; symbiotic methods is accomplished via the cooperation or collaboration of several robots (Slice B). Infrastructural sensors provide an opportunity for corroboration as in Slice C. The devices are often used for localization to validate (corroborate) the position of a robot relative to its environment. Asset integrity inspection is represented by slice D and represents a symbiotic relationship under rapid developed and is discussed within this chapter. Cooperation with a DT ensures that asset integrity data is shared for an accurate representation of faults to the, often remote, end-user. Lastly, we create a novel symbiotic relationship represented in System of Systems (Slice E), where symbiosis is achieved between systems onboard an RAS. The approach uses bidirectional communications for assessment of mission updates/status and certification of a RASs own systems via a run-time reliability ontology. With this perspective, present "Symbiotic systems" can be described as symbiotic partnerships between a pair of sub-elements, for example, a DT and sub-element as in portions A-C. These usually also simply feature a single element of corroboration, cooperation or collaboration. This enables the designed SSOSA to represent all symbiotic partnerships to achieve C^3 governance, as displayed by the hatched area in Fig. 13.8, with connections to a single, shared DT acting as the SSOSA boundary. Bidirectional means of communication between each symbiotic relation to the symbiotic ecosystem controlled via the DT ensures full symbiotic digitalization is achieved. A SSOSA is transferrable to ensure the integration of a range of RAS and infrastructural devices and sensors under the same framework. This work, and the relevant case study conducted by the ORCA Hub, has allowed Mitchell et al. [79] to construct the theory around the hypothesis and to show whether safety and trust is to be created via self-certification to work in an autonomous mission evaluation.

This section presents a SSOSA to ensure resilient autonomy as defined in Fig. 13.9. Symbiosis is achieved across systems within a RAS and via a DT utilizing bidirectional communications for run-time data interaction and representation. A symbiotic system is defined as the co-evolution and lifecycle learning with shared knowledge for mutualistic gain. We also describe a set of systems or system aspects which work together to provide a unique capability that none of the fundamental systems can achieve on its own as a system of systems approach [79]. This

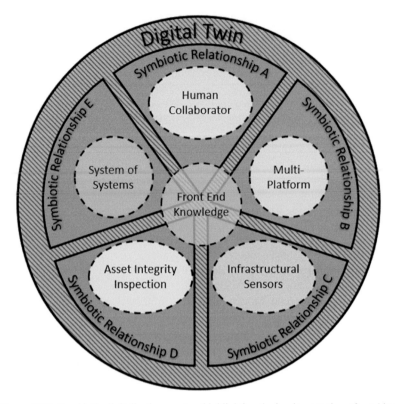

Figure 13.8: Symbiotic digitalised ecosystem highlighting the implementation of symbiotic interactions within the SSOSA.

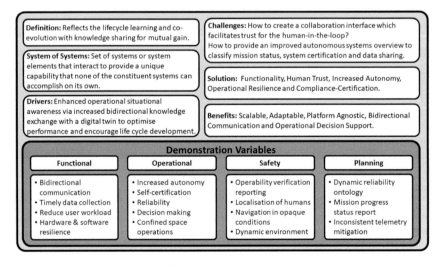

Figure 13.9: SSOSA definitions highlighting the challenges, solution, benefits and mission evaluation variables.

methodology is motivated with the perspective that an improvement in operating awareness can be accomplished via bidirectional exchange of knowledge from a DT, to enhance execution and promote life cycle advancement. The aggregation of data from across the RAS, environment, infrastructure and human operator will ensure this is completed.

The barriers which symbiotic systems will encounter include the creation of collaborative governance via a DT interface which creates confidence and trust for the human operators and the provision of an improved DT to classify system certification, operations report and shared data across systems without inducing information overload for the operator. Within the SSOSA, the DT elements are created to perform as the base of command-and-control for a mission which creates functionality, increases autonomy, enhances human trust, resilience during operations and compliance certification. A SSOSA secures several advantages due to the platform agnosticism within the SDA which is adaptable and scalable, featuring the bidirectional network for enhanced visibility or data-driven solutions during autonomy. This enables the architecture to be utilized to any commercial off-the-shelf robotic platforms, such as SPOT from Boston Dynamics. The SDA and system implementation process is modified appropriately depending on the sensors and actuators specific to the robotic platform.

Mutualism and commensalism is captured under the first tier, '*Adapt and Survive*', of the SSOSA as defined at the start of the previous section. The utilization of a real-time ontology for reliability allows the symbiotic architecture created to assess the effects of a situation from variables across environment, infrastructure, RAS reliability and interaction for a remote operator. The incorporation of shared data from numerous deployed devices allows for data collected to be routed to the DT to allow collaboration and an overview for a remote human-in-the-loop. This allows for mitigation of unknown and known hazards and threats to the resilience and safety of the autonomous mission. A mission can be evaluated due to the closing of goals within the mission envelope whilst confirming safety compliance of the RAS under a survivability viewpoint.

In the future development of our SSOSA, we include a roadmap to tier 2, '*Adapt and Thrive*', where a number of RAS employ a map of distributed knowledge to create recommendations for the human-in-the-loop on new mission priorities which have multi-objectives. This newly created information can be shared for many CPS autonomously and seamlessly integrated for mutualistic, commensalistic or parasitic advantage, however, by no means at the detriment of another CPS mission envelope. An example of this parasitic gain could include the data sharing of battery state of charge, where a RAS (symbiont) could deprive a host robotic platform of battery charge, but where the symbiont leaves enough charge for the host to still complete its planned mission objectives. We include the definition of a 'Thriving' SSOSA in our future objectives, where a robotic platform can overcome unforeseen events, necessitating autonomous departure from the mission objective, yet still achieving an optimized mission profile. The system can autonomously suggest solutions to threats to ensure mission permanence and continuity.

The creation of a run-time reliability ontology via edge analytics improves the visibility to present and imminent signs of failure. The quick evolution of different types of failure requires different revival strategies and should be designed into a reliability ontology. In the design of our ontology, this includes a recovery element that instructs the RAS to proceed to an accessible and safe area in the event of a warning fault or future failure. This can become important as discussed in "Confined Environments" implementation, where humans may not be able to access a zone to recover a robot. Therefore, if a robot can make itself safe in a designated recovery zone, this may be a more effective option when compared to a robot stranded in an area inaccessible to humans.

Mutualism is achieved for safety compliance as the human and robot may communicate and interact via bidirectional communication systems. This is accomplished via human access to the DT for the assessment of mission status, whilst the RAS simultaneously prompts the human operator with fault diagnoses in real-time. The operator can terminate the mission at any point however, the reliability ontology gives the robotic platform the capability to make autonomous decisions to ensure a successful and safe mission envelope.

To verify the successful implementation of a SSOSA, demonstration variables must be fully considered and are listed under functional, operational, safety and planning of Fig. 13.9. A successful testing of our SSOSA within a confined space autonomous inspection evaluation is shown in the pilot studies section. Functional variables include ensuring run time data collection and bidirectional communications for a completely synchronized system architecture, precisely matching the representation within the DT. Operational variables are addressed via the system self-certification, which increase the autonomy and resilience onboard a robotic platform. Safety is a key variable in our SSOSA due to the requirement to support localization of humans, route planning and execution in opaque/challenging environments and operational verification reporting. Lastly, the design of a plan ensures that the reliability ontology is accurate to the deployed CPS. The ontology represents the decision-making hierarchy for the CPS and for reporting the status of a mission to the DT.

Our SSOSA incorporates a system integration process which is displayed within Fig. 13.10. The illustration presents the aspects of the sub-elements of the system and focuses on the symbiosis and resilience across the layers due to the C^3 of data. The colour coding included in the figure is also utilized in Fig. 13.11 and Fig. 13.17 and provides a common differentiator between the different elements of the symbiotic architecture and robotic platform. The links between all subsystems are displayed within each layer and represent the addressed mission variables. The human interaction layer represents the human operator with the capabilities to interact with the mission via the DT. The DT user interface comprises of the functions for the operator to increase their operational overview of the deployed CPS. The data gathered from the FMCW radar is fed to the DT. The sensor represents a non-destructive asset integrity inspection payload employed on the robotic platform and can be used for surface and subsurface evaluation of materials. The Planning Domain Definition Language (PDDL) is the decision-making layer of the ontology and is connected to the software packages onboard the RAS. The Simultaneous Location and Mapping (SLAM) stack, ontology and motion planning are linked with the decision making as identified in the system integration process. Diagnostics from the actuators and internal sensors onboard the RAS and is processed by the ontology where the data collected from the cameras and LiDAR sensors is fed to the SLAM stack. The mobile base and manipulators receive the commands calculated from the motion planning element. The system integration process improves the resilience of each element, as each when functioning independently would have been unable to determine the required

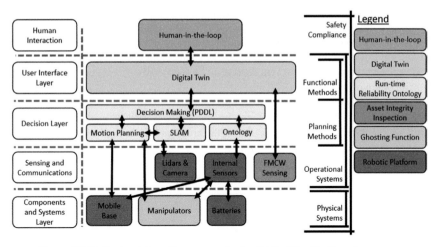

Figure 13.10: System integration process for the RAS utilized in the autonomous mission envelope.

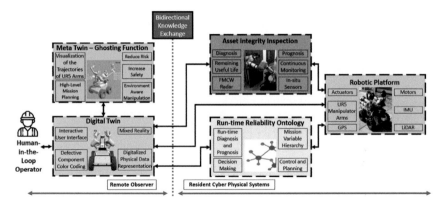

Figure 13.11: SDA representing sub-elements from RAS to the remote human operator via bidirectional knowledge exchange.

answer. Therefore, with an applied SSOSA, mutualism via knowledge sharing and C^3 is achieved across all systems.

With a focus on addressing the top-down requirements, alongside ground-up capability challenges, a SSOSA supports reliability in autonomous missions. To ensure actionable and time-critical information, the top-down requirements are mapped onto an architecture for reliable and trustworthy systems through the SDA (Fig. 13.11), which captures planning, safety compliance, operational and functional requirements of the SSOSA. The SDA also enables resilient intra symbiosis (within the robotic platform) and inter symbiosis (across robotic platforms and other systems). This includes the systems engineering with the incorporation of up to 1000 different sensors and architectures to be included under the same architecture.

The SDA is initiated by the user via the human-in-the-loop symbol. This permits the user to utilize the synthetic environment provided by the DT to gain actionable information from the resident CPS via the Graphical User Interface (GUI), demonstrating bidirectionality. The DT has been designed to ensure knowledge can be obtained from MR devices, producing improved operational reporting, also available via a standard laptop. The asset data and all the information are presented within the digital environment of the real-world asset. Logical colour coding enables information such as components which present defects, to be displayed easily and identified by the human operator quickly.

The ghosting function is a meta-function of the DT and reduces the associated risks with any robotic arm operations by increasing safety. A visualization of the arms is accessible via the interface, where the arm trajectories can be simulated in the synthetic environment prior to operational deployment. This builds confidence across the SDA, as the human operator may identify any risks within the simulation via the visualization of the manipulation task prior to executing the planned path to the real-world robot. This leads to increased assurance for effective operation.

We include a novel radar sensing payload on-board the robotic platform which is included in our SDA. The FMCW radar sensor features the ability to distinguish humans through barriers which include walls and doors, thereby expanding the operational awareness of a robotic platform. The payload also provides support in opaque environments or when poor visibility impedes localization and where collision avoidance sensors become less capable. The sensor can also be utilized for asset integrity inspection, specifically when the sensor is used for the analysis of air to material interface, in addition to internal properties. This has been applied to integrity inspection of wind turbine blades, detection of corrosion precursors (with or without insulation) and inspection of metals within low dielectric civil infrastructures [57, 111].

The run-time reliability ontology block within the SDA supports adaptive mission planning which enables robustness, diagnosis, decision making, and prognosis. For a human observer who is remote to the field, this is useful as an improved understanding of the remaining useful life and state of health of important subsystems is provided, both at the mission planning stage and during run-time. To ensure effective operation of the ontology, front-end data and edge analytics is fed into rear-end functions via the DT. Bidirectional communications, supports connectivity and awareness via these data streams. The data collected from actuating systems and associated sensors are converted into actionable data when passed through the ontology to be presented to the human-in-the-loop. Actionable information includes recommended remedial action for the human operator to solve the problem. This could include stopping the mission or replacing components upon failure.

A diagnosis automaton within the AI-driven ontology is constructed for each critical element in the robotic platform including motor, batter, wheel, motor driver, integrated devices or single component. This includes components which are sensed or non-sensed. Distinct states can be designed for each segment of a system as displayed in Equations 1-4. C^3 governance is outlined via the full adherence of the robot to the rules set in the ontology which minimize risk [41].

$$\text{States} = \{\text{sensed, possible, normal}\} \tag{1}$$

$$\text{Sensed states} = \{\text{low current, high temperature, ...}\} \tag{2}$$

$$\text{Possible states} = \{\text{broken, aging, degrading, abnormal behaviour, ...}\} \tag{3}$$

$$\text{Normal states} = \{\text{on, off, ready, working, ...}\} \tag{4}$$

Event transitions are scenarios or events which changes the state of a component or system. These include temporal, internal, external or spatial events (each with differing degrees of probability). These transition events are:

$$\text{Events} = \{\text{internal, time-driven, space-driven, external}\} \qquad (5)$$

Hierarchical relationships are utilized to convey the reliability ontology models, which include: '*is-linked-to*' and '*is-type-of*' or '*is-connected-to*' relationship. For example, '*x is-connected-to y*' [115].

$$\text{Binary relationship} = \{\text{causality, implication, prevention, hierarchical,} \\ \text{composition, aggregation, optional}\} \qquad (6)$$

The defining logic within the ontological binary interrelationship enables the C^3 across all sub-elements and systems under the SSOSA. Zaki et al. express a detailed formalism in [115].

Three types of binary relationships are linked to display the level of confidence in the relationship. These are: '*causality*', '*implication*' and '*prevention*' [115]. E.g. '*x must-cause y*', '*x might-cause y*'. Modalities combined with those relations include the following verbs:

- *could* (less possible)
- *might/may* (possibly)
- *should* (very likely)
- *would* (really certain)
- *must* (absolutely certain)

Each segment attains its own distinct properties, each having an influence on the inter- intrarelations within the system, such as: '*reusability*', '*dependency*', '*availability*' and '*validity*'. E.g. x (is) *reusable*, x (is) *stand-alone*, x (is) *available* and x (is) *valid* [115].

A summary of these steps include:

A. Creation of an automaton for diagnosis,as built for each key segment of the CPS.
B. A description of the transitional connection across the states.
C. A description of the binary relationships across the states in differing elements.
D. Creation of the hierarchical model of the specified CPS.
E. Creation of a standard model of elements of the CPS.

5. Pilot Studies

The following section covers examples of cyber-physical implementation applicable to the energy sector. The pilot studies are confined environments, an onshore wind turbine test dock and nuclear storage tank decommissioning. These pilots showcase the SSOSA, and its components depicted in Fig. 13.17.

5.1 Confined Environments

Confined space environments present significant challenges to personnel and robotic maintenance regimes. A confined space typically has restricted access, leading to increased safety concerns; potential noxious fumes, reduced oxygen levels or risk of fires and more. Vigilance is paramount for both personnel and deployed autonomous systems [116, 117].

The piloting of the SDA to enhance safety compliance and resilience a physical onshore training facility was arranged to present similar challenges as an offshore substation platform. The environment included complex arrays of cabling and piping which included large elements of infrastructure such as a high-capacity transformer or offshore generator as in Fig. 13.12 seen here with a robotic platform deployed in a BVLOS confined space inspection mission. To ensure reliable communications a wireless base station was combined alongside a pair of wireless transceivers integrated with the robotic platform to mitigate wireless communication challenges.

The transit area includes a narrow corridor with a small amount of clearance on each side for the RAS, which resulted in an area of increased risk of collision. The confined space operational area consisted of a minimal area for manoeuvrability for the robotic platform. Path parameters were modified to enable for increased functionality during the navigation through the confined space whilst preserving safety via the avoidance of collisions. The case study discussed utilized an environment to replicate the highly challenging environment for sensors and accuracy of the path planning (SLAM) functions.

Figure 13.12: Photo of the mission environment with the RAS during run-time on route to enter the confined space.

To demonstrate autonomous confined space asset integrity inspection and how the SDA services symbiotic collaboration across the cyber-physical elements (robotic platform, sensors, reliability ontology and the DT) readers are encouraged to view the videos available through Mitchell et al. [118–120].

An autonomous inspection mission can be divided into eight phases, with each phase having distinct objectives. They are:

A. Pre-mission planning
B. Mission start at base point
C. Transit to asset integrity scan 1
D. Perform asset integrity scan 1
E. Transit to asset integrity scan 2
F. Perform asset integrity scan 2
G. Return transit to base point
H. Mission end

Three major system issues were generated on the CPS to simulate symbiotic collaboration dynamics. This would ensure the assessment of whether the RAS reassess the mission symbiotically via intra-inter system certification and adhere to rules which ensure their safety during a mission. The autonomous mission evaluation aimed to demonstrate '*Adapt and Survive*' where the run-time and dynamic conditions imposed on the CPS enable the AI-assisted ontology to diagnose a fault and ensure the correct decision is made or fed to the human operator via the DT. This ensures commensalistic collaboration with the designed reliability ontology to ensure the robot can complete the following:

- Detect hazards or obstacles to accomplishing the mission via on-board sensing.
- Detect risks or obstructions to ensure safety of the RAS within the surrounding environment and nearby human presence detection via integrated sensing mechanisms.
- Support real-time C^3 with the DT to pass on obtained asset integrity management data and advise the human operator and other robotic systems and software packages during run-time via knowledge sharing which is enhances via bidirectional communications.
- Trusted autonomy and corroborated decision making via low latency, wireless communications through both the AI and/or the human operator.

A significant component of this case study is to display resilience and reliability during autonomous operations whilst maintaining a mission envelope within safety compliance. Success is created through C^3 in the SSOSA methodology to provide collaborative governance between the systems that enable the robot to operate safely and autonomously and provide an increased awareness for a remote human operator.

The run-time reliability ontology enabled symbiotic assessment of the RAS for certification of its own systems where in the case of potential significant deterioration, the mission could be autonomously terminated. Each autonomous mission aspect was evaluated and in this section, we focus on the robustness and resilience of the robotic platform and its run-time reliability ontology. The mission plan is illustrated in Fig. 13.13, highlighting the main stages of the asset integrity inspection and induced faults on the robotic platform. The applied methodology is presented within Fig. 13.17 and

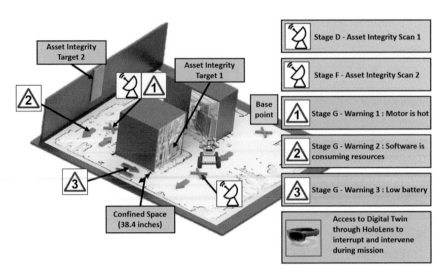

Figure 13.13: 3D model of a mission plan within an industrial facility stressing the key stages of the mission scenarios and route taken by the autonomous system.

displays the operations, symbiotic decisions, and interactions between systems. The resulting flow chart is discussed throughout the following subsections.

A. Pre-Mission Planning

An essential event to ensure a safe mission includes pre-planning. Reconnaissance is first conducted to map the mission area to establish the working environment. Cyber-physical sensing is provided by both 2D and 3D LiDAR to assist the human operator to navigate the autonomous system around the infrastructure and environment for the creation of a map which can then have waypoints assigned to it (Fig. 13.14). Therefore, under COVID-19 requirements, personnel do not have to be on-site to complete the autonomous missions. The cooperation between robot and human operators establishes low obstacles and raised surfaces such as pipework. A schematic displays the resulting reconnaissance map layered on the 3D model as in Fig. 13.13. For asset integrity inspection of corrosion, the FMCW radar was used.

For the autonomous mission evaluation, the Robotic Operating Software (ROS) planning and navigation stack was implemented on-board the autonomous system.

To achieve the assigned objectives of the autonomous mission, the robotic platform acted upon tasks assigned to it by the human operator. The decision making in these tasks was based on PDDL associated relational sequential system actions [121]. This represents the future remote working conditions as engineers can access missions remotely in a COVID-19 climate. Waypoint goals are positioned and received at the navigation stack from the planner. Simultaneous Location and Mapping (SLAM) is used for the navigation. A DT provided both graphical interface and dashboard for the operator/planner to create the waypoints. The integration of computation, data and process analysis ensures the selected robotic platform can complete the required mission. From the point of the mission being initiated, the RAS actively certifies its on-board systems. This is achieved through watchdog nodes, which are subscribed to fault and warning diagnostic data from the robotic platform ontology.

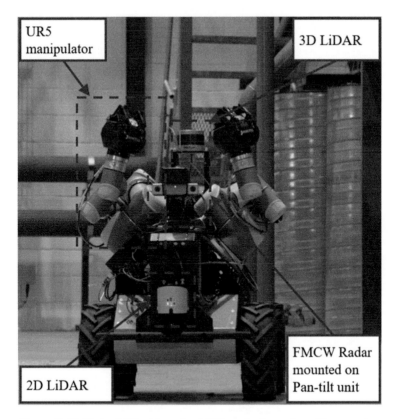

Figure 13.14: Husky A200 with a pair of UR5 manipulators alongside annotations
for the onboard payloads.

B. Mission Start at Basepoint

The autonomous system will remain inactive at an authorized home position until
the robot is initiated by the human-in-the-loop. A resilient wireless connection is
required between the DT and CPS to ensure mission start. Intra-system corroboration
is achieved by the system continuously self-certifying its systems from the mission
start. This network is a central feature of cyber-physical systems that ensures the
human operator has an overview that the robot is fully deployable and operational.
Watchdog nodes have been implemented to provide another level of autonomous self-
certification. The most efficient routes are calculated by the autonomous navigation
and mapping systems.

C. Transit to Asset Integrity Scan 1

A low-level path planner is utilized in conjunction with SLAM for transit to the first
waypoint. The costmap represents the map generated to ensure collision avoidance
and path planning between waypoints is achieved; this is created from the onboard
LiDAR sensors (Fig. 13.15). The PDDL produces a waypoint action including x, y and
θ locations and are utilized for autonomous navigation by feeding this information to
the ROS move_base.

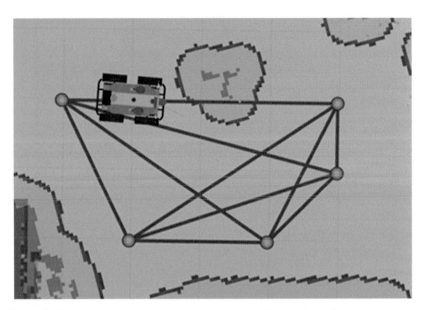

Figure 13.15: A local costmap emphasising waypoint positions set by the human operator and the possible routes for the robot to complete.

D. Perform Asset Integrity Scan 1

For this pilot, the K-Band FMCW radar sensor was utilized as a non-contact asset integrity inspection method for the detection of corrosion. The challenge for this inspection pertains to the safe manoeuvre of the robot and the FMCW payload whilst avoiding collisions with infrastructure. The CPS provides information to the remote human observer with data from the physical environmental sensing to the DT to ensure C^3.

E. Transit to Asset Integrity Scan 2

The transition to the second asset integrity inspection begins the confined space mission. The infrastructure has a narrow corridor and a space with minimal room for manoeuvrability of the robot. To ensure accurate manoeuvrability, autonomous navigation of the confined space was setup through the motion planner. Maintaining the ability to avoid collisions allowed the robot to adapt with the dynamic mission space where personnel could be within the workspace for certain areas. This ensured a safe mission envelope.

F. Perform Asset Integrity Scan 2

At this point, the second waypoint has been reached by the autonomous system. The system is now ready to carry out the second asset integrity inspection for corrosion precursors. The parameters of this inspection are comparable to the first inspection highlighted in stage D.

G. Return to Base Point

Upon the return to the base point, three faults were induced via simulation on-board the autonomous system through code which was initiated within the robotic platforms hardware on this phase of the mission. The fault severity levels increase upon each induced fault.

The goal of the run-time reliability ontology is to discover or detect invalidities or anomalies within the autonomous system whilst it operates and under stress. This system can corroborate the CPS behaviour relative to the required specifications and ensure performance is as expected.

Several semi-automated mission envelopes were implemented in the confined space asset integrity inspection including:

- A potential warning or fault within an element which is not sensed, for example, a tyre failure.
- A low battery voltage prediction.
- Root cause evaluation for a third module affected by a failure in a pair of other modules.
- Predictions for elevated temperature within the driver of the motor.

The implementation of the ontology prioritizes fault thresholds over warning thresholds (Fig. 13.17G) in all instances to safeguard the reliability of the CPS. Figure 13.17G represents the final stage of the autonomous mission where the methodology of the decision making is displayed to highlight the connections of the SSOSA across systems within the architecture.

The remote operator is notified of the mission status in real-time though the DT with a precise estimation of the system status via diagnosis and prognosis. This ensures a SSOSA due to the systems engineering from the SDA to ensure the resilience of the platform and allow the remote operator to have an operational overview of the robotic platform.

H. Mission End

This case study of an autonomous mission evaluation demonstrates the advantages of a real-time reliability ontology. The induced warning indications were accurately detected by the run-time reliability ontology as expected alongside the anticipated decisions as designed within the ontology. These warnings allow the operator to make decisions as to terminate or continue the mission and is another layer of protection and interaction for the human-in-the-loop. To ensure obedience to the safety rules, the robot would still continuously evaluate its capacity to function efficiently after each subsequent warning, ensuring the survivability of the RAS. From the perspective of symbiosis, the DT serves to corroborate human-in-the-loop actions with respect to real-time mission status and fault prognosis. The twin presents representation and descriptions of data, which is transformed into selected ontology updates. These updates are presented as human readable text describing hardware and system faults and warnings. A red colour is used on the text to highlight the presence of a warning or fault. In the evaluation of the autonomous mission discussed in pilot study, a watchdog node linked to oversee battery state of health alerts detected a low battery fault. The fault during the autonomous mission evaluation is pictured as in the DT within Fig. 13.16, where the system was created to ensure the human operator is aware of all red high ranked alerts. The DT also describes operating information and diagnostic information including battery status and motor parameters. The integration, decision making and coordination of all system subcomponents and operator objectives are achieved via collaborative governance as within the SSOSA.

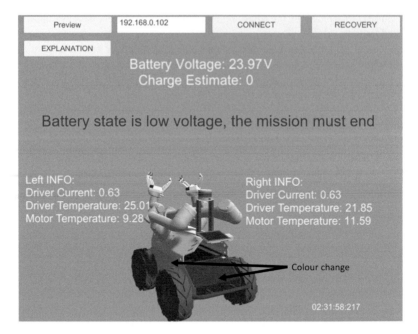

Figure 13.16: Error message displaying a low battery within the DT. The section marked colour change on the base of the robotic platform indicates the health status of the platform.

The motor temperature symbiotic safety compliance modes of the RAS are presented in the taxonomy structure in Table 13.4. This identifies the levels of safety compliance modes corresponding to the collaborative governance aspects of operation, provision, and outcome and system awareness corresponding to the following relationships: Mutualism, Commensalism and Parasitism (MCP). MCP is critical for the SSOSA for the creation of exchanges across or between the autonomous systems (DT, ontology, robotic platform) and operator. The capability for the CPS to create system awareness enables the RAS to monitor self-preservation without disturbing the human operator unless necessary. In this case, although the mission could be terminated by the human operator, self-certification ensures the integrity of the robotic platform. Mutualism is moderate whereas parasitism is low, and commensalism is high in the mission envelope as the autonomous system continuous with its list of objectives with a low chance of adverse consequences to state of health of the RAS system.

Table 13.4: Taxonomy of symbiosis to achieve safety compliance and autonomous systems temperature of the motors

Collaborative governance (C³)	Safety compliance modes		
	Mutualism	**Commenalism**	**Parasitism**
System Awareness	Moderate	High	Low
Human-in-the-loop Provision	High	Moderate	Low
Operation	Self-certification (Implication)	Augmentation (Causality)	Instructional (Prevention)
Outcome	Positive Anticipation	Indeterminacy	Negative Anticipation

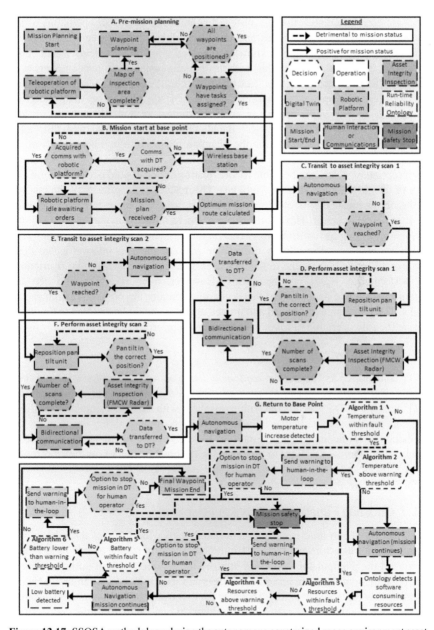

Figure 13.17: SSOSA methodology during the autonomous constrained space environment asset integrity inspection highlighting the system of system interactions, decisions and operations. An identical colour coding has been employed to pinpoint elements as also displayed in Figure 13.10 and Figure 13.11.

Human miscalculations are reduced within a mission due to the implementation of run-time reliability ontology. Under human-in-the-loop provision as in Table 13.4, Parasitism is low as fault thresholds for all problems that may risk the integrity of the

RAS are established such that the system automatically ceases all operations of the real-world robot if any hazardous operational conditions are discovered. Mutualism exists due to the SSOSA due to knowledge shared throughout systems which could previously not have been feasible without the augmentation of subcomponents at both data and information levels. For this example, the human operator is updated via warning messages (information), and a new threshold for fault detection (data) is triggered which causes an emergency mission stop. Commensalism and parasitism includes a balance between the alteration of fault and warning thresholds which should be minimized during the planning phase. To minimize parasitism, an experienced operator should only alter the thresholds. If they are altered too leniently/ inappropriately, deterioration of the robotic platform (host) could occur resulting in a benefit for the human operator (symbiont). This results in the priority of the mission at the detriment of the robot. Commensalism is achieved when faults are adjusted by a proficient operator. This results in a mission termination,in the case the risk the thresholds present have a minimal impact on the mission. This is corroborated by the reliability ontology. The robot can therefore still complete its mission where there is a benefit to the human due to the increased safety of the robot or less restrictions on performance, hence commensalistic. However, there is a fine line between commensalism and parasitism in this scenario when altering ontology warnings and faults. Therefore, an experienced and trained operator should be certified to do this to ensure the safe operation of robot over the mission priorities.

5.2   Digital Twin

A DT is identified as *"digital replications of living as well as non-living entities that enable data to be seamlessly transmitted between the physical and virtual worlds"* [51]. A "stage 4" DT was utilized within this work with extensive simulation abilities and data analytics, in particular influencing edge-processing during run-time for the prediction of forthcoming behaviours (Fig. 13.18). Positive interdependencies across external and internal functions of the DT allow the combination of run-time processes from sensors and payloads with operational AI services. Legitimacy is supported within and between existing technologies by following this paradigm.

5.2.1 Ghosting Function for Dual Manipulators

The creation of run-time evaluation and collaborative functions of the robotic arm manipulators was achieved via the DT interface, allowing for the user to observe and command the manipulator operations onboard the robotic platform during run-time. The reliability ontology can generate messages and are displayed in a similar manner to as previously discussed in Fig. 13.16 where the user can intuitively command the arms on the CPS to mirror their real-world condition in real-time. Run-time connectivity between the client machines and robot is achieved via a DT server package which is utilised onboard the ROS core of the robotic platform. A key advantage of the DT discussed includes the interchangeability between operating devices as the user is not tied to using a ROS based system. The SDA allows the user to connect to the DT via a mobile, tablet, MR device or standard laptop from anywhere whilst remote to the CPS. The Graphical User Interface (GUI) of the DT offers the visualization and interaction required to demonstrate the SSOSA for manipulation of processes. Run-time prognostics verify the significance of the implementation of bidirectional

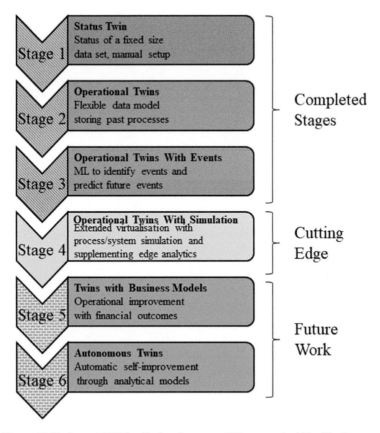

Figure 13.18: Stage 4 DT identified as the current DT presented within this chapter alongside descriptions of other DT models.

interaction and communications. This is enabled by a physics-based operational view, which encourages trustworthy interactions with the DT and system health status via C^3 governance.

The synchronized robotic platform in the real-world and DT is displayed within Fig. 13.19. The ROS core provides the data necessary for the DT to position the robotic arms to reflect the real-world platform. Synchronization of all system parameters is achieved upon mission start, which is maintained for the duration of the mission.

The preview function integrated in the DT allows the remote human operator to plan and control the manipulators as displayed in Fig. 13.20. Planned positions and trajectories of the arms are rendered as translucent 'ghost' models. This allows the operator to preview and analyse the requested operations. The use of sliders within the DT GUI enables intuitive control of the 'ghost' manipulator arms by simulating each axis of the manipulators. This allows for verification of safe robotic arm motions via simulations for remote operators, before executing the movements to the field robotic platform. This increases the trust levels for the human that the manipulators will operate as planned.

Figure 13.19: Left: Robotic arm as displayed in the DT. Right: Synchronized with the real-world robotic arm during the mission.

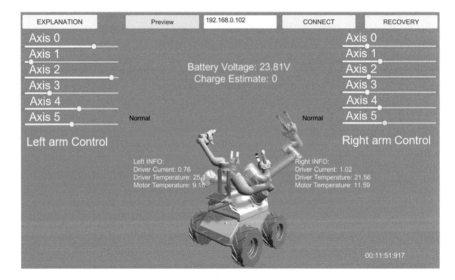

Figure 13.20: Meta ghosting function of the robotic arms within the DT, displaying the desired trajectories of the arms. Also displayed are the axis controls within the user interface.

Run-time fault prognosis was also evaluated within the DT. Figure 13.21 shows a scenario in which a motor fault is induced upon the robotic arm within the ROS core. The location of this fault is shown in the DT by colour coding the arms red (Fig. 13.21). Colour coding in this manner allows for the rapid identification of an arm which has a diagnosed fault.

5.3   Mixed and Augmented Reality

Utilising MR and AR devices, such as the Microsoft HoloLens, allows for prompt evaluation of the health status or a RAS, whether the operator is on-site or working remotely. The AR interface presented in Fig. 13.22 highlights the health status where

Figure 13.21: Meta warning function of the DT. Arms are colour coded, with a colour change showing a motor fault.

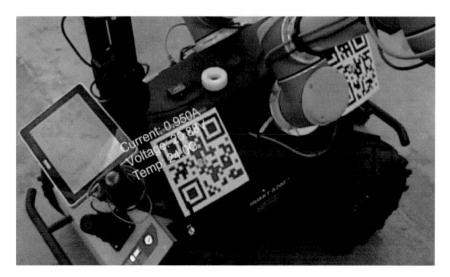

Figure 13.22: QR codes are recognized by an MR device and enable human-readable health status information to be overlaid on the robotic platform.

natural language indicates the RAS state of health using the information from a Quick Response (QR) code. The colour coding as presented in Fig. 13.23 highlights the health status of the component within the autonomous system. In this scenario, the base is depicted red to enable rapid visualization of a fault when viewed through the headset. Customization of the displayed colour coding is possible to reflect different systems and fault types.

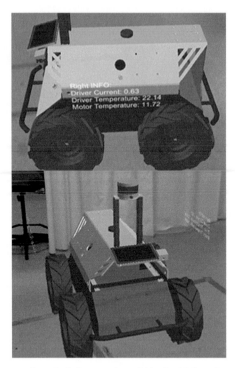

Figure 13.23: A demonstration of a defect warning within the AR interface. Top: Live diagnostics of the robotic platform. Bottom: Colour coded defect warning displayed upon detection of defect within the robotic platform.

6.　FMCW Radar Sensing for Integrated Offshore Environmental Sensing

6.1　Asset Integrity Inspection

Sensing with Frequency Modulated Continuous Wave (FMCW) is reliant on the interaction of transmitted microwave radiation with a material. The properties of the reflecting surface can be obtained from analysis of the reflected electromagnetic (EM) wave, which are a result of the scattering, emission, absorption and phase change, and are unique to the reflecting object. Microwave sensing offers rapid measurements for edge analytics, high resilience to ambient environmental conditions and non-invasive evaluation of materials. The hardware is low power and a solid-state electronic device which is certified as ATEX compliant. Millimetre-wave radar technology, in both the X and K bands, have tuneable EM outputs and have proven harsh environment capability,which include high temperature or high pressure operating conditions [122–130]. In addition to having the capability to operate resiliently in opaque conditions, such as mist, fog, smoke and dust.

　　This case study demonstrates the capability of the FMCW system for asset integrity inspection and was utilized as a run-time device on the deployed CPS, a Husky autonomous ground vehicle [131]. The demonstration of the sensor in this role returned critical asset integrity information in real-time to our DT and represented the inspection of an asset in a simulated offshore environment. We discuss in detail the successful deployment of two use cases: corrosion inspection on steel infrastructure targets and integrity monitoring for wind turbine blades via a specially developed Asset Integrity Dashboard (AID). The FMCW sensor was utilized for both mission profiles. The implementation of this inspection device further advances the SSOSA, where information was relayed to the DT and represented to achieve C^3 governance.

Improved manoeuvrability of the FMCW radar sensor for asset inspection was achieved via the gripping of the sensor as a payload within one of the dual UR5 robotic arms, as pictured in Fig. 13.24, allowing raster scanning motions for a wide area of fault assessment, while the other robotic arm may be used for manipulation and asset intervention manoeuvres.

Figure 13.24: Dual UR5 husky A200 with the FMCW millimetre-wave sensor in the gripper during a corrosion inspection.

6.1.1 Structural Corrosion

Steel structures in the offshore environment are prone to surface corrosion, reducing the operational lifetime of the infrastructure. The quantification and detection of corrosion on the surface of structures is therefore essential to ensure efficient and effective O&M schedules [132]. The robotic platform was used during an integrity inspection of the steel sheet for corrosion and is pictured in Fig. 13.24. The observed reflected wave amplitude response for different concrete and metallic targets, at a consistent sensor-target separation of 10 cm, are shown in Fig. 13.25. Distinct contrasts in the return signal amplitude are observed for the lightly corroded and non-corroded steel sheets, in addition to substantial differences when comparing the polished aluminium and different areas of the concrete floor.

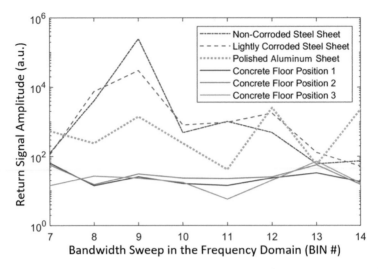

Figure 13.25: Reflected wave amplitude responses observed for multiple concrete and metal targets. The peaks observed at bin 9 represent the targets responses at 10 cm from the sensor tip.

A DT facilitates a remote perspective for asset health management and customized O&M scheduling as data from an inspection device can be fed to the DT, where the human operator gains an increased understanding of the asset. This allows for an enhancement of C^3 with an increase in corroborative compliance, as the data from the inspection device can be viewed in the synthetic environment alongside historical data and past decisions on maintenance.

6.1.2 Wind Turbine Blades and the Asset Integrity Dashboard

Wind turbine blade defects can be categorized into distinctive types, as detailed in Table 13.5. This includes delamination, water ingress and cracking. The use of high-resolution cameras via UAV platforms (visual and infrared) represents current state-of-the-art in the inspection of wind turbine blades and requires post-processing from experts to identify/infer regions with notable damage. The FMCW radar sensor may be deployed as a handheld device or as part of a robotic platform mounted wider sensor suite. This subsection presents the FMCW radar sensor for inspection of a wind turbine blade removed from operations, exhibiting an internal delamination defect (type four), where the defect is situated within the structure of the blade, as displayed in Fig. 13.26A, and where the FMCW radar was positioned external to the blade facing the target as illustrated in Fig. 13.26B. The technology evaluates the ability for the millimetre-wave sensor to detect defects which can accelerate asset degradation in adverse weather conditions. The subsurface faults within the wind turbine blade used for this study are highlighted in the Asset Integrity Dashboard (AID), as displayed in Fig. 13.27. A remote operator can access key information from the offshore inspection via interaction with the synthetic. Colour coding aids easy identification of faults, with green representing a healthy baseline area and red identifying an area of the blade containing a defect. Interaction is achieved by clicking on the defective area, revealing layered information blocks for the user to interrogate. Within the synthetic environment, the operator can view further information, including graphs of the radar response, which is displayed within Fig. 13.27 within the AID tool but also as a clearer illustration in Fig. 13.28. The graph displays the FMCW response to the following:

- An undamaged baseline area of the wind turbine blade structure.
- A type four delamination defect
- The inclusion of 3 millilitres of fresh water within the same type four defect at 3 minutes and 40 seconds into the experiment duration.

A summary video presented by Mitchell et al. [133], highlights the interaction between the layers of the AID.

Table 13.5: Wind turbine blade failure modes listed by description [111]

Type	Description
1.	Adhesive layer failure and growth in the bond joining external structure and main spar flangers (debonding)
2.	Adhesive layer failure in the external structure along leading/trailing edges (adhesive or joint failure)
3.	Failure at the interface between external and core sandwich panels in external structure and main spar
4.	Internal failure and growth in laminated structures comprising skin and/or main spar flanges, under tensile or compressive loading
5.	Laminated external structure and main spar debonding of fibres (fibre failure in tensile load conditions; laminate failure in compressive loading conditions)
6.	Buckling of external laminated structure due to debonding and growth in the external structure and main spar bond under compressive load
7.	Formation and growth of cracks in the external protective layering resulting in detachment of the gel-coat from the laminated external structure

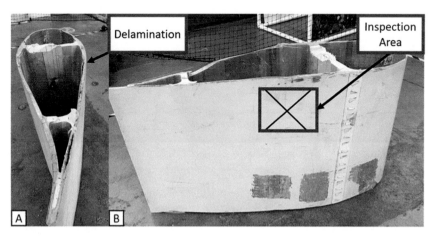

Figure 13.26: A – Wind turbine blade section end elevation view highlighting the internal delamination defect. **B** – Elevation view of the wind turbine blade section detailing the external inspection area.

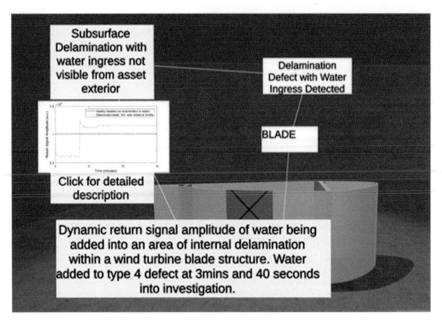

Figure 13.27: AID indicating the synthetic environment of the sandwich composite blade, where a cross indicates a defective area, while providing a human operator with options to view or extract detailed fault information.

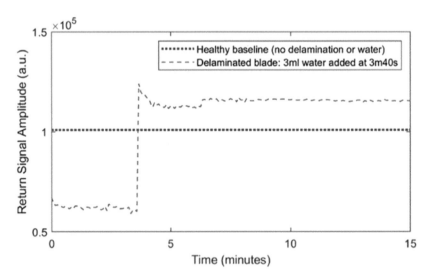

Figure 13.28: Observed signal return amplitude of 3 ml water added within an area of internal delamination.

An improvement of C^3 is generated from the AID post-processing tool via data collected from the FMCW sensor. This helps wind farm operators to gain an operational overview of O&M data collected from the real-world asset, leading to easy detection and localization of problems which occur on wind turbine blade structures.

This application demonstrates the capabilities of millimetre-wave radar sensing, via the edge analysis of non-destructive evaluation sensors in the offshore environment, and their role in the wider integration of data to DTs via robotic deployment. This integration capability also extends to foresight monitoring for RAS to ensure safety compliance and trust.

6.2   Foresight Monitoring of Safety and Mission Environment Conditions

Service robots are intended to be deployed in difficult situations, which include hazardous and complex scenarios, such as visually opaque and GPS denied areas with restricted communications. To overcome these challenges, the use of accurate sensors and payloads are crucial for RAS to ensure they can '*Adapt and Survive*' by having the capability to assess a scenario rapidly and effectively. Sensors must therefore have extended capabilities to localize infrastructure and environment (current state-of-the-art such as LiDAR), but also to identify differing types of surface condition, materials and variables that affect external mapping, such as the detection of hazards through solid, low to medium dielectric structures, such as walls (future state-of-the-art capabilities). This allows safety precautions to be followed by a robotic platform for a range of surface conditions, or if an engineer enters the same workspace.

Humans can rapidly lose trust in RAS if a major fault occurs in a system, CPS enables assurance due to the data-driven approach. Regulators require *defence in-depth*, resulting in trusted autonomous services and a high level of foresight in autonomy, alertness with intervention strategies to mitigate unanticipated threats to the CPS, ensuring health and safety requirements are preserved. Within the SSOSA, the FMCW radar sensor ensures that foresight monitoring ensures safety governance. Due to this approach, risks are reduced in the operation of AS around humans as humans can be detected when deployed offshore. This leads to an increase in C^3, allowing RAS to action decision making at an earlier stage, depending on the scenario.

6.2.1 Surface and Waypoint Condition Analysis

Inherent risks are associated with the surface of the ground which autonomous vehicles will have to overcome. The FMCW radar sensor enables non-contact monitoring and analysis of surface waypoints, ensuring compliance to safety requirements and to prevent failure in areas where surface ice, oil are present or are unstable. This capability forewarns a wheeled robot or vehicle of areas which have less traction. The millimetre-wave sensor was tested on a section of hot rolled asphalt, following the application of a brown salt brine solution at an ambient laboratory temperature of 24.8°C. The peak interfacial reflection at 10 cm from the sensor was extracted via fast Fourier transform (FFT) from time-domain data and is displayed within Fig. 13.29. Iterative applications of brown salt brine solution of 20% weight by volume were then placed in the field of view of the radar sensor, where a sufficient duration of time was allowed for the solution to fully evaporate before reapplying the same volume (30 ml/m^2) and concentration of salt solution. Residual salt in the field of view was seen to accumulate during the four applications of brine. The brine solution concentration was mixed to the same standards stipulated for highway maintenance during winter operating conditions between –7 and –10°C [134–136]. The deposition of the initial brine solution provides a return signal baseline. The subsequent applications show

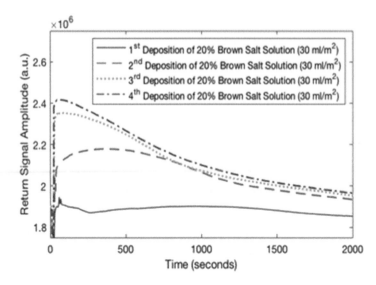

Figure 13.29: Return signal amplitude for applications of 20% brown salt liquid brine mixture onto hot rolled asphalt surface in a laboratory environment and subsequent evaporation.

increases in amplitude response, which are consistent with the presence of increased residual salt following the deposition of the previous brine solution within the sensor field of view. The observed deterioration in signal response over time links to the evaporation of water content in the brine solution, leaving residual salt levels incrementally higher than the previous application [137].

Symbiosis between an environment and robotic platform improves as a robotic platform could scan nearby waypoints to assess the terrain conditions on a given route. This information would then be relayed to a DT and distributed between local robots to ensure paths are planned to avoid areas which are unstable or with traction issues that could impede or harm the mobility of the robotic platform. This symbiosis would represent multi-platform mutualism in a fleet of autonomous ground vehicles acting in unison.

6.2.2 Safety in Low Visibility or Opaque Environments

When deploying RAS, two key factors for consideration are resilience and safety compliance. Autonomous systems are created for deployment in dangerous situations, such as opaque or severely restricted visual conditions. Limitations in state-of-the-art sensing, such as LiDAR etc., mean that robots experience difficulty navigating in areas where steam, smoke, or misty conditions are prevalent. Therefore, systems solely reliant on visual spectrum sensors lack the resilience to operate fully autonomously in the oil and gas sector, offshore renewable energy sector, search and rescue or mining sectors. RAS requires supporting or secondary navigational payloads which can guarantee the robustness of operations during a mission to ensure that an '*Adapt and Survive*' framework provides the required safety of the resource, as outlined in the SSOSA.

The FMCW payload is a critical and promising radar sensor to ensure the resilience of robotics in challenging operational conditions. The following subsections present the application of the FMCW to detect and distinguish humans within shared workspaces and to ensure a robot can comply with safety procedures and rules via low to medium dielectric detection of human targets through walls or doors.

6.3 Human Proximity Alerting

The investigation of human proximity alerting took place in the following evaluation. This enabled the autonomous platform to detect and distinguish between a human and an autonomous system or structure. This demonstrates improvements in the situational awareness of the platform, which ensures safe robot proximity to infrastructure and humans in adherence to safety compliance requirements. This represents a significant enhancement of SLAM in the presence of humans, where safety compliance is maintained via C^3 governance. This application summarizes the utilization of the millimetre-wave sensors to differentiate between a human and a metallic target over a range sensor to target distances. Figure 13.30 shows the FMCW amplitude response for both targets as a function of range.

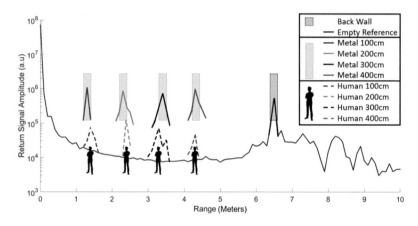

Figure 13.30: Return signal amplitude versus distance for human and metal sheet targets.

The human test subject was positioned in the centre of the sensor field of view and moved from 1 metre to 4 metres from the sensor in one-metre increments. This procedure was repeated for the aluminium metal sheet, which measured 700 mm by 500 mm. Relevant annotations have been made to Fig. 13.30 to more effectively present the findings from the data collected. The diagram firstly presents an empty reference signal via the solid blue line and blue rectangular block at 6.5 m for when no objects are in the field of view of the antenna. The metal sheet has been represented in the diagram via yellow blocks and solid lines, where humans are represented as human silhouettes and dashed lines. The results shown indicate a clear contrast in the return signal amplitude of a human when compared to a metal sheet. The peaks collected within the data were passed through an algorithm to calculate the reflection magnitude relative to the set baseline, which was taken to be the laboratory wall at 6 metres from the sensor. The calculated reflection magnitudes are presented in Table 13.6 [138]. Note: the distance calculated does not account for the length of the waveguide, resulting in target distances increased by 0.5 metres, as shown in Fig.

13.30. The application of the FMCW radar sensor for human detection results in increased symbiosis between a robotic platform and its environment.

Table 13.6: Calculated reflection magnitudes for contrast identification between aluminium sheet and human targets

Target type and distance from sensor	Relative magnitude
"No Target" Reference (or Lab Wall at 600 cm)	1
Human at 100 cm	1.54709657
Human at 200 cm	1.875306979
Human at 300 cm	1.519923948
Human at 400 cm	1.322427315
Aluminium Sheet at 100 cm	14.92893924
Aluminium Sheet at 200 cm	10.79030341
Aluminium Sheet at 300 cm	7.516517468
Aluminium Sheet at 400 cm	13.51913174

6.3.1 Through-wall Detection

This case study investigates the unique application of the FMCW radar for through-wall detection of a target. The challenge addressed by this work is whether the FMCW sensor can improve the operational awareness of a RAS to signal contrasts which indicate whether a human or robot has entered the mission space or is blocking a doorway, while unseen from the other side of that doorway or wall. Constricted high foot-traffic areas would benefit from this type of situational assessment mapping, as it promotes enhanced safety compliance of the CPS. A specific example is where a human is in close proximity to a door, through which a robot requires passage. If the robot unknowingly operates the door in close proximity to the human, this could result in an accident. Therefore, if the FMCW radar was employed, the radar could detect the human whilst obscured by the door and advise the robot to utilize another entry door. This increases the safety compliance by reducing the chance for collisions to occur during transit through doors and avoiding getting stranding between doors which would render it unusable.

An illustration, where the sensor was situated 10 cm from a partition wall within the laboratory, is presented in Fig. 13.31. The human test subject held a 30 × 30 cm copper sheet on the far side of the concrete partition wall. Consequently, the copper sheet was completely obscured from the sensor by the partition wall during this test. The copper sheet was then moved from position A to position D whilst the radar continuously scanned. The results are displayed in Fig. 13.32, where an empty reference baseline was taken, represented by the space between the wall 1 and wall 2. The human test subject positioned their back to wall 2, while holding the copper sheet in the field of view of the sensor. This correlates to Position A (solid black peak). As the human test subject and copper sheet advanced towards wall 1, peaks are observed at Position B (solid grey peak), Position C (dashed black peak) and Position D (dashed grey peak). Each peak represents the return signal amplitude from the interface of the copper sheet to the radar. This is represented as a distance to the target.

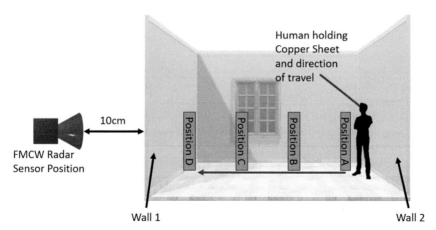

Figure 13.31: Through wall detection using FMCW radar highlighting positions of the human test subject and copper sheet relative to the sensor.

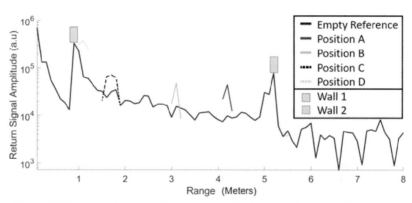

Figure 13.32: Return signal amplitude responses for the metal sheet at positions A-D.

Robotic manipulator arms represent "ground-up" technology and are progressively being used to operate entrance/access points autonomously. The Boston Dynamics SPOT Arm [139] has an inbuilt LED and 4K camera, which can be used for inspection, however, the arm has no mechanism to detect key contrasts through a door. Therefore, if the arm were to push a door, this could result in an injury to a human in close proximity to that door or if an unseen object was leaning against the door. This represents a new challenge in the safe transition of robots into unmapped workspaces. Current autonomous systems are not required to assess whether areas beyond obstructions are clear, such as behind a doorway. This is due to the limits imposed by current, visual spectrum SLAM systems. The application of FMCW radar in this role facilitates improvements in safe operating procedure when a robot is required to pass through visually opaque doors. Symbiosis is accomplished via commensalism as the robotic platform can interact with the human or obstruction without the need to inform the human.

6.4   Search and Rescue

Search and rescue environments are often represented as harsh and highly variable conditions, often with extreme thermal contrasts, low visibility, constrained spaces, noxious fumes combined with the threat of significant infrastructural failures. These are often major contributing factors in human disorientation. In the previous subsections, we discussed the capability of the FMCW sensor to detect static and dynamic measurands for human detection through walls in the built environment. The FMCW system evaluated within this chapter has demonstrated operational proficiency when in environments known to cause severe impediments to conventional SLAM technologies, including LiDAR systems and visual or thermal spectrum imaging.

We identify applications where millimetre-wave sensing may be further developed to improve symbiotic relationships across systems used for search and rescue. These are:

1. Differentiation between infrastructure and humans, allowing for the implementation of vital rescue strategies in zones where standard communications are rendered ineffective, such as obstructive terrain, GPS-constrained locations, and situations with communications dead zones.
2. Detection of humans obscured by collapsed infrastructure or in low visibility situations within a search and rescue mission area, including opaque or extreme environments.
3. Detection of crucial vital signs for rapid review of casualties [140–143] and real-time communication of casualty data to medical facilities.
4. Accurate real-time situational reporting and incident area mapping to support navigation of dynamic disaster areas.

7.   A Systems Approach to Real-World Deployment of Industrial Internet of Things

Deploying CPS's, specifically, sensors in a real industrial setting are often hampered by unpredictable challenges that are not encountered in a controlled environment. Using a bottom-up systems approach to identify, integrate, and install an IIoT system, the challenges can be mitigated [144].

7.1   Challenges in IIoT Deployment

Every industrial site has a set of unique challenges; however, the majority of these will be the same across sites and sectors.

1. Current IIoT systems are often inflexible in their data acquisition which can prove difficult to adapt to the range of industrial sites they are required for.
2. Industrial sites are dynamic, they go through periods of upgrades and repairs, and the IIoT systems are required to be robust enough to handle these upheavals.
3. Network connectivity can vary unpredictably on industrial sites, whether this is due to wireless communication being protected with firewall systems, the range of materials used to construct such site blocking wireless signals or the distance a signal is required to cover.

7.1.1 Bottom-up Approach

Step (1) High-Level Abstraction: Identify the critical assets, then assign them to two classes:

    a. Class-1: Passive Assets (e.g., crates, walkways, and walls)
    b. Class-2: Active Assets (e.g., power generators, wasteducts, air conditioners)

The aforementioned generalization is essential as in order to be able to apply the bottom-up approach in a generic way to other situations which share a set of common features.

Class-1 assets do not generate continual vibrations or high-frequency movements, while Class-2 assets do. The measurements gathered from the assets via the sensors need to be transmitted to a central repository stationed in a secure location. A secure area was created with the receiver and edge equipment, allowing for the readings from each of the asset's sensors to be stored. If the asset is within a close proximity to the secure location (sub 100 m), Bluetooth, Zigbee, and Wi-Fi can be employed. If the asset is located further than 100 m, either LoRa (Long Range) [145] or Long-Term Evolution (LTE) is required. If communicating using LoRaan area ideally with a line of sight to the sensor platforms or assets to be monitored should be setup as LoRa signal quality is greatly reduced by obstructions.

Often the assets that are of interest are remotely located, and thus the battery life of the CPS should be in the order of months to years in length. LoRa provides a method of long-distance communication and which has a lower power requirement than other wireless methods of communication. However, it has bandwidth restrictions and cannot be deployed where high-sample and communication rates are required.

Because Class-1 assets do not generate high-frequency measurements, each asset is ideal for using LoRa as its mode of communication. However, with Class-2, assets are more varied and thus, so are the required communication methods. Additionally, the assets surface materials determine how the unit can be mounted, which can also be configured into the asset description.

Step (2) Module Selection: Typically, an IIoT system consists of multiple discrete active and passive elements such as sensors, communication devices, batteries, encapsulations, etc. The Step (1) classification determines the modules to be used. For example, a Class-2 could use a Hall effect sensor to record its magnetic field, determining the communication module needed.

7.2 System Components

7.2.1 Sensing Platform

To monitor the structures at this industrial site, the Limpet platform [55] was deployed. Every Limpet has an array of sensors that include optical, temperature, sound, magnetic field, distance, pressure, humidity, and IMU. ROS is integrated into each Limpet, allowing joint operations with a broad range of robotic systems. As the assets to be monitored were spread over an expansive area (over 100 m), LoRaWAN was used to overcome the range and power issues.

To enable the Limpet to take advantage of the extended range of LoRaWAN, a LoPy4 expansion board was added. As offshore platforms are the desired environment for the Limpet to be deployed, data security is essential. Therefore, a local LoRaWAN communication system was deployed. Deploying such a communication system also removes any reliance on existing or commercial communication connectivity.

The local communications system integrates the LoRa Server project developed by CableLabs [145]. The Limpet transmits its sensor data over a UART connection to the LoPy [146], then data packets are transmitted to the securely located data hub via the LoRaWAN wireless protocol. To provide an adequate power supply for the deployment duration, a 5 V lithium polymer battery was integrated with the Limpet. To allow a concise reference to the complete system, each combination of Limpet, LoPy, and a battery is designated an L-node. Figure 13.33 shows a complete L-node.

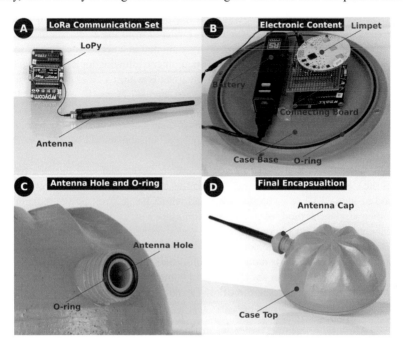

Figure 13.33: The Limpet V1, **(A)** The LoPyBoard and antenna, **(B)** Limpet V1 mounted on the LoPy expansion board connected to a rechargeable battery, **(C)** External antenna hole and watertight O-ring, **(D)** Complete Limpet V1 encapsulation [144].

The Limpet is both required to be able to adhere reliably to multiple surfaces and to withstand harsh environmental conditions. For this reason, the outer encapsulation is 3D printed with an infill of 95% in Polylactic acid before a coat of acrylic spray paint is applied, followed by an epoxy sealant, all gaps are compressed sealed with O-rings. During lab tests, the encapsulation achieved the targeted level of IP54 rating [147]. The adhesion for the Limpet came from an arrangement of five to six neodymium magnets arranged as required for the surface it was fitted to or via a steel strap.

7.3   Data Acquisition, Visualization, and Querying

7.3.1 Data Acquisition

The L-nodes were installed at distances up to 100 m away from the secure area. As LoRaWAN was the predominant method of communication, the data hub system was composed of a Sentrius™ RG1xx series LoRa-Enabled gateway from Laird™, a NETGEAR® Nighthawk R7000 Wi-Fi router, and an Intel® NUC.

The gateway operates a packet-forwarder software that forwards the incoming packets to a network server via a User Datagram Protocol (UDP). The LoRa gateway and network server are given IP addresses by a local Domain Name System (DNS) server. Typically, an IIoT generates a constant stream of data, in prestigious amounts and in an unstructured format. Relational database methods are the standard in data storage for many applications. However, they are deemed inadequate for IIoT applications due to the restrictive computational rates and steep storage expansion costs [20]. Therefore, MongoDB, a NoSQL (Not only SQL) database, was used to store the data received from the sensor nodes. Creating the optimal schema for the deployment scenario is fundamental for future scalability. A schema is away the unstructured data is sorted in the database. Each L-node was sending data every five seconds, an average of 12 data packets per minute during this scenario. The data schema wrote 720 packets to a single document over an hour. This schema has a considerably fewer number of reads than one that writes a separate document for every data packet received. As large amounts of data queries are expected of an IIoT system, the optimization of the read rate is crucial, especially for high scalability.

7.3.2 Data Query and Visualization

The primary purpose of data aggregation is the smooth retrieval and visualization of critical information. A dashboard-with-query processing engine that visualized the status of the sensors for the L-node chosen was created. As the dashboard is limited and only able to illustrate a finite amount of information, it incorporated a drop-down interface to question previously recorded data. The dashboard-with-query engine was created using a Python library called Dash running as a service app. The app was hosted on the data hub and could be viewed via a secure URLngrok7 was used [148].

7.4 On-Site Deployment

The data acquisition system was deployed alongside the L-node in locations visible in Fig. 13.34. Each L-node was placed on a different type of machinery or infrastructure within the LoRa's range and had the required line of sight to guarantee optimal LoRa data transmission. Across the whole site and on multiple different types of asset, a total of seven L-nodes were deployed. To optimize each L-node location, the Signal to Noise Ratio (SNR) was used. During this deployment, the LoRa SNR stayed in the range of –10 dB and +10 dB. A positive and significant SNR reading indicated a suitable location with sufficient signal strength. As every data packet sent via LoRa carries an SNR value as a complement with the actual data requested, the appropriate location of each L-node was straight forward to find and monitor. Due to the L-nodes being deployed with the expectation to operate for extended periods, uninterrupted reliability is a key element. Preliminary tests were run on the L-nodes once they were mounted on each asset to assess their ability to stay mounted and test and record their delay in transmission, SNR and signal reading. Once the initial testing was completed, each L-node was calibrated against the recorded values.

7.5 Results

The core idea from the work conducted was the development of a straight forward technique that could help in the integration and installation of multiple heterogeneous units within an IIoT system.

The bottom-up flowchart shown in Fig. 13.35 illustrates the process to follow from asset identification through categorization of the asset to the module selection finishing at the endpoint of integration into an IIoT system. An example wind turbine is selected as the desired asset to be monitored, and the flow of the decisions is shown

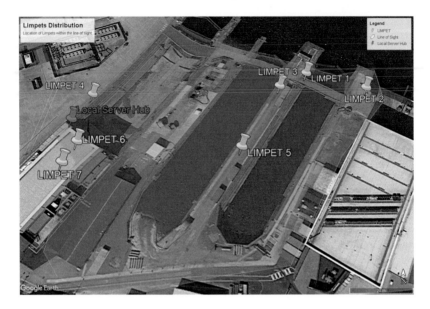

Figure 13.34: Each pin marked L-(X) designates the installation location of an L-node and their corresponding number, while the location of the secure area is labelled separately [144].

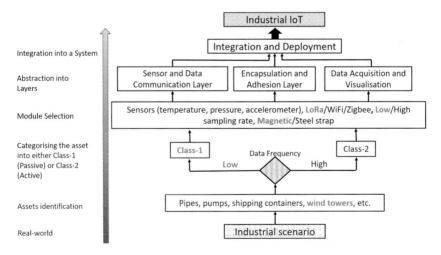

Figure 13.35: A bottom-up flow chart visualization of the demonstrated technique [144].

in the bold text. The first stage is to categorize the wind turbine into a suitable class. From this classification, the sensors required, and the communications modalities are found. Typically wind turbines should be a passive infrastructure and thus require a low sampling rate. As wind turbines can be situated far from the control centre, often offshore or on mountainous terrain, the only usable form of communication would be LoRaWAN. Predominantly wind turbines towers are of a steel structure, and therefore a magnetic adhesion can be used. After all the low-level modules are chosen, the required layers can be extracted and then combined and installed as a complete and functional IIoT system.

For ease of data understanding and access, a dashboard-with-query application was created. Initially, a Dashboard application was developed, shown in Fig. 13.36, allowing for an efficient and concise view of the status of the L-nodes and the relevant sensors.

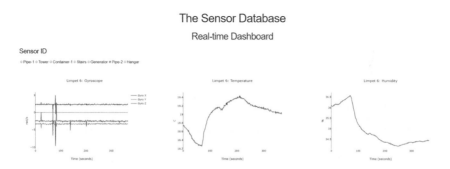

Figure 13.36: Real-time sensor database dashboard [144].

Using a radio-style button (shown in Fig. 13.36), the users can pick the corresponding desired asset, and a visualization of the previous hour of data recordings from each sensor of the selected L-node will be displayed.

Only using a dashboard can limit the volume of data that can be shown. The ability to see the historical data of an asset is critical. So, a second interface was created, where once the user inputs the relevant L-node ID, time and date, the desired information will be displayed.

Data is often shown graphically; however, other representations can also be applicable, as mentioned in previous sections. If a user is required to consult the database frequently, a mouse-oriented interface can be clumsy. To compensate for this clumsiness, a chatbot was added and configured to interpret questions aimed at the databases. The chatbot was built using RASA8 [149], an open-source machine learning framework to develop contextual chat assistants. An example question and answer from the chatbot is shown in Fig. 13.37.

Over the whole of the industrial demonstration, data was collected. To evaluate the capability of each unit used, data from each sensor on each L-node was analysed.

As an example, vibration monitoring is an essential part of industrial asset monitoring. Figure 13.38 shows readings from the gyroscope (X, Y, Z) gathered during the operation of a diesel pump (Class-2 asset). Noise is often generated in industrial environments, and to compensate for it and smooth it,a moving average filter with a ten-second period was applied to the raw data.

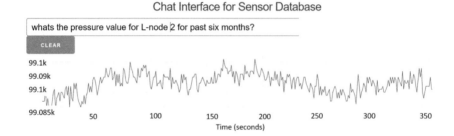

Figure 13.37: RASA chatbot interface for the sensor database [144].

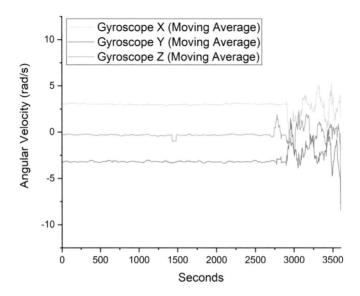

Figure 13.38: Structural vibrations monitoring and filtering using a moving average [144].

7.4.1 Problems in IIoT Deployment

1. **Accessibility:** Industrial sites can be heavily restricted due to heavy machinery operating and other health and safety risk. During the installation of the L-Node, finding qualified personnel to provide aid was an issue.
2. **Line-of-sight:** LoRa wireless communication signal degrades when passing through dense infrastructure, which can be the typical setup in industrial areas. Thus, it is essential to find a secure site that is ideally visible to the location of interest to be monitored.
3. **Adhesion:** Different shapes, materials and biofouling can prove problematic for magnets or steel-straps to be used in conjunction with.
4. **Site Access Time:** All sites were active and carry out other activities from regular maintenance to new installations, and therefore the time allocated to test external 3rd party systems is restrictive even when deployed by external parties.

7.4.2 Solutions

To be to adapt and overcome the challenges faced in the deployment of IIoT systems in an active site a number of solutions were generated and given next:

1. **Accessibility:** Advanced planning and negotiation with the facilities staff can avoid unnecessary delays and issues.
2. **Line-of-sight:** Pre-mapping of the site and locating areas for optimal line-of-sight and locations where signal repeaters could be installed if required.
3. **Adhesion:** Where possible, pre-cleaning any biofouling would aid in the adhesion or the application of drilling or welding for a more permanent method.
4. **Network Connectivity:** Deploying a secure network separate from the facilities owner's network ensures a connection and reassures the owners there is no data at risk.
5. **Site Access Time:** As with accessibility, advanced planning and negotiation can reduce this risk.

Applying all the previous solutions and the bottom-up systems approach shown in Fig. 13.35 to the process of designing of an industrial deployment of one or more CPS allows for the following:

- Problems to be spotted and neutralized before they occur (poor line of sight – repeaters required)
- Optimize the in-situ data (Recording frequency and length, visualization, and query method)
- Planned avoidance of human interaction to minimize viral transmission risk.

8. Connect-R

Decommissioning structures, for example, gas platforms or nuclear storage tanks, is challenging and the cost of the dismantling, as well as the effect and impact of the surrounding environment, are among some of the factors that must be included and anticipated on an asset management system as these can be extremely costly and environmental conservation standards must be met.

There is pressure for oil, nuclear and gas, and similar industries to increase their profitability whilst growing the business. Here, the correct IAM strategy will maintain and service their equipment in a time-effective manner whilst increasing equipment lifetime and maintaining low costs as it is essential that they keep their critical assets working efficiently whilst being effectively serviced.

These types of industries are filled with heavy-duty assets and they can be often sizable or located at great distances from the other, hence remote and accurate real-time data is essential in these circumstances for effective and adequate asset management.

As mentioned previously, technological advances, through the digital transition, have enhanced maintenance operations. Some of these technologies include 3D scanning, mapping and predictive maintenance, which allow for much-improved monitoring and maintaining industrial assets.

In these industries, in particular, the working environments can often be hostile and extreme. Such situations and environments create challenges in maintaining monitoring assets as they can often pose health risks to personnel and therefore should not be performed by personnel. This is particularly true in the nuclear industry due to the risk of personnel being exposed to high radiation levels as well as unstructured environments. Operating in an extreme environment can have an effect on asset management structures and management strategies due to risk to human life and the increasing cost of operations. However, this can be mitigated through the use of robots and in-situ sensor technology.

Connect-R is an industrial sized self-building modular robotic solution that provides access to hazardous environments on industrial work sites through a multi-robot system (MRS). The system is a resilient and robust autonomous robotic system. This modular robot is a structural robot that can form into a variety of, required, physical structures to allow access to an extreme environment without the requirement of a human. The structure that is formed by the modular robots creates a path for other robots to traverse regardless of the unstructured environment surrounding it. Once in the environment, these smaller robots are able to perform a number of tasks such as repair and diagnostics to provide real-time data and mapping through the use of various, suitable sensors and end effectors [150].

9. Future Challenges

While some future challenges can be predicted, such as dealing with an increasingly large number of ageing and failing industrial assets coming to the end of their predicted life, others such as the COVID-19 pandemic could not have been foreseen. However, it can be observed throughout this chapter that the greatest challenge is still to keep humans safe, whether that is from a virus, storms or radiation. To keep them safe the continued deployment of CPS is essential, but it must go further, as at present humans are still required to deploy the robots and to retrieve them. Two different methods can be used to separate humans further from danger, (1) Resident Robots and (2) Fluidic Logic Systems.

9.1   Resident Robots

Instead of a robot being stored and then deployed manually by a human, resident robots are already situated "in residence" close to or on the asset itself. A simulation can be seen in Fig. 13.39. These robots can be autonomous but also can be operated from the shoreline remotely. Minimal human interaction either with the asset or robot is required unless remedial action cannot be completed by a robot. Resident robots would also provide enhanced operational overview due to DTs, therefore an allowing for a greater understanding of what status is and what is going on with an asset. Within these expansive DT asset management methodologies are built-in as well as robot fleet integration.

9.2   Fluidic Logic Robots

An issue when deploying RAS in areas of radiation can be the degradation or failure in the performance of the on-board electrical control systems and thus the entire robot itself. While sensitive systems can be shielded and often are, they will still degrade and will also become contaminated and un-retrievable. One approach to dealing with this degradation issue is by removing the electronics in their entirety. As mentioned previously, there are groups working in the area of fluidic logic where typical electrical systems are replaced with a functional fluidic analogue. If the fluid

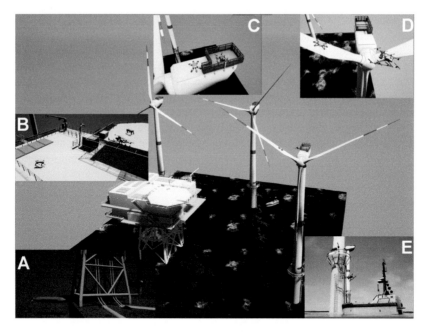

Figure 13.39: Resident robots deployed on offshore platforms and turbines, **(A)** Hugin and BlueROV, **(B)** Boston Dynamics Spot, **(C)** Crawler Robot and Intel Falcon 8+, **(D)** Crawler Robot and Intel Falcon 8+ and **(E)** ASV Global C-Worker 7 and Intel Falcon 8+.

and structural material were non-ionizing in nature, this would alleviate one aspect of the degradation problem [153].

10. Conclusion

It can be seen from the trends that the incorporation of RAS and CPS into industrial asset management was progressing. However, the COVID-19 pandemic has driven this deployment to rapidly advance the approach for CPS (due to the requirement to work remotely) in achieving the roadmap to trusted and safe autonomy within robotics and asset management methodologies.

At the start of the chapter, a question was posed "How can the new dangers of a pandemic and the past dangers of the extreme environments can be mitigated using cyber-physical systems?" A theoretical SSOSA and multiple pilot studies were given as examples of ways in which these dangers can be reduced if not mitigated fully.

The SSOSA acts as the theoretical model, which ensures the mutualistic approach enhancing the interaction across human, infrastructure, robot and the environment. The SDA represents system engineering to enable the interaction via bidirectional communications with knowledge sharing across the system elements, which are required to be integrated for advanced CPS. This can encompass asset management methodologies, O&M, deployment and fleet management which can be seen in an operational overview within a DT.

The bottom-up systems approach provided a foundation for how to assess potential issues and pit falls on industrial sites, which can be easily modified to incorporate COVID-19 specific restrictions allowing for straight forward deployment of CPS with minimal risk to the operators.

Both of these implementations featured CPS be they robots or sensors being used for scanning and monitoring of infrastructure, while the third implementation discusses the work being done on how to use MRS in areas where humans cannot tread, and standard robots require help to allow for an adaptable robotic structure to be custom fabricated made of itself for other robotic systems to traverse.

The system engineering discussed display how both current and future work environments can be created with the idea in mind of minimal to no human intervention being required. This reduces the risk of accident or injury coming from dangerous environments or viral transmission from COVID-19, or future pandemics.

Acknowledgement

This research was funded by the Offshore Robotics for the Certification of Assets (ORCA) Hub [EP/R026173/1], EPSRC Holistic Operation and Maintenance for Energy (HOME) from Offshore Wind Farms and supported by MicroSense Technologies Ltd (MTL) in the provision of their patented microwave FMCW sensing technology (PCT/GB2017/053275) and decommissioned wind turbine blade section and Connect-R: Providing Structure in Unstructured Extreme Environments [Innovate UK (TS/S017623/1)].

References

1. E. and I. S. Department for Business, UK Energy Statistics, Q1 2020. Accessed: Apr. 13, 2021. [Online]. Available: www.gov.uk/government/collections/road-transport-consumption-at-regional-and-local-level, (2020).
2. Department of Energy and Climate Change, UK Renewable Energy Roadmap, (2011).
3. Evans, W. and E. and I. S. Department for Business, Energy Trends, (2020).
4. E. and I. S. Department for Business, Statistical Release Energy Prices 2021, (2021).
5. Bell, R.J., S.L. Gray and O.P. Jones. North Atlantic storm driving of extreme wave heights in the North Sea. J. Geophys. Res. Ocean., 122(4) (Apr. 2017): 3253–3268, doi: 10.1002/2016JC012501.
6. Management of Hydrogen Sulphide (H_2S) Gas in Wind Turbine Sub-Structures: Identifying and Managing H_2S, (2016). ORE. Catapult, https://ore.catapult.org.uk/wp-content/uploads/2017/12/Management-of-Hydrogen-Sulphide-H2S-Gas-in-Wind-Turbine-Sub-Structures.-Identifying-and-managing-H2S.pdf
7. Malone Rubright, S.L., L.L. Pearce and J. Peterson. Environmental toxicology of hydrogen sulfide. Nitric Oxide, 71 (Dec. 2017): 1–13, doi: 10.1016/j.niox.2017.09.011.
8. Griggs, J.W. BP Gulf of Mexico Oil Spill. Accessed: Apr. 13, 2021 [Online]. Available: http://www.ktiv.com/Global/story.asp?S=13386062, (2011).
9. Li, Y. Role of ventilation in airborne transmission of infectious agents in the built environment – A multidisciplinary systematic review. Indoor Air, 17(1) (2007): 2–18, doi: 10.1111/j.1600-0668.2006.00445.x.

10. Leclerc, Q.J., N.M. Fuller, L.E. Knight, S. Funk and G.M. Knight. What settings have been linked to SARS-CoV-2 transmission clusters? Wellcome Open Res., 5 (2020), doi: 10.12688/wellcomeopenres.15889.2.
11. Fennelly, K.P. Particle sizes of infectious aerosols: Implications for infection control. Lancet Respir., 8 (2020): 914–924, doi: 10.1016/S2213-2600(20)30323-4.
12. F.V. and D.J. Team. Lockdowns compared: Tracking governments' coronavirus responses. Financial Times, (2021), https://ig.ft.com/coronavirus-lockdowns/ (accessed Apr. 13, 2021).
13. Crow, D. and A. Millot. Working from home can save energy and reduce emissions. But how much? IEA, (2020). https://www.iea.org/commentaries/working-from-home-can-save-energy-and-reduce-emissions-but-how-much (accessed Apr. 13, 2021).
14. IEA, Covid-19 impact on electricity, Paris [Online]. (2021). Available: https://www.iea.org/reports/covid-19-impact-on-electricity.
15. Komonen, K., H. Kortelainen and M. Räikkonen. An asset management framework to improve longer term returns on investments in the capital intensive industries. *In:* Proceedings of the 1st World Congress on Engineering Asset Management (WCEAM), (2016): 418–432.
16. Vanier, D.J. Why industry needs asset management tools. J. Comput. Civ. Eng., 15(1) (Jan. 2001): 35–43, doi: 10.1061/(ASCE)0887-3801.
17. Vanier, D.J. ASSET MANAGEMENT 101: A PRIMER [Online]. (2000). Available: www.nrc.ca/irc/uir/apwa.
18. Gavrikova, E., I. Volkova and Y. Burda. Strategic aspects of asset management: An overview of current research. Sustain., 12(15) (2020). doi: 10.3390/su12155955.
19. ISO, ISO 55000:2014. (2014).
20. Wang, B., Y. Liu, J. Qian and S.K. Parker. Achieving effective remote working during the COVID-19 pandemic: A work design perspective. Appl. Psychol., 70(1) (Jan. 2021): 16–59, doi: 10.1111/apps.12290.
21. Brynjolfsson, B., J. Horton, A. Ozimek, D. Rock, G. Sharma and H.-Y. TuYe. COVID-19 and Remote Work: An Early Look at US Data. Cambridge, MA, (Jun. 2020). doi: 10.3386/w27344.
22. Kylili, A. The role of remote working in smart cities: Lessons learnt from COVID-19 pandemic. Energy Sources, Part A Recover. Util. Environ. Eff., (Oct. 2020): 1–16, doi: 10.1080/15567036.2020.1831108.
23. Parlikad, A.K. and M. Jafari. Challenges in infrastructure asset management. IFAC-PapersOnLine, 49(28) (2016): 185–190, doi: 10.1016/j.ifacol.2016.11.032,
24. Abuzayan, K.M.A., A. Whyte and J. Bell. Asset-management framework(s) for infrastructure facilities in adverse (post-conflict/disaster-zone/high-alert) conditions. Procedia Econ. Financ., 18 (2014): 304–311, doi: 10.1016/s2212-5671(14)00944-7.
25. Nel, C.B.H. and W.J.L. Jooste. A technologically-driven asset management approach to managing physical assets – A literature review and research agenda for 'smart' asset management. South African Journal of Industrial Engineering, 27(4) (2016): 50–65, doi: 10.7166/27-4-1478. South African Institute of Industrial Engineering.

26. Jónasdóttir, H., K. Dhanani, K. McRae and J. Mehnen. Upgrading legacy equipment to Industry 4.0 through a cyber-physical interface. Advances in Production Management Systems. Smart Manufacturing for Industry 4.0. (2018): 3–10.

27. Liu, Y. and X. Xu. Industry 4.0 and cloud manufacturing: A comparative analysis. J. Manuf. Sci. Eng. Trans. ASME, 139(3) (2017): 1–8, doi: 10.1115/1.4034667

28. Candón, E. Implementing Intelligent Asset Management Systems (IAMS) within an Industry 4.0 manufacturing environment. IFAC-PapersOnLine, 52(13) (2019): 2488–2493, doi: 10.1016/j.ifacol.2019.11.580.

29. Balali, F., J. Nouri, A. Nasiri and T. Zhao. Industrial asset management and maintenance policies. *In:* Data Intensive Industrial Asset Management, (2020): 21–41. Cham: Springer International Publishing

30. Costa, M.J., P. Goncalves, A. Martins and E. Silva. Vision-based assisted teleoperation for inspection tasks with a small ROV. *In:* 2012 Oceans, (Oct. 2012): 1–8, doi: 10.1109/OCEANS.2012.6404915.

31. Elvander, J. and G. Hawkes. ROVs and AUVs in support of marine renewable technologies. *In:* 2012 Oceans, (Oct. 2012): 1–6, doi: 10.1109/OCEANS.2012.6405139.

32. Bogue, R. Robots in the offshore oil and gas industries: A review of recent developments. Ind. Robot Int. J. Robot. Res. Appl., 47(1) (Nov. 2019): 1–6, doi: 10.1108/IR-10-2019-0207.

33. Reid, M. The piper alpha disaster: a personal perspective with transferrable lessons on the long-term moral impact of safety failures. ACS Chem. Heal. Saf., 27(2) (Mar. 2020) 88–95, doi: 10.1021/acs.chas.9b00022.

34. Mahon, S.T., A. Buchoux, M.E. Sayed, L. Teng and A.A. Stokes. Soft robots for extreme environments: Removing electronic control. *In:* 2019 2nd IEEE International Conference on Soft Robotics (RoboSoft), (Apr. 2019): 782–787, doi: 10.1109/ROBOSOFT.2019.8722755.

35. Bartlett, N.W., K.P. Becker and R.J. Wood. A fluidic demultiplexer for controlling large arrays of soft actuators. Soft Matter, 16(25) (2020): 5871–5877, doi: 10.1039/C9SM02502B.

36. Drotman, D., S. Jadhav, D. Sharp, C. Chan and M.T. Tolley. Electronics-free pneumatic circuits for controlling soft-legged robots. Sci. Robot., 6(51) (Feb. 2021): eaay2627, doi: 10.1126/scirobotics.aay2627.

37. Xu, K. and N.O. Perez-Arancibia. Electronics-free logic circuits for localized feedback control of multi-actuator soft robots. IEEE Robot. Autom. Lett., 5(3) (Jul. 2020): 3990–3997, doi: 10.1109/LRA.2020.2982866.

38. Garrad, M., G. Soter, A.T. Conn, H. Hauser and J. Rossiter. A soft matter computer for soft robots. Sci. Robot., 4(33) (Aug. 2019): eaaw6060, doi: 10.1126/scirobotics.aaw6060.

39. Abidi, H. and M. Cianchetti. On intrinsic safety of soft robots. Front. Robot. AI, 4 (Feb. 2017), doi: 10.3389/frobt.2017.00005.

40. Galloway, K.C. Soft robotic grippers for biological sampling on deep reefs. Soft Robot., 3(1) (Mar. 2016): 23–33, doi: 10.1089/soro.2015.0019.

41. Li, G. Self-powered soft robot in the Mariana Trench. Nature, 591(7848) (Mar. 2021): 66–71, doi: 10.1038/s41586-020-03153-z.

42. Aracri, S. Soft robots for ocean exploration and offshore operations: A perspective. Soft Robot., (2021): 1–15, doi: 10.1089/soro.2020.0011.

43. Binti Sulaiman, S., S.S.A. Ali, S.H. Adil, M. Ebrahim and K. Raza. Virtual Reality Training and Skill Enhancement for Offshore Workers. *In:* 2020 International Conference on Computational Intelligence (ICCI), (Oct. 2020): 287–292, doi: 10.1109/ICCI51257.2020.9247819.

44. Major, P., H. Zhang, H. Petter Hildre and M. Edet. Virtual prototyping of offshore operations: A review. Sh. Technol. Res., (Oct. 2020): 1–18, doi: 10.1080/09377255.2020.1831840.

45. Marino, E., L. Barbieri, B. Colacino, A.K. Fleri and F. Bruno. An augmented reality inspection tool to support workers in Industry 4.0 environments. Comput. Ind., 127 (May 2021): 103412, doi: 10.1016/j.compind.2021.103412.

46. Hastie, H. The ORCA Hub: Explainable Offshore Robotics through Intelligent Interfaces. arXiv preprint arXiv:1803.02100.

47. Anderson, T. and M. Rasmussen. Aging Management: Monitoring of Technical Condition of Aging Equipment. ICMES, Helsinki, (2003).

48. Pettinghill, H. and P. Weimer. Worldwide deepwater exploration and production: Past, present and future, Lead. Edge, 21(4) (2002): 371–376.

49. Havard, B. Reliability Management of Deepwater Subsea Field Developments. Offshore Technol. Conf. Houston, U.S.A., (2003).

50. Mobley, R. Maintenance Engineering Handbook. New York McGraw-Hill Educ., (2014).

51. Miguelañez-Martin, E. and D. Flynn. Embedded intelligence supporting predictive asset management in the energy sector. *In:* IET Conference Publications, 2015(CP669) (2015): 7.-7, doi: 10.1049/cp.2015.1752.

52. Blackburn, S. The Oxford Dictionary of Philosophy, Oxford Univ. Press, (1996).

53. Gruber, T. Towards Principles for the Design of Ontologies Used for Knowledge Sharing, Int. Work. Form. Ontol. Italy, (1993).

54. Fuchs, F., S. Henrici, M. Pirker, M. Berger, G. Langer and C. Seitz. Towards Semantics-based monitoring of large-scale industrial systems. *In:* 2006 International Conference on Computational Intelligence for Modelling Control and Automation and International Conference on Intelligent Agents Web Technologies and International Commerce (CIMCA'06), (2006): 261, doi: 10.1109/CIMCA.2006.220.

55. Sayed, M.E., M.P. Nemitz, S. Aracri, A.C. McConnell, R.M. McKenzie and A.A. Stokes. The limpet: A ROS-enabled multi-sensing platform for the ORCA hub. Sensors (Switzerland), 18(10) (2018), doi: 10.3390/s18103487.

56. Sayed, M.E., J.O. Roberts, R.M. McKenzie, S. Aracri, A. Buchoux and A.A. Stokes, Limpet II: A modular, untethered soft robot. Soft Robot., (Aug. 2020): soro.2019.0161, doi: 10.1089/soro.2019.0161.

57. Mitchell, D., J. Blanche and D. Flynn. An Evaluation of Millimeter-wave Radar Sensing for Civil Infrastructure Citation for published version, (2020).

58. Ivan, V., A. Garriga-Casanovas, W. Merkt, F.B. Cegla and S. Vijayakumar. Autonomous non-destructive remote robotic inspection of offshore assets. *In:* Proceedings of the Annual Offshore Technology Conference, (May 2020), doi: 10.4043/30754-ms, (2020).

59. Clearpath, Husky UGV – Outdoor Field Research Robot. https://clearpathrobotics.com/husky-unmanned-ground-vehicle-robot/ (accessed Apr. 12, 2021).

60. ANYmal C – Autonomous Legged Robot | ANYbotics. https://www.anybotics. com/anymal-legged-robot/ (accessed Apr. 12, 2021).

61. Xin, G. Variable Autonomy of whole-body control for inspection and intervention in industrial environments using legged robots. IEEE Int. Conf. Autom. Sci. Eng., (2020-August): 1415–1420, Apr. 2020, Accessed: Apr. 11, 2021. [Online]. Available: http://arxiv.org/abs/2004.02996.

62. Jarvis, R., A. Farinha, M. Kovac and F. Cegla. NDE sensor delivery using unmanned aerial vehicles. Insight - Non-Destructive Test. Cond. Monit., 60(8) (Aug. 2018): 463–467, doi: 10.1784/insi.2018.60.8.463.

63. Nguyen, H.-N., R. Siddall, B. Stephens, A. Navarro-Rubio and M. Kovac. A passively adaptive microspine grapple for robust, controllable perching. *In:* 2019 2nd IEEE International Conference on Soft Robotics (RoboSoft), (Apr. 2019): 80–87, doi: 10.1109/ROBOSOFT.2019.8722779.

64. Dams, B., S. Sareh, K. Zhang, P. Shepherd, M. Kovac and R.J. Ball. Remote three-dimensional printing of polymer structures using drones. Proc. Inst. Civ. Eng. - Constr. Mater., (Jul. 2017): 1–31, doi: 10.1680/jcoma.17.00013.

65. Sareh, P., P. Chermprayong, M. Emmanuelli, H. Nadeem and M. Kovac. Rotorigami: A rotary origami protective system for robotic rotorcraft. Sci. Robot., 3(22) (Sep. 2018): eaah5228, doi: 10.1126/scirobotics.aah5228.

66. Zufferey, R. Consecutive aquatic jump-gliding with water-reactive fuel. Sci. Robot., 4(34) (Sep. 2019): eaax7330, doi: 10.1126/scirobotics.aax7330.

67. Seaeye, S. Falcon. https://www.saabseaeye.com/solutions/underwater-vehicles/ falcon (accessed Apr. 12, 2021).

68. Blue Robotics – Underwater ROVs, Thrusters, Sonars, and Cameras. https:// bluerobotics.com/ (accessed Apr. 12, 2021).

69. Pairet, E., P. Ardón, X. Liu, J. Lopes, H. Hastie and K.S. Lohan. A digital twin for human-robot interaction. *In:* ACM/IEEE International Conference on Human-Robot Interaction, (March, 2019): 372, doi: 10.1109/HRI.2019.8673015.

70. Hastie, H., F.J. Chiyah Garcia, D.A. Robb, A. Laskov and P. Patron. MIRIAM. *In:* Proceedings of the 20th ACM International Conference on Multimodal Interaction, (Oct. 2018): 557–558, doi: 10.1145/3242969.3266297.

71. Nesset, B., D.A. Robb, J. Lopes and H. Hastie. Transparency in HRI: Trust and Decision making in the face of robot errors. *In:* Companion of the 2021 ACM/ IEEE International Conference on Human-Robot Interaction, (Mar. 2021): 313–317, doi: 10.1145/3434074.3447183.

72. Hastie, H. Challenges in Collaborative HRI for Remote Robot Teams, (May 2019) [Online]. Available: http://arxiv.org/abs/1905.07379, accessed: Apr. 12, 2021.

73. Wu, M. Gaze-based intention anticipation over driving manoeuvres in semi-autonomous vehicles. *In:* IEEE International Conference on Intelligent Robots and Systems, (Nov. 2019): 6210–6216, doi: 10.1109/IROS40897.2019.8967779.

74. Lopes, A.R.F.J., K. Lohan and H. Hastie. Symptoms of Cognitive Load in Interactions with a Dialogue System. (2018), doi: 10.1145/3279810.3279851.

75. Ahmad, M.I., D.A. Robb, I. Keller and K. Lohan. Towards a multimodal measure for physiological behaviours to estimate cognitive load. *In:* Engineering Psychology and Cognitive Ergonomics. Mental Workload, Human Physiology, and Human Energy, (2020): 3–13.

76. Coradeschi, S. and A. Saffiotti. Symbiotic robotic systems: Humans, robots,

and smart environments, IEEE Intell. Syst., 21(3) (2006): 82–84, doi: 10.1109/ MIS.2006.59.

77. CK-12. Symbiotic Relationships (Mutualism, Commensalism and Parasitism), CK-12 Foundation, (2016).

78. Zainal, N.A., S. Azad and K.Z. Zamli. An adaptive fuzzy symbiotic organisms search algorithm and its applications. IEEE Access, 8 (2020): 225384–225406, doi: 10.1109/ACCESS.2020.3042196.

79. Mitchell, D. Symbiotic System of Systems Design for Safe and Resilient Autonomous Robotics in Offshore Wind Farms, (Jan. 2021). arXiv preprint arXiv:2101.09491.

80. Flynn, D. Interactive digital twins framework for asset management through Internet. IEEE Global Conference on Artificial Intelligence and Internet of Things. IEEE, (Dec. 2020).

81. Overstreet, R.M. and J.M. Lotz. Host-symbiont relationships: Understanding the change from guest to pest. *In:* The Rasputin Effect: When Commensals and Symbionts Become Parasitic, 3 (2016): 27–64. Nature Publishing Group.

82. Sapp, J. Evolution by Association: A History of Symbiosis. Oxford University Press (OUP), (1994).

83. Sokolov, M., O. Bulichev and I. Afanasyev. Analysis of ROS-based visual and lidar odometry for a teleoperated crawler-type robot in indoor environment. *In:* ICINCO 2017 – Proceedings of the 14th International Conference on Informatics in Control, Automation and Robotics, 2, (2017): 316–321, doi: 10.5220/0006420603160321.

84. Kono, H., T. Mori, Y. Ji, H. Fujii and T. Suzuki. Development of perilous environment estimation system using a teleoperated rescue robot with on-board LiDAR*, *In:* 2019 IEEE/SICE International Symposium on System Integration (SII), (2019): 7–10, doi: 10.1109/SII.2019.8700382.

85. Walker, M.E., H. Hedayati and D. Szafir. Robot Teleoperation with augmented reality virtual surrogates. *In:* ACM/IEEE International Conference on Human-Robot Interaction, (Mar. 2019): 202–210, doi: 10.1109/HRI.2019.8673306.

86. Eggers, W.D., N. Malik and M. Gracie. Natural Language Processing Examples in Government Data. Deloitte Insights, (2019).

87. Oshikawa, R., J. Qian and W.Y. Wang. A survey on natural language processing for fake news detection. Lr. 2020 – 12th Int. Conf. Lang. Resour. Eval. Conf. Proc., (Nov. 2018): 6086–6093.

88. Redden, E., C.B. Carstens and R.A. Pettitt. Intuitive Speech-based Robotic Control. Army Research Laboratory, (2010).

89. Pettitt, R.A., E.S. Redden and C.B. Carstens. Scalability of robotic controllers: Speech-based robotic controller evaluation (2009). Army Research Lab Aberdeen Proving Ground MD, Human Research and Engineering Directorate.

90. UploadVR, HoloLens 2 AR Headset: On Stage Live Demonstration – YouTube, (2019).

91. Naumann, A., I. Wechsung and J. Hurtienne. Multimodality, inclusive design, and intuitive use. Is prior experience the same as intuition in the context of inclusive design. (2009).

92. Grieves, M. and J. Vickers. Digital Twin: Mitigating unpredictable, undesirable emergent behavior in complex systems. *In:* Transdisciplinary Perspectives on Complex Systems, (2017): 85–113.

93. Ferguson, S., Apollo 13: The First Digital Twin. SIMCENTER, (2020).

94. Deloitte, Tech Trends 2021: A Government Perspective, (2021) .
95. Panetta, K. Gartner Top 10 Strategic Technology Trends for 2020. Smarter With Gartner, (2019) .
96. Lheureux, B., A. Velosa, M. Halpern and N. Nuttall. Survey Analysis: Digital Twins are Poised for Proliferation (2019). Gartner Research Notes.
97. L3Harris, Pilot Training Locations. https://www.l3harris.com/all-capabilities/ pilot-training-locations.
98. Clark, G., J. Campbell, S.M.R. Sorkhabadi, W. Zhang and H.B. Amor. Predictive modeling of periodic behavior for human-robot symbiotic walking. *In:* 2020 IEEE International Conference on Robotics and Automation (ICRA), (2020): 7599–7605, doi: 10.1109/ICRA40945.2020.9196676.
99. Onggo, B.S., N. Mustafee, A. Smart, A.A. Juan and O. Molloy, Symbiotic simulation system: Hybrid systems model meets big data ANALYTICS. *In:* 2018 Winter Simulation Conference (WSC), (2018): 1358–1369, doi: 10.1109/ WSC.2018.8632407.
100. Bilberg, A. and A.A. Malik. Digital twin driven human-robot collaborative assembly. CIRP Ann., 68(1) (2019): 499–502, doi: https://doi.org/10.1016/j. cirp.2019.04.011.
101. Pairet, E., P. Ardón, X. Liu, J. Lopes, H. Hastie and K.S. Lohan. A digital twin for human-robot interaction. *In:* 2019 14th ACM/IEEE International Conference on Human-Robot Interaction (HRI), (2019): 372, doi: 10.1109/ HRI.2019.8673015.
102. Tsokalo, I.A., D. Kuss, I. Kharabet, F.H.P. Fitzek and M. Reisslein. Remote robot control with human-in-the-loop over long distances using digital twins. *In:* 2019 IEEE Global Communications Conference (GLOBECOM), (2019): 1–6, doi: 10.1109/GLOBECOM38437.2019.9013428.
103. Lei, L., G. Shen, L. Zhang and Z. Li. Toward intelligent cooperation of UAV swarms: When machine learning meets digital twin. IEEE Netw., 35(1) (2021): 386–392, doi: 10.1109/MNET.011.2000388.
104. Ramachandran, R.K., N. Fronda and G. Sukhatme. Resilience in multi-robot multi-target tracking with unknown number of targets through reconfiguration. IEEE Trans. Control Netw. Syst., (2021): 1, doi: 10.1109/TCNS.2021.3059794.
105. Bolu, A. and Ö. Korçak. Adaptive task planning for multi-robot smart warehouse, IEEE Access, 9 (2021): 27346–27358, doi: 10.1109/ACCESS.2021.3058190.
106. Khropatyi, O., O. Lohinov and V. Kazymyr. Embedded models realization platform in IoT. *In:* 2020 IEEE 5th International Symposium on Smart and Wireless Systems within the Conferences on Intelligent Data Acquisition and Advanced Computing Systems (IDAACS-SWS), (2020): 1–6, doi: 10.1109/ IDAACS-SWS50031.2020.9297061.
107. Suhail, R. Hussain, R. Jurdak and C.S. Hong. Trustworthy digital twins in the industrial Internet of Things with Blockchain. IEEE Internet Comput., (2021): 1, doi: 10.1109/MIC.2021.3059320.
108. Wang, W., H. Hu, J.C. Zhang and Z. Hu. Digital twin-based framework for green building maintenance system. *In:* 2020 IEEE International Conference on Industrial Engineering and Engineering Management (IEEM), (2020): 1301– 1305, doi: 10.1109/IEEM45057.2020.9309951.

109. Sofia, H., E. Anas and O. Faïz. Mobile mapping, machine learning and digital twin for road infrastructure monitoring and maintenance: Case study of Mohammed VI Bridge in Morocco. *In:* 2020 IEEE International Conference of Moroccan Geomatics (Morgeo), (2020): 1–6, doi: 10.1109/Morgeo49228.2020.9121882.
110. Mitchell, D., J. Blanche and D. Flynn. An evaluation of millimeter-wave radar sensing for civil infrastructure. *In:* 2020 11th IEEE Annual Information Technology, Electronics and Mobile Communication Conference (IEMCON), (2020): 216–222, doi: 10.1109/IEMCON51383.2020.9284883.
111. Blanche, J., D. Mitchell, R. Gupta, A. Tang and D. Flynn. Asset integrity monitoring of wind turbine blades with non-destructive radar sensing. *In:* 2020 11th IEEE Annual Information Technology, Electronics and Mobile Communication Conference (IEMCON), (2020): 498–504, doi: 10.1109/IEMCON51383.2020.9284941.
112. Borth, M., J. Verriet and G. Muller. Digital twin strategies for SoS 4 challenges and 4 architecture setups for digital twins of SoS. *In:* 2019 14th Annual Conference System of Systems Engineering (SoSE), (2019): 164–169, doi: 10.1109/SYSOSE.2019.8753860.
113. SEBoK, Systems of Systems (SoS), (2020).
114. Nagothu, K., T. Shaneyfelt, P. Benavidez, M.A. Jordens, S. Kota and M. Jamshidi. Systems of systems communication for heterogeneous independent operable systems. *In:* 2009 IEEE International Conference on System of Systems Engineering (SoSE), (2009) 1–6.
115. Zaki, O., M. Dunnigan, V. Robu and D. Flynn. Reliability and safety of autonomous systems based on semantic modelling for self-certification. Robotics, 10(1) (Jan. 2021), doi: 10.3390/robotics10010010.
116. H. and S. Executive. Working in confined spaces. HSE, (2021), https://www.hse.gov.uk/toolbox/confined.htm.
117. Fly Ability. Confined spaces inspection, (2021). https://www.flyability.com/articles-and-media/confined-spaces-inspection.
118. Guillen, S. and Clearpath Robotics. Heriot-Watt University Develops Autonomous Environments for Offshore Energy Sector – Clearpath Robotics, Mar. (2021).
119. Mitchell, D. Symbiotic System of System Approach – Autonomous Confined Space Asset Integrity Inspection: Summary Video, (Jan. 2021), https://www.youtube.com/watch?v=QG04Q-W0bvY (accessed Mar. 22, 2021).
120. Mitchell D. Symbiotic System of Systems Design for Safe and Resilient Autonomous Robotics in Offshore Wind Farms: Full Video, (Jan. 2021), https://youtu.be/3YzsEtpQMPU (accessed Mar. 22, 2021).
121. Cashmore, M. Rosplan: Planning in the robot operating system. Proc. Int. Conf. Autom. Plan. Sched. ICAPS, (Jan. 2015): 333–341.
122. Blanche, J., D. Flynn, H. Lewis, G. Couples and R. Cheung. Analysis of geomaterials using frequency modulated continuous wave radar in the X-band. *In*: 2017 IEEE 26th International Symposium on Industrial Electronics (ISIE). IEEE. (2017): 1376–1381.
123. Blanche, J., D. Flynn, H. Lewis, G. Couples and R. Cheung. Analysis of geomaterials using frequency modulated continuous wave radar in the X-band. IEEE 26th Int. Syposium Ind. Electron. ISIE, doi: https://doi.org/10.1109/ISIE.2017.8001446.

124. Blanche, J., D. Flynn, H. Lewis, G.D. Couples and R. Cheung. Analysis of geomaterials using frequency modulated continuous waves. 13th International Conference on Condition Monitoring and Machinery Failure Prevention Technologies, (2016).

125. Desmulliez, M.P.Y., S.K. Pavuluri, D. Flynn and D. Herd. Microwave Cavity Sensor, US 2015/0097561, (2013).

126. Jones, R.E., F. Simonetti, M.J.S. Lowe and I.P. Bradley. Use of microwaves for the detection of water as a cause of corrosion under insulation. J. Nondestruct. Eval., 31(1) (2012): 65–76, doi: 10.1007/s10921-011-0121-9.

127. Blanche, J. Analysis of sandstone pore space fluid saturation and mineralogy variation via application of monostatic K-band frequency modulated continuous wave radar. IEEE Access, 6 (2018): 44376–44389, doi: 10.1109/ACCESS.2018.2863024.

128. Blanche, J. Dynamic fluid ingress detection in geomaterials using K-band frequency modulated continuous wave radar, IEEE Access, (2020), doi: 10.1109/ACCESS.2020.3002147.

129. Blanche, J., J. Buckman, H. Lewis, D. Flynn and G. Couples. Frequency modulated continuous wave analysis of dynamic load deformation in geomaterials, (2020), doi: 10.4043/30479-ms.

130. Blanche, J. Frequency Modulated Continuous Wave Sensing for Static and Dynamic Material Analysis. (2020). PhD Thesis, Heriot-Watt University, Edinburgh.

131. Robotics, C. Husky unmanned ground vehicle. https://www.clearpathrobotics.com/husky-unmanned-ground-vehicle-robot/ (accessed Mar. 06, 2018).

132. Herd, D.S. Microwave Based Monitoring System for Corrosion Under Insulation. (2016). Doctoral Dissertation, Heriot-Watt University.

133. Smart Systems Group, D. Mitchell, J. Blanche, S. Harper and D. Flynn. Asset Integrity Dashboard for FMCW Radar Inspection of Wind Turbine Blades – YouTube, (2020).

134. B.S. Institution. Specification for Sat for Spreading on Highways for Winter Maintenance, BS 3247:2011. (2011).

135. National Winter Services Research Group. Section 2: Planning for Winter Service Delivery, (2019) .

136. National Winter Services Research Group. Section 8: Treatments for Extreme Cold, (2019) .

137. Blanche, J., D. Mitchell and D. Flynn. Run-time analysis of road surface conditions using non-contact microwave sensing. IEEE Global Conference on Artificial Intelligence and Internet of Things 2020. (Dec. 2020), doi: 10.1109/GCAIoT51063.2020.9345917.

138. Zaki, O.F. Self-Certification and Safety Compliance for Robotics Platforms, (2020), OTC-30840-MS, doi: 10.4043/30840-ms.

139. Spot Arm | Boston Dynamics.

140. Ahmad, A., J.C. Roh, D. Wang and A. Dubey. Vital signs monitoring of multiple people using a FMCW millimeter-wave sensor. *In:* 2018 IEEE Radar Conference (RadarConf18), (2018): 1450–1455, doi: 10.1109/RADAR.2018.8378778.

141. Wang, S. A novel ultra-wideband 80 GHz FMCW radar system for contactless monitoring of vital signs. *In:* 2015 37th Annual International Conference of the

IEEE Engineering in Medicine and Biology Society (EMBC), (2015): 4978–4981, doi: 10.1109/EMBC.2015.7319509.

142. Kiuru, T. Movement and respiration detection using statistical properties of the FMCW radar signal, *In:* 2016 Global Symposium on Millimeter Waves (GSMM) & ESA Workshop on Millimetre-Wave Technology and Applications, (2016): 1–4, doi: 10.1109/GSMM.2016.7500331.

143. Alizadeh, M., G. Shaker and S. Safavi-Naeini. Experimental study on the phase analysis of FMCW radar for vital signs detection. *In:* 2019 13th European Conference on Antennas and Propagation (EuCAP), (2019): 1–4.

144. Semwal, T., S. Aracri, A.C. McConnell, M.E. Sayed and A.A. Stokes. A Systems Approach to Real-World Deployment of Industrial Internet of Things. (2020), doi: 10.1109/CEC48606.2020.9185790.

145. ChirpStack. ChirpStack, open-source LoRaWAN® Network Server stack, (2020), https://www.loraserver.io/.

146. pycom, LoPy3, (2020), https://docs.pycom.io/datasheets/development/lopy4/.

147. IEC. IP Ratings, (2020), https://www.iec.ch/ip-ratings.

148. ngrok, ngrok, (2020), https://ngrok.com/.

149. RASA. The Future of Conversational AI is Open, (2020), https://rasa.com/open-source/.

150. Modular Robots for Enabling Operations in Unstructured Extreme Environments. Advanced Intelligent Systems, (2021), doi: 10.1002/aisy.202000227.

Transforming a Standalone Machine Tool to a Cyber-Physical System: A Use Case of BEMRF Machine Tool to Tackle the COVID-19 Restrictions

Faiz Iqbal, Zafar Alam, Madhur Shukla, Jitin Malhotra and Sunil Jha*

1. Introduction

Ball end magnetorheological finishing (BEMRF) is a nanofinishing technology developed by Singh et al. [1] at the beginning of this decade. It is a variant of magnetic field assisted finishing processes that make use of smart magnetorheological polishing fluid to smoothen the roughness peaks in a controlled manner [2]. BEMRF process has the capability to finish plane, nonplanar and free form surfaces up to the order of nanometers [3]. Since its inception, this technology has been employed by various researchers to finish a list of materials having a ferromagnetic nature like mild steel [4] to those with a nonmagnetic nature like additive manufactured polylactic acid (PLA) workpiece [5], copper mirrors [6], polycarbonates [7], etc. The capability of the BEMRF process to finish free form complex surfaces of a variety of materials can be attributed to its unique tool design with an electromagnetic core mounted on a five axes CNC machine tool. Further, it is controlled by a customized controller developed by Alam et al. [8] with the capability to control in-process finishing forces by changing the electromagnet-based tool's input current values. Archival literature shows the potential of the BEMRF process established by various reported works [9–13].

Recently engineered products need a precise finish (up to the order of nanometers) due to their enhanced surface characteristics in high-tech applications such as aerospace, biomedical, laser, optical etc. Since the demand for these types of products are increasing rapidly, the machines that manufacture these products are in the spotlight to cater to these demands. The BEMRF process is a breakthrough technology in the field of nanofinishing because of its ability to finish the free form surfaces of a variety of materials. A five axes CNC BEMRF machine, developed by Iqbal and Jha

*Corresponding author: suniljha@mech.iitd.ac.in

[14], is fully capable of nanofinishing precise and complex parts all automatically as a standalone system and is an industry ready prototype. However, with the current rise in Industry 4.0 and requirements of enhancing digital manufacturing there is a need for cyber-physical systems in the nanofinishing sector as well.

2. Cyber-Physical Systems

The term cyber-physical systems (CPS) was coined in 2006 by Helen Gill of USNSF (United States National Science Foundation) [15]. This term is basically a combination of two different worlds i.e., cyber (software world) and physical (mechanical world), further with a joining layer of communication and control in between them [16]. These systems are responsible for supporting the critical infrastructure by founding the basis for establishing the links in between two different worlds and further improve the life quality in almost all the areas starting from healthcare to smart cities, smart grids, smart manufacturing, etc. CPS is an engineering focused discipline with an aim to solve the problems by providing the next generation systems utilizing varied technologies, modeling techniques and mathematical abstractions. CPS is about adding the modern computing elements, sensors to the physical actuators and monitoring the big data generated through those sensors, analyzing them, and taking the respective control actions based on them [17].

The CPS is a similar concept to various other terms like Internet of Things (IOT), Industrial Internet of Things (IIOT) etc. sharing the common idea behind them i.e., adding cyber to physical components. CPS has a very wide application area like the automotive sector, manufacturing, electric power grids, healthcare, city infrastructure, aircraft domain and smart buildings. Focusing more on the smart manufacturing sector, this sector has seen the new industrial revolution i.e., 4th industrial revolution which is focused on the development of the technologies to boost the productivity of the goods manufactured, delivery of the services, the mass customization concepts and manufacturing in the batch size of one [18].

CPS plays a key role in the manufacturing sector starting from the design phase of a product to its manufacturing, maintenance, and further disposal. The CPS spans from a small component of a machine to complete production systems and its main aim is to make the components self-aware and self-predict; and self-compare; and production systems self-configure, self-maintain, and self-organize. All of these can only be achieved by merging the cyber parts with the physical systems and giving them a self-awareness, self-comparison, self-predicting, self-configuring, self-optimizing, and self-organizing capabilities to make them more independent and more efficient both in terms of power and production with minimum wastage [19].

Few researchers have previously developed and demonstrated the concepts of CPS in the manufacturing sector like Lee et al. [20] who presented the first CPS architecture called 5C architecture for CPS targeting the manufacturing sector. The first level is the Connection level which has a job of acquiring raw data from individual machines and their sub-systems which is transferred to its second level called a Conversion level, where the acquired raw data is converted to useful information by intelligent algorithms. The third level is a Cyber level which pretends to be a central hub among various levels inside and outside the factory and transfers data between heterogenous networked machines. Fourth level is the Cognition level, where the useful information is presented to users and experts in a graphical form for further analysis and decision making. The last level is the Configuration level which generates supervisory commands from the Cyber level to Connection level and acts in a commanding role to make machines self-configure and self-adaptive.

In another report Lee et al. [21] proposed an architecture for a cyber manufacturing system, in which the data from machine tools and the environment is transferred to cyber space for analysis and feedback through a cyber-physical interface. In addition to analysis and feedback, the useful information is also visible on mobile and web. Some design challenges for implementation of CPS are also presented like the lack of standards, huge raw data and disconnected analytics, cyber security, etc. A comparison among cyber and E-manufacturing is also presented in this article.

Morgan and O'Donnell [22] presented a cyber-physical process monitoring architecture and implementation for CNC turning machine tools. The process monitoring system acquires spindle current, spindle acceleration and cutting forces data from three sensors and are passed on to a computing unit which is connected to the cloud through a router. Also, a database client, and a signal pre-processing unit is connected to this computing unit. On the second computing unit the complex event processing units are connected which then does the time and frequency domain signal extraction and decision making and shows the results on a connected HMI screen. Some cutting patterns for a CNC machine are also shown in the end by analyzing the data coming from the connected sensors and extracting the features. Furthermore,various initiatives are running in the world for virtual representation of the types and instances of objects. These components need to be depicted in a form of reference architecture as shown in [23].

This chapter shows the transformation of a standalone CNC BEMRF system into a cyber-physical system in line with the concepts of Industry 4.0 providing an example for cottage industries and micro-SMEs to act in a similar manner to tackle challenges enforced by the COVID-19 crisis.

3. Materials and Methods

To transform a standalone CNC BEMRF machine tool into a cyber-physical system it is required to develop an advanced connection between machines and the cloud for ensuring a real time data transmission from physical devices to cyberspace and to get information feedback from it. The cyberspace performs smart data management, detailed analytics, and computation on raw data. It also stores machine data, which is to be analyzed so that uncertainties arising and/or resulting in the degradation of product quality can be eliminated. A user interface (UI) is also to be developed for easy access of the machine and machine data remotely and to integrate the customer in the process.

3.1   Understanding of the Subsystems Involved

3.1.1 Physical System: Motion and Process Controls

The CNC BEMRF machine tool has the following specifications as listed in Table 14.1, the motion and process controls of the physical system are standardized and governed by one of PLCopen frameworks. For Industry 4.0, an administration shell as shown in Fig. 14.1 is defined, where the physical aspects of all assets are defined in e-Class. These PLCopen specifications imparts a detailed list of functionalities, covering the basic range.

Table 14.1: Specifications of CNC BEMRF machine tool

- Footprint: 1000 mm × 1000 mm, Height = 1500 mm.
- Axes designations and respective travel limits:
  - X: 150 mm.
  - Y: 150 mm.
  - Z: 300 mm.
  - B: +45° to −45° (software limit).
  - C: 0° to 360°.
- 5 axes CNC interpolation (TwinCAT software).
- Confocal sensor for in-situ roughness measurement.
- Intel i3 processor-based IPC system with Windows operating system and 12-inch multitouch screen.
- BEMRF tool with temperature measurement sensors at three levels.
- Range of spindle speed: 300 RPM – 3000 RPM
- Range of electromagnet current: 0-10 A.
- Polishing fluid preparation and fluid delivery system.
- Workpiece cleaning system.

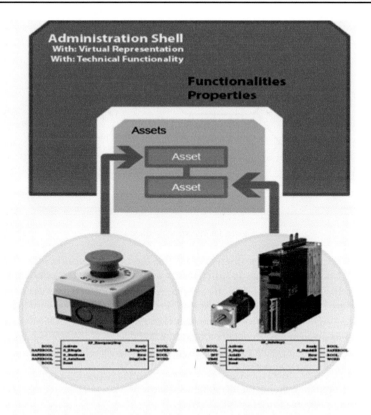

Figure 14.1: Administration shell defined by PLCopen.

In addition to the above, there is an open source framework defined by PLCopen which has the details about the function blocks with a special focus on defining user specific libraries. With this framework, higher levels of integration with larger functionalities in machine tools can be easily done. This framework further expedites the engineering of new machines with ease and provides a modular and reusable structure to software making it easier for future additions. For facilitating this framework, PLCopen even started a new working group to prepare a proposal on how to map the existing PLCopen functionalities to the Industry 4.0 administration shell, which was to be submitted to the Industry 4.0 initiative. Previously, PLCopen had also standardized the behavior of axis-state diagram as shown in Fig. 14.2.

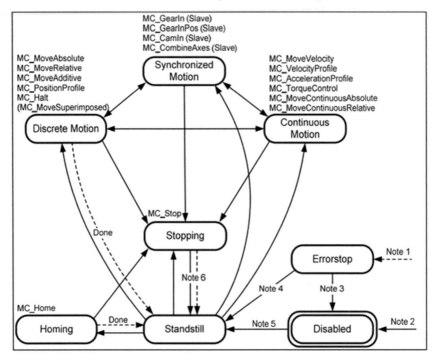

Figure 14.2: Axis state diagram.

There are several software systems available for motion controllers like Codesys, TwinCAT etc. Each software is different in using the same concept or logic. The CNC BEMRF machine tool also uses TwinCAT for motion and process control as the hardware in the machine tool is compatible to TwinCAT. It has a very interesting feature the "ADS (Automation Device Specification) over MQTT (Message Queue Telemetry Transport)". ADS details a field bus and device-independent interface for governing the type of access to various ADS devices.

The ADS interface permits:

- communication with other ADS devices
- implementation of an ADS device

The TwinCAT system is a software-based controller whose framework permits individual modules, i.e., TwinCAT PLC, user HMI, etc. to be served as independent devices. The messages among these modules are interchanged through a robust and responsive ADS interface via the message router which helps to manage and distribute all the in/out messages present in the system and is available over the TCP/IP connections.

ADS over MQTT means the same ADS commands are communicated over MQTT as other communication protocols. For this the TwinCAT router needs to establish a connection to a broker for sending and receiving ADS protocol commands.

3.1.2 Cyber System: The Cloud

To successfully develop a cyber-physical system of a machine an understanding of the basic principal components of the internet of things (IoT) is required. These components are:

Big Analog Data

Big analog data is big data derived from physical analog world. Everything in industrial internet of things is analog phenomenon such as vibration, sound, location, acceleration, moisture, and speed etc. all these phenomena must be digitized. The data collected is huge (big) and is sensor acquired which is further digitized via analog to digital conversion.

Perpetual Connectivity

One of the main ideas of Industry 4.0 is to perpetually connect to products or customers. If one can monitor the condition and usage of products, devices, people in marketplace or industry, one can control things and devices to push upgrades, fixes, patches, and management and one can compel an employee or consumer to take some action,buy, accessorize, etc. By this one can avoid risk, discover more about the consumer, become more efficient and generate more revenue. Figure 14.3 schematically shows how data is captured and relayed to cloud.

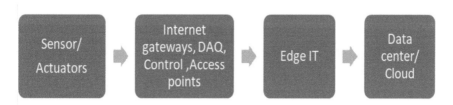

Figure 14.3: Data capture and transfer to the cloud.

Cloud Services

There are various organizations that are providing cloud services viz. Microsoft Azure, Amazon web services, IBM Bluemix, things Board etc. Some of these services are paid and some of them are open source. Preliminary experiments were performed to verify machine to cloud connectivity on the Intel cloud platform, IBM Bluemix and Firebase (Google mobile platform). An embedded control board (Intel Edison) is exclusively used to upload and collect data and interact with the cloud.

Communication Protocols

Most of the cloud services use MQTT which is a connectivity protocol for machine-to-machine communication or Internet of Things. It is a lightweight client/server transfer protocol which works on the publish/subscribe architecture as shown in Fig. 14.4. It is extremely dense with a small footprint on the device making it preferable for constrained devices.

Figure 14.4: MQTT transfer protocol.

3.2 Establishing Communication between the Controller and Cloud Services

An embedded controller (Intel Edison) is integrated with the standalone CNC BEMRF system as a bridge between the machine PLC and the cloud services. Initial communication is setup between the two. The CNC BEMRF system has temperature sensors embedded into the BEMRF tool head, these sensors read the temperature of the tool and provide real time values to the PLC controller. The PLC is programmed through TwinCAT has this data in the form of volts which is calibrated and converted to temperature with help of code in Intel XDK. A two-way communication of PLC to the embedded controller and the embedded controller to the cloud server (IBM cloud services) is done in which the temperature readings are available to the PLC in the form of volts. These values are calibrated and converted to temperature readings in the embedded controller program. For cloud communication testing the readings from sensors are uploaded to the cloud in both volts as well as temperature. Figures 14.5 and 14.6 show the volt vs time plot and temperature vs time plots received by the cloud server with time stamp. The uploading of data to IBM cloud services is done with the help of the API key generated by creating an application in IBM Watson.

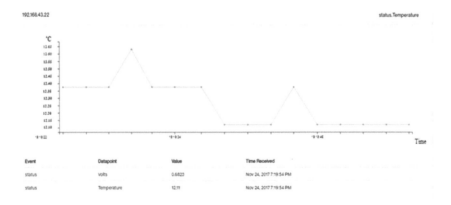

Figure 14.5: Temperature data uploaded to the cloud.

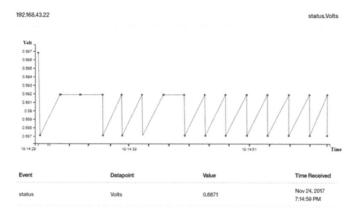

Figure 14.6: Voltage data uploaded to the cloud.

3.3   Webpage: A UI for User and Customer

A webpage is developed that acts as the UI where interaction between customers and manufacturers occurs. Through the website (shown in Fig. 14.7), the customer is required to provide essential inputs so that manufacturer can obtain the target parameters of products. The customer orders the product or services and manufacturer provides service for the same. Inputs required from the customer are the CAD model of their product, target roughness parameters and other miscellaneous information. After all the desired information from the customer has been uploaded the web portal will generate a financial quotation for the order placed. The customer will pay for the services as per the terms and conditions laid, once the payment is confirmed the order is confirmed and the order number is generated with a QR code (shown in Fig. 14.8) corresponding to each product. The customer through this web portal gets continuous updates for his order and can track the delivery of the products after completion.

Figure 14.7: Website developed as a UI for customers.

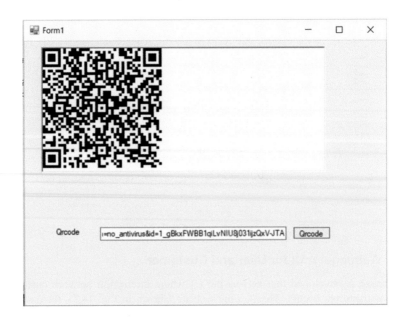

Figure 14.8: QR code generated.

For safety purposes a login interface as shown in Fig. 14.9 is created for machine users as it should technically only be accessed by someone who is an expert of the machine. For that the SQL database is created which contains the login credentials of the authorized users. After a successful login from an authorized user of the machine the machine menu (Fig. 14.10) appears which guides the user to the next pending order for the machine.

Figure 14.9: Login window.

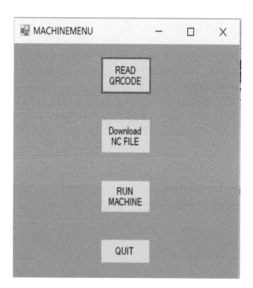

Figure 14.10: Machine menu.

The menu has options viz. read QR code, download NC file, run machine, and quit. Since the machine is a nano-finishing expert the products that are to be dealt with are already manufactured and must be sent by the customers to the manufacturer with a specific QR code attached to it.

Once the product is received the read QR code option is selected. QR code is a type of matrix barcode which uses four encoding nodes for efficiently storing data, which in this case is read with the help of an imaging Webcam integrated with the BEMRF panel PC. The QR code containing details required for downloading NC file for the finishing of the product, is to be read to extract details, a windows form application is made with help of which the read QR code extracts further information stored on the cloud (Google drive). The QR code thus read is transferred to a Windows form application which downloads file the from google drive with the help of Web Client library in C#. File which is stored in a predefined path given in code. Figure 14.11 shows a successful QR code being read and Fig. 14.12 shows a successful attempt at downloading the NC file from the information extracted from QR code.

ADS communication is established between a Windows form application and the TwinCAT motion controller. ADS commands are communicated over MQTT like other communication protocols, where the TwinCAT router setups a connection to the broker for sending and receiving ADS protocol commands. The end point of such broker is further configured on the respective local device. The result of this exercise is a creation of the one to one relationship between an ADS route and the matching broker. Successful communication in ADS depends on the right certificate exchange and port number given in code of windows form application and TwinCAT motion controller. The file stored is read from the TwinCAT motion controller which is programed to perform the required motion described in NC code. It also transfers status of motors into the cloud. Figure 14.13 shows a screen grab from the TwinCAT program used for extracting the .NC file from the Windows form application and performing a motion control according to the NC file.

Figure 14.11: QR code read by a Webcam.

Figure 14.12: NC file successfully downloaded.

Once the machine has a .NC file and related process parameters the finishing process can start after the product is mounted on the machine fixture. The machine conducts a closed loop finishing of the product as per customer requirements [closed loop]. After the successful completion of the finishing process the machine indicates the same and the product can proceed further for dispatch.

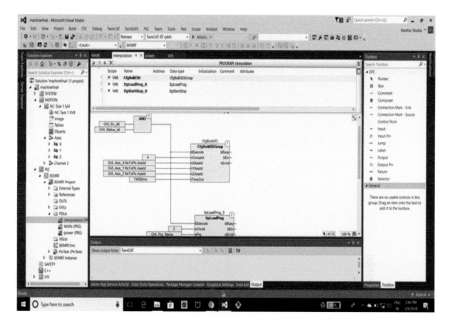

Figure 14.13: Twin CAT program for .NC file extraction.

3.4   Prediction of Machining Time and Cost

One of the main applications of Artificial Intelligence (AI) is Machine Learning (ML) that provides a system with prowess to autonomously learn and improve from experience without any need for explicitly programming it. Machine learning targets the development of smart models (computer programs) that can access and learn from data collected automatically. A ML trained model is developed for predicting machining time and cost for the orders placed by customers, this enables the quick billing for the customer at the time of check out. Labelled data is collected which is having the values of R_a and process parameters. This data is stored in Microsoft Azure Blob storage in Comma Separated Values (CSV) files. The trained model for the prediction of machining time and cost is generated with the help of Microsoft Machine Learning Studio. Figure 14.14 shows a schematic of the trained ML model for the prediction of machining time and cost.

4.   Results and Discussions

In the physical world, methodology described can be implemented in lab experiments or for manufacturing. According to the methodology described in the previous section, the machine will come closer to both the customer as well as the manufacturer. Customers can customize their product and the manufacturer will have enhanced insight during the manufacturing process. From the website a customer can place an order and schedule its time on the machine remotely, receive the predicted time and cost of machining generated from the past experience of the machine i.e., algorithm generated in the Microsoft Machine learning studio from the time machine (data collected from runs on the machine in the past).

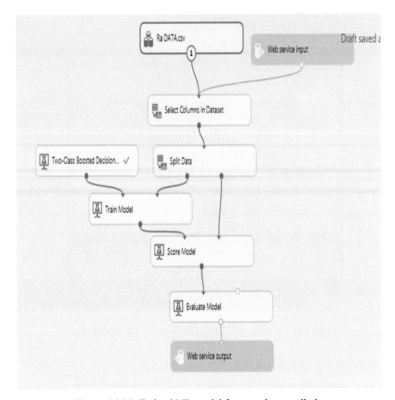

Figure 14.14: Trained ML model for cost-time prediction.

For the manufacturer it is the deal to increase its productivity by reducing setup time, maintenance time, human errors etc. The machine is independent of human interventions only major decisions are to be made by the operator otherwise the machine is capable of thinking and interacting with the ecosystem and to work efficiently. With the help of this methodology the manufacturer can make different products in same run rather than making different products in different runs which increases the cost of product for the customer because of the increased setup cost every change brings. Moreover, manufacturers will have the enhanced insight into the working of the machine, as data from all sensors will be available to conclude the important results by performing analytics on the data collected. Concluded results could be predicting machine failure, predicting optimal parameters for finishing, etc. By converting the machine tool into a cyber-physical system, the manufacturer can keep records like the operation conditions for past products, maintenance records etc. to make the machine learn from its past and gain experience which will help the machine in decision-making.

5. Conclusions

The work in this chapter described the transformation of a standalone CNC BEMRF machine tool to a cyber-physical system. The following points conclude the work:

1. Transformation of standalone systems to cyber-physical systems is required for the Industry 4.0 and post COVID-19 survival of existing setups, the same is done in this work for the standalone CNC BEMRF system.
2. An embedded controller (Intel Edison) is integrated with the standalone CNC BEMRF system as a bridge between the machine PLC and the cloud services.
3. Standards like PLCopen, MQTT have been used to ensure reliability.
4. A web-based user interface is developed for customer interaction.
5. The customer can monitor the whole process throughout its journey from the start and back to the customer.
6. A cost-time prediction algorithm based on machine learning concepts is developed to give the customer an estimate of the two entities.
7. More sensors can be included to the newly transformed cyber-physical system to develop a digital twin of the same.
8. This transformation work can be used as a guide for small scale enterprises to do the same to their stand-alone systems and stay in business when Industry 4.0 completely takes over.

References

1. Singh, A.K., S. Jha and P.M. Pandey. Magnetorheological ball end finishing process. Materials and Manufacturing Processes, 27(4) (2012): 389–394.
2. Alam, Z. and S. Jha. Modeling of surface roughness in ball end magneto-rheological finishing (BEMRF) process. Wear, 374–375C (2017): 54–62.
3. Iqbal, F. and S. Jha. Nanofinishing of free form surfaces using BEMRF. *In:* Jain, V.K. (Ed.), Nanofinishing Science and Technology: Basic and Advanced Finishing and Polishing Processes. CRC Press, Florida, (2017): 235–263.
4. Iqbal, F. and S. Jha. Experimental investigations into transient roughness reduction in ball-end magneto-rheological finishing process. Materials and Manufacturing Processes, 34(2) (2019): 224–231.
5. Kumar, A., Z. Alam, D.A. Khan and S. Jha. Nanofinishing of FDM fabricated components using ball end magnetorheological finishing process. Materials and Manufacturing Processes, 34(2) (2019): 232–242.
6. Alam, Z., D.A. Khan and S. Jha. MR fluid-based novel finishing process for nonplanar copper mirrors. The International Journal of Advanced Manufacturing Technology, 101(1-4) (2019): 995–1006.
7. Khan, D.A., J. Kumar and S. Jha. Magneto-rheological nano-finishing of polycarbonate. International Journal of Precision Technology, 6(2) (2016): 89–100.
8. Alam, Z., F. Iqbal, S. Ganesan and S. Jha. Nanofinishing of 3D surfaces by automated five-axis CNC ball end magnetorheological finishing machine using customized controller. The International Journal of Advanced Manufacturing Technology, 100(5–8) (2019): 1031–1042.
9. Iqbal, F., Z. Alam and S. Jha. Modelling of transient behaviour of roughness reduction in ball end magnetorheological finishing process. International Journal of Abrasive Technology, 10(3) (2020): 170–192.

10. Alam, Z., F. Iqbal and S. Jha. Automated control of three axis CNC ball end magneto-rheological finishing machine using PLC. International Journal of Automation and Control, 9(3) (2015): 201–210.

11. Khan, D.A., Z. Alam, F. Iqbal and S. Jha. A study on the effect of polishing fluid composition in ball end magnetorheological finishing of aluminum. *In:* 39th International MATADOR Conference on Advanced Manufacturing, July 2017, University of Manchester, UK, (2017).

12. Iqbal, F. and S. Jha. Closed loop ball end magnetorheological finishing using in-situ roughness metrology. Experimental Techniques, 42(6) (2018): 659–669.

13. Iqbal, F., Z. Alam, D.A. Khan and S. Jha. Part program-based process control of ball-end magnetorheological finishing. *In:* Advances in Unconventional Machining and Composites. Springer, Singapore, (2020): 503–514.

14. Iqbal, F. and S. Jha. Closed loop control of ball end magnetorheological finishing process using in-situ roughness feedback. Doctoral thesis submitted to Indian Institute of Technology Delhi, India, (2019).

15. Wan, J., M. Chen, F. Xia, L. Di and K. Zhou. From machine-to-machine communications towards cyber-physical systems. Computer Science and Information Systems, 10(3) (2013): 1105–1128.

16. Sadiku, M.N., Y. Wang, S. Cui and S.M. Musa. Cyber-physical systems: A literature review. European Scientific Journal, 13(36) (2017): 52–58.

17. Gunes, V., S. Peter, T. Givargis and F. Vahid. A survey on concepts, applications, and challenges in cyber-physical systems. KSII Transactions on Internet & Information Systems, 8(12) (2014).

18. Kotakorpi, E., S. Lähteenoja and M. Lettenmeier. Household MIPS. Natural resource consumption of Finnish households and its reduction, 43 (2008).

19. Koziolek, H., R. Weiss, Z. Durdik, J. Stammel and K. Krogmann. Towards software sustainability guidelines for long-living industrial systems. Software Engineering 2011 – Workshopband, (2011).

20. Lee, J., B. Bagheri and H.A. Kao. A cyber-physical systems architecture for industry 4.0-based manufacturing systems. Manufacturing Letters, 3 (2015): 18–23.

21. Lee, J., B. Bagheri and C. Jin. Introduction to cyber manufacturing. Manufacturing Letters, 8 (2016): 11–15.

22. Morgan, J. and G.E. O'Donnell. Cyber physical process monitoring systems. Journal of Intelligent Manufacturing, 29(6) (2018): 1317–1328.

23. Malhotra, J., F. Iqbal, A.K. Sahu and S. Jha. A cyber-physical system architecture for smart manufacturing. *In:* Advances in Forming, Machining and Automation. Springer, Singapore, (2019): 637–647.

Index